The Films of
Victor Mature

ALSO BY JAMES MCKAY

Dana Andrews: The Face of Noir
(McFarland, 2010)

The Films of Victor Mature

JAMES MCKAY

McFarland & Company, Inc., Publishers
Jefferson, North Carolina, and London

LIBRARY OF CONGRESS CATALOGUING-IN-PUBLICATION DATA

McKay, James, 1959–
The films of Victor Mature / James McKay.
  p.   cm.
Includes bibliographical references and index.

ISBN 978-0-7864-4970-5
softcover

1. Mature, Victor.
2. Actors — United States — Biography.
I. Title.
PN2287.M5435M36 2013   791.4302'8092—dc23   [B]   2012046014

BRITISH LIBRARY CATALOGUING DATA ARE AVAILABLE

© 2013 James McKay. All rights reserved

No part of this book may be reproduced or transmitted in any form or by any means, electronic or mechanical, including photocopying or recording, or by any information storage and retrieval system, without permission in writing from the publisher.

Front cover: Victor Mature in *Kiss of Death* (1947)
(Photofest)

*McFarland & Company, Inc., Publishers
Box 611, Jefferson, North Carolina 28640
www.mcfarlandpub.com*

In loving memory of my sister Liz.

Acknowledgments

I would like to thank my wife Christine for proofing the manuscript and helping with the selection of photographs; fellow film enthusiast and friend Pete Farley for his valued thoughts on content; the helpful staff at the British Film Institute for providing some of the research material; the prompt and friendly services of Photofest in supplying the great photographs; the wonderful Victor Mature Fan Club, and last but not least Victor Mature for his wonderful film legacy.

Table of Contents

Acknowledgments vi
Preface 1
Biography 5

THE FILMS 23
(Chronologically)

Appendix: Select Radio Appearances 179
Notes 182
Bibliography 187
Index 191

Preface

"I accepted the roles they offered and put the money in the bank. After all, it wasn't brain surgery, and I never lost my sense of humor about what I was doing." Candid words from Victor Mature, a fine, iconic actor who, through a great zest for living and an infectious sense of humor, never lost his perspective on life, particularly where his career was concerned. He was an honest, gregarious and fun-loving man, and his motto on this worldly existence was "Take it easy. If the time is ripe, it'll all break for you. Everything eventually breaks right for me; I just relax."

Indeed, Mature combined relaxation, or loafing, as he put it, with a devil-may-care attitude that barely concealed a deeper, sensuous vitality, and at times fragility, that infused his film characterizations with depth and color. Added to this persona, his dark, rugged Mediterranean looks, accentuated by heavy-lidded eyes, full lips and thick, wavy black hair, made him one of the most distinctive-looking actors in Hollywood. Throw in a six-foot, two-and-a-half-inch, solidly built frame and a memorably husky voice, and you have a star who simply oozed screen presence out of every pore. His appeal was such that he made a vital contribution to four musicals without being able to sing or dance. Dubbed a "Beautiful Hunk of a Man" and "King of Beefcake," Mature had to work that much harder to prove himself as an actor, but the labels didn't worry him. With his wonderful self-deprecating sense of humor, he simply took it all in his stride.

His arrival in Hollywood helped to usher in a new breed of star, one who combined an outdoor ruggedness with earthy sex appeal, far removed from the debonair types of the 1930s. In his personal life and professional endeavors, he appeared larger than life, an image no doubt fueled by his extrovert nature and appetite for self-publicity, which set him up as a target for many of the film critics, who chose not to see beyond his powerful build. He dated a series of beautiful women, many of whom he starred with, causing his legend to grow, making him a household name throughout the world. Once seen, he was never forgotten.

As well as being a versatile actor, Mature had a good head for business, successfully balancing his film career with his many business interests. He was also smart enough to quit his film career when he was at the top of his game, which enabled him to fully enjoy the fruits of his labors through early retirement. In retirement, he pursued his passion for his favorite pastime, golf. In retiring when he did, Mature was spared some of the poorer quality roles that other great veteran stars of the silver screen fell victim to in the 1960s onwards. Instead, he left us with a wonderful legacy of 56 films, many of them classics that are still highly praised today. His film career may have included some routine features, but one can't deny their entertainment value, and none of them can be classed as bad.

And if, like Robert Mitchum, he could occasionally be accused of sleepwalking through a handful of roles, with his strong screen magnetism it mattered not, because you still thoroughly enjoyed them.

Possessing a broad acting range, he could convincingly convey upbeat, cocky self-assuredness or downbeat, anguished stoicism. His precision timing and broad grin found the ideal home in musicals such as *Song of the Islands*, *My Gal Sal* and *Wabash Avenue*, where he was perfectly matched alongside the likes of Betty Grable and Rita Hayworth. His magnificent physique and craggy face, that looked like they had been carved out of a slab of marble, made him the perfect choice to play in the biblical epics *Samson and Delilah* and *The Robe*. In such films, which became his hallmark, he proved that he could express strength and emotion, with an underlying fragility. Through his expressive eyes, he could also convey pent-up anger, despair and, in some cases, a melancholic fatalism that really got under your skin, particularly in the roles of Doc Holliday in *My Darling Clementine* and as the reformed crook Nick Bianco in the classic film noir *Kiss of Death*—two of his greatest performances. He could also express a softer, tender side to his tough guy persona when the occasion demanded, as he did in *Violent Saturday*, *China Doll* and *Escort West*. Mature was equally adept in the dark, claustrophobic spaces of film noir or in the big, colorful outdoors of Westerns and actioners, where his imposing screen presence perfectly lent itself to Technicolor and the widescreen process.

Mature shares some quality time with his "best girl," his mother, Clara (circa 1940s).

But as well as looming large, Mature could also skillfully underplay his parts, or in some cases take a back seat if the role demanded, allowing other actors to come to the fore, such as when he ably supported Betty Hutton in *Red, Hot and Blue*, David Wayne in *Stella* and Edmund Gwenn in *Something for the Birds*.

When they made Mature, they threw away the mold. He was certainly a "one off" in many ways, but, for me, his most endearing quality, apart from his inimitable acting style, was his wonderful ability to poke fun at himself both on and off screen. Watch his terrific performance as the over-the-hill actor in the comedy *After the Fox* and witness a perfect example of self-parody. Not many actors steal a film from Peter Sellers, but Mature did. With such a sense of humor, he would have been the sort of guy you'd love to have whiled away a lazy summer's afternoon with, sharing a few cold beers. If ever an actor deserved more credit than he received for his unique contribution to cinematic history, it was Victor Mature.

Biography

Blessed with a ready-made Hollywood screen name, Victor John Mature was born January 29, 1913, in Louisville, Kentucky, to Austrian immigrant Marcellus George Mature and his wife Clara. The couple had two other children before Victor, a daughter who died in infancy and an older son who died in 1918 at age 11.[1] Settling in Louisville, his father made a living as a knife sharpener and scissors grinder. Victor enjoyed a happy childhood, later in life describing his father as "a wonderful man; colorful, dynamic, a real man," and his mother as "a thoroughly down-to-earth type, possessing of great vivacity and charm." Although Victor had respect for both his parents, he was closer to his mother, who understood him better than his father, who Victor felt was too constrained by his strict country ways and manner. Mature would always regard his mother as his best girl, who saw right through him, particularly when he regularly feigned illness to avoid going to school.

Schooling was definitely something the young Mature didn't care for. At an early age, he nurtured a stubborn, rebellious streak within him, which would create many a problem in his education. On his first day at George H. Tingley Public School, he was sent home for biting his teacher. Further expulsions followed when he attended St. Paul's and St. Xavier's parochial schools. On one occasion, the priest at St. Xavier's summoned his mother Clara and told her, "Your son is a perfect nuisance. When I go back into the room, he is the comedian. The place is an uproar. They sit there entranced." Mature once mused that his mother was summoned so often that the other students thought she worked there.[2] Mature was certainly a born entertainer, much to the despair of his parents. He took his disruptive behavior to two other places of learning, St. Josephs Academy in Bardstown and the Kentucky Military School, who only put up with his conduct for a short while. Mature clearly had no time for formal education, particularly where exams were concerned, once confessing that he simply answered questions by writing a big zero for each one.

Mature's wild exploits were not confined to school. Not quite 12, he and several other boys were once caught in a squall when they were returning from an island picnic across a large river. When the boat capsized, Mature helped two of the weaker swimmers to safety. For his efforts, one of the mothers gave him a tongue-lashing for having torn her son's shirt during the rescue, complaining, "You're the ringleader in these crazy pranks and you're simply too reckless."[3] In his high school days, he took up the hazardous hobby of racing down hills on coaster wagons, on one occasion hitting a truck doing sixty which smashed his buggy. Luckily, two seconds earlier, Mature had bailed out.[4] Such high spirits would continue beyond childhood into his formative adult years, as Mature would fondly recall later in life: "There was a period in my life when everything was just a lark. I would do things that caused me to be tagged a mad hatter. The result was the wrong sort of publicity."

Having thoroughly tested the patience and tolerance of the education authorities, he was allowed to leave school at the age of 14, or as Mature put it, "I was kicked out of a couple before I finally quit." In later life he would admit, "I was absolutely wrong. I could have wound up workin' awfully hard to make a living with that kind of a start, if I didn't have my luck."

Freed from the confines of educational life; the world was now his oyster, and there would be no stopping him. But first he needed to develop a head for business, which he achieved helping out his father in his door-to-door grinding and sharpening business. When his father bettered himself by buying into a commercial refrigeration plant, Mature continued to work for him for a short while, before getting a job as a salesman for a wholesale candy company. A scribe once remarked, "You couldn't expect Mature, with his face and physique, to be in refrigeration, of all things! He'd defrost the things while installing them! But he's a salesman nevertheless." A natural salesman he clearly was, in the candy business doing the work of three candy salesman. "I was an eager beaver when I was 14. I was always big for my age and looked around 18, so I got work as a candy jobber." He further explained that in the summer he'd get up at 5 A.M., go to the jobber and load up his orders, deliver them, and get home around 11 P.M. Mature was always of the opinion that such perseverance was the main factor behind his film success.

His sales patter, which earned him up to $150 per week, made full use of his charm. He would tell customers, "Just let me leave the candy. If you don't sell it, I'll take it back." Encouraged by his success and looking for new challenges, Mature left the candy business, using his profits to buy into a Louisville restaurant when he was 19. It was to prove a less than successful venture, which lost him $300 in the first month. As Mature explained it, "The help was stealing me blind, and I didn't have the sense to know it." To combat the problem, Mature briefly employed the services of a Childs Restaurant manager, who started out by firing everyone. When the restaurant broke even after two months, Mature sold the business.

The year was now 1935, and the young Mature had certainly reached a crossroads in his life. He had tried many activities to earn an honest crust, including a stint selling magazines and operating the elevator at the Brown Hotel, until he was sacked for dancing on the roof garden while he was on duty. But he had yet to find his niche in life, which made him restless. As a small boy he had held aspirations towards becoming a playwright, starting to write plays at the age of 11. At 15, he wrote *The Incorrigible One*, which was put on by some of the youngsters of the neighborhood. Mature described the play as pretty bad; it ended his playwriting career, but it did instill in him a liking for acting.[5] Fueled by a desire to fulfill this passion, Mature decided to pack his bags and head for Hollywood. Some sources suggest that Mature's decision to leave Louisville was perhaps prompted by a rebuff by one of the city's socialites, who in response to being asked for a dance by Mature at a debutante's ball held in 1935, reportedly called him, "a dirty son of a common knife grinder," before slapping him in the face.[6] In an interview with *Life* magazine in 1941, Mature commented, "I told myself I'd never return until the name Mature was so big that those society people would eat dirt."

His father was opposed to his son's plans, but knew it would prove fruitless to try and stop him, waving him off with a piece of homespun advice: "As long as people think you're dumber than you are, you'll make money." It was a piece of advice that the young Mature heeded much to his benefit when his career took off.

Loading his car up with some of the sweets stock he had left over from his candy venture, and accompanied by a pal, he set off for California. Without having planned a route or timetable, they stopped wherever and whenever the mood took them, exchanging the sweets for oil and gas along the way.[7]

When they eventually arrived in Hollywood a week later, Mature had eleven cents to his name. He wired his dad, "Am in Hollywood, have eleven cents, what can I do?" His father wired back, "When I arrived in this country I had six cents in my pocket and couldn't speak English. Good luck."[8] Having made his money the hard way and disapproving of his son's decision to become an actor, his father was of the firm opinion that if he persisted in becoming an actor then he would have to pay for "the funny business himself."

But it would take more than empty pockets to dampen Mature's spirits. Selling off the rest of his candy stock, he found a roof for their heads, a partly burnt-out garage, before registering with all the casting agencies in town. One of the agencies suggested he get some stage experience under his belt, and that the best place to get it was the Pasadena Playhouse (the starting point for many of his contemporaries such as Dana Andrews and Robert Preston), where one night a week they held auditions open to everyone. Mature attended the Sunday night open audition where he found the place packed with young hopefuls. One after another read his or her lines and then it came to Mature's big moment. Brimming with confidence, he gave a good account of himself with his reading, which much impressed Gilmor Brown, the playhouse's director. Inviting him over for a chat at the end of the evening, Brown told Mature that he liked his audition and inquired as to whether he had the means to support himself, explaining that his actors received no payment. When Mature told him he had yet to secure employment, Brown thought it over, and after a couple of days offered him the chance to do some odd jobs about the playhouse for a small wage that would help pay for his tuition. Mature eagerly accepted.[9] After a few weeks his pal went back to Louisville but Mature stayed on, determined to make a go of it in California. Never afraid of hard toil, he took on all sorts of work (in addition to his theater jobs) including mowing lawns, dish washing, and waxing floors at the local YMCA. He even tried his hand at janitorial work but soon gave it up because it "paid meagerly and kept me up all night, which didn't make for alertness in school classes during the day." With his keen business mind, Mature soon hit on the most profitable use of his time — waxing and polishing cars. The money and the hours certainly suited him, but as he would later recall, "It was hard work and gave me more exercise than I bargained for."[10]

In an effort to cut down his overhead, he moved from the garage to a tent fashioned out of an old canvas, which he pitched in the backyard of the theater — a move which some columnists simply saw as a publicity stunt to promote an image of the struggling, homeless actor. Shameless self-publicity or not, Mature was definitely living hand to mouth, but despite his frugal existence, nothing seemed to faze him. He once told a friend, "This acting business interests me. If I make it, I make it. If not, there's always plenty of time to make money."

Being a novice, he spent his first four days in the routine school learning such things as how to walk on stage and what to do with his hands. Soon he was transferred to the small Playhouse theater, where he remained until he was ready to tread the boards in the main theater. Mature felt that the classes, which covered speech, English, stage presence, boxing, fencing and set building, were harder than polishing cars. Up until this point he had rarely read a book, and now he was compelled to study scores of plays.

His big break came on November 16, 1936, when he made his acting debut in the theater's production of *Paths of Glory*. Anxious to share the good news, he sent a message to his father proclaiming, "I now have more than an ambition. I have a career."

In the spring of 1937, he received a playhouse scholarship, which released him from paying his tuition in cash. In 1938, after a succession of fifty or so small parts, he was offered a lead role in *Autumn Crocus,* a story of a single headmistress, who when on holiday in the Tyrol falls in love with the married owner of the hotel in which she is staying. Love was also in the air for Mature when he married a fellow Playhouse student, the beautiful red-haired Frances Evans (professional name: Frances Charles) in Yuma on January 30, 1938. It was done on impulse and cloaked in secrecy, with Mature continuing to live in his tent and she in the girl's dormitory at the theater. Their union was doomed from the start, culminating in divorce in 1940.

But if his marriage was on the slide, his professional career was quite the opposite. After appearing in over sixty plays, he finally caught the attention of a representative from one of the film studios while playing the lead in *To Quito and Back* in 1939. The representative in question, Frank Ross, was the vice-president of the Hal Roach film studio. Very taken by Mature's impressive performance, he told Hal Roach about the new kid on the block, showing him a program which featured a picture of Mature on the cover — an image which clearly oozed sex appeal and virility. Instantly recognizing his star potential, Roach said, "Victor Mature. I've never heard of him, but maybe I'd better."

After signing him up, Roach immediately put him to work, casting him in 1939 as the lovesick gangster Lefty in his debut film the comedy thriller *The Housekeeper's Daughter.* When offered the part, Mature jumped at it, confidently informing the producer, "Actors make parts — parts don't make actors." It was a small part with Mature speaking only a handful of words, but it did allow him to play opposite the first in a long line-up of beautiful leading ladies, in this instance, Joan Bennett. Upon its release in September 1939, it also prompted a deluge of fan mail for the studio, some twenty thousand letters, by all accounts, all inquiring about their new actor. When the film was premiered in his home town, Louisville, Hal Roach's publicity man Jules Seltzer had to lock the actor in his changing room to stop him from running off to avoid making a speech to a home crowd. Mature felt that as these were the same people he had sharpened knives for and sold candy to, that they'd probably walk out, not wanting to listen to anything he had to say. He was proved wrong when the audience heartily applauded and remained in their seats.[11]

Boosted by this success, and with money in his pockets, Mature moved out of his tent to share a house with Jules Seltzer and two fan magazine editors, Carl Schroeder and Walt Ramsay; all three helped to build the Mature image as a virile actor with great sex appeal. Seltzer and Schroeder would become two of Mature's closest friends, with the actor regarding Seltzer as the smartest publicity man in town and Schroeder as the best editor and writer.

Roach certainly knew he had hit gold with his new prospect, instructing his writers to pull together something that would really put the star in the limelight. The result was the starring role as a caveman in *One Million B.C.* (1940) opposite Carole Landis. Set in prehistoric times, the film made full use of the special effects department, featuring a slew of magnified monsters, but there was no fakery required where Mature's physique was concerned. Wearing animal skins and loincloths, his solid frame and dark handsome looks were shown to great effect, particularly opposite the blonde Landis, turning him into an overnight sensation, and substantially adding to the coffers of the studio. However, the critics were less than impressed with the film, with the *New York Times* commenting that Mature "is perhaps lucky that his first assignment is in a very immature picture." Mature would later comment that many of his early films, such as *One Million B.C.*, gave him little opportunity to act, and like many of the small parts he played at the Pasadena Playhouse, were possibly won on his muscular merits as opposed to his dramatic talent. He said, "One scantily dressed role I remember was in George Bernard Shaw's *Back to Methuselah*, in which I was clad only in a bearskin — and carried a spear.... I wasn't ashamed of my muscles, and still don't mind showing them off if that's what the ladies like, but that isn't acting."[12]

Striking while the iron was hot, Roach put the star in his first costume drama, the swashbuckling, rip-roaring actioner *Captain Caution*, set during the British-American War of 1812. Although he presented no threat to Errol Flynn, Mature cut a dash as the commander of an American Merchant vessel in a role that gave him some real dialogue to learn and another fine opportunity to show off his manly torso. Once again, if it had been down to the critics, his career might have gone into a tailspin at this juncture, with one or two of them circling like vultures. Archer Winsten of the *New York Post* was probably one of the least damning when he mused, "He is equipped for the role only in physical aspects."

When asked for his thoughts on the great Hal Roach, Mature described him as a very nice man who appeared to have lots of confidence in his team, willingly handing the directorial reins to his assistant, with little concern, if the mood took him, particularly if there was a race meeting that he didn't want to miss.[13]

For his next assignment, Mature found himself vying with Richard Carlson for the affections of English actress Anna Neagle in *No, No, Nanette*, a 1940 screen adaptation of the 1925 stage musical, with most of the tunes relegated to background music. On paper Mature and Neagle seemed an odd combination, but it worked, even though Mature loses the girl to Carlson in the end. The film was the first of a six-picture loanout deal the cash-strapped Roach made with RKO for Mature's services, with the producer taking most of the fee.

At this point in his life, Mature was very much a "man about town," escorting a succession of beautiful women around the local night spots. Among them were such luminaries as Betty Grable, Carole Landis, Alice Faye and Lana Turner. Women simply adored his looks and devil-may-care manner, but the Hollywood old guard, perhaps green with envy, saw him as nothing more than a self-promoting upstart, with little talent. In time, like the society set back home who had also belittled him, they would eat their words. But to make them do this, he would first need to prove himself as an actor — and what better way than on Broadway?

With no projects lined up after *No, No, Nanette*, Mature convinced Roach to let him go east to try his luck on the New York stage, arguing that it would make him a more bankable investment if the audience took him more seriously as an actor. He would later tell reporters, "One of the reasons I was anxious to get away from Hollywood was to slay, while it was still in the process of growing, the legend that I was just a glamour boy with a lucky streak." The gamble certainly paid off because in the role of Randy Curtis, one of Gertrude Lawrence's suitors in *Lady in the Dark*, he won the unconditional plaudits of the drama critics, many of whom had little time for Hollywood stars, or indeed glamour boys. The *New York World-Telegram* wrote that Mature acted "with an engaging manner, simply, directly and effectively." Mature was full of admiration for Lawrence, describing her as "a stimulating and exciting personality."

Through his character's introductory description, the role was also responsible for tagging Mature as "a beautiful hunk of man," a label that would stick to him for the rest of his screen career. In like manner, the press would later dub him "King of Beefcake," "Mr. Beautiful," "Glamour Boy," and "The Hunk."

While in New York, Mature met 22-year-old Martha Stephenson Kemp, the widow

Mature (as Randy Curtis) makes his presence felt opposite Gertrude Lawrence in the 1941 Broadway production *Lady in the Dark.*

of the late bandsman Hal Kemp, who had been killed in a car accident in December, 1940. He was smitten with the former model, because as he explained, "She is very easy to get along with. Without losing any of her mystery, you know where you stand with her at all times."[14] Martha had a baby girl, Helen (fathered by Hal Kemp), whom Mature adored. Mature was convinced he had met his soulmate; they were married after a six-week romance at the bride's home on Park Avenue on June 17, 1941. But the course of true love never did run smooth, and less than a year later they separated, the marriage ending with a divorce on February 10, 1943. Mature put it down to the fact that perhaps he was a little too earthy for the sophisticated Martha.

With his popularity gaining with each performance, Mature helped it along by indulging in a certain amount of self-publicity, which he regarded as an important part of being a movie star. Many years later, in an interview for *Picturegoer* magazine, he had this to say on the subject: "A while back someone called me a big show-off. That's just what I am, professionally speaking. In one sense all show business folk are. It's part of their existence. I know there are some stars who prefer to shun the limelight. They are entitled to that view and I respect them for it. That's not my way however. I believe an actor has to sell himself hard and, if it's publicity he's after, he's just gotta take the kicks with the kisses."[15]

Back in Hollywood, Mature got his first taste of film noir when he was loaned out to producer Arnold Pressburger for his sumptuous production *The Shanghai Gesture*, which was directed by Josef von Sternberg and released by United Artists. Starring alongside Gene Tierney, Mature was cast as the mysterious Arab Dr. Omar, a role that allowed him to show off his expressive face and sensuous persona. Perhaps a little too rich for the tastes of the day, the film was undeservedly panned by the critics and the box office takings were poor.

Mature, on loanout to 20th Century–Fox, tried his hand at another noir with the murder mystery *I Wake Up Screaming* (1941), starring two former dates, Betty Grable and Carole Landis. When praising Mature's acting ability in an article for *Picturegoer* magazine in 1953, Elspeth Grant described the film as a brisk little thriller in which Mature stood up splendidly to formidable competition from Laird Cregar. Audience reaction to the film was generally positive, helping to swell Mature's fan base. With his star on the rise, Mature demanded that Roach pay him a larger share of his loan-out fee. (The producer reportedly received $3,000 a week for the actor's services in *The Shanghai Gesture*, out of which he paid Mature a flat weekly rate of $450.)[16] However, his dissatisfaction was cut short when 20th Century–Fox took over his contract from Roach in November 1941, for a reputed $80,000, increasing the actor's salary to $1,200 a week.[17]

At this juncture, Mature's career was certainly on the up, but his personal life hit a low point on October 19, 1941, when his 64-year-old father Marcellus died of a heart attack in Louisville. Before he died, Marcellus wanted to will all his money to his son, because he

Under suspicion of murder, promoter Frankie Christopher (Mature, center) finds himself in a "hot spot" when the cops crowd him in the early film noir *I Wake Up Screaming* (1941), Mature's first film for 20th Century–Fox. From left: Laird Cregar as Police Inspector Ed Cornell and Tim Ryan, Dick Rich and James Flavin as detectives.

thought his wife wouldn't know how to look after it, and might lose it. However, Victor insisted that it all be placed at his mother's disposal because, as he explained in a 1942 interview, she would have become dependent on him, which would have made her unhappy. He added, "Mother should have it outright. What if she does lose it? I'll make my own anyway. All that dough might make me lazy."

Fox thought Mature would make the perfect leading man to play opposite the likes of Betty Grable in their glossy Technicolor musicals. And they thought right, with the star's winning smile and engaging presence working a treat in three of the best from their 1942 crop: *Song of the Islands* and *Footlight Serenade,* both starring Betty Grable, and *My Gal Sal* with Rita Hayworth. Starring opposite two of the loveliest stars of the day proved too much of a temptation for the red-blooded Mature, who promptly fell in love with both of them both on and off screen — feelings that the girls reciprocated. In later years, being the perfect gentleman, Mature would always speak respectfully of his former romances, remembering Grable as having the greatest laugh in the world. "It comes from way down inside her. And you can hear it a block away. It bubbles." When Grable was laid up in hospital awaiting an operation, Mature sent flowers with a message to cheer her up: "Dear Betty, I hope by now you're singing 'The Song of the Islands' (because you were 'Strictly Dynamite' doing that) and that your days of 'Waking Up Screaming' are all over now. Love." The two stars would always remain friends. Of Hayworth, he was once quoted as saying to Louella Parsons, "Rita Hayworth is the only girl I ever felt I truly loved."

To top off 1942, Mature continued his RKO loan-out deal with the comedy *Seven Days' Leave,* playing alongside Lucille Ball. The film was a pleasant enough filler, but the reviews were disappointing. Mature took it all in his stride, informing a reporter that he knew that Hollywood had yet to accept him, because other players in the studio didn't invite him to their parties. "To be invited to parties in Hollywood, you have to amount to something. You have to be important. I will know when I am important when I am invited to parties."[18]

During the war, Mature served in the United States Coast Guard, enlisting on July 2, 1942. As a seaman, second class, he saw duty overseas in various locations including the North Atlantic, the Philippine Islands and Europe. Before serving 14 months aboard a Coast Guard cutter in the North Atlantic patrol, he gave Rita Hayworth a diamond and ruby ring as a token of his love. With the end of his marriage to Martha in early 1943, Mature's love life took a further tumble when Hayworth met Orson Welles, who used her as part of his USO magic act; their affair culminated in marriage on September 7, 1943. Mature heard the news by radio in the North Atlantic and, although heartbroken, in true Mature style he idly quipped, "Now I know that the way to a woman's heart is by sawing her in half." Mature might have been unlucky in love at this juncture in his life, but lady luck was certainly looking down on him in other ways, particularly where flying was concerned. Stuck at an Eastern airport during the war, on a spot of leave, and keen to get back to Hollywood, he hitched a ride aboard a courier flight to an airfield not far from Los Angeles. Twenty-four hours later the plane in which he had made the trip was lost, swallowed up in a storm over the mountains.[19]

During his tour of duty ashore, Mature's acting skills were put to good use in a Coast Guard revue which opened in Miami, Florida, in 1944, before playing across the nation. Throughout his travels he also promoted war bonds. On November 26, 1945, he received an honorable discharge, having reached the rank of chief boatswain's mate.

With his Coast Guard duty behind him, Mature returned to Hollywood, living in his dressing room for the first ten months. When a reporter asked him if he couldn't find a place to live, Mature responded, "I could have, but I thought it was rather crummy of me to rent myself a place when veterans with families were sitting on the curbs."

With the war over, Hollywood entered a new phase, with changing audience tastes, new aspirations and the looming threat of television on the horizon. For many returning stars, it was indeed a period of great uncertainty, as they tried to re-establish their film careers, and Mature was no exception. Fox signed him to a new contract, but the critics were still poised to belittle his acting ability. "I'm identified in print as a 'lush Lothario,' 'Technicolor Tarzan,' and an 'overripe Romeo,'" he explained in a 1940s interview. "Directors who make pictures for the ages and actors who make pictures with one eye cocked on the Academy Award dismiss me as ham—uncured and uncurable." With his engaging, self-deprecating humor, Mature laughed it off, knowing that one day he would prove his critics wrong. And that day dawned in 1946 when director John Ford starred him in his classic Western *My Darling Clementine*, which culminated in the gunfight at the OK Corral. Mature played Doc Holliday to Henry Fonda's Wyatt Earp, an inspired piece of casting that tested the actor with his most complex role to date. As the fatalistic Doc, all consumed with inner bitterness, Mature gave it his all, delivering a powerhouse performance that was simply awesome. Some of the critics were clearly taken aback, with *Variety* commenting, "Improvement in Mature's thesping is marked by a degree of emotional expression and facial animation not seen in his former roles." The *New York Sun* wrote that Mature "forgets about his good looks and actually does some acting.... It's a good part and a good performance." Mature would later praise Ford as "the greatest director, the greatest Irishman, the greatest human being..."[20]

Mature's acting range was tested again the following year, when he took the part of a mysterious aristocratic figure in the intriguing Victorian thriller *Moss Rose* with the British actress Peggy Cummins. (It was his first of four films with Vincent Price.) And to prove that his incredible take on Doc Holliday was not a one off, in the same year he turned in another excellent brooding performance in Henry Hathaway's cult film noir *Kiss of Death*, which co-starred Richard Widmark in his debut film role as a psychotic killer. The role of Nick Bianco, a petty thief turned good, was one of Mature's favorites, proving to one and all that there was more to this guy than the glamour boy image. The *New York Tribune* commented, "Mature has been growing in acting stature so immensely that it is no surprise to find him playing ... with persuasion and finesse." Forever the joker, Mature, during location filming in New York, signed autographs for the prisoners at Sing Sing with a flourishing, "This entitles you to a three-day pass."[21]

Despite his rising star, Mature never forgot who his real friends were, always finding time to be with them, and help sort out their problems if necessary. Mature drew friends from a variety of professions, including a New York doctor, a magazine editor, a publicity man and several actors including Richard Widmark, Jim Backus, Richard Egan and Bill Talman. Mature's close circle of friends also included stuntman Fred Carson, who appeared with Mature in many of his films. As a measure of Mature's kindness, when he left the Coast Guard he took one of his best buddies, Bud Evans, from the service with him, doing some alterations to his house (Mature's) to provide living space for Bud and his wife Ella. Mature commented, "Friendship means a lot to me—perhaps more than it does to most people. I hate being alone. Why, once when I had a perfectly new house to myself, I just couldn't stand it. I closed it up and went to live with a neighbor."[22] Mature's generosity was exercised on many occasions; he once loaned an in-debt studio employee $2,500, telling the man to pay it back a $1 week.[23] Matching this generosity, Mature displayed an amusing frugality, once taking half a dozen high-button shoes from *Million Dollar Mermaid* to convert into golf shoes. He was also noted for buying old cast-off studio clothes at half price for personal use.

In 1948, Mature turned in sterling performances in *Fury at Furnace Creek*, his second Western, and *Cry of the City*, his fourth film noir. Both films were well received, proving he was a natural in both the wide western expanse and the confined urban jungle. Buoyed by success, Mature was ready to try his hand at anything, even another go at marriage, tying the knot with Dorothy Stanford Berry on February 28, 1948. Once again it was love at first sight when Mature met Dorothy shortly after making *Cry of the City*. A pretty blonde, Dorothy had a five-year-old-son, Mike, from her previous marriage. Not one for reading, Mature jokingly remarked in a 1953 interview that when he accompanied Dorothy to a Shakespearean Festival, he had to take a dictionary along to understand half the words. It proved to be another marriage that would eventually end up on the rocks. After a series of breakups, the couple divorced on November 8, 1955. As usual with Mature, the end of this marriage came without the furor of publicity usually associated with celebrity breakups.

The actor's next two films in 1949 were loanouts, *Easy Living* for RKO and *Red Hot and Blue* for Paramount. The former, an offbeat sleeper directed by Jacques Tourneur, saw Mature as an aging pro football star with a heart problem and a wayward wife (Lizabeth Scott). The latter was a more routine affair, a noisy musical comedy with Mature in another theater director role, pretty much playing the straight man to the wild but fun bombshell Betty Hutton.

That same year (1949), while on the Paramount lot, Mature took on the defining role of his film career; a role that would immortalize his name and secure his screen legend: Samson in Cecil B. DeMille's glorious epic *Samson and Delilah*. Over time, much would be said and written about this wonderful film, some good, some bad, but one can't deny its sheer spectacle as screen lovers, Mature and Hedy Lamarr (an awesome combination) play out their doomed love affair. The film was a huge commercial hit, raking in $12 million at the box office.[24] If ever a role fitted an actor like a glove, it was this one, kicking off Mature's association with stories set in the ancient world.

When DeMille first approached him about the role, Mature was initially concerned that it would be a tall order for any actor to bring the character to life, particularly as Samson was such a giant of a man. He told an interviewer, "To give the impression of height, it had to be managed by thought and I had hard work to sustain the illusion of height and power."[25]

With Samson under his belt, Mature was certainly at the top of his game, but despite all his success he always kept things in perspective, commenting in one interview, "I check Victor Mature at the sound stage door. I play the parts straight. I try to become the guy the script says I am. When the job is done though, then I relax. Life should be a ball, you know."

His penchant for relaxing was nicely balanced with his natural business mind. Always on the lookout for an opportunity, and never one to let the grass grow under his feet, Mature went into the retail television business, even selling discount sets from his Fox dressing room, where he would escape to when things got tough at home on the marital front. Mature would find much amusement when, between scenes of his historical films, he would often be called to the phone to deal with a problem concerning his television business. As he aptly put it, "Imagine leaving a scene in which a lion and I are at odds and I am wearing armor and a pleated skirt, to be suddenly plunged into a discussion of amplifiers, resistors

With his renewed strength, Samson (Mature) topples the Philistine temple in the film that set a new benchmark for biblical epics, *Samson and Delilah* (Paramount, 1949).

and solenoids." In a typical moment of self-deprecation, Mature once quipped that people's first thoughts when they wanted a television set were, "Guess I'll call that jerk actor, Vic Mature." Humor aside, Mature was definitely no jerk when it came down to business:

In 1953 he was appointed to the board of directors of Douglas J. Roesch, manufacturers of electronics. In the same year, he was in the running for the honorary Mayor of West Los Angeles.[26] He also judiciously invested in several restaurants and a nightclub.

Throughout the 1940s, Mature's movies greatly added to the coffers of 20th Century–Fox, but the king of the studio during the decade was still Tyrone Power, prompting Mature to comment, "I wasn't pampered the way Tyrone Power was. Zanuck would say to producers, 'If you're not careful, you son of a bitch, I'll give you Mature for your next picture.'" According to the Mature legend, the actor had a neighbor with four children who had hit hard times. The man was exactly the same size as Power, so Mature took two of the neighbor's suits into the Fox wardrobe department and hung them on Power's rack, taking two of the actor's suits in exchange.[27]

The dawn of a new decade, 1950, saw Mature reunited with Betty Grable in Fox's turn-of-the-century musical *Wabash Avenue*, their fourth and final film together. Simply bursting with great songs, eye-catching choreography and sharp, lively banter between Mature and Grable, the film is a treat. Later that year, in the equally tuneful *I'll Get By*, he played himself in a cameo slot.

His laid-back charm found a suitable outlet in the comedy thriller *Stella* (1950) playing an insurance investigator opposite Ann Sheridan, followed by another offbeat role, that of a foreign-born crook facing deportation in *Gambling House* (1950), this time ably supported by Terry Moore and William Bendix.

From 1940 onwards, Mature's distinctive husky voice was also used to good effect on the radio, with many of the shows (*Lux Radio Theater*, *Suspense* and *Hollywood Star Time*) airing adaptations of his films such as *My Gal Sal*, *Kiss of D*eath and *Samson and Delilah*.

In 1951, he extended his business interests to include real estate, returning to the screen in RKO's much underrated noir *The Las Vegas Story* (1952) an enticing tale of lost love and intrigue set against the backdrop of the gambling mecca. The shapely stunner Jane Russell played Mature's former lover, singing two of Hoagy Carmichael's catchy tunes, "I Get Along Without You Very Well" and "My Resistance Is Low" (worth the entrance fee alone), with the great composer himself singing "The Monkey Song." And if that wasn't enough, we are also treated to an incredible, death-defying helicopter chase.

Having been absent from the screen the previous year, Mature was kept busy for the rest of 1952 with three other films: the screen version of George Bernard Shaw's fable *Androcles and the Lion*, marking the Hollywood debut of Jean Simmons; the romantic comedy *Something for the Birds* with Patricia Neal; and the splashy musical biopic *Million Dollar Mermaid* with Esther Williams, with whom the romantic interest was not purely confined to the screen. In her autobiography, Williams was quite candid about her brief affair with Mature, describing him as a strong and fulfilling lover. She added, "He adored the romance of it, too, offering me a surprisingly vulnerable and gentle side that was irresistible."[28]

Mature conceded in an 1950 film magazine interview that women were smarter than men, explaining, "Women are smart because they never make a frontal attack. If they want something, they build up to it gradually. They throw in little hints and suggestions from time to time and conduct a propaganda campaign that would do justice to a government expert. They've infinite patience. And then, when the stage is all set, they score a touchdown before the unsuspecting male knows what has happened."[29]

As the diversity of his relationships continued, so did that of his film roles in 1953, ranging from high drama to comedy. *The Glory Brigade*, a Korean War drama, saw Mature playing his first combat soldier; in *Affair with a Stranger* he returned to light romantic comedy as a playwright in his second feature with the winsome Jean Simmons. But although these films (and the past half dozen) were entertaining enough vehicles, at this point in his career Mature needed another big hit like *Samson and Delilah* to keep him on top: Cue another biblical blockbuster, The *Robe*. As The first feature to make use of Cinema Scope, *The Robe* lent itself perfectly to Mature's imposing screen presence, with the widescreen process fully capturing his statuesque physique and look of anguished heroism. Mature took third billing to Richard Burton and Jean Simmons, but it is his powerful and heartfelt performance as the Greek slave Demetrius that clearly defines the film, which received excellent reviews and box office receipts totaling $17.5 million. If ever Mature deserved an Oscar or at the very least a nomination for his acting, it was in this film, but alas it was not to be. On his role, Mature would later comment, "I had to give up golf during the time I played *The Robe* and later in *Demetrius and the Gladiators*. It was a case of knuckling down to business. I was up against excellent actors. In *The Robe* Demetrius was only a supporting character, so, to make him convincing I had to bring everything I had to the part."[30]

His determination to make the most of his parts in the "toga and sandal" epics didn't go unnoticed by one reviewer who wrote that "he played most of them convincingly because he approached parts like these seriously while other players tended to send up their lines in despair of the script."

To round off 1953, Mature stayed in costume, but on a much lighter note in *The Veils of Bagdad*, providing the actor with another opportunity to stamp his unique style on the swashbuckling genre (after *Captain Caution*).

With his star continuing to shine bright, Mature was still a magnet for female admirers, once happily obliging a good-looking lady who asked if he could teach her to swim at the pool of the Del Mar Hotel (a favorite Hollywood haunt) where he was staying. For an hour, he patiently showed her how to use her arms and legs in the water, only to later learn that he had been giving swimming lessons to Barbara Langan, the swimming coach at the hotel and daughter of the proprietor.[31]

Maintaining a steady stream of four films a year, Mature kicked off 1954 with the action adventure *Dangerous Mission*, filmed in 3-D amidst the breathtaking beauty of Montana's Glacier Park, and co-starring the equally beautiful Piper Laurie. Next came *Demetrius and the Gladiators,* an awesome sequel to *The Robe*, in which the actor gave another incredible performance as the Greek slave. With Mature in his prime taking on gladiators in fights to the death, and coping with palace intrigue and a lustful Susan Hayward, the film certainly ticked all the boxes on the entertainment front. Mature would later praise the director Delmer Daves for creating the right dramatic effect, commenting that he "gave it that deft touch which made every situation come off so it had life." Cashing in on the appetite for tales from the ancient world, Fox pulled out all the stops for *The Egyptian*, which saw Mature at his most opportunist as an ambitious soldier who becomes a pharaoh. Grand to look at, but sluggish in pace, the film was poorly received by critics and audiences alike. As Horemheb, Mature once again recognized the secondary nature of his role, explaining in an interview, "Again, like Demetrius in *The Robe*, I am party to the major conflict — this time between Edmund Purdom and Bella Darvi. It is another instance of a type of part that is not vital to the storyline, and I had to work hard to establish the character and make it memorable."[32]

Extending his repertoire of screen nationalities, Mature played a Dutch resistance fighter in the wartime drama *Betrayed*, which reunited him with one of his old girlfriends, Lana Turner, and gave him an opportunity to work alongside the great Clark Gable in Gable's final film for MGM.

To relax in between film assignments, Mature played golf, which became a major passion in his life. His interest in the game had flourished when he rented a house for two months (while recovering from a leg injury) at Rancho Santa, which was located near one of the best golf courses in California. Mature put much of his good luck down to golf, once commenting, "Golf kept me out of trouble pretty well—the sort I used to get into in my early days in pictures. It also helped to keep me in physical shape. The hours in the fresh air were good. I developed patience, and found time to think as I walked between shots." When later in life, he was asked on the state of his game, Mature, in typical modest style, quipped, "Just say it's legendary."

Mature would regularly recount the story of the time he tried to join an exclusive golf club. When told that they didn't accept actors, he replied that he was no actor and he had 28 films and many reviews to prove it. Apart from swimming, golf was the only keep fit pastime Mature indulged in, because as he once explained, "I'm allergic to exercise." On his dietary habits, he once mused, "I eat what I feel like eating and when I feel like eating it." He added that he smoked like a stove and took a drink when he felt like it. And that said, he lived to the ripe old age of 86.

As the Mature legend gathered pace, so did the bank of stories the actor would joyfully recall, one of which involved being presented to Queen Elizabeth alongside Marilyn Monroe. As the queen approached, Mature noticed that Monroe's bosom was slipping free from her strapless gown. Being the perfect gentleman, he tried to hold up the back of her dress during the ceremony, but had to let go when it was his turn to shake hands. With gravity taking over, Mature said that Monroe remained unperturbed as she chatted with the queen.[33]

In 1955, Mature added another three impressive outdoor action dramas to his CV. *Chief Crazy Horse* saw him proud and resolute in the title role as the legendary Indian leader. It was a sympathetic treatment, and one of the rare occasions where Mature's character dies in the final reel. *Violent Saturday*, a compelling blend of film

Mature in the mid–1950s, indulging his love of golf.

noir and soap opera, showcased his compassionate side as a loving father; it was his final film for 20th Century–Fox. *The Last Frontier*, directed by the highly acclaimed Anthony Mann, cast the actor as a primitive but resourceful trapper, a role that few other actors at the time could have done justice to. All three films saw Mature at his best, with each of his fearless characters barely concealing suppressed pent-up energy and emotion.

In 1955, he hit choppy waters in his home life. Following several rocky years, his marriage to Dorothy Berry came to an end. Next Mature agreed a six-film deal with United Artists, which allowed his production company to take a cut of the profits. In tandem with this package, he made several films under a contract with Britain's Warwick Productions, who made actioners for Columbia. With these two deals under his belt, he was kept fully employed for the rest of the decade, starring in a mixed bag of films; although routine at times, they were all thoroughly entertaining. At this point in his career, Mature was reportedly making approximately $196,000 a picture, plus 25 percent of the profits.[34]

His 1956 program took him to a variety of exotic locations, first to the wilds of Kenya as a revenge-driven big game hunter opposite Janet Leigh in the riveting drama *Safari* (Warwick), followed by a trip to Cuba as a naval officer in *The Sharkfighters* (United Artists). Topping off the year, he traveled to England, India and Burma to play an Afghan bandit in the "boy's own" adventure *Zarak* (Warwick). While in London (a city he fell in love with) shooting scenes for *Safari*, Mature told an interviewer for a big British newspaper that due to certain financial obligations, including private, business and tax commitments, he wasn't exactly rolling in money at that moment. The reporter made a big thing of it, which prompted weeks of letters from his fans containing money and notes of sympathy. Mature returned the money, commenting, "I've never been more moved by anything in my whole life."

The years 1957 and 1958 were lean ones for Mature, output-wise, with only two film releases in each year, both made by Warwick. In 1957, Mature made the narcotics drama *Interpol* with co-producer Albert (Cubby) Broccoli, who would go on to give us the James Bond films. Likeably conveyed like a pulp novel, the film's action moved all around the world and included a brilliant turn from Trevor Howard as a deranged killer. The excellent British film noir *The Long Haul* followed next, with Mature giving one of his best anguished performances as a trucker whose married life is put to the test when he falls for femme fatale Diana Dors.

Nineteen fifty-eight added another two World War II stories to Mature's résumé. Back at Warwick, he played an American soldier serving in a British tank crew fighting in the Libyan desert in *Tank Force* (a.k.a. *No Time to Die* in the U.K.), a routine actioner which did little to test the actor. By contrast, *China Doll* (United Artists), which marked director Frank Borzage's return to the screen after a ten-year absence, was an a touching, offbeat love story in which Mature's battle-weary pilot falls in love with a Chinese girl. In it, his character is fully developed, enabling the actor to convey a range of emotions as he grapples with the demands upon him. Mature and Borzage had planned to form a production company, but nothing came of it.

With the decade drawing to a close and early retirement looming, Mature bowed out in style in a mixed collection of derring-do adventures, all familiar tales but great fun nonetheless. Fulfilling his United Artists obligations, at the start of 1959 he was cast in *Escort West* as an ex–Confederate soldier heading west through hostile territory with his daughter, along the way picking up Indian attack survivors Elaine Stewart and Faith Domergue. As the caring father, Mature gave a sincere and subtle performance in a Western that deserves better recognition. Next, Warwick decided to do another take on *Zarak*, casting

Mature as an Indian chieftain in *The Bandit of Zhobe*. Another "boy's own" adventure yarn followed, with Mature working up a sweat as an adventurer in *Timbuktu* (United Artists), a gloriously camp tale involving the French Foreign Legion and love interest Yvonne De Carlo. Mature firmly put his stamp on the circus genre in Allied Artists' appropriately titled *The Big Circus* (released before *Timbuktu*), a wonderfully colorful, star and action packed big-top drama, which saw Mature in a tailor-made role as the circus owner who must keep the show on the road.

On September 27, 1959, Mature gave marriage another try, tying the knot with wife number four, Adrienne Joy Urwick, the 25-year-old-actress-daughter of a London physician. Earlier that year, his mother Clara passed away.

Not quite ready to hit the golf courses on a daily basis, Mature headed off to Italy in 1960 to prove he still had what took to convince in the "sword and sandal" genre. (The Italian film companies were churning out them as low-budget quickies between 1957 and 1965, usually starring American imports such as Steve Reeves and Gordon Scott.) In *Hannibal*, he gave a solid, respectable performance as the Carthaginian general who takes on the might of Rome. Two years later, in the role of a Viking, he was pitted against his Rita Hayworth love adversary, Orson Welles, in *The Tartars*. The film was described as trash, but one can't deny that it was highly enjoyable trash, with the presence of two screen giants enough to put butts in seats.

With these two foreign ventures behind him, Mature went into semi-retirement, continuing to look after his business interests. On his retirement, he explained, "I thought it would be a good idea to sort of enjoy what I had worked so hard for and see how the other half of the world lived."

In 1966, he was coaxed out of retirement to parody himself as an aging actor in the Neil Simon comedy *After the Fox,* which was shot in Italy and Yugoslavia. Mature was on cracking form in the role, literally stealing the show from star Peter Sellers. Thereafter, his appearances were rare, and for the most part in cameo roles. In 1968, he appeared in the Monkees' surreal comedy *Head* as a giant aptly called "The Big Victor," a role which he said he only took because he said he was bored with retirement and never took any of his movie star image seriously. The comedy *Every Little Crook & Nanny* (1972) saw him once again sending himself up, this time as a Mafia godfather opposite Lynn Redgrave, followed by yet more self-parodying in the "spot the star" spoof *Won Ton Ton, the Dog Who Saved Hollywood* (1976). In 1978, he appeared in possibly the shortest cameo on record at the end of Michael Winner's action thriller *Firepower* starring James Coburn and Sophia Loren. His last role was as Samson's father in the 1984 television version of *Samson and Delilah*, with largely unknown actor Antony Hamilton in the title role that Mature made his own 35 years previously. Asked how he felt about playing Samson's father, Mature, in typical glib style, responded, "If the price is right, I'll play his mother." Mature was also asked to play Sylvester Stallone's father in a movie, but the project never came off, which is a great shame, because in many ways, Mature was the forerunner of the great action stars such as Stallone. I can just see Mature playing Rocky, or perhaps Stallone playing Nick Bianco or Samson. Ah, the endless possibilities.

After ten years of marriage, Mature and Joy Urwick divorced on February 6, 1969. Fox publicist and long-term friend Johnny Campbell proffered a possible explanation as to why Mature's marriages were always destined to failure: "These gals marry him and they think they're going to change his lifestyle, and they don't. He stays the same and they get disillusioned."

It would be another five years before the actor was tempted to give marriage one more try, this time to former opera singer Loretta "Lorey" Sebena. Married on February 22, 1974, Mature finally found his soulmate in Loretta, with the couple enjoying a happy marriage which was blessed in 1975 with Mature's first and only child, Victoria.

Mature spent the rest of his retirement in relative privacy, whiling away the days with his wife, daughter, a few good friends and the everpresent golf clubs. Despite all his loafing (as he described it), Mature displayed a zest for life, making the most of each day, informing one interviewer, "I never slept until noon in my life. Rarely miss a sunrise."

Having reached a state of pure happiness, Mature commented in a 1987 interview, "Hell, I'm a lucky guy. My wife and I are as happy as can be. Our little girl was born when I was 60. I came into fatherhood late in life, and I love it." When Victoria was seven in 1982, Mature proudly remarked that she played golf with him "every once in a while, but I don't want her to get too good. The way I play, that would be embarrassing."

Mature's happy state was interrupted in 1989 when his best friend and fellow actor Jim Backus, of Mr. Magoo fame, died. Mature was devastated by his death, but fortunately he had Lorey and Victoria around to help him through his grief. Towards the end of the 1990s Mature's health deteriorated and after a three-year battle with leukemia, he passed away on August 4, 1999, aged 86, at his beloved home Rancho Santa Fe, California, with his wife and daughter at his side.

Despite all his fine, and in some cases outstanding performances, Mature, at the height of his career, was never asked to put his footprints in the cement at Grauman's Chinese Theater. Acknowledging the rebuke in glorious Mature style, he lowered his rear end into wet concrete in front of his Fox dressing room. At age 55, in an interview with Aijean Harmetz, he explained that he took acting a lot more seriously than anyone else but, perhaps due to a complex, he found it difficult to show it. He added that going to premieres scared him to death, and that when appearing, he would put on a brave, spirited stance to suggest otherwise.

Mature certainly lived a full life, leaving behind a wonderful film legacy which we still enjoy today. He was a larger-than-life character who always seemed to remain positive and upbeat. One of his remarks may perfectly sum up his outlook. When an interviewer wrapped up by inquiring as to whether Mature was going to work, the actor jovially responded, "No. I'm going to a party. Gonna have some fun. You've gotta have fun, boy, or life becomes a bore."

What more can I say, other than "Victor Mature, we salute you!"

THE FILMS
(Chronologically)

The Housekeeper's Daughter

United Artists, 1939

Cast: Joan Bennett (Hilda); Adolphe Menjou (Deakon Maxwell); John Hubbard (Robert Randall); William Gargan (Ed O'Malley); George E. Stone (Benny); Peggy Wood (Olga); Donald Meek (Editor Wilson); Marc Lawrence (Floyd); Lilian Bond (Gladys); Victor Mature (Lefty); John Hyams (Professor Randall); Leila McIntyre (Mrs. Randall); Luis Alberni (Tony Veroni); Rosina Galli (Mrs. Veroni); Tom Dugan, Gene Morgan (Gangsters).

Credits: Hal Roach (Producer-Director); Donald Henderson Clarke (Story); Rian James, Gordon Douglas (Screenplay); Norbert Brodine (Cinematography); Amedeo De Filippi (Music); Lud Gluskin (Music Director); Charles D. Hall (Art Direction); Harry Black (Wardrobe); Roy Seawright (Special Effects); Bernard Carr (Assistant Director); William Randall (Sound); William Ziegler (Editor). Running time: 81 minutes

Hilda ends her association with a racketeering gang headed by Floyd, and returns home to her mother, a housekeeper to the wealthy Randall family. The Randalls' son Robert has a craving to be a reporter and stumbles upon some clues that could lead to a murder indictment for Floyd, when the body of Floyd's girlfriend, Gladys, is found in the river. Gladys had accidentally been poisoned by her friend Benny, a meek flower vendor, who had intended the poison for Floyd. With the assistance of a hard-drinking reporter, Deakon Maxwell, and his photographer pal Ed O'Malley, Robert sets about pulling the case together, despite attempts by Floyd's henchmen, headed by Lefty (Victor Mature), to have him silenced. Lefty is sweet on Hilda, but she only has eyes for Robert. All ends in a final showdown, in which Benny is shot by Floyd (after revealing that he had set out to poison him). Floyd is shot by a dying Lefty (he, too, inadvertently samples Benny's poisoned coffee) in a final act of retribution, and the rest of the members of the mob are rounded up by the police. Robert and Hilda announce their engagement.

"5 Men Ran After THE HOUSEKEEPER'S DAUGHTER ...
Who Treated Them Like She Hadn't Oughter!"

"5 Men Tried to Keep House with THE HOUSEKEEPER'S
DAUGHTER ...But Keeping House Was Not in Her Line!"

"She Couldn't Cook, She Couldn't Sew,
but Oh how she could so and so!"

With such titillating plugs, who could fail to get excited? The lead star, Joan Bennett, by all accounts. Hailing from a respectable acting dynasty, she didn't see the funny side and promptly harnessed the support of 2,600 women's clubs countrywide in her objection to the "tongue-in-cheek" slogans. The press had a field day with the protests, which simply fueled the publicity for the film.[1] Such an unexpected marketing boost would have not gone unappreciated by the producer Hal Roach. Mature, the king of self-publicity, must have been grinning from ear to ear.

Perhaps Bennett's apparent lack of humor was a little understandable, when one considers that in the previous year, she was shortlisted for the part of Scarlett O'Hara in *Gone with the Wind*, with the likes of Paulette Goddard, Jean Arthur and English candidate Vivien Leigh, who of course went on to win the much coveted role and a place in Hollywood Valhalla as a consequence. From *GWTW* contender to the low-key comedy feature *The Housekeeper's Daughter*, in less than a year, must have been quite a climb-down for Bennett, although in between, she did manage to slip in the respectable *The Man in the Iron Mask*.

The Housekeeper's Daughter simply can't make up its mind whether it's a romantic comedy, screwball comedy, black comedy, zany crime comedy, thriller comedy or an outing in slapstick mayhem. However, whatever the label, the frantic pace of the film, crammed with incident, keeps you heartily amused throughout, as one should rightfully be by a Hal Roach feature.

Like many of the early Hollywood pioneers, Roach's career was a fascinating story in itself. He drifted into films after a stint as a mule skinner and an Alaskan gold prospector.

Mature pulls in the fan mail in his debut role as gangster Lefty, who is sweet on reluctant mobster's moll Hilda (Joan Bennett), in the Hal Roach comedy *The Housekeeper's Daughter* (United Artists, 1939).

Rising from stuntman and extra to minor actor, he went on to become one of the great Hollywood producers (also taking in directing and screenwriting), successfully transcending the silent era to sound, and along the way launching the careers of Harold Lloyd, Laurel and Hardy, Charlie Chase, Our Gang — and Victor Mature. In the late 1930s, Roach moved away from short comedies and started to produce feature films such as the successful *Topper* series and *The Housekeepers Daughter*. Going strong to the end, he lived to see his 100th birthday.

During a 1972 interview, Mature recalled his days with Roach and a particularly amusing incident involving Bennett. Instructed to slap her in one scene, he overdid it and accidentally knocked off her wig, which made Bennett extremely angry. When Roach approached Mature with a serious expression, the actor feared the worst, but the mogul simply whispered to him, "Next time hit her a little harder."[2]

In one of the reviews for the film, Bennett's looks were compared to one of Mature's future leading ladies, Hedy Lamarr. However, as a sign of her versatility, she could easily turn femme fatale, as she seductively proved in two of Fritz Lang's greatest noirs, *The Woman in the Window* (1944) *and Scarlet Street* (1945), both featuring Edward G. Robinson. Bennett holds the distinction of starring in five Fritz Lang films, more than any other American actress or actor. Her career took a tumble in the early 1950s when her third husband, producer Walter Wanger, in a jealous rage, shot and wounded Bennett's agent, who he assumed was having an affair with his wife.

Although Bennett was the star of the film, it was Mature who received all the attention. Female audience members swamped the Hal Roach studies with thirty thousand letters praising the new boy on the block. It was hard for the 6'2½" Mature to go unnoticed as he towered above the other henchmen. In his opening scene, with his exotic Mediterranean looks and imposing physique, nattily decked out in a black tuxedo, he clearly looked like a guy who was going places.

Mature's imposing frame had not always been in evidence. During his starvation years at the Pasadena Community Playhouse, he dropped down to 160 pounds, which is almost "Gandhi weight" for a guy his size, and he'd have dropped lower if it wasn't for a hash house waitress who took pity on him, making out checks for dime Cokes while slipping him full meals. To repay her kindness, when he got his first break with *The Housekeeper's Daughter*, he sent her sixty dollars which she pasted in her memory book, later commenting, "He's got a break in Hollywood — seventy-five bucks a week! So out of his first check, he sends me sixty!"[3]

In an early scene in the film, we get a slight hint of Mature's likable heroic potential when his gangster boss growls at Bennett, "You know, for two cents I'd slap your teeth out." We hear Mature's first screen words, as he rides to her defense, "Take it easy, will you, chief?" Okay, it's not exactly the Gettysburg Address, but Mature delivered it with great confidence, as he did with much of his dialogue in the film. He was on screen for about five minutes.

The rest of the supporting cast was also top-notch, including the suave Adolphe Menjou, William Gargan, Donald Meek, Marc Lawrence and Peggy Wood. And we mustn't forget George E. Stone's wonderfully sensitive performance as the wacko poisoner Benny. (Got a part for a furtive-looking little guy, and Peter Lorre and Elisha Cook, Jr., are both out of town? Get George E. Stone's agent on the line.)

As debut roles go, Mature's Lefty (a gangster who's not all bad) was a respectable one, and it gave him an opportunity to play his first death scene, albeit a brief one, when he unwittingly savors a cup of Benny's lethal brew in the last reel, and then shoots his mobster boss to stop him from plugging Bennett.

Variety commented, "*The Housekeeper's Daughter* is a wacky farce, not to be taken seriously, and audiences will accept it on that basis."

Halliwell pretty much summed up today's view: "Zany crime farce which often lets its zip fade, but atones in a crazy firework finale."

One Million B.C.

United Artists, 1940

Cast: Victor Mature (Tumak); Carole Landis (Loana); Lon Chaney, Jr. (Akhoba); Conrad Nagel (Narrating Archaeologist); John Hubbard (Ohtao); Nigel De Brulier (Peytow); Mamo Clark (Nupondi); Inez Palange (Tohana); Edgar Edwards (Skakana); Jacqueline Dalya (Ataf); Mary Gale Fisher (Wandi); Norman Budd, Harry Wilson, John Northpole, Lorraine Rivero, Harold Howard, Ricca Allen, Adda Gleason, Edward Coxen (Rock People); Ben Hall, Creighton Hale, Audrey Manners, Rosemary Theby, Patricia Pope, Chuck Stubbs (Shell People).

Credits: Hal Roach (Producer-Director); Hal Roach, Jr. (Director); Mickell Novack, George Baker & Joseph Frickert (Screenplay); Norbert Brodine (Cinematography); Werner R. Heymann (Music): Charles D. Hall (Art Direction); Harry Black (Wardrobe); Roy Seawright (Special Effects); Bernard Carr (Assistant Director); William Randall (Sound); Ray Snyder (Editor). Running time: 80 minutes.

Caught in a rainstorm, a group of wanderers find shelter in a cave where they meet an archaeologist, who entertains them with his interpretation of the story depicted by prehistoric drawings on the cave walls. He tells of the caveman Tumak, (Victor Mature), a member of the primitive Rock tribe, who following an argument with his father, Akhoba, is exiled from the community. On his travels he meets Loana, a member of the more civilized Shell tribe. The shell tribe takes him in, and she teaches him good manners and a gentler way of life. But he is forced to flee the camp for stealing, and makes his way back to his own people in the company of Loana. Threatened by a series of calamities including an erupting volcano and rampaging dinosaurs, both of the tribes are brought together to fight the common danger.

"UNBELIEVABLE! The World at the Dawn of Time!"

Unbelievable is right: dinosaurs co-existing with cavemen (just a few million years out I guess, but hey, I'm no expert), the perfectly coiffured Landis chased from pillar to post by all types of beasties without a hair out of place, and Mature in his first starring role, cleanly shaven when all around are sporting beards (with the exception of the ladies of course). Was he possibly christened Tumak Remington?

But joking aside, this film is a pure delight, wonderfully camp and well worth a view. Prior to *One Million B.C.*, only a handful of films had tackled the subject of our prehistoric past (all of them silent). Inspired by Sir Arthur Conan Doyle's *The Lost World* (1912) and Edgar Rice Burroughs' *The Land That Time Forgot* (1915), the silents included D.W. Griffith's *Man's Genesis* (1912), Charlie Chaplin's *His Prehistoric Past* (1914), Buster Keaton's *Three Ages* (1923) and Laurel and Hardy's *Flying Elephants* (1928).

Tumak (Mature) and Loana (Carole Landis) experience the perils of outdoor life in the caveman saga *One Million B.C.* (United Artists, 1940).

But no one had attempted a serious sound feature on the subject, perhaps because of the difficulty of realistically conveying a story through caveman grunts and groans. Roach decided to give it a go, and managed to coax the legendary silent film director D.W. Griffith out of retirement to help handle the reins of the production. With a keen eye on box-office returns, Roach believed that Griffith's name still had great marquee value which would help to pull in the audiences. However, Griffith left the film at an early stage and it is difficult to discern exactly how much of the film he was responsible for. Some suggest he was disappointed to discover that Roach was really in charge of the direction and that his name was simply being used for prestige purposes. In response to his objections, the film went into general release in 1940 with his name conspicuously absent from the credits. Instead, Roach credited himself as producer and director with his son Hal Roach, Jr.

Roach may have been a wheeler dealer type, but he certainly knew how to pull a great cast together for this prehistoric epic: Victor Mature, Carole Landis and Lon Chaney, Jr. Who could ask for more? As well as giving Mature his first starring role, the film also gave Landis her first big break. A favorite pin-up girl of World War II, Landis started out as a hula dancer and dance band singer before Hollywood beckoned. Unfortunately, for much of her film career she tended to be relegated to B movie roles, and after a series of failed marriages, health issues, financial problems and a disastrous liaison with married Rex Harrison, she committed suicide in 1948 at age 29. Her screen legacy lives on including three memorable outings with Mature: *One Million B.C., I Wake Up Screaming* (1941) and *My Gal Sal* (1942).

Although Mature and Chaney had been first choice for their parts, this was not so with Landis, who according to Roach only got the part because Griffith thought she was the most athletic barefoot runner out of a group of fifty females he had running back and forth to his command.[1] As Roach put it, "That's a hell of a way to find a leading lady." Griffith felt that the ability to run like a deer was vitally important in a film where the girl is constantly chased by all manner of prehistoric animals. With the amorous Mature on set, you'd think that those fast feet would have been put to good work for other reasons, but that was not the case as Landis revealed in a 1942 interview: "Vic and I are really close friends. After all we both started in *One Million B.C.* We both had a long hard climb to 20th Century–Fox together and both are still appearing in the same pictures. We protect and praise each other and we're conscientious about our jobs. When we're working on a picture we don't kid around — it's home, study, and early to bed for each of us." Landis further recalled how Mature and co-star John Hubbard tried to shock her one day on set, while dressed in their cavemen attire. They were eating lunch at the time and as soon as they saw her, they reverted to cavemen eating habits, plastering their hair and faces with butter and mustard. Landis also described how one day during filming, Mature sprained his ankle scrambling over some mountain terrain, but because he was a good sport he insisted on working rather than holding up the production.[2] Mature would later describe Landis as a wonderful girl and a "regular fellow."

In addition to her sprinting prowess, Landis, when being auditioned, probably also scored heavily in the drop-dead gorgeous department — particularly when kitted out in a skimpy cave girl costume. She was definitely up there with the likes of Raquel Welch's eye-catching furry bikini-clad cave girl from the 1966 remake *One Million Years B.C.* (with John Richardson in the role of Tumak) and Maureen O'Sullivan's censor-baiting thigh-cut loincloth from *Tarzan and his Mate* (1934).

With Mature's solid frame, 15-inch biceps and confident handling of a primitive man character shaped by the challenges of his environment, he would have made a great Tarzan if the opportunity had arisen, which it didn't. This enabled Mature to escape typecasting and go on to a wide variety of roles — although possible caveman sequels such as *Tumak and the Amazons* or *Tumak and the Leopard Woman* certainly get my vote. Fortunately for Mature and his fans, Johnny Weissmuller and Jon Hall had these type of one-dimensional roles nailed down at the time.

Although the dialogue was gibberish, both Mature and Landis conveyed a lot of emotion in their scenes together, in a slender plotline that was essentially Romeo and Juliet meet the Flintstones. But the acting honors had to go to Lon Chaney, Jr., who in the role of Tumak's deposed father gave it all he had. Playing it like a silent movie, his range of facial expressions would have made his father, "Man of a Thousand Faces" Lon Chaney, proud. The look on his face when Tumak brings home a blonde babe to teach them table manners is a hoot. However, like Griffith, Chaney was also disappointed with the end result, *One Million B.C.* coming hot on the heels of the success of his impressive performance as Lennie in the Steinbeck classic *Of Mice and Men* (1939). Following in the footsteps of his father, Chaney devised his own makeup for the part, but was blocked from using it by the cosmeticians union, whose rules stipulated that actors could not create their own makeup.[3] Supporting player John Hubbard starred in Mature's debut film *The Housekeeper's Daughter.*

The film opened to mixed reviews with many deriding some of the dinosaur special effects employed. Griffith had wanted to use the type of dinosaur animation that made *The Lost World* (1925) and *King Kong* (1933) such successes, but Roach, keen to keep costs down, insisted on using miniature sets populated by lizards and alligators with sail-fins stuck on their backs. Griffith thought this would look phony, and it is perhaps another reason why he disappeared from the scene.[4] That said, the special effects did win an Oscar nomination, perhaps mainly for the impressive volcanic eruption and earthquake scenes. Personally, I think the enlarged beasties work well, and the fight to the death duel (quite literally — animal welfare was clearly not high on the agenda) between a lizard and an alligator is simply awesome. Equally impressive was the music score by Werner Heymann, which also secured an Oscar nomination. Due to claims of animal cruelty, many of the scenes were heavily edited when the film was released in England.

B.R. Crisler of the *New York Times* lapped up the entertainment on offer, commenting "[I]t is the most delightfully amusing tableau from a museum of unnatural history in the history of the cinema....." The *New York Post* said that Mature "is good in a brunette primitive way." *The A to Z of Science Fiction & Fantasy Films* called it "[d]ated, anachronistic monster pic, of interest chiefly for the talent involved." In *Science Fiction in the Cinema*, John Baxter wrote, "The ineptly organized battles between lizards are less impressive than Mature's shambling ardor."

Captain Caution

United Artists, 1940

Cast: Victor Mature (Daniel Marvin); Louise Platt (Corunna Dorman); Leo Carrillo (Lucien Argandeau); Bruce Cabot (Lehrman Slade); Robert Barrat (Capt. Dorman); Vivienne Osborne (Victorine Argandeau); Miles Mander (Lieut. Strope); El Brendel (Slushy); Roscoe Ates (Chips); Andrew Tombes (Sad Eyes); Aubrey Mather (Mr. Henry Potter); Alan Ladd (Newton); J. Pat O'Malley (Fish Peddler); Lloyd Corrigan (Capt. Stannage); Ted Osborne (Capt. Steve Decatur); Ann Codee (Landlady); Romaine Callender (English Officer); Pierre Watkin (American Consul); Clifford Severn (Travers — English Drummer Boy); Bud Jamison (Blinks).

Credits: Hal Roach, Richard Wallace & Grover Jones (Producers); Richard Wallace (Director); Kenneth Roberts (Novel); Grover Jones (Screenplay); Norbert Brodine (Cinematography); Phil Ohman (Music); Nicolai Remisoff (Art Direction); Walter Plunkett (Wardrobe); Charles D. Hall & Roy Seawright (Special Effects); Harve Foster (Assistant Director); William M. Randall, Jr. (Sound); James E. Newcom (Editor). Running time: 86 minutes.

In the year 1812, the *Olive Branch*, an American merchant ship on its way home with a valuable cargo from the Far East, is fired upon by a British ship, as unbeknownst to the crew of the *Olive Branch*, their country is now at war with England. The shelling results in the capture of the American ship and the death of its captain, whose daughter Corunna vows vengeance on the British. Her sweetheart, sailor Dan Marvin, urges caution, for which she scornfully titles him Captain Caution. Upon recapture of the ship, Corunna spurns Dan, whom she considers a coward, and makes the treacherous sailor Slade her first mate. She then sets out to use her ship to do battle with the British, but Slade has ambitions to take the ship and the feisty Corunna for his own. Following a bout of double dealing and a full-blooded sea battle, Dan proves to Coruuna that she misjudged him when he regains control of the ship after dispensing with the dastardly Slade, and all ends well.

Having flexed his muscles, to great effect, in *One Million B.C.*, prompting a deluge of fan mail, Mature fittingly followed it up with another rousing adventure yarn, *Captain Caution*. With Errol Flynn, Douglas Fairbanks, Jr. and Tyrone Power drawing in the crowds with their swashbucklers, Roach decided to carve his own initials on the genre with this adaptation of Kenneth Roberts's 1934 novel of the same name. Roberts scored with another historical novel, *Northwest Passage*, that same year when it was made into a film by MGM with Spencer Tracy in the lead role.

Taking charge of production, Roach handed the reins of direction to Richard Wallace, whose initial ambitions to become a surgeon were curtailed during medical training due to lack of funding. After a stint as a merry-go-round operator with a carnival company, he worked for Max Sennett as a scene cutter before joining the Hal Roach Studios. More renowned for "B" movies than "A," his memorable credits include *The Little Minister* (1934), *A Night to Remember* (1943), *Bombardier* (1943) and a handful of Shirley Temple films.

With the exception of Lewis Milestone, who directed Roach's crowning glory *Of Mice and Men*, eminent directors eluded the producer due to the precarious financial standing of his studio. And with the company facing financial ruin in 1940, Wallace really had his work cut out to deliver the goods with *Captain Caution*. Alas, despite great efforts by all concerned, the film did poor business at the box office, with many critics going for the jugular where Mature's performance was concerned. The *New York World-Telegram* moaned, "His work is, bluntly, amateurish." The *New York Post* was equally scathing, claiming, "He is equipped for the role only in physical aspects."

Such criticism was perhaps a trifle harsh for the youthful-looking Mature. When it came to derring-do, nobody could surpass Errol Flynn, the master of high adventure and reckless action, but Mature brought a new vigor to the action, one based on the use of his fists and sheer brawn. Lacking the nimble athleticism associated with fancy sword play (perfected by Flynn and Power), Mature heroically slugs his way out of trouble to save the crew and win the hand of the fair maiden. Roach initially had his eye on John Wayne for the role of Dan Marvin,[1] and Wayne no doubt would have chewed up the scenery and the bad guys in like manner. But all great swashbucklers are only as good as the villains that feature in them, and *Captain Caution* had one of the best: Wayne's drinking buddy and fellow hell-raiser, the inimitable Bruce Cabot, whose many pre–Hollywood jobs included that of a sailor. With his robust frame and tough guy looks, he made the perfect adversary for Mature, with both actors quite literally matching each other pound for pound in stature and in the muscle stakes. Both actors also shared a similar distinction in that Mature made his mark in *One Million B.C*, while Cabot scored a big hit in another epic monster movie, *King Kong* (1933). Mature's scrap with Cabot took two and a half days to film, with Mature losing seven pounds in the process to Cabot's five. The film also has Mature pitted against a hulking brute, decked out in Arabian Nights fancy dress and given to bouts of hysterical laughter. Twice the size of Mature, this guy is clearly off his trolley, but, fear not, our gallant hero comes out on top.

Mature's character is clearly a man who will only resort to violence when it is absolutely necessary (hence his character's name Captain Caution), but push him too far and he's a force to be reckoned with, as we witness in an early scene. After his courage is questioned, he lays out two belligerent sailors with his fists, snarling, "I said I wouldn't fight. I didn't say I couldn't." Mature's ability to convey restraint when under pressure would be developed to greater effect in later movies.

Bearing proud torso, Captain Caution (Mature, right) prepares for action alongside feisty Corunna Dorman (Louise Platt) and Frenchman Lucien Argendeau (Leo Carrillo) in the rousing seafaring adventure *Captain Caution* (United Artists, 1940).

In addition to Mature's dashing two-fisted hero, which marked a notable departure from the genre norm, it was refreshing to see a privateer movie set during the War of 1812; the majority of entries were usually set in the West Indies during the sixteenth to eighteenth centuries. With Britain at war during filming, Roach was careful not to show the British in a bad light, with the real villain of the piece clearly that no-good double-crossing varmint Lehrman Slade played by Cabot.

The rest of the cast members are also good value. Louise Platt had, a year earlier, acquitted herself admirably as the officer's pregnant wife in John Ford's *Stagecoach* (1939). In 1942, aged 27, she married and retired from acting. As is the way with sea-going heroines, Platt was feisty as they come, although of course not quite in the same league as the queen of swashbuckling piracy Maureen O'Hara. Due to the misunderstandings that abound between the two lovers in the film, Mature's scenes with Platt are, at times, both tender and intense.

The film's comic relief came courtesy of Leo Carrillo, possibly the most stereotypical Latino in screen history. Such was the large cast on offer (it seems that all of Central Casting got in on the act), there was even a place for a pre-stardom Alan Ladd who played one of several sailors pressed into service by the British and mercilessly punished with a constant diet of smoked herrings. With his wild long hair and slightly startled, "faraway" look, Ladd clearly thought he was in *Treasure Island* playing Ben Gunn.

Although the film is as rousing as they come, I have to admit that there are times when the fast-paced plot, which entails the capturing and recapturing of the ship on numerous occasions, leaves you in a whirl, wondering just exactly who has possession of it (don't pop out to make a cup of tea or you'll never keep up).

Variety commented, "Although the picture holds plenty of robust action, excitement and knockabout battles, it never quite makes up its mind to be a straight adventure drama or a Gilbert and Sullivan operetta presentation of the subject." The *New York Times* agreed on the action element ("the carnage is great"), but assessed the plot as meandering: "*Captain Caution* is a slapstick version of the long voyage home without a compass."

Mature's Dan Marvin was in no doubt what it was all about, pretty much summing it up in the final scene: "There will always be war, but there's only one time in a life that the right girl comes along." So to hell with liberty, duty, fraternity, democracy, nationhood, and all that inconsequential stuff; what it really boils down to (as we always suspected) is getting the gal. If you don't find any enjoyment in this film, you're certainly one tough nut to crack.

Constantly plagued with debt, the Roach Studio was re-established for television in 1948, but when Roach went into retirement in 1955, it finally succumbed to creditors, closing its doors in 1961.

No, No, Nanette

RKO, 1940

Cast: Anna Neagle (Nanette); Richard Carlson (Tom Gillespie); Victor Mature (William Trainor); Roland Young (Jimmy Smith); Helen Broderick (Mrs. Susan Smith); Zasu Pitts (Pauline Hastings); Eve Arden (Kitty); Billy Gilbert (Styles); Tamara (Sonya); Stuart Robertson (Stillwater, Jr. & Stillwater, Sr.); Dorothea Kent (Betty); Aubrey Mather (Remington); Mary Gordon (Gertrude); Russell Hicks (Hutch).

Crew: Herbert Wilcox (Producer-Director); based on the musical comedy by Frank Madel, Otto A. Harbach, Vincent Youmans and Emil Nyitray; Ken Englund (Screenplay); Russell Metty (Cinematography); Anthony Collins (Musical Director); Vincent Youmans, Otto Harbach & Irving Cesar (Songs); Lawrence P. Williams (Art Direction); Darrell Silvera (Set Decorations); Edward Stevenson (Costume Design); Vernon L. Walker (Special Effects); Aida Broadbent (Choreography); Kenneth Holmes & Lloyd Richards (Assistant Directors); Richard Van Hessen (Sound); Elmo Williams (Editor). Running time: 96 minutes.

Nanette, a busy "Miss Fix-It," tries to save the marriage of her wealthy uncle, "Happy" Jimmy Smith, and help him out of his financial difficulties by ending his commitments to three gold-diggers, whom he has got entangled with over the years through his innocent flirtations. To this end, she enlists the services of theatrical producer William Trainor (Victor Mature) and artist Tom Gillsepie, who both promptly fall in love with her. Having saved the marriage of her uncle by diverting the girls down other theatrical and financial avenues, Nanette chooses Tom over Bill as her husband-to-be.

Broadly speaking, Mature's film career, with one or two exceptions, fell into four genres: musical, film noir, religious epic and general outdoor adventure. (The latter category sub-divided into several further categories: war, Western etc.) With *No, No, Nanette*, Mature took his first tentative steps into the realms of the first category, the Hollywood musical. And surprisingly, for an actor devoid of any dancing or singing talent, he proved a success

"Little Miss Fix It" Nanette (Anna Neagle) arm in arm with both her suitors, theater producer William Trainor (Mature, left) and artist Tom Gillespie (Richard Carlson), in the Herbert Wilcox musical comedy *No, No, Nanette* (RKO, 1940).

in the genre, for what he lacked in crooning or hoofing skills, he more than made up for with his striking good looks, infectious grin and lightness of comedy touch. Like Don Ameche and John Payne, he made the ideal musical companion to the great musical pin-ups of the period, most notably Betty Grable. However, his first musical outing, *No, No, Nanette*, saw him in support of British box office sensation Anna Neagle — a teaming which, on paper, seems just as bizarre and mismatched as Neagle's collaboration with Errol Flynn in two later musicals, *Lilacs in the Spring* (1955) and *King's Rhapsody* (1955). But oddly enough, in both cases, the combinations work a treat.

The sophisticated Neagle started out as a dancer before being discovered by the founder of Elstree Studios, producer-director Herbert Wilcox, who became her husband in 1943. Although highly adept at musicals and comedies, it was the historical drama where she really made her mark: *Nell Gwynn* (1934), *Victoria the Great* (1937) and *Nurse Edith Cavell* (1939).

During World War II, she appeared in several Hollywood productions including three frothy musical comedies: this movie, *Irene* (1940 and *Sunny* (1941). Neagle commented in her autobiography, *There's Always Tomorrow*, that she and Wilcox chose these escapist films "to cheer up the troops and munitions workers." She further recalled that Wilcox had another reason for the choice: "So far American audiences had seen me only in character parts and believed me to be a middle-aged character actress. These new films were to blow that 'middle-aged' image sky high and present me as myself." They clearly had that effect. Later, when Neagle was on a continental ENSA tour, a young American soldier was heard to remark, "Cor — last time I saw her she was Queen Victoria. I never knew she had legs like that."[1]

Neagle may have not been middle-aged when she made *No, No, Nanette*, but at 36 she was no youngster. As a testament to her natural beauty, she looked the same age as her fellow co-stars Mature, aged 27 at the time, and Richard Carlson, aged 28.

The role of Broadway producer William Trainor gave Mature his first opportunity to hone an image as a self-satisfied, overly confident, brash "man about town" type, which he memorably played in the later features *My Gal Sal* (1942), *Seven Days' Leave* (1942), *Footlight Serenade* (1942), *Wabash Avenue* (1950) and *Million Dollar Mermaid* (1952). It was during this period that the media tagged him a "Glamour Boy," which didn't perturb Mature in the slightest, as he explained in a 1941 interview: "I woke up one morning and found myself a 'Glamour Boy,' then a 'Matinee Idol,' then a 'Beautiful Hunk of Man.' It grew and grew.... [I]t's none of my doing, but it's okay, it's harmless. ...The whole thing is ridiculous. I am revolting to look at, actually. I'm about as glamorous as Wally Beery."

Mature's casting in the part only came about because of Roach's dire financial plight, which prompted him to share the actor's contract with RKO, who immediately put him under a six-picture deal starting with *No, No, Nanette*.[2] This was the second screen adaptation of the 1925 Broadway musical following a 1930 Warner version starring Bernice Clare. Zasu Pitts played the role of the maid in both the 1930 and 1940 screen versions. In 1950, the film was remade again, this time as a Doris Day vehicle entitled *Tea for Two*.

Neagle's previous Wilcox collaboration *Irene* (another remake of an earlier musical) was a top box office picture for RKO, but unfortunately the magic did not rub off where *No, No, Nanette* was concerned, mainly due to Wilcox's decision to relegate the catchy score to the background and concentrate on the wafer-thin storyline. As one reviewer remarked, "If the audience paid close attention, they could hear snippets of 'Tea for Two,' 'I Want to Be Happy,' 'Where Has My Hubby Gone?' 'Take a Little One-Step' and 'No, No, Nanette.'" This is a great shame because, in addition to her light comedy skills, the versatile Neagle was an enticing singer and dancer. The only real opportunity she gets to reveal the latter attribute is in a wonderful dream-induced dance sequence, which put me in mind of the later film *Lady in the Dark* (1944) with Ginger Rogers. Although the light escapist aspect of the film works well, I have to say that the understated score does frustrate one at times. In one scene with Mature looking dapper in a tux, you want someone to toss him a straw hat and cane and then have him belt out "Gotta Dance!" Alas, this was not to be as Mature has little to do in the film except hone his ability to lift his eyebrows and roll his eyes. This is used to great effect in the funniest scene when, in the company of Nanette, he auditions the "bubble girl," prompting Nanette to exclaim, "Isn't she marvelous?" to which he responds through gritted teeth and beaming smile "Terrible." Indeed, the songs may be few, but the laughs are plentiful. When Eve Arden is asked "Tea for two?" in a café, she instinctively cracks, "Make mine a vodka with a dash of gin." And let's not forget the comic talents of the inimitable Roland Young, everyone's favorite bewildered and quaintly lecherous socialite. Who can forget his ghost-beset banker in the brilliant *Topper* series and his unforgettable bottom-pinching Uncle Willy in *The Philadelphia Story* (1940)? His reasoning for his character's shameless philandering *in No, No, Nanette* is a beaut: "to spread a little happiness," he explains to his understanding niece.

Bosley Crowther of The *New York Times* was clearly not amused, "From a cast of dependable comics, which includes Roland Young, Helen Broderick, Zasu Pitts and Eve Arden, Mr. Wilcox has derived about as much mirth as there is in an ancient joke book. He's an Irishman by birth, but his humor has the body of a Yorkshire pudding. Richard Carlson and Victor Mature go dutifully through the motions of conventional romantic foils."

The film also failed to impress *Variety*: "Musical comedies rarely have much story. That's all right. No one expects them to. Plot is compensated for in a hit show by good music. That's an elementary show business lesson taught in a class that producer Herbert Wilcox must have skipped." The review bestowed the only honors to the older generation including Young, Broderick and Pitts, stating that "Miss Neagle and the youngsters, Richard Carlson, Victor Mature and Eve Arden, show to no advantage against such a trio of comedy vets."

The Shanghai Gesture

United Artists, 1941

Cast: Gene Tierney (Victoria "Poppy" Charteris) Walter Huston (Sir Guy Charteris); Victor Mature (Dr. Omar); Ona Munson ("Mother" Gin Sling); Phyllis Brooks (Dixie Pomeroy); Albert Bassermann (Van Elst); Maria Ouspenskaya (The Amah); Eric Blore (Caesar Hawkins); Ivan Lebedeff (Boris); Mike Mazurki (The Coolie); Clyde Fillmore (Percival Montgomery Hower); Grayce Hampton (Lady Blessington); Rex Evans (Mr. Jackson); Mikhail Rasumny (Mischa Vaginisky); Michael Dalmatoff (The Bartender); Marcel Dalio (The Croupier); John Abbott (Poppy's Escort).

Crew: Arnold Pressburger (Producer); Josef von Sternberg (Director); John Colton (Play); Josef von Sterberg, Geza Herczeg, Jules Furthman, Karl Vollmoller (Screenplay); Paul Ivano (Cinematography); Richard Hageman (Music); Boris Leven (Art Direction); Oleg Cassini (Miss Tierney's Costumes); Royer (Miss Munson's Costumes); Hazel Rogers (Makeup); Harry Redmond, Jr. (Special Effects); Charles Kerr & Fred Pressburger (Assistant Directors); Jack Noyes (Sound); Sam Winston (Editor). Running time: 98 minutes.

36 • *The Shanghai Gesture*

"Mother" Gin Sling is threatened with the shutdown of her gambling casino by English financier Sir Guy Charteris, who is buying up property in the district. His daughter Poppy, newly arrived in Shanghai, visits the casino and is seduced by its atmosphere with the capable assistance of mysterious gigolo Dr. Omar (Victor Mature), who leads her on a downward spiral. At a party Gin Sling throws on New Year's Eve, she reveals to her guests that Charteris had married then abandoned her and her infant child many years previous, absconding with her dowry. To humiliate him even further, she invites a doped-up and drunken Poppy to the table. Taken aback, Charteris denies abandoning Gin Sling, who he now recognizes as his former wife, explaining that he thought that she was dead, and that he never touched her money, but instead deposited it in a bank account made out to her name. He further admits that Poppy is Gin Sling's daughter, who he rescued from a hospital where she had been abandoned. When she confronts her daughter with the news that she is her mother, Poppy sneers at her in disgust, which provokes Gin Sling into shooting her.

"Shanghai — where almost anything can happen and does!"
"POPPY...the Victim of Vengeance! Her love of life and laughter led her to a most amazing doom!"
"Lured into a world of vice there was no turning back!"

Opening lines: "Years ago, a speck was torn away from the mystery of China and became Shanghai. A distorted mirror of problems that beset the world today. It grew into a refuge for people who wished to live between the lines of laws and customs — a modern Tower of Babel."

The play *The Shanghai Gesture* having enjoyed huge Broadway success, a screen adaptation, on paper, had everything going for it: great director, great cast and a sumptuous, exotic setting. Understandably, all concerned were happy to be on board, and very excited about the prospects of working with a living legend, Austrian director Josef von Sternberg, in this, his comeback movie. But for reasons only known to the gods, the film was slammed by the critics on its release. If there was ever a film that was stifled at birth, but is recognized by modern audiences as a masterpiece of its type, it's this heady slice of the Far East.

A visual feast, this is the type of film, like an intoxicating piece of music, you can savor time and time again. Much has been said about Ona Munson's wonderful Dietrich-styled "Mother" Gin Sling, but for me, the cast member who really added a spark was Mature's brilliant portrayal of Dr. Omar. There was simply no one on the Hollywood scene, at the time, who could have played the part to such effect. In a pinch, Charles Boyer, who looked a natural in a fez, could have had a stab at it, but he was simply too French and urbane for the part. No, what it needed was a newcomer who could convey a mystical, enigmatic character of no fixed abode, whose origins were questionable and difficult to pin down. Somebody with smoldering good looks, who oozed sex appeal out of every pore. Enter Victor Mature.

His Omar could have been Rick from *Casablanca* or Pepe from *Algiers*. Corrupted at an early stage, he simply lost his way — or perhaps he was born immoral. We simply don't know, for all his character tells us is that he is a "thoroughbred mongrel." From his few words, we see a man not quite sure of himself, but clear in his contempt for life. He refers to himself as the Doctor of Shanghai and Gomorrah. When Gene Tierney asks "Doctor of what?" he nonchantly responds, "Doctor of nothing.... It sounds important and hurts no one — unlike most doctors." His lazy self-assurance is all-pervasive, and we hang on his every seductive word, even though most of them are packaged up as clichés and riddles. We get the distinct impression that he is driven more by a desire to relieve his boredom of life, than by the victory of any human or monetary conquest. He casually boasts, "I cheat at nothing except at cards"—not out of any real need or financial necessity we feel, but simply because cheating is more fun, all part of the game.

In some aspects, this is simply Mature playing himself, a charming, relaxed man who attracts beautiful women like moths to a flame. A description of Mature in a 1963 article could have equally been applied to the character Omar: "He had those great soulful eyes and that sexy mouth, and the women of America just flipped. Coupled with his physical appeal was his manner: it was just so darn self-indulgent and hedonistic, like a large contented cat, that girls just swooned. He epitomized a sort of complacent, calm masculinity." Omar's artful laziness is certainly something that Mature could associate with, the actor once commenting in an interview during his retirement (at age 55), "I loaf very gracefully. There's a lot to be said about loafing if you know how to do it gracefully." And when it comes to looking bored as is the case with Omar, Mature once acknowledged that in the absence of a big smile, his facial expression could suggest that he either looked bored or self-impressed.[1]

As with most of von Sternberg's movies, there are no heroes or heroines in *The Shanghai Gesture*, just a melting pot of degenerate human flotsam and lost souls washed up on the shore. The master of seductively flamboyant films, von Sternberg was the caricature of the autocratic early Hollywood director: Attired in riding clothes and high leather boots, clutching a riding crop, he cut quite a dash on set. He is best remembered for discovering Marlene Dietrich when in Germany looking for an actress to star in *The Blue Angel* (1930). They went on to make a

Publicity poster from Josef von Sternberg's *The Shanghai Gesture* (United Artists, 1941). Mature plays a role that was tailor-made for him as the enigmatic Dr. Omar, here seducing Gene Tierney (as "Poppy").

further six pictures together—*Morocco* (1930), *Dishonored* (1931), *Shanghai Empress* (1932), *Blonde Venus* (1932), *The Scarlet Express* (1934) and *The Devil Is a Woman* (1935).

Based on a 1925 Broadway play by John Colton, the story of *The Shanghai Gesture* went through 30 revisions before the screenplay was sufficiently sanitized to get past the Hays Office censors, with the original brothel setting changed to that of a gambling den (the censors must have taken a convenience break when they played the scene with the girls suspended in basket cages).

As well as some great technicians at his disposal, von Sternberg also gathered a stellar cast for *The Shanghai Gesture,* which in addition to Mature included Gene Tierney, Walter Huston, Ona Munson and Phyllis Brooks. And let's not forget Eric Blore, Mike Mazurki and Michael Dalmatoff. I can't figure out which of these three is the craziest in the movie, as they are all memorably barking mad.

On loan to United Artists for the film, Tierney looks absolutely stunning as the fallen Poppy. In her autobiography *Self-Portrait: Gene Tierney,* she commented that she looked forward to making the film because it gave her an opportunity to not only work with the great von Stenberg, but also with her husband Oleg Cassini who was hired to design all of the costumes. As a memento of filming, Tierney asked the director if she could have the carved figurines that feature in the scene when all are seated at the dining table for the final showdown. He agreed, and she proudly took them home. However, when the film bombed, Cassini, unbeknown to Tierney, used them for target practice in the back yard, blowing off their heads with a hunting rifle and smugly declaring to his wife, "I have executed them. Now you won't be reminded of that dreadful movie."[2]

Mature would later call Tierney "light, breezy and fascinating. For me, she was a 'different' kind of girl. She didn't conform, and that, I think is the secret of her fascination."

Ona Munson, whose "Mother" Gin Sling's outrageous hairstyle has to be seen to believed, made her mark as another madam: Belle Watling in *Gone with the Wind* (1939). In the final years of her life, she suffered ill health, committing suicide with an overdose of sleeping pills at age 51 in 1955.

And how do you sum up Canadian-born actor and former engineer Walter Huston in a few sentences? Answer: You don't. To admire his artistry, catch his Academy Award performance in *The Treasure of the Sierra Madre* (1948) directed by his equally talented son John Huston.

Phyllis Brooks, whose appearance in the opening scene prompts Mature's Omar to declare, "Allah be praised for providing new women," also looks like a million dollars in the film, her streetwise, sassy blonde neatly contrasting with Tierney's naive brunette. She was nicknamed the "Ipana Toothpaste Girl" due to her work as a model; her career didn't go beyond B movies in the 1940s and 1950s with the exception of such films as this and *In Old Chicago* (1937).

As a measure of Mature's growing popularity, Hal Roach was able to lend him out to United Artists for $3000 per week for *The Shanghai Gesture*, although at the time Roach was only paying the actor $450 per week. Despite being mauled by the critics, *The Shanghai Gesture* did receive Academy Award nominations for Best Art Direction (Boris Leven) and Best Original Music Score (Richard Hageman).

The *New York Times*: "Victor Mature as the roving Egyptian who lures little Poppy to her doom describes himself as a 'thoroughbred mongrel'—a description which his performance justifies." *Variety* thought otherwise: "Victor Mature as the matter-of-fact Arab despoiler of Miss Tierney's honor provides a standout performance that will enhance his popularity."

With his great lingering looks and knowing facial expressions, Mature certainly made the role of Dr. Omar his own, and his fine delivery of the wonderful dialogue was simply icing on the cake. Indeed, the dialogue throughout is a pure joy, with Tierney telling Munson, "You're no more my mother than a toad," and Mike Mazurki's bare-chested coolie (possibly the biggest Chinaman in history) having the final word in the closing street scene: With firecrackers going off, he turns to Walter Huston's Sir Guy Charteris and asks, "Likee Chinnee New Year?"

I Wake Up Screaming

20th Century–Fox, 1941

Cast: Betty Grable (Jill Lynn); Victor Mature (Frankie Christopher); Carole Landis (Vicky Lynn); Laird Cregar (Police Insp. Ed Cornell); William Gargan (Jerry McDonald); Alan Mowbray (Robin Ray); Allyn Joslyn (Larry Evans); Elisha Cook, Jr. (Harry Williams); Morris Ankrum (Assistant District Attorney); Chick Chandler & Cyril Ring (Reporters); Charles Lane (Keating — Florist); Frank Orth (Cemetery Caretaker); Gregory Gaye (Headwaiter); May Beatty (Lady Handel).

Crew: Milton Sperling (Producer); H. Bruce Humberstone (Director); Steve Fisher (Novel); Dwight Taylor (Screenplay); Edward Cronjager (Cinematography); Cyril J. Mockridge (Music); Richard Day, Nathan Juran (Art Direction); Thomas Little (Set Decorations); Gwen Wakeling (Costume Design); Guy Pearce (Makeup); Bernard Freericks, Roger Heman, Sr. (Sound); Robert L. Simpson (Editor). Running time: 82 minutes.

Sports promoter Frankie Christopher (Victor Mature) is accused of murdering Vicky Lynn, a beautiful girl he had been grooming for stardom. Maintaining his innocence, he hides out with the girl's sister Jill, who is also under scrutiny. The police investigation, led by detective Ed Cornell, takes in a number of other suspects including one of her admirers, hotel clerk Harry Williams. With the help of Jill, Frankie tries to clear his name, but Cornell is determined to frame him for the crime. Finally Williams confesses to the murder, revealing that Cornell told him to stay silent on the matter because he wanted the finger of blame to point at Frankie. It turns out that Cornell was secretly in love with Vicky, and due to his jealously wanted Frankie to be executed for stealing his girl. The truth revealed, Cornell takes his own life and Frankie goes off with new love, Jill.

With a dearth of good producers in Hollywood, Fox mogul Darryl F. Zanuck plucked Milton Sperling out of the writers pool, and gave him a chance to prove himself as a producer. Rather daringly for his debut assignment, he decided to put Betty Grable in her first dramatic, non-musical role — a straight part that Mature said Grable was happy to play. Other actresses had been considered for the part, including Rita Hayworth and Gene Tierney, with Lucille Ball an early consideration for the part played by Carole Landis.

At a sneak preview in Pasadena under the title *Hot Spot* the movie bombed because the audience, understandably, expected (with such a title and leading star) a musical. Having great faith in his protégé, Zanuck took Sperling back to the studio cutting room that same night and fixed the problem. The title was changed to *I Wake Up Screaming* and a tagline was added to the publicity posters: "Betty Grable as you've never seen her before!"[1] As a consequence, many of the critics gave it the thumbs-up, the film made money and Sperling went on to make a number of solid features including *Pursued* (1947), *The Courtmartial of Billy Mitchell* (1955) and *Battle of the Bulge* (1965).

Zanuck signed up Grable when his big female star, Alice Faye, retired briefly following an illness. Noted for having Hollywood's most beautiful legs (famously insured for one million dollars), Grable became the number one pin-up girl of World War II with her legendary bathing suit photo. Fox's top star, she appeared in many Technicolor musicals including three with Mature: *Song of the Islands* (1942), *Footlight Serenade* (1942) and *Wabash Avenue* (1950). Just as she had taken over where Alice Faye has left off, her light was later eclipsed by Marilyn Monroe at the Fox studio.

For her first serious role, Grable found herself partnered with Fox newcomer Victor Mature, on loan-out from Roach. The role of the leading male had also attracted the interest of George Raft (a former love of Grable) and Cesar Romero.[2]

Confidently in control of the situation in his previous early film noir *The Shanghai Gesture*, Mature now found himself playing an equally resourceful noir-type character, who nonetheless gets bounced around like a pinball as events conspire to undermine his self-assurance. With each scene, Mature's character becomes less cocky and more perplexed and anxious as the ruthless detective (Cregar) out to nail him increases the pressure. But along the way, he does get to flatter his tormentor with some great one-liners. Awakening in his bedroom to find Cregar lying in wait in the darkness, he quips, "First time I ever had a bad dream with my eyes open." And when later Cregar asks for a lift, he responds, "Sure, always happy to oblige a ghoul," later followed by, "You make me feel like I'm driving a hearse."

However, by way of an interlude to keep cheesecake fans happy, the film finds an excuse to put Grable and Mature in swimsuits at the local swimming baths. During an interview with Gladys Hall while filming, Mature dismissed his first three films, citing *I Wake Up Screaming* as the real beginning of his film career. Even though he was pleased with the outcome, he would later recollect that the swimming insert was the only phony scene in the film. Referring to Zanuck's decision to use the scene, he mused, "He kept wanting to inject things into the script that he thought seemed like Betty.... He just had to get Betty Grable out of her clothes."[3] Grable apparently loathed the scene, but Zanuck's idea paid off with the film receiving a positive response from her fans.

With its brooding atmosphere and sharp performances from all concerned, *I Wake Up Screaming* marked a departure from director Bruce H. Humberstone's usual lightweight features, and is rightfully considered one of his most notable films. He may not have been the most inspired of directors, but he certainly drew inspired performances from Grable, Mature, Landis and Laird Cregar, with each reveling in their parts. The role of Frankie Christopher marked Mature's first performance as a freewheeling huckster type — a character association he would refine and adapt over time.

Tapping into Mature's screen presence, Gladys Hall commented during her on-set interview with Mature: "He's been compared to Robert Taylor, Nils Asther and Gargantua. And is said to possess the best qualities of all three. My opinion, he's more the type of Clark Gable, lusty, sane, debunking, honest."

Mature may well have scored a high mark with *I Wake Up Screaming*, but as with many of his noirs, his great performance would be overshadowed by a scene stealing villain, in this instance Laird Cregar's brilliant portrayal of the menacingly obsessive detective Police Inspector Cowell. In later years, Richard Widmark's bad guy would steal the show in *Kiss of Death* (1947), followed by Richard Conte in *Cry of the City* (1948) and Lee Marvin in *Violent Saturday* (1955).

Great as a hulking psychopath cop (Orson Welles would play a similar character in *Touch of Evil*—1958), Cregar further excelled as Jack the Ripper in *The Lodger* (1944) and as the demented pianist in *Hangover Square* (1945). For the latter role, he tried to lose a hundred pounds on a crash diet, which resulted in his death from a heart attack at age 31. Carole Landis, like her *I Wake Up Screaming* character, died tragically, committing suicide in 1948.

I don't know about you, but I had Elisha Cook, Jr. down as the murderer at the start, not from any intuitive reasoning or deduction, but simply because having watched Mature's earlier thriller *The Housekeeper's Daughter*, the shifty-looking little guy in the tale is always a good bet. Cook excelled at playing nervous small-time losers, taking it to an art form in his fatal showdown with Jack Palance in *Shane* (1953). He was also brilliant in *The Maltese Falcon* (1941) and *Phantom Lady* (1944). In his later years, he lived a reclusive life in the Californian desert, without an agent, only returning to work when anyone could track him down.

Variety wrote, "This picture is first rate entertainment.... Victor Mature plays in a tougher groove than usual and this seems a desirable switch."

Like an old family photograph, the film still looks good today:

The *Radio Times Guide to Films*: "A crackling good film, superbly cast with forties icons such as Victor Mature..."

The *TV Times Film & Video Guide*: "The sense of threat surrounding the 'framed' hero (another serviceable performance from the undervalued Victor Mature) is very well sustained."

With its memorable shadowy photography, enriched by variations of Alfred Newman's brilliant *Street Scene* score (further laced by snippets of "Over the Rainbow") *I Wake Up Screaming* is highly acclaimed by modern-day critics as a great example of early pre-war noir. According to Silver and Ward, "*I Wake Up Screaming* is exemplary of what the developing noir style could do to a movie."

Fox successfully remade *I Wake Up Screaming* as *Vicki* in 1953 with Jean Peters in the title role, Jeanne Crain as her sister, Richard Boone as the cop and Elliott Reid playing Mature's part.

Song of the Islands

20th Century–Fox, 1942

Cast: Betty Grable (Eileen O'Brien); Victor Mature (Jefferson Harper); Jack Oakie (Rusty Smith); Thomas Mitchell (Dennis O'Brien); George Barbier (Jefferson Harper, Sr.); Billy Gilbert (Palola's Father); Hilo Hattie (Palola); Harry Owens and His Royal Hawaiians; Lillian Porter (Paulani—Palola's Cousin); Hal K. Dawson (John Rodney); Amy Cordone (Specialty); Bobby Stone, Rudy Robles (Native Boys); Bruce Wong (House Boy); Harold Lishman (Old Native); Alex Pollard (Valet).

Crew: William LeBaron (Producer); Walter Lang (Director); Joseph Schrank, Robert Pirosh, Robert Ellis, Helen Logan (Screenplay); Ernest Palmer (Cinematography); Alfred Newman (Musical Director); Mack Gordon and Harry Warren, Gordon and Harry Owen (Songs); Richard Day, Joseph C. Wright (Art Direction); Thomas Little (Set Decorations); Gwen Wakeling (Costume Design); Guy Pearce (Makeup); Roger Heman, Sr., E. Clayton Ward (Sound); Robert Simpson (Editor). Running time: 75 minutes.

Cattle baron Harper feuds with an Irish beachcomber, Dennis O'Brien, over a strip of beach owned by O'Brien; the baron needs it to transport his cattle. The baron's son Jefferson Harper (Victor Mature) arrives on the Hawaiian Island with his buddy Rusty Smith and promptly goes about romancing O'Brien's daughter Eileen. Both fathers initially object to the liaison, but after a series of mishaps they set aside their quarrels and come to terms, leaving the two love birds to set their thoughts on marriage.

"Betty's Even Got the Palm Trees Swaying!"

And that she has from the wonderfully inviting opening sequence, sailing toward shore, blonde hair blowing in the breeze as she sings "Sing Me a Song of the Islands" you know that you're going to come away from this film with a big smile on your face.

Smart cookie that he was, Zanuck, when pulling the film together, must have checked out Paramount's gold mine Dorothy Lamour, who sent pulses racing in a sarong. Going one better, Zanuck put Grable in a grass hula skirt to show off her shapely pins. She has looks to die for; no wonder Mature in the film utters, "If you see me in the moonlight, you better yell aloha and start running."

In the wake of Grable's *I Wake Up Screaming* success, Milton Sperling and a few other producers wanted to put her in some more dramatic roles, but Zanuck played safe and decided to keep her in musicals.[1]

Grable was happy to team up again with the likes of Mature and Oakie, but initially had her reservations about working alongside serious character actor Thomas Mitchell, who

Starry-eyed lovers Eileen O'Brien (Betty Grable) and Jeff Harper (Mature) share a quiet moonlit moment in the enduring 20th Century–Fox musical *Song of the Islands* (1942).

had never starred in a musical before. Luckily, they got on like a house on fire, and she often sought his advice on how to act out certain scenes.[2]

The natural chemistry between Grable and Mature shines through in the film, but director Walter Lang initially wasn't at all happy with the choice of Mature as leading man in the movie, apparently from what he'd heard about the actor's temperament. Going to the front office, he threatened to leave the set if the actor proved to be difficult, but the following week he burst into the office again claiming that the rumors about Mature were unfounded, because he'd never worked with a sweeter guy.

A fashion designer, artist and clerk in earlier years, Lang was responsible for some of the big glossy Technicolor Fox musicals of the 1940s and 1950s, coaching six actors to Oscar nominations, with one of them, Yul Brynner, winning the award for his performance in *The King and I* (1956), a film for which Lang received a Best Director nomination.

Mature's easygoing Jeff Harper was by no means any sort of Oscar contender, but under Lang's guiding hand, and a simple "boy meets girl, then loses girl, then wins back girl" premise, it did enable him to turn in one of his most carefree, likable performances. With his beaming smile constantly on show, Mature certainly looks like the cat who got the cream, which is not altogether surprising as he was dating Grable at the time.

Joining in the festivities was fast-talking comedian Jack Oakie, whose most notable performance was possibly as the boisterous dictator Benzino Napaloni in Charlie Chaplin's *The Great Dictator* (1940). When describing his studio career, he delivered one of the best quotes in Hollywood history: "The pictures I made were called the bread and butter pictures of the studio. They cost nothing and made millions, and supported the prestige productions that cost millions and made nothing." Ably assisting Oakie in the laughs department was Hawaiian Hilo Hattie in, this, her screen debut.

Song of the Islands ran contrary to Oakie's' quote, in that it was a big-budget film that made Zanuck a tidy sum. With most of the South Seas swarming with the Japanese at the time, location shooting was out, so the whole two acres of Fox's Stage 14 became a Hawaiian paradise, with imported palm trees, the construction of a 30-foot waterfall and the use of 300 Polynesian extras.[3]

According to Fox records, the studio had been trying to develop a screenplay for *Song of the Islands* since 1937, with Joan Davis down as the star. In 1938, the film was earmarked as a potential vehicle for Alice Faye and Don Ameche. Subsequent screenplay rewrites saw John Payne and Robert Cummings as candidates to star opposite Grable. According to a pre-production memo from Zanuck, he dallied with the idea that the film should be a *Philadelphia Story*–type of picture in a Hawaiian setting.[4] Instead the script evolved into lightweight escapism, which set the trend for Grable movies thereafter and gave Mature another opportunity (after *No, No, Nanette*) to prove his credentials as a light romantic leading man, following the serious business of *The Shanghai Gesture* and *I Wake Up Screaming*.

An obligatory romantic beach scene gave Grable and Mature another opportunity to show off their perfect physiques in swim suits. And not to be completely outshone by Grable in her grass skirt, the studio put Mature in a series of short-sleeved, chest-hugging net sweaters to capitalize on his natural assets. However, such attractions did not impress the *New York Times*: "As a movie, *Song of the Islands* is a great bathing suit advertisement." Of Mature's performance, the reviewer was particularly scathing: "Mr. Mature, who is not so flexible, is content to look godlike in sundry sweaters and flowered garments which neatly expose his rugged contours—and that apparently is all his contract called for. If it also required a performance, Twentieth Century–Fox could demand a refund."

The film also provided some catchy song and dance numbers including "Blue Shadows and White Gardenias," "O'Brien Has Gone Hawaiian," "Sing Me a Song of the Islands," "Down on Ami Ami Oni Oni Isle," "Maluna Malolo Mawaena," "What's Buzzin' Cousin," "Cockeyed Mayor of Kaunakakai," "Hawaiian War Chant," and "Home on the Range."

Taking five months to produce at a cost of just over one million dollars, the film took four millions dollars in the U.S. box office alone.

Whilst Grable's figure kept the male members of the audience happy, *Variety* wrote that "the athletic Victor Mature will get the attention of the women customers."

My Gal Sal

20th Century–Fox, 1942

Cast: Rita Hayworth (Sally Elliot); Victor Mature (Paul Dresser); John Sutton (Fred Haviland); Carole Landis (Mae Collins); James Gleason (Pat Hawley); Phil Silvers (Wiley); Walter Catlett (Col. Truckee); Mona Maris (Countess Mariana Rossini); Frank Orth (McGuiness); Stanley Andrews (Mr. Dreiser); Margaret Moffatt (Mrs. Dreiser); Libby Taylor (Ida — Sally's Maid); John Kelly (John L. Sullivan); Curt Bois (Monsieur De Rochemont), Hermes Pan (Specialty Dancer); Gregory Gaye (Monsieur Garnier); Andrew Tombes (Corbin); Albert Conti (Henri the Chef); Charles Arnt (Janson the Tailor).

Crew: Robert Bassler (Producer); Irving Cummings (Director); Theodore Dreiser (Story "My Brother Paul"); Seton I. Miller, Karl Tunberg, Darrell Ware (Screenplay); Ernest Palmer (Cinematography); Richard Day, Joseph C. Wright (Art Direction); Thomas Little (Set Decorations); Gwen Wakeling (Costume Design); Guy Pearce (Makeup); Alfred Bruzlin, Roger Heman, Sr. (Sound); Robert L. Simpson (Editor). Running time: 103 minutes.

A musical set in 1890s America, based on the life of songwriter Paul Dresser (Victor Mature). Anxious to make a name for himself in music, rather than pursue a career in the ministry, Paul leaves Indiana and takes up with a cheap medicine show, then joins a traveling carnival where he entertains on the piano and has a brief fling with showgirl Mae Collins. Before long he's off to New York to make his fortune as a songwriter. In the big city, he takes up with musical star Sally Elliot, who had previously mocked his carnival antics. As Dresser becomes the toast of the town with his musical numbers, his relationship with Sally has the usual ups and downs and misunderstandings before a happy union is assured.

Now under contract to Fox, Mature found himself in another big splashy musical, starring opposite another big World War II pin-up, Rita Hayworth. The search for an actress to play the lead opposite Mature in *My Gal Sal* reads like the hunt to find Scarlett O'Hara; those originally considered for the part of Sally Elliot included Alice Faye (who withdrew from film work due to pregnancy), Irene Dunne (busy schedule), Mae West (not interested), Betty Grable (overworked) and Carole Landis. Zanuck finally decided to borrow Hayworth from Columbia after her excellent performance in *Blood and Sand* (1941).[1] Mature's role as the songwriter Paul Dresser (born Paul Dreiser) was by no means certain itself, with George Montgomery and Don Ameche initially in the running. Ameche looked like the favorite, but was replaced by Mature because Fox thought that it might not be good box office for the actor to play another composer after taking the part of Stephen Foster in *Swanee River* a few years previously.[2]

The legendary Fritz Lang had been first choice to direct the film, but after a week of pre-production he asked to be replaced and Irving Cummings took over the directorial reins.[3] Cummings was a popular leading man in silent movies before turning his hand to directing. Like his Fox colleague Walter Lang, he will fondly be remembered for his Technicolor musicals. MGM may have reigned supreme with the musical genre, but Fox certainly gave them a run for their money in the 1940s with their splashy productions like *My Gal Sal*.

Although inspired by the life of songwriter Paul Dresser, the film is, for the most part, a fictitious romantic cant through Fox's take on the Gay Nineties, which audiences lapped up as the ideal form of escapism with the world at war. The daughter of a flamenco dancer, Hayworth had already made her mark with this type of turn-of-the-century entertainment the year before in *The Strawberry Blonde* (1941). One of the love goddesses of the 1940s, she was always guaranteed to light up the screen with her sensuous presence. The musical *Cover Girl* (1944) with Gene Kelly established her as one of Columbia's top stars of the 1940s, but the film that without doubt sealed her legendary status was *Gilda* (1946). Married five times (including to Orson Welles and Dick Haymes), she fought a long battle with alcoholism for much of her life and died from Alzheimer's disease in 1987.

Mature wonderfully conveys the simple country boy who gains sophistication through his association with singer Sally Elliot. Like his promoter character from *I Wake Up Scream-*

Mature, in the role of songwriter Paul Dresser, shares a tender moment with real-life love Rita Hayworth (playing Sally Elliot) in the memorably tuneful musical biopic *My Gal Sal* (20th Century–Fox, 1942).

ing, Mature's Dresser is a self-assured type, who could sell ice to the Eskimos. Fueled by desire for the feisty Sal, he confidently informs us, "Someday, I'll write a song. And she'll come begging to sing it." And write them he did, but in the film not all the numbers came from the pen of Dresser, because many of his were not deemed worthy of big production numbers. The Dresser songs included "My Gal Sal," "On the Banks of the Wabash," "I'se Your Honey, If You Wants Me, Liza Jane," "Come Tell Me What's Your Answer (Yes or No)," "Blue and Gray," "The Convict and the Bird," and "Mr. Volunteer." They were supplemented by songs by Leo Robin and Ralph Rainger, including "Me and My Fella," "On the Great White Way," "Oh, the Pity of It All," "Here You Are," and "Midnight at the Masquerade." Alfred Newman was nominated for an Academy Award for the film's music score, but the award went to *Yankee Doodle Dandy*. However, *My Gale Sal* did win awards for art and set decoration.

In terms of physique, Mature bore little resemblance to the real-life, 300 pound Paul Dresser but, for a non-musician, he did look convincing tickling the ivories, particularly in the glorious scene where he plays two pianos at the same time. (One critic commented on his portrayal, "He plays it with remarkable assurance and manages to get away with playing and singing with a minimum of awkwardness.") In the film, Mature's singing was dubbed by Esther Williams soon-to-be second husband, radio singer Ben Gage. Hayworth's singing was dubbed by big band singer and actress Nan Wynn. But no stand-in was required where romantic chemistry was required on screen, with Mature and Hayworth literally lighting up their every scene together, which was no doubt helped by the fact that off-screen they were a hot item. In one love scene, their kiss reportedly went on a lot longer than intended, and had to be reshot. Both their marriages to other people were on the rocks at the time, ultimately leading to divorce shortly after.

By all accounts, Hayworth was swept off her feet by Mature's comical behavior. He could make her laugh by turning up outside her dressing room during breaks in shooting and going through a minstrel routine. Mature's later rival for Hayworth's affections, Orson Welles, explained Hayworth's attraction to Mature: "He's very funny in real life and that amused her."[4] Hermes Pam, the film's choreographer, recalled that Mature "was sort of hammy. He'd come in with loud shirts that said 'The Genius.'"[5] Mature also gave some of the crew coveralls with "Assistant Genius" stitched on their backs, and was occasionally accompanied by a Boxer dog named Genius.

The supporting roles were ably filled by the likes of John Sutton, Carole Landis, James Gleason and Phil Silvers. After an early career managing plantations in British colonies, Sutton went to Hollywood, excelling as swashbuckling villains, and more often than not, like in *My Gal Sal*, finding himself on the losing end of a romantic triangle. Silvers, who went on to great television fame as Sgt. Bilko, recalled that during the making of *My Gal Sal* there was very little tension on set because the Fox films were doing well at the box office. The only tension Silvers experienced was when he had to board a giant Ferris wheel, with many others, for the final number. Suffering from acrophobia, he tensed up and had to be eased out of the cab after the shot, breaking into welts when he got home that day.[6]

With its wonderful song and dance routines, great supporting cast, and electric performances from Hayworth and Mature, *My Gal Sal* couldn't fail to be a hit, finally earning Mature some good reviews, and setting him up nicely for his next musical extravaganza, *Footlight Serenade*.

The *New York Times*: "Mr. Mature, whose weight is shy about 120 of that of Mr. Dresser, cuts a dashing figure as the hail-fellow, brassy composer."

Picturegoer: "Victor Mature is well cast as the musically minded son of a Puritanical father…"

Dresser, who was born in 1857 in Indiana, wrote more than 400 songs in his lifetime. He died, aged 49, in 1906 from heart disease.

Footlight Serenade

20th Century–Fox, 1942

Cast: John Payne (Bill Smith); Betty Grable (Pat Lambert); Victor Mature (Tommy Lundy); Jane Wyman (Flo La Verne); James Gleason (Bruce McKay); Phil Silvers (Slap); Cobina Wright (Estelle Evans); June Lang (June); Frank Orth (Mike the Doorman); Mantan Moreland (Amos); Irving Bacon (Stagehand); Charles Tannen (Charlie — Stage Manager); George Dobbs (Frank — Dance Director); Harry Barris (Composer); John Dilson, James Craven (Clerks), Trudy Marshall (Secretary); Bud Spencer, Jim Mercer (Dance Specialty); Wilbur Mack (Boxing Commissioner); Frankie Van, Russ Clark (Referees); Allen Wood, Frank Coghlan, Jr. (Ushers).

Crew: William LeBaron (Producer); Gregory Ratoff (Director); Kenneth Earl, Fidel LaBarba (Story "Dynamite"); Robert Ellis, Helen Logan, Lynn Starling (Screenplay); Lee Garmes (Cinematography); Charles Henderson (Musical Director); Leo Robin, Ralph Rainger (Songs); Richard Day, Albert Hogsett (Art Direction); Thomas Little (Set Decorations); Earl Luick (Costume Design); Guy Pearce (Makeup); Hermes Pan (Dance Director); Bernard Freericks, Roger Heman, Sr. (Sound); Robert L. Simpson (Editor). Running time: 80 minutes.

Conceited boxer Tommy Lundy (Victor Mature) sets his sights on Broadway, taking the central role in a play where he falls for dancer Pat Lambert, who is secretly dating another one of the actors, Bill Smith. When Bill and Pat get married, Pat maintains the secrecy of their relationship for fear it will adversely impact on her career, much to the annoyance of Bill, who grows weary of Tommy's advances towards his wife. Cast as Tommy's sparring partner in the show, Bill finally gets to vent his anger when in the ring he deals Tommy a knock-down blow. When Tommy discovers that he's been chasing a married woman, he does the decent thing and bows out of the picture.

Once Betty Grable proved herself a natural at musical comedy, Zanuck put her to work in *Footlight Serenade* which, unlike the norm for Fox musicals, was shot in black and white. With the war on, color stock was in short supply and the studio had already used up its allocation on other features. However, with the film's runaway success, it proved that all a good musical needed was bouncy song and dance numbers and a fabulous cast to woo audiences, and that Technicolor was simply icing on the cake. Zanuck was pleased with the end result, but inserted a clause into Grable's contract ensuring that all her future films were to be shot in Technicolor.[1]

This time, Grable had two of Fox's leading men chasing after her, Mature and John Payne. A well-established star at Fox, Payne took top billing over Grable and Mature. But with Mature's over-the-top role, as an extrovert boxer, and his natural ability to ham it up "good style" he simply stole the show. Grable, Payne and Mature had been scheduled to play in a lighthearted drama titled *White Collar Girl*, but persistent script problems mothballed the project. With cast, crew and resources already committed, another production was quickly needed, and *Footlight Serenade* nicely fitted the bill.

For direction, Zanuck assigned Russian-born Gregory Ratoff, who had served in the czar's army and fought in World War I. Escaping the Bolshevik revolution, he eventually settled in America. Starting his Hollywood career as actor in the 1930s, he later moved into direction, his most notable film being *Intermezzo* (1939), which saw Ingrid Bergman in her first Hollywood role.

As Phil Silvers recalled, Ratoff's thick Transylvanian-gypsy accent, which led to his hilarious distortion of the English language, was a constant source of amusement on set. Silvers described how in one scene, Ratoff was instructing Grable how to play up to Mature's character to secure a part in the show: "You arr chorruss girrl and he ees beeg star from price fighting, but now in show, you want to make heem think he's terrific. You want to play up to heem. You want to suck heem." What he meant was to flatter him, by sucking up to him, but everyone interpreted it another way, which led to much laughter and the suspension of work for five minutes, with Ratoff innocently inquiring, "What did I sayed?" Grable never let him forget it, for in subsequent scenes, before the camera rolled, she would lean toward Mature's belt and ask, "I do it now?"[2]

By all accounts, Mature's character was based on the colorful former heavyweight champion Max Baer, who had a reputation as a bit of a partygoer, often at the expense of his training, which cost him dearly when he was knocked out in 1935 by unemployed longshoreman Well Braddock, "The Cinderella Man" (possibly the inspiration behind Sly Stallone's *Rocky*). Mature was trained by former contender Jack Roper before stepping into the ring with Payne, who already had some boxing experience. For the three fight scenes, Lloyds of London had to write $50,000 policies on both Mature and Payne.[3] But injury during production was to occur elsewhere, when Grable tore her abdominal muscles when she hit the deck while carrying out a dance movement with Mature. Her other dance scenes were postponed to allow her time to heal.[4]

Mature certainly looks the part of a boxer, and it would have been great to have seen him in a serious boxing film of the noir genre. The closest we get to this type of sporting characterization is his over-the-hill pro football player in *Easy Living* (1949). Despite looking the part, Mature was a big softie at heart, as co-star Phil Slivers recalled: "Mature, a virile womanizer and very intelligent, was surprisingly gentle for a muscleman. He abhorred violence, couldn't stand anyone hitting him with a glove or even touching him."[5]

This larger-than-life character was certainly in the Mature mold, giving the actor a great opportunity to convey an over-emphasized impression of himself, a role he truly enjoyed judging by his energetic performance, particularly in the hilarious scene where he dispenses unexpected electric shocks during every handshake with his hand-held buzzer. Ratoff kept the pace brisk and Mature proved that he was more than up to it with his superb comic timing and a brash way with a line. When Grable accuses him of chasing her, he idly quips, "Lady, I've been trying to sprinkle salt on your tail for a long time, but I can't get near you." But it takes more than sharp patter to win Grable's character over. When Mature asks her, "'Will you come into my dressing room?' said the spider to the fly," she responds, "Oh, thank you, Mr. Spider, but I'm very, very shy."

The film's other hunk, John Payne, had a lot going for him, ruggedly handsome and equally adept in light musicals and action films, but he never quite joined the ranks of the major stars of the day. Like Dick Powell, he was another singer turned tough guy, and will always be remembered for his part in *Miracle on 34th Street* (1947), but for my money, his best roles were in film noir: *The Crooked Way* (1949), *Kansas City Confidential* (1952), *99 River Street* (1953), *Hell's Island* (1955) and *Slightly Scarlet* (1956). Interestingly, he was the first person in Hollywood to show an interest in making the James Bond novels into a film series, but dropped the project when he couldn't secure the rights to the entire 007 series. In 1961, he suffered life-threatening injuries when he was struck by a car in New York, and had to have six hours of surgery on his face. In 1943, during a spot of leave while serving in the U.S. Coast Guard service, Mature dated Payne's ex-wife, actress Anne Shirley, and there was even talk of marriage, but nothing came of it.

Such was the talent on offer, we also had Jane Wyman playing Grable's straight-laced friend and fellow chorus girl. Wyman was not only an excellent actress, receiving an Academy Award for her performance in *Johnny Belinda* (1948), but she was also the first wife of Ronald Reagan, in a marriage that lasted from 1940 to 1948. In 1984, she was quoted as saying, "Women are like tea bags. You never know how strong they are until you put them in hot water." In *Footlight Serenade*, Wyman, on her first encounter with Mature's character Tommy Lundy, dismissively describes him as a "fresh guy," and he later sarcastically refers to her as, "hatchet face." Further verbal sparring between these two would have worked a treat, in my opinion, but it was not to be.

With James Gleason and Phil Silvers on hand once more, providing solid light-hearted support, the show moved along at a lively clip. And in the choreography department, Hermes Pan again proved he was a force to be reckoned with, providing Grable with some truly memorable dance routines. Particular mention should be made of the novel boxing sequence where Grable boxes with herself and the brilliant dance duet she does with Pan. The songs, which came courtesy of Leo Robin and Ralph Rainger, included "Are You Kidding?" "I'm Still Crazy for You," "I Heard the Birdies Sing," "Living High," "I'll Be Marching to a Love Song," and "Land on Your Feet."

Mature took third billing after Payne and Grable, so it was a dead certainty that he'd end up losing the girl, just as his third billing in *No, No, Nanette* lost him Anna Neagle to Richard Carlson. As well as giving Grable ample opportunity to show off her legs (or gams, as she referred to them), the film provided Mature with a rare opportunity to dance when Grable tries to teach him how to waltz, which included him hoisting her onto his shoulder and catching her when she descends (a routine that resulted in her abdominal injury). Mature was certainly no threat to Gene Kelly, but what he lacked in hoofing skills, he more than made up for with his breezy manner and his amazing ability to flip cigarettes into his mouth, catching them neatly between the lips each time. This is Mature at his most brash and conceited, adding that final touch to a great musical; they certainly don't make 'em like this any more. A *Newsweek* reviewer wrote that the high point of the film is "probably Mature's confident interpretation of the brash, immature lady killer. While there are those who will discount this performance as a triumph of type casting, Mature manages the role with the saving grace of humor and self-kidding."

Variety: "Although Mature successfully pictures the egoistic and swaggering fight champ for reverse angles, he's painted with lily-white duco for the finish, which will be alright with the women customers."

The *Radio Times Guide to Films*: "This film contains some very pleasing performances, including a lightly self-mocking one from hulk Victor Mature as a Broadway-bound boxer."

Mature would once again take to self-mocking, to glorious effect, 24 years later in the film that brought him out of retirement, *After the Fox* (1966).

Seven Days' Leave

RKO, 1942

Cast: Victor Mature (Johnny Grey); Lucille Ball (Terry Havalok-Allen); Harold Peary (The Great Gildersleeve); Mapy Cortes (Mapy); Ginny Simms (Herself), Freddy Martin (Himself); Les Brown (as Les Brown and his Orchestra); Marcy McGuire (Mickey Havalok-Allen); Arnold Stang (Bitsy Slater); Lynn Royce & Vanya (Themselves); Ralph Edwards & Co. (Themselves); Peter Lind Hayes (Private Pete Jackson); Walter Reed (Ralph Bell); Wallace Ford (Sergeant Mead); Buddy Clark (Clarky); Charles Victor (Charles); King Kennedy (Gifford); Charles Andre (Andre — Terry's Butler); Harry Holman (Justice of the Peace — Percy Gildersleeve); Addison Richards (Captain Collins); Ralph Edwards (Himself).

Crew: Tim Whelan (Producer-Director); George M. Arthur (Associate Producer); William Bowers, Ralph Spence, Curtis Kenyon, Kenneth Earl (Screenplay); Robert De Grasse (Cinematography); C. Bakaleinikoff (Musical Director); Charles Walters (Choreography); Frank Loesser, Jimmy McHugh (Songs); Carroll Clark, Albert S. D'Agostino (Art Direction); Michael Ohrenbach, Darrell Silvera (Set Decorations); Sam Ruman (Assistant Director); Vernon L. Walker (Special Effects); Renie (Costumes); Robert Wise (Editor). Running time: 87 minutes.

Army private Johnny Grey (Victor Mature) has seven days to marry a girl he has never met in order to claim an inheritance of $100,000 from his grandfather's will. The girl, Terry, a wealthy socialite, initially proves resistant to Johnny's love play, but after a series of trials and tribulations, featuring a number of big acts of the day, she finally succumbs to his charms and agrees to be his girl, before he heads off for a tour of duty overseas.

Seven Days Leave was pretty much a wartime reworking of Lucille Ball's earlier romantic comedy *Next Time I Marry* (1938) with its emphasis on all the fun and frolics associated with inheritance, but on this occasion Ball is on the receiving end of someone else's plans to secure a legacy through a conveniently timed marriage — that someone else, yes, Vic Mature. Filming got underway on June 17, 1942, under the working title of *Sweet or Hot*.[1]

Although it is not apparent in their scenes together, by all accounts neither Ball or Mature enjoyed making the film. At the time, Ball was struggling to make an impression as a contract player with RKO and her days at the studio were coming to an end. Work on *Seven Days' Leave* started four days after Ball had finished *The Big Street* with Henry Fonda, her favorite film, for which she received much praise, but unfortunately it was a flop at the box office. To follow critical acclaim with a "B" feature like *Seven Days' Leave* must have been disappointing for her. To make matters worse, Mature (on loan from Fox) was to have had approval of his leading lady and he wanted Rita Hayworth, with whom he was having an affair. When Harry Cohn, Columbia's studio head, refused to loan her out, Mature took out his frustration on Ball, which soured their relationship on set.[2] It is, perhaps, a testament to their acting skills that both stars still look great together on screen, despite the falling-out. A critic for the *Radio Times Guide to Films* certainly liked the pairing, commenting, "This endearing RKO romp effectively teams a pre–*I Love Lucy* Lucille Ball and handsome hunk Victor Mature, both of whom seem to be having a jolly good time and manage to convey that pleasure to the audience."

Arnold Stang, who played Mature's pipsqueak buddy Bitsy, recalled that when Ball wasn't incensed by Mature, she was lovesick over husband Desi Arnaz who was away a lot fundraising for army and navy relief.[3] While away, Arnaz, by all accounts, chased other women, which would have greatly added to Ball's distress.[4]

Stang was an underage performer and needed someone to keep an eye on him during production. His mother had his good friend Victor Mature down as the ideal candidate; Mature found a room for him at Rita Hayworth's house. Stang commented that even though Ball knew he was staying with Mature, she was still very friendly and courteous towards him.[5] Stang went on to become the voice of various animated characters, including Top Cat.

After *Seven Days' Leave*, Ball signed a contract with MGM, who dyed her brown hair red, which, in a way, marked a turning point in her career, as she went on to become Hollywood's foremost female clown and a powerful producer, with a succession of extremely successful television comedy shows. She would team up with Mature again in the football drama *Easy Living* (1949).

Mature plays his cocky soldier like an early prototype for Sgt. Bilko, all fast patter and brimming with self-confidence. When one of his buddies remarks, "Get this guy, he likes himself and he has no rivals," Mature glibly responds, "Say, I resemble that remark." And like Bilko, he has himself down as a ladies' man. When the lovesick Bitsy (Stang) is jokingly accused of being a one-woman man, Mature quips, "So am I, one tonight, one tomorrow night." Such is his performance, there are times that you get the distinct feeling that Mature is simply playing a speeded-up version of himself, but it all adds to the screwball entertainment on offer, which sees Mature indulge in a marching song and dance routine in the barracks, sing a duet with Mapy Cortes (with Mature's voice dubbed), play a trumpet in a big band (once again, mimicking), chase Ball up onto a chair with a dueling sword, and take a cold dip with her in a country pool. Incidentally, whether decked out in formal attire or swimsuit, Ball looks a million bucks in this movie.

With Fox's other big stars Preston Foster, Dana Andrews and George Montgomery already flying the flag for the studio in a slew of serious war propaganda films, there was little need for Mature to don the attire of a serviceman on active duty. It is possible that the actor was excluded from such parts because with his smoldering Mediterranean good looks, he wasn't sufficiently representative of the "All American" type of guy required for combat movies at the time. But that aside, there was no doubting his natural ability as the perfect romantic foil for the pin-ups of the day. And with romantic musical comedy offering another form of propaganda, highlighting what the guys were fighting for back home, films like *Seven Days' Leave* also played their part in the war effort.

Although a "B" musical, the film marked a first for Mature in several ways. Up until this point he had always got on well with his leading ladies, dating many of them, but his frostiness towards Lucille Ball ended this trend. Private Johnny Grey was also his first stint in the role of a serviceman, and although he would have been very convincing as a battle-hardened soldier type, he would have to wait eleven years before getting the opportunity in the Korean War actioner *The Glory Brigade* (1953), followed by *China Doll* and *No Time to Die* (both 1958). *Seven Days' Leave* also saw him as one of the guys, as opposed to the rather detached, self-centered types he had played up until this point.

Although there are some excellent comic sparring moments between Ball and Mature, who both ham it up in good style, the real value in the film lies in the colorful assortment of supporting characters and the great music. Many of the characters came from radio shows and variety acts of the day, including the jitterbug comedian Marcy McGuire, Harold Peary (radio's "Great Gildersleeve"), Ralph Edwards (shown hosting *Truth or Consequences*), Charles Victor (hosting the *Missing Heirs* radio program), comedian Peter Lind Hayes (doing excellent impressions of Ronald Colman and Charles Laughton), Puerto Rican actress Mapy

Cortes (in her only American appearance), and big band leaders Freddy Martin and Les Brown.

After the "A" status of his previous films, *Seven Days' Leave* could be seen as a slightly backwards step in Mature's career. However, any lost ground would be swiftly won back on his return to Hollywood in 1946 with the role of Doc Holliday in John Ford's classic *My Darling Clementine*.

The *New York Times*: "With rugged, dimpled, eye-rolling Victor Mature and the nearly as beautiful Lucille Ball to provide the romantic hide-and-seek, *Seven Days' Leave* is an unsteady melange. But on a thin tire the producers are still getting a little mileage. The audience seemed to enjoy the ride."

Brooklyn Daily Eagle[,] "Loaded with music, hot, sweet and solid *Seven Days' Leave* made a whole lot of local audiences happy...."

Despite some lukewarm reviews, *Seven Days' Leave* was one of RKO's top moneymakers of 1942.

My Darling Clementine

20th Century–Fox, 1946

Cast: Henry Fonda (Wyatt Earp); Linda Darnell (Chihuahua); Victor Mature (Dr. John "Doc" Holliday); Cathy Downs (Clementine Carter); Walter Brennan (Old Man Clanton); Tim Holt (Virgil Earp); Ward Bond (Morgan Earp); Alan Mowbray (Granville Thorndyke); John Ireland (Billy Clanton); Roy Roberts (Mayor); Jane Darwell (Kate Nelson); Grant Withers (Ike Clanton); J. Farrell MacDonald (Mac the Barman); Russell Simpson (John Simpson), Don Garner (James Earp); Francis Ford (Town Drunk); Ben Hall (Barber); Arthur Walsh (Hotel Clerk); Louis Mercier (Francois the Chef); Mickey Simpson (Sam Clanton); Fred Libby (Phin Clanton); Earle Fox (Gambler); William B. Davidson (Owner of Oriental Saloon); Harry Woods (Marshal); Charles Stevens (Indian Charlie); Aleth "Speed" Hanson (Townsman and Guitar Player); Frank Conlan (Piano Player).

Crew: Samuel G. Engel (Producer); John Ford (Director); Sam Hellman (Story); Stuart N. Lake (based on his book *Wyatt Earp, Frontier Marshal*); Samuel G. Engel, Winston Miller (Screenplay); Joseph MacDonald (Cinematography); Cyril J. Mockridge (Music); Alfred Newman (Musical Director); James Basevi, Lyle R. Wheeler (Art Direction); Thomas Little (Set Decorations); Rene Hubert (Costume and Wardrobe); Ben Nye (Makeup); Fred Sersen (Special Effects); William Eckhardt (Assistant Director); Jack Montgomery, Gil Perkins (Stunts); Eugene Grossman, Roger Heman, Sr. (Sound); Dorothy Spencer (Editor). Running time: 97 minutes.

After bringing law and order to Dodge City, Wyatt Earp and his brothers Virgil, Morgan and James make their way to Tombstone on a cattle drive. On the outskirts of town they come into contact with Old Man Clanton, who offers to buy their cattle at a knockdown price. Refusing the offer, the Earps head into town, where Wyatt is offered the job of sheriff after tackling a troublesome drunken Indian. At first he refuses the job, but takes it up when he discovers that their cattle has been stolen, and that his youngest brother James, left behind to keep an eye on them, has been murdered. In his efforts to clean up the town and bring the killers to justice, he falls foul of the town's gambling boss, former surgeon Doc Holliday (Victor Mature). Originally an Eastern aristocrat, Holliday is suffering from consumption and his life is now following a fatalistic course. The two men promptly develop a mutual respect for one another and become friends. Complications ensue when Holliday's former love from the East, Clementine, arrives in town, much to the annoyance of his current girlfriend, Mexican firebrand Chihuahua. Wyatt falls in love with Clementine, but keeps his feelings to himself out of respect for his friend. When the Clantons are revealed as the killers, it's off to the OK Corral for the final shootout. With guns blazing, the Earps aided by Holliday get the better of the Clantons, but Holliday is fatally wounded.

"The Roaring West at Its Reckless Best!"

And on his return to the screen, with the war behind him, this was Mature at his most dramatic best, in by far his most demanding role to date.

While away from the screen on war service, his youthful looks had become weatherbeaten, giving his demeanor a more defined, rugged edge, which would provide the perfect facial canvas for a number of muti-faceted parts far removed from the two-dimensional characters which had tagged him the "Glamour Boy." Mature was back, and back with a vengeance. And what a role to mark his comeback, the fatalistic Doc Holliday, perhaps one of the most complex and enigmatic characters in western history. The role finally allowed him to jettison his light image and prove to one and all that he could tackle the dramatic meaty parts as well, if not better, as some of his Hollywood contemporaries.

In addition to a peach of a role, Mature also found himself in the company of Hollywood's finest craftsmen, including director John Ford and co-star Henry Fonda, who were also looking to re-establish themselves in Hollywood following war service. During the conflict, Ford was appointed chief of the Field Photographic Branch of the OSS, while Fonda had spent four years in the navy.

In Ford's silent Western days, Wyatt Earp had acted as the director's technical advisor. Some of Ford's memories from these encounters would find service in *My Darling Clementine,* which was primarily based on Stuart N. Lake's creative 1931 book *Wyatt Earp: Frontier Marshal,* which received contributions from the legendary lawman himself before his death in 1929.[1] Lake's story provided the basis for two previous Fox productions in 1934 and 1939, both entitled *Frontier Marshal* and starring George O'Brien and Randolph Scott, respectively. Although Lake's book claims to be an accurate account of the life of Earp, there are some fictitious elements, further embellished by Ford in his screen adaptation for *My Darling Clementine,* which was shot in Monument Valley.

According to records, Earp was a gambler and a law enforcement officer who served in several frontier towns. In 1876, he met fellow gambler Doc Holliday in Dodge City, and in 1880 the two rode out to join Wyatt's brothers in Tombstone, where Virgil Earp was appointed marshal. The famous 1881 gunfight against the Clantons ended with everyone but Wyatt either wounded or dead. Contrary to Ford's film, Doc Holliday (a dentist and not a surgeon as depicted in the film), although wounded, survived the final shootout, passing away in 1887 in Glenwood Springs, Colorado, where he had hoped to tale advantage of the reputed healing powers of the waters.

The role of Earp always belonged to Fonda, but the rest of the casting was not so straightforward. Early considerations for the role of Clementine included Jeanne Crain, Donna Reed and Anne Baxter, before Zanuck and Ford agreed on newcomer Cathy Downs. A former model, Downs' career went downhill after *My Darling Clementine,* with most of her subsequent work of the low-budget variety, but she is fondly remembered for her 1950s sci-fi movies *The Amazing Colossal Man* (1957) and *Missile to the Moon* (1959).

Returning from war service, Mature gave his most powerful performance to date as the brooding Doc Holliday (center), here meeting Wyatt Earp (Henry Fonda, with badge) for the first time in John Ford's Western masterpiece *My Darling Clementine* (20th Century–Fox, 1946).

James Stewart was seriously considered for the role of Doc Holliday,[2] but Stewart, who also returning from war duties, preferred to make his comeback in *It's a Wonderful Life* (1946). Ford's list of early possibilities for the role also included Tyrone Power, Douglas Fairbanks, Jr. and Vincent Price.[3]

When Zanuck put forward his preference Victor Mature, Ford penned a note to the mogul expressing his concern on such a choice. In a 1948 interview, Mature recalled how Ford had invited him to his office one day and told him that he had heard about him ... much of it not good. Ford had heard that Mature threw his rank on set, for instance, and that he ordered the crew around. In defense, Mature angrily responded, "Mr. Ford, I may be a character, but so help me I've never stepped on any human being up or down. That's one thing I don't do." Following the meeting, Ford wrote to Zanuck, "I am not at all worried about Mature. I really wrote the note to see that a little discipline was performed on Junior."[4] Zanuck wrote back, "I am pleased that you like [Fox contract player] Victor Mature. Personally, I think the guy has been one of the most underrated performers in Hollywood. The public is crazy about him and strangely enough every picture that he has been in has been a box-office hit. Yet the Romanoff's* round table has refused to take him seriously as an actor. A part like Doc Holliday will be sensational for him as I know you will get a great performance out of him and I agree with you that the peculiar traits of his personality are

A popular restaurant of the time frequented by motion picture executives and players.

ideal for a characterization such as this."⁵ Ford believed that Mature's decadent sensuality suited Holliday's self-destructive personality.⁶

According to Scott Eyman's *Print the Legend. The Life and Times of John Ford,* the director was surprisingly easy on Mature during production, perhaps because the actor had served in the Coast Guard during the war and was on active convoy duty in the North Atlantic for fourteen months. Eyman further recorded that when Mature started to run a high fever, Ford insisted that he should leave the cramped studio dressing room he had been living in since returning to Hollywood, and take up residence in his (Ford's) house for the remainder of the production.⁷

Mature certainly benefited from Ford's wealth of filmmaking experience, delivering by far one of his finest performances. His entrance in the film is unforgettably dramatic, marked with a heavy silence as he makes his way to the bar, to be shortly joined by Fonda's Earp. Aware of each other reputations, a mutual respect soon develops:

> DOC HOLLIDAY: I know all about you and your reasons for being here.
>
> WYATT EARP: I've heard a lot about you, too, Doc. You left your mark around in Deadwood, Denver and places. In fact, a man could almost follow your trail goin' from graveyard to graveyard.
>
> DOC HOLLIDAY: There's one here, too ... the biggest graveyard west of the Rockies. Marshals and I usually get along much better when we understand that right away.

In common with Fonda, Mature has a presence that dominates the screen, his pent-up energy and inner turmoil all pervading throughout his entire performance. Like Mature's Dr. Omar from *The Shanghai Gesture,* Doc Holliday is a mysterious and complex character who is difficult to pigeonhole. Although he has come west to drink himself into oblivion, we are reminded of his Eastern sophistication in a memorable scene where he finishes a soliloquy from *Hamlet*— a scene which Mature powerfully performs with heartfelt sincerity. The fatalistic nature of the character is also squarely driven home by Mature's natural ability to convey raw anguish and pained emotion in his facial expressions, showcased to good effect in the scene where he tries to persuade Clementine to go back east, declaring to her, "The man you once knew is no more, there's not a vestige of him left. Nothing!"

Zanuck would later comment that the film enjoyed "an unforgettable performance by Henry Fonda, and even a strong one by Victor Mature."

Stirring performances were also given by Walter Brennan, Ward Bond, John Ireland, Tim Holt and Linda Darnell. Brennan and Ford shared a mutual dislike, which was clearly evident when Ford, noticing Brennan struggling with a horse, yelled, "Can't you mount a horse," to which Brennan coldly replied, "No, but I got three Oscars for acting." Bond, who did the film back to back with *It's a Wonderful Life,* appeared in the aforementioned *Frontier Marshal,* which also depicted the events leading up to the famous gunfight. On a similar note, John Ireland, who played Billy Clanton in the film, returned later as Johnny Ringo in *Gunfight at the OK Corral* (1957). Tim Holt, best remembered for *The Treasure of the Sierra Madre* (1948), received a Purple Heart for his war service in the Army Air Corps. During the making of *Clementine,* he broke seven ribs and had to be airlifted to medical facilities in Tucson, Arizona. At his peak in the 1940s, he was the fastest draw in the movies. Linda Darnell's portrayal of the Mexican Indian saloon girl Chihuahua won her some of the best reviews of her career, but her crowning glory will always be her subsequent film *Forever Amber* (1947).

Mature's performance found favor with many critics with the *New York Sun* writing that Mature "forgets about his good looks and actually does some acting.... It's a good part and a good performance." *Variety*'s critic wrote, "Playing counterpoint to Fonda, Victor Mature registers nicely as a Boston aristocrat turned gambler and killer."

There is much myth wrapped up in fantasy with Ford's retelling of the lawman's story, but it still makes for one of the timeless Western classics, providing Mature with an ideal platform to relaunch his career.

Moss Rose

20th Century–Fox, 1947

Cast: Peggy Cummins (Belle Adair); Victor Mature (Michael Drego); Ethel Barrymore (Lady Margaret Drego); Vincent Price (Police Inspector R. Clinner); Margo Woode (Daisy Arrow); George Zucco (Craxton); Patricia Medina (Audrey Ashton); Rhys Williams (Deputy Inspector Evans); Felippa Rock (Liza); Carol Savage (Harriett); Patrick O'Moore (George Gilby); Billy Bevan (White Horse Cabby); Michael Dyne (Assistant. Hotel Manager); Gilbert Wilson, Stanley Mann (Footmen); Paul England (Pub Owner).

Crew: Gene Markey (Producer); Gregory Ratoff (Director); Joseph Shearing (Novel *The Crime of Laura Saurelle*); Niven Busch (Adaptation); Jules Furthman, Tom Reed (Screenplay); Joseph MacDonald (Cinematography); David Buttolph (Music); Alfred Newman (Musical Director); Richard Day, Mark-Lee Kirk (Art Direction); Paul S. Fox, Thomas Little (Set Decorations); Rene Hubert (Costume Design); Charles Le Maire (Wardrobe); Ben Nye (Makeup); Fred Sersen (Special Effects); Ad Schaumer (Assistant Director); Roger Heman, Sr., George Leverett (Sound); James B. Clark (Editor). Running time: 82 minutes.

A Victorian whodunit set against the backdrop of a fogbound London. When a chorus girl is killed by an unknown person who leaves behind a Bible marked with a Moss Rose, her roommate, Cockney singer-dancer Belle Adair, suspects her former date, the mysterious aristocrat Michael Drego, as being the murderer. Determined to advance herself and see how the other half lives, she blackmails Drego into letting her spend two weeks at the family estate. On arrival, she discovers that Drego is engaged to Audrey Ashton, who becomes the killer's next victim. With yet another Moss Rose left at the scene of the crime, Scotland Yard sends Inspector Clinner to investigate. When Belle falls in love with Drego, she becomes the next intended victim when the killer is revealed to be Drego's deranged and overly protective mother Lady Margaret, who wants to keep her son for herself and will kill anyone who threatens to take him away. Having pieced the clues together, Clinner and his men arrive in the nick of time to apprehend Lady Margaret before she can claim another victim.

"Gripping Action...

Weird Murder....

Pulse-Pounding Suspense!"

"No Stranger Bond!

No Stronger Love!"

"Was This Love a Thing of Evil?"

"Deadly ... The Flower of Evil That Stood Between Them!"

In the 1940s, the big screen saw some excellent examples of the Victorian melodrama genre. Britain, usually in the form of Gainsborough productions, gave us the likes of *Fanny by Gaslight* (1944), *The Seventh Veil* (1945), *Jassy* (1947) and *Madeleine* (1949), with Hollywood coming up with *Gaslight* (1944), *The Lodger* (1944), *Hangover Square* (1945), *Dragonwyck* (1946), *Britannia Mews* (1949) and the suspense laden *Moss Rose* (1947).

Adapted from the novel *The Crime of Laura Saurelle*, by Gabrille Margaret Long, writing under the name Joseph Shearing, *Moss Rose* is loosely based upon the murder of a prostitute in 1873, a crime which was never solved.

With his dark, brooding Continental looks, Mature was the ideal candidate to lurk in the shadowy recesses of fogbound Victorian London. In common with his enigmatic Omar from *The Shanghai Gesture*, his Michael Drego has a mysterious foreign look about him that is hard to pin

All is not as it seems when Cockney chorus girl Belle Adair (Peggy Cummins) suspects mysterious aristocrat Michael Drego (Mature) of murder in the riveting Victorian melodrama *Moss Rose* (20th Century–Fox, 1947).

to a country. When Peggy Cummins asks about his nationality, a male friend dismissively responds, "Probably some Italian or Portuguese prince, the town's crawling with them." The film certainly marked a new type of role for Mature, prompting one contemporary reviewer to comment, "Victor Mature, making his second film since his return from war service, reveals a greater depth in his acting than filmgoers had previously known."

A foreign-looking gent, hansom cabs, the London Embankment, swirling fog, bobbies on the beat, tripe, Waterloo Bridge, music-hall gals, bustles, Scotland Yard, dark cobbled alleys, ancestral estates, an arranged marriage, a possessive mother — this film has it all, and then some. Throw in Gregory Ratoff's brisk direction and David Buttolph's suitably atmospheric score and the heady concoction is complete. Well, *nearly*, but let's return to the script in a minute.

As the chorus girl from Shoreditch, East London, who wants to sample the good life of a family estate, Welsh actress Peggy Cummins holds center stage, literally lighting up the screen with her presence. On her splendid performance, the *New York Times* commented that she had "spirit, humor and brass — and a surprisingly tender quality which nicely rounds the role." A few months before, Cummins missed out on the lead role in *Forever Amber*

(1947), but she did go on to thoroughly entertain us in the likes of *The Late George Apley* (1947), *Gun Crazy* (1949) and *Night of the Demon* (1957).

In complete contrast to Cummins' infectious exuberance, Mature plays his part straight and four-square, making up for lack of incisive dialogue with a series of menacing, disdainful stares, particularly in his early encounters with Cummins. Thinking perhaps that the Cockney sprite has flipped her lid when she sets out her stall, he idly threatens, "If you weren't more of a fool than a blackmailer, I'd go to the police myself and have you put away." (Dangerously naïve, and all of five-foot-one and a half, petite Cummins squaring up to hulking Mature, a possible murderer and all of six-foot-two and a half, purely so she can see how the other half lives—perhaps the sprite has flipped her lid after all.)

Cummins recalled that she got on well with both Mature and Price, and that the height differences between her and these tall leading men were overcome by ramps. As she described, they were all prone to giggling, which made it difficult for her to walk up the ramps to do a scene without the three of them breaking into laughter. To maintain order, she would jokingly plead with them, "We'll all be sacked if we don't stop, I'm sure!"[1] She further recounted that in one London fog scene, they put too much fog in, which made it difficult for her and Mature to see each other.[2]

Cummins added, "The script came down, and that was it, and we had to do it. By the time you'd fought your way through to get it changed, the fight was too great, perhaps. Time was money."

But what the film lacks in script, it more than makes up for in great performances and a wonderfully atmospheric setting, which all add up to the tension and suspense which is skillfully maintained throughout. And, let's face it, any film with Vincent Price and Ethel Barrymore is worth the price of admission. As if one British beauty wasn't enough, the film also features Liverpool-born actress Patricia Medina as Mature's fiancée (her first Hollywood role). Medina was married to actor Richard Greene from 1941 to 1951 and to Joseph Cotten from 1960 until his death in 1994.

Playing against type as a sophisticated gent, Mature gave a good account of himself, which didn't go unnoticed by the critic for *Variety*: "Victor Mature handles his somber character of a well-bred Englishman expertly and thoroughly pleases."

The *New York Times*: "[A] suave and absorbing mystery thriller, neatly plotted and deliciously played."

The trade press were certainly impressed:

Daily Film Renter: "Absorbing story, excellently acted. Has definite claim to rank high among recent features of this type."

Kinematograph Weekly: "Novel and intriguing romantic crime melodrama, set in Edwardian England. The result is one of the most exciting and colorful 'whodunits' seen for many a day. Grab it! Capital thriller."

As well as providing Mature with a rare opportunity to play a gent, the film also enabled him to prove his prowess as a fireman when, according to the film's pressbook, he put out a fire caused by a faulty heater. When a wall near where Mature, Barrymore and Cummins were playing out a dramatic scene began burning, Mature spotted the fire first, thrusting Cummins to one side, before he fell to with an axe, preventing thousands of dollars of damage. Everything happened so fast that the whole scene was photographed before the director had time to call "Cut." In the same press article, Mature proudly commented, "I have a print of the film, so that I can show it to my grandchildren if they show signs of disbelieving my story."[3]

Kiss of Death

20th Century–Fox, 1947

Cast: Victor Mature (Nick Bianco); Brian Donlevy (Assistant D.A. Louis D'Angelo); Coleen Gray (Nettie); Richard Widmark (Tommy Udo); Taylor Holmes (Earl Howser); Howard Smith (Warden); Karl Malden (Sgt. William Cullen); Anthony Ross ("Big Ed" Williams); Mildred Dunnock (Ma Rizzo); Millard Mitchell (Max Schulte); Temple Texas (Blondie); J. Scott Smart (Skeets); Wendell Phillips (Pep Mangone); Lew Herbert, Harry Kadison (Policemen); John Kullers (Prisoner); Victor Thorley (Sing Sing Guard); Iris Mann (Congetta); Marilee Grassini (Rosaria); Norman McKay (Capt. Dolan); Robert Karnes (Hoodlum); Harry Carter, Robert Adler (Detectives); Jack Rutherford, Lawrence Tiernan, Bernard C. Sell, Arthur Holland (Policemen); John Marley (Al); Gregg Martell (Turnkey); Lee Sanford (Chips Cooney); John Stearns (Harris); Eda Heinemann (Mrs. Keller); Arthur Kramer (Mr. Sulla); Jesse White (Taxi Driver); Tito Vuolo (Luigi).

Crew: Fred Kohlmar (Producer); Henry Hathaway (Director); Eleazar Lipsky (Story); Ben Hecht, Charles Lederer (Screenplay); Norbert Brodine (Cinematography); David Buttolph (Music); Leland Fuller, Lyle R. Wheeler (Art Direction); Thomas Little (Set Decorations); Charles Le Maire (Costume and Wardrobe); Fred Sersen (Special Effects); Abe Steinberg (Assistant Director); Rod Amateau, Herbert Holcombe (Stunts); W.D. Flick, Roger Heman, Sr. (Sound); J. Watson Webb, Jr. (Editor). Running time: 98 minutes.

Small-time crook Nick Bianco (Victor Mature) is caught by the police robbing a jewelry store at Christmas time. District attorney D'Angelo offers him a reduced jail sentence if he informs on other criminals; he refuses, believing his criminal friends will take care of his family. In prison, Nick cooperates with D'Angelo when he discovers that his poverty-stricken wife has committed suicide and that his two children have been placed in an orphanage. Out on parole, he marries Nettie, who used to babysit his kids. D'Angelo keeps pressuring him to provide information on the criminal fraternity. Working undercover for the law, Nick ingratiates himself with sadistic killer Tommy Udo. To appease D'Angelo, Nick testifies against Udo, but the killer is acquitted. Sending his family away for their safety, Nick confronts Udo and is badly wounded. Udo is shot dead by the police.

"It will mark you for life as it marked him for ... Betrayal!"

Capitalizing on his strong showing in *My Darling Clementine*, Fox assigned Mature to an even meatier role in *Kiss of Death*. The film marked a career best, securing him a place as one of the noir greats.

Nick Bianco, a troubled and vengeful character, was one of Mature's favorites, it again proved his versatility as an actor. Mature remarked, "Such roles got me out of the 'jerk' department, and I'm going to stay out of it from now on." That he was tailor-made for the part was summed up in a missive from Zanuck to the production team (including director Henry Hathaway): "The idea of Victor Mature for the leading role of Nick Bianco is a sensational idea.... He has made a big personal hit for his performance in *My Darling Clementine*.... This will be a great thing for Mature, and for once he fits the part perfectly."[1]

"Perfect casting" could also be applied to Mature's adversary in the film, played by Richard Widmark, fresh from Broadway. This was Widmark's debut role. Just as Orson Welles would steal the show as villain Harry Lime in *The Third Man* (1949), Widmark would do the same as the giggling psychopathic killer Tommy Udo in *Kiss of Death*. Certain movie scenes will always be sealed in your mind and none more so than when Udo pushes an elderly lady in a wheelchair down the stairs. In fact, the scene was deemed too violent for British audiences of the day and was cut when the film was released in the UK. Widmark also gets to rattle off one of the best lines in the film when he utters, "I wouldn't give you the skin off a grape."

Widmark's Udo was certainly memorable, but all memorable villains need a perfect foil, in the form of a compassionate good guy, to emphasize their evil ways. Whereas Welles' Harry Lime had to contend with the sensitive Holly Martin (wonderfully underplayed by Joseph Cotten), Widmark benefited from a sympathetic performance from Mature, who (playing his first family man) gave a warm and emotive performance that truly got under the skin of the audience. Playing such a tormented character enabled Mature to convey a wide range of emotions such as anger, despair, frustration, disappointment and bitterness, which all neatly contrasted with the moments of love and tenderness he shares with his family. As with Doc Holliday, events have made Nick Bianco a forlorn fatalist, which is clearly stated in a heartfelt moment when, drained of emotion following the death of his wife, he informs Nettie, "I'm the kind of guy you can't hurt. It doesn't matter." Later in the film, we experience a frustrated Bianco: When the police are unable to keep a tail on Udo, he says this of the killer to the D.A.: "He's nuts and he's smarter than you are."

In addition to the fine leading performance, the film also benefited from a great Ben Hecht screenplay, Norbert Brodine's superb photography and director Hathaway's taut direction. Hathaway was a true professional, but like many of the great directors he was prone to temper outbursts on set. Mature recalled how Hathaway invited him to his office to forewarn him about this short fuse. After expressing admiration for Mature's work, Hathaway explained, that when he got angry he would say things that he didn't really mean. Not at all fazed by this forewarning, Mature responded that when someone around him explodes with anger, he would react in the same way; he finished the conversation by telling Hathaway that he didn't need the part and that perhaps he should seek out the services of Cesar Romero instead.[2] Luckily, Hathaway didn't take him up on his suggestion, and Mature went on to deliver possibly the best performance in his career.

Widmark was another actor who had little time for fire-breathing directors. When Hathaway bawled him out, Widmark (who had been forewarned by Mature about the director's temper) simply gave him the finger and sat down, informing the director that he was a professional and expected to be treated as such.[3]

After that, the director was well behaved with Widmark, who received an Academy Award nomination for his performance. Widmark would go on to deliver many other great performances in his long career, but my favorite has to be that other noir classic *Night and the City* (1950), closely followed by *Panic in the Streets* (1950).

Fine support in the film was also provided by Brian Donlevy as D.A. D'Angelo and Coleen Gray as Nettie. Initially, Darryl Zanuck had his sights on Edward G. Robinson for the part of D'Angelo. Years later, Coleen Gray said that *Kiss of Death* was Mature's best film and that she had fun working with him. She further recalled how Mature would claim he wasn't an actor; "He deprecated his talent — but I was pleased for him that in his career he had *Kiss of Death* to point to."[4] Patricia Morison played Mature's first wife, but her scenes were cut from the final print as the producers reputedly felt audiences of the time were not ready for a scene that depicted suicide.

In common with Hathaway's *The House on 92nd Street* (1945) and *13 Rue Madeleine*

(1946), *Kiss of Death* was filmed in a semi-documentary style shooting scenes on actual exterior locations, in this case New York, taking in the likes of Sing Sing Prison and the Tombs. Location shooting posed two problems: crowd control and the transportation of equipment. To prevent spectators from mingling with the actors, the studio employed the services of 50 policemen. For the latter problem, six large trucks were in constant use transporting forty tons of equipment (including two miles of special cable to cope with filming in moving elevators) to the 76 different sets used in the film's production.[5]

On Mature's performance, Hathaway emphatically commented that rugged realism was Mature's forte. He also remarked that the thing Mature would most likely be apt to say when asked for his own serious comment on his performance in the film, is that he only regrets that the neighborhood grouch back in Louisville who'd always predicted, "That Mature boy will wind up in prison someday," didn't live to see it.[6]

Reformed petty criminal Nick Bianco (Mature, right) has his work cut out when he befriends psychopathic killer Tommy Udo (Richard Widmark) to gain incriminating evidence that will bring Udo to account in the nail biting film noir classic *Kiss of Death* (20th Century–Fox, 1947).

Silver and Ward commented, "Victor Mature's interpretation of Nick—although like Widmark's celebrated, leering portrayal of Undo overly dramatized in context—suggests a character trapped by his compulsive behavior and elicits viewer sympathy despite his criminal past."

Variety: "Victor Mature, as the ex-convict does his best work to date." The *New York Times* agreed, citing Nick Bianco as "Mature's best character, " adding, "Victor Mature, has, if you'll pardon the pun, really matured as an actor in *Kiss of Death*.

Time magazine felt that Mature "apparently needed nothing all this time but the right kind of role—for once, he has it."

The *New York Herald Tribune*: "Mature has been growing in acting stature so immensely that it is no surprise to find him playing ... with persuasion and finesse."

5001 Nights at the Movies: "Victor Mature gives an unexpectedly, subdued, convincing performance."

Mature, Widmark and Gray reprised their film roles for Lux Radio Theater on January

12, 1948. Mature and Widmark also featured in three broadcasts of the story for *The Screen Guild Theater*, the first going out on October 28, 1948.

In 1958, the film was remade in a western setting, entitled *The Fiend Who Walked the West*. Another remake, *Kiss of Death* (1995), starred David Caruso in the Mature role and Nicolas Cage as the villain.

Fury at Furnace Creek

20th Century–Fox, 1948

Cast: Victor Mature (Cash Blackwell aka Tex Cameron); Coleen Gray (Molly Baxter); Glenn Langan (Capt. Rufe Blackwell aka Sam Gilmore); Reginald Gardiner (Capt. Grover A. Walsh); Albert Dekker (Edward Leverett); Fred Clark (Bird); Charles Kemper (Peaceful Jones); Robert Warwick (Gen. Fletcher Blackwell); George Cleveland (Judge); Roy Roberts (Al Shanks); Willard Robertson (Gen. Leads); Griff Barnett (Appleby); Frank Orth (Evans); J. Farrell MacDonald (Pops); Charles Stevens (Artego); Jay Silverheels (Little Dog); Robert Adler (Leverett Henchman); Harry Carter (Clerk); Mauritz Hugo, Howard Negley (Defense Counsels); Harlan Briggs (Prosecutor); Si Jenks (Jury Foreman); Edmond Cobb, Guy Wilkerson (Court Clerks); Kermit Maynard (Scout); Jerry Miley, Al Hill, George Chesebro (Card Players); Minerva Urecal (Mrs. Crum); Ray Teal (Sergeant); Oscar O'Shea (Jailer); Al Bridge (Lawyer).

Crew: Fred Kohlmar (Producer); H. Bruce Humberstone (Director); David Garth (Story); Charles G. Booth (Screenplay); Winston Miller (Additional Dialogue); Harry Jackson (Cinematography); David Raksin (Music); Alfred Newman (Musical Director); Albert Hogsett, Lyle R. Wheeler (Art Direction); Thomas Little (Set Decorations); Rene Hubert (Costume Design); Charles Le Maire (Wardrobe); Ben Nye (Makeup); Fred Sersen (Special Effects); Ted Mapes, Kermit Maynard, Chuck Roberson (Stunts); Eugene Grossman, Harry M. Leonard (Sound); Robert L. Simpson (Editor). Running time: 88 minutes.

General Blackwell is court-martialed on the charge of conspiring with Indian renegades and causing the massacre of his command at Fort Furnace Creek. When he dies of a heart attack during the trial, his two sons Cash Blackwell (Victor Mature) and Capt. Rufus Blackwell, incognito, set out to prove his innocence. Cash finds romance along the way with Molly Baxter, whose father died during the massacre. Having spent years apart, the two brothers go about their mission in different ways, which only serves to alienate them from each other. But when the chips are down they join forces to reveal and bring down the real traitor, Edward Leverett, the head of a mining syndicate, who had their father framed so that they could buy up Indian land to exploit its mineral value. In the final showdown at the fort, a wounded Cash is saved by Indian Little Dog, who shoots Leverett.

Better known for his Charlie Chan thrillers and light Technicolor musicals, director H. Bruce Humberstone tried his hand at a Western in 1948 with the sadly, forgotten crowd-pleaser *Fury at Furnace Creek*. Although his work has been described as uninspired by many commentators, Humberstone certainly knew how to keep an audience thoroughly entertained, and *Fury at Furnace Creek* did just that, in thrilling oater style. It is fair to say that at this point in his career, the two most notable departures from his typical output, the brilliant early film noir *I Wake Up Screaming* and the action-packed *Fury at Furnace Creek*, both starring Mature, suggest that he was capable of giving more than was asked of him. Anyone compiling the best of Humberstone's work would undoubtedly have to include these two on their list.

Apart from its taut pacing, lively plot and host of great Western bad guys, *Fury at Furnace Creek* boasts another fine, moody performance from Mature. Like Humberstone, Mature was a relative newcomer to the Western genre. Admittedly, he already had one under his belt with his memorable performance as Doc Holliday in *My Darling Clementine,* but his fatalistic Doc is essentially an Easterner trying to lose himself out west. Mature's Cash Blackwell (incognito as Tex Cameron) is more of a westerner, but in some ways a variation on Doc: Both men are black sheep of the family, getting by on the turn of a card as sharp-suited gamblers, but Blackwell is less embittered and showy, perhaps mirroring a slightly younger Doc before the rot set in. Resolute and fixed in purpose, he has a poker face that cleverly conceals his real intentions. When Leverett talks of the rumors that implicate him (Leverett) in the massacre, Blackwell maintains his guise as a gun for hire when he informs him, "I never listen to small talk unless I'm paid to."

Western loner Cash Blackwell (Mature) shoots it out with bad hombres during his quest to clear his father's name in the taut oater *Fury at Furnace Creek* (20th Century–Fox, 1948).

Like *My Darling Clementine*, and indeed all the great Westerns, *Fury at Furnace Creek* is distinguished by a colorful array of bad hombres and a stunning looking, wholesome heroine. Raising land grabbing and treachery to an art form, Albert Dekker, Fred Clark and Roy Roberts share the honors as "shoot 'em in the back" varmints. And delivering the lethal bullets on their behalf, we have Charles Stevens as the obligatory Mexican killer Artego, who sportingly jangles his spurs to forewarn victims of his approach (clearly ignoring the silent assassin's handbook). And just as Cathy Downs lit up the screen with her sensitive performance and innocent beauty in *Clementine*, so did Coleen Gray in *Furnace Creek*. Although her screen career never really took off after Fox ended her contract in 1950, Gray has the distinction of starring in two of the best film noirs of 1947, *Kiss of Death* (once again with Mature) and *Nightmare Alley* with Tyrone Power. In that same year, she was quoted as saying, "When I got my contract at 20th I was in seventh heaven, but I found that a movie career is mostly hard work, laced with disappointments."

As in *Kiss of Death*, Mature's character is on a vengeful quest but his hard-driven nature is refreshingly softened by the endearing presence of Gray and the promise of her uncle's lip-smacking Mulligan stew. We are also treated to a comical turn from Charles Kemper as the lovable town drunk — Peaceful Jones.

And if those guys weren't enough, we also have Reginald Gardiner as the washed-up and extremely nervous Capt. Walsh and the exceptionally tall Glenn Langan as Mature's estranged brother Capt. Rufe Blackwell. According to *The Hollywood Reporter* (September 1947), George Montgomery had asked to be released from his contract to play Rufe Blackwell before it went to Langan. Like Vincent Price, Langan was one of the few actors who could tower over Mature. A handsome "B" leading man Langan (married to actress Adele Jergens from 1951 to his death in 1991) will forever live on in our memories as the title character in *The Amazing Colossal Man* (1957), one of the cult 1950s sci-fi classics, which also featured another Mature co-star, Cathy Downs from *My Darling Clementine* (1946).

Filming got underway with nearly two weeks of location work near Kanab, Utah. According to studio publicity, it was the first Fox film to use planes to transport cast, crew and equipment from Hollywood to a location set.[1] Good use was made of Kanab Movie Fort, which saw service in many a Western including *Fort Apache* (1948), *She Wore a Yellow Ribbon* (1949), *Fort Yuma* (1955), *Fort Dobbs* (1958) and *Fort Bowie* (1958). Mature's 1959 actioner *Timbuktu* was also shot in the Kanab area.

This was the studio's second adaptation of David Garth's novel, with John Ford's *Four Men and a Prayer* (1938) placing the story in India, and on that occasion starring Richard Greene (in the Mature role), David Niven and Loretta Young. A *Fury at Furnace Creek* radio adaptation followed, with Mature, Charles Kemper and Reginald Gardiner reprising their roles for the 30-minute *Screen Guild Theater* broadcast on February 10, 1949.

The *New York Times*: "Arrogant in his manner, Mr. Mature is adept at romance, at twirling a shiny six shooter or at facing a villain in his lair."

Variety: "Victor Mature sits easily in the hero's saddle and pleases mightily with his interpretation of the outdoor character. It's a forthright performance that adds credence to the dramatic goings."

Maurice Speed Film Review (1948): "First-class Western with Victor Mature excellent as an itchy-fingered hero."

Cry of the City

20th Century–Fox, 1948

Cast: Victor Mature (Lt. Candella); Richard Conte (Martin Rome); Fred Clark (Lt. Collins); Shelley Winters (Brenda Martingale); Betty Garde (Miss Pruett); Berry Kroeger (W.A. Niles); Tommy Cook (Tony Rome); Debra Paget (Teena Riconti); Hope Emerson (Rose Given); Roland Winters (Ledbetter); Walter Baldwin (Orvy); June Storey (Miss Boone); Tito Vuolo (Papa Roma); Mimi Aguglia (Mama Roma); Konstantin Shayne (Dr. Veroff); Dolores Castle (Rosa); Claudette Ross (Rosa's Daughter); Howard Freeman (Sullivan); Tiny Francone (Perdita); Elena Savonarola (Francesca); Thomas Ingersoll (Priest); Vitto Scotti (Julio); Robert Karnes, Charles Tannen (Interns), Oliver Blake (Caputo); Antonio Filauri (Vaselli); Joan Miller (Vera); Emil Rameau (Dr. Niklos); Eddie Parks (Mike); Jane Nigh, Ruth Clifford (Nurses); Michael Sheridan, Ken Christy (Detectives); Michael Stark, Davison Clark (Cops).

Crew: Sol C. Siegel (Producer); Robert Siodmak (Director); Henry Edward Helseth (Novel *The Chair for Martin Rome*); Richard Murphy (Screenplay); Lloyd Ahern (Cinematography); Alfred Newman (Music); Albert Hogsett, Lyle R. Wheeler (Art Direction); Ernest Lansing, Thomas Little (Set Decorations); Bonnie Cashin (Costume Design); Charles Le Maire (Wardrobe); Ben Nye (Makeup); Fred Sersen (Special Effects); Jasper Blystone (Assistant Director); Eugene Grossman, Roger Heman, Sr. (Sound); Harmon Jones (Editor). Running time: 95 minutes.

Wounded cop killer Martin Rome is visited in the hospital by crooked lawyer Niles, who tries to persuade him to confess to a jewel theft and a murder his client carried out, since Rome is going to the chair anyway. Rome refuses. Fearing for the safety of his girlfriend, Teena, who Niles threatens to frame as a female accomplice to the crime, he escapes his imprisonment. Out on the streets, hotly pursued by boyhood pal turned police detective Lt. Candella (Victor Mature), he protects the woman he loves. Along the way, he encounters a number of characters, including menacing masseuse Rose Given and former girlfriend Brenda. A wounded Candella (previously taking a bullet meant for Rome, fired by Given) eventually catches up with Rome, fatally shooting him during the pursuit.

"From the heart of its people comes the Cry of the City."

By 1948, film noir was really hitting some high notes, and this uncompromising Robert Siodmak classic was certainly one of them. Originally going under the working titles *The Chair for Martin Rome* and *The Law and Martin Rome*, *Cry of the City* was Mature's fourth noir (after *The Shanghai Gesture*, *I Wake Up Screaming* and *Kiss of Death*), and once again through his subdued, hard-boiled performance, he proved he was a natural in the genre. As the relentless cop Candella he clearly takes the lesser of the two leading roles in the film, but he is still quite effective.

Looking as Italian as they come, both Conte and Mature work well together as boyhood friends brought up in a tough New York neighborhood, who eventually go their separate ways. But on paper I would have had Mature down as the Martin Rome character. He was a bigger star at the time than Conte, and with the success of *Kiss of Death* behind him, it could be argued that he was tailor-made for the part of the charismatic villain who could have just as easily turned good if circumstances had been different. Mature's naturally showy, flamboyant nature has much in common with Rome's charming personality, but on closer inspection, perhaps Conte is better able to convey the character with the necessary callous, "smart-guy on the edge" treatment that wouldn't have suited Mature's more affable, laid-back persona. Career-wise, it was thought unwise for Mature to play two criminals in succession. J. Greco in his book *The File on Robert Siodmak in Hollywood: 1941–1951* (an essential guide) commented that Mature was first cast in the role of Martin Rome because he had played Nick Bianco so well in *Kiss of Death*, "but that Bianco's seriousness best suited Candella, whom Mature consciously drains of any charm, yielding in every instance to Conte's charisma."[1]

At the top of their game, both stars make the most of their well-defined roles, turning in career-best performances for one of noir's most iconic directors, Robert Siodmak.

Siodmak was to film noir what John Ford was to Westerns and Alfred Hitchcock to thrillers — a master craftsman in his genre. Born in 1900 in Dresden, Germany, he left the country for Paris and then Hollywood, to escape the rising tide of Nazism. After directing a string of "B" movies for various studios, he landed a seven-year contract with Universal

Charming criminal Martin Rome (Richard Conte, left) gets a hospital visit from boyhood pal turned police detective Lt. Candella (Mature) in the atmospheric Robert Siodmark noir *Cry of the City* (20th Century–Fox, 1948).

in 1943. For various studios he turned out a succession of great noirs including *Phantom Lady* (1944), *The Spiral Staircase* (1946), *The Killers* (1946), *The Dark Mirror* (1946), *Cry of the City* (1948), and *The File on Thelma Jordon* (1950). He was one of the first refugee directors to return to Europe after his Hollywood success, arriving in France in 1953 before heading back to Germany in 1954.

Based on the novel *The Chair for Martin Rome* by Henry Edward Helseth, the movie tells a familiar tale of boyhood friends who grew up on opposite sides of the law, in much the same way James Cagney and Pat O'Brien played it out ten years earlier in *Angels with Dirty Faces* (1938). Like O'Brien's priest, Mature's police lieutenant is an easygoing type, comfortable in his surroundings and well respected by the community (young and old) in which he plays an integral part. A "people person," he plays it straight and by the book, unlike Conte, who for all his charisma and bravado is very much an insecure loner, exploiting people for his own purposes and deep down probably hating himself for doing so. The tale is pretty much a battle of wills between these two protagonists, from which a number of other characters emerge, some good, some bad and others just about unsavory as a slug on a cracker.

To flesh out these roles, *Cry of the City* enjoys a quirky supporting cast with Debra Paget, Shelley Winters (in one of her dumb broad roles), and Hope Emerson ably accompanied by Fred Clark and Berry Kroeger. Emerson and Kroeger vie for the most unpleasant noir villain, with perhaps Emerson's hideous masseuse stealing an edge over Kroeger's crooked lawyer.

All these characters dwell in the dark underbelly of New York, with most of the scenes taking place at night against rain-washed pavements. Various location scenes were filmed in New York, but many of the night shots were actually taken in Los Angeles. (The original script adaptation had San Francisco down as the setting, but Zanuck thought it better suited to Brooklyn.) The cityscape is all-pervasive in the film, with Siodmak making great use of lighting to convey mood and emotion. According to *Time Out Film Guide*, "Rarely has the cruel, lived-in squalor of the city been presented in such telling detail, both in the vivid portrayal of ghetto life and in the astonishing parade of corruption uncovered in the night..." In a similar vein, the *New York Times* praised the film as "taut and grimly realistic."

To infuse this street realism, Zanuck was very much in favor of on-location shooting which had been showcased to great effect in films such as *The Naked City* (1948) and *Call Northside 777* (1948). Siodmak, however, preferred to shoot indoors, and given the choice would have shot *Cry of the City* entirely within the studio, because as he once explained, it gave him more control over action and artists. This lack of control was highlighted by an incident involving Mature towards the end of filming, when a piece of heavy machinery being transported on the "New York" street set fell on Mature's foot, breaking some of the actor's toes.[2] As a consequence, Mature played out his final scenes with the camera shooting above his ankles.

To emphasize the cityscape, the film opens to the familiar sound of Alfred Newman's *Street Scene* score, which was used in many Fox noirs including *I Wake Up Screaming* (1941), *The Dark Corner* (1946), *Kiss of Death* (1947) and *Where the Sidewalk Ends* (1950). Veteran noir scribe, Ben Hecht took a hand in the writing department but his contribution is not credited. Siodmak also rattled off a handful of lines when he decided that the script needed some explanatory information on the condition of Rome, who recuperates from a bullet wound in the story. The lines involving respiration, transfusions and other medical terms were sent to the studio physician, who sent them back with a perfect score for accuracy. Mightily impressed, Mature complimented Siodmak, saying that the director must have had medical experience. Siodmak replied, "None at all. It's just that I've been such a hypochondriac in my time."[3]

Mature's womanizing reputation was the least of Shelley Winters' concerns during filming. She had made friends with Mature's dog, Genius II (an in-joke with Mature, who was Genius I), who in between scenes rushed at her with enthusiastic, but rough, affection. When she showed Mature the claw marks, pleading with him to keep the dog on a leash for a while because she was exhausted, he apologetically responded, "I can't. He's trained to retrieve blondes."[4]

Playing an upbeat cop, Mature's innate vulnerability is not as clearly evident as in his previous two noir outings, *I Wake Up Screaming* and *Kiss of Death*, but just to prove that nobody's bulletproof, he still manages to catch a slug in the shoulder in the final reel, but not before he gets to rattle off some classic lines in the pursuit of Rome.

"Look at him, Tony, he's a dead man."

"They got an idea that a cop is someone who pinches an apple off a push cart and chases kids."

"He's out there somewhere, in an alley, on a roof, looking for a way out. He's not asleep."

"I've been lucky, I've never had to kill a man in my life. But I'll get you, Rome. I'll get you because I've got to."

The *New York Times* wrote, "Victor Mature, an actor once suspected of limited talents, turns in a thoroughly satisfying job as the sincere and kindly cop, who not only knows his business but the kind of people he is tracking down." The *Los Angeles Examiner* went even further, describing his performance as "excellent."

Maurice Speed Film Review: "First class crime thriller, all the more interesting because it is photographed on the actual New York locations in which the incidents took place."

His performance is still heartily applauded today with the *Radio Times Guide to Films* commenting, "For those who have been unable to take Mature seriously as an actor, this ranks with his best work."

Red, Hot and Blue

Paramount, 1949

Cast: Betty Hutton (Eleanor Collier aka Yum-Yum); Victor Mature (Danny James); William Demarest (Charlie Baxter); June Havoc (Sandra); Jane Nigh (Angelica Roseanna aka No-No); Frank Loesser (Hair-do Lempke); William Talman (Bunny Harris); Art Smith (Laddie Corwin); Raymond Walburn (Alex Ryan Creek); Onslow Stevens (Capt. Allen); Barry Kelley (Lieutenant Gorman); Jack Kruschen (Steve); Joseph Vitale (Carr); Percy Helton (Mr. Perkins); Erno Verebes (Waiter); Philip Van Zandt (Louie); Henry Guttman (Frankie); Don Shelton (Hamlet); Herschel Daugherty (Laertes); Dorothy Abbott (The Queen); Julia Faye (Housekeeper); John Marchak (Guard); Lester Dorr (Workman).

Crew: Robert Fellows (Producer); John Farrow (Director); Charles Lederer (Story); John Farrow, Hagar Wilde (Screenplay); Daniel L. Fapp (Cinematography); Joseph J. Lilley (Musical Director); Frank Loesser (Songs); Franz Bachelin, Hans Dreir (Art Direction); Sam Comer, Ross Dowd (Set Decorations); Edith Head (Costume Design); Wally Westmore, Bill Wood, Charles Boerner (Makeup); William H. Coleman (Assistant Director); Gene Garvin, Hugo Grenzbach (Sound); Eda Warren (Editor). Running time: 84 minutes.

Aspiring chorus girl Eleanor Collier is dating stage director Danny James (Victor Mature), who is planning a Broadway show. Their simple life is thrown into turmoil when she naively accepts an invitation to visit the apartment of one of the show's backers, gangster Bunny Harris. When he is bumped off during her stay by rival gangsters, she becomes the chief suspect. Danny is curious as to what she was doing in the apartment in the first place, and so are Harris' gang who kidnap her to get some answers. But all ends well when she is rescued by Danny.

On screen, Betty Hutton has been described as a frantic but good-natured screwball. With a wartime shortage of men, she was usually cast as man-hungry whirlwinds following her Hollywood debut in Paramount's *The Fleet's In* (1942). Baby-faced comic Eddie Bracken tended to be the object of her affections, but in 1949 for *Red, Hot and Blue*, she upped her sights and set her cap for a more red-blooded type — Victor Mature. On paper such a combination, like Mature's teaming with Anna Neagle in *No, No, Nanette* seemed odd to say the least, but the screen teaming only came about because Mature was already on the Paramount lot on loanout, having just finished filming on the DeMille epic *Samson and Delilah*, which was released after the Hutton vehicle. On the entertainment front, the film hits all the right buttons with Hutton belting out her over-the-top musical numbers for all their worth. But for Mature it was, perhaps, his first experience of miscasting.

Other than its name, *Red, Hot and Blue* bears no relation to the 1936 Cole Porter Broadway musical starring Ethel Merman, Jimmy Durante and Bob Hope. In fact, just what the title refers to is anyone's guess. Songwriter Frank Loesser, who went on to write the score for the Broadway hit *Guys and Dolls* in 1950, penned the tunes for the film, each lending themselves perfectly to Hutton's supercharged song-and-dance delivery—"I Wake Up" (where she literally bounces off the ceiling), "That's Loyalty" (where she bounces off the street), "Hamlet" (a zany take on Shakespeare, where she bounces off everything) and "Now That I Need You" (a ballad, where she slows down to take a much-deserved breather). Hutton continued a long line of blondes who partnered up with Mature on screen, but she was simply too far off the radar to have any chemistry with the actor. Clearly unsure how to tackle the part, Mature plays it safe and goes for the straight no-nonsense type of guy he played in *No, No, Nanette*, who simply wants to hang onto his girl and put on a show. However, there are times where you get the impression from some of Mature's intense and pained expressions that he thinks he's in another film altogether. In many ways, Mature got to do his male impression of Hutton with his over-the-top, "this guy's got a screw loose" boxer in *Footlight Serenade*. It can never be said that Hutton didn't give her fans just want they wanted, with *Red, Hot and Blue* once again giving her a great opportunity to put over numbers in her inimitable style.

There's top-notch support from the likes of June Havoc as Hutton's roommate, William Demarest as her fast-talking agent, Walter Winchell as a columnist, William Talman as a mobster, Raymond Walburn as a befuddled, inebriated old letch (what else) and Percy Helton as the stage manager, who in his unique hoarse rasping voice pulls no punches when he tells "Yum-Yum" what he thinks of her act. Director John Farrow also managed to squeeze in a small part for Frank Loesser as one of the gangsters.

Born in Sydney, Australia, Farrow began writing short stories and plays during a four-year stint in the navy. In the late 1920s, he arrived in Hollywood as a naval technical advisor, working his way up as a director of "B" movie productions to "A" features such as *Wake Island* (1942), the Ray Milland thrillers *The Big Clock* (1948) and *Alias Nick Beal* (1949) and the John Wayne Western classic *Hondo* (1953). He was married to Tarzan's Jane, Maureen O'Sullivan, and was the father of Mia Farrow.

At times, Hutton's hilarious antics need to be seen to be believed, particularly the scene where she puts over her memorably, wacky rendition of "Hamlet" after highjacking Mature's serious rehearsals. This easily has to be Mature at his most tolerant and restrained, for just when you think he's going to sock her in the jaw for disrupting proceedings, he simply smiles and lets her take to the floor, as if she's going to surprise us and deliver Shakespeare as the Bard intended it.

And when he is well and truly exasperated by Hutton's natural ability to be taken in by all concerned, he lets loose his best line in the picture when he angrily remarks to her, "And when you buy the Brooklyn Bridge, be sure to take the river with you, and that's a very expensive job." But the film's finale does at least allow him to get back on familiar ground when he and Hutton round up the gangsters in slapstick fashion, which puts you in mind of the equally madcap ending in Mature's first film *The Housekeeper's Daughter*, where once again the mob prove they are dumber than dumb when it comes to a final showdown in Hollywood comedies.

With production wrapping up in the early months of 1949, the film was released on November 25 to a lukewarm reception. The *New York Times* wrote that Hutton's brand of "comical T.N.T., which has been known, on certain occasions, to blast people out of their seats, explodes with mild detonation in Paramount's *Red, Hot and Blue* ... Mr. Mature has a patient, solemn air...."

Variety noted that Mature "handles a straighter role as co-star.... It's a very competent personable delivery that supplies some substance to support the fuss-'n-feathers script."

In her autobiography *Backstage You Can Have: My Own Story*, Hutton wrote that she had her own misgivings about the film, commenting that at this point in her career she was discontented with the poor scripts that Paramount put her way: "I didn't care so much if the studio went belly-up from the bad movies it was suddenly turning out, I just didn't want to take the rap for it."[1]

Picturegoer: "Betty Hutton's loud voice is too prominent; Victor Mature, William Demarest and Frank Loesser have a difficult time being heard. There are some good cracks at the 'arty crafty' community and some well presented 'screwy' slapstick but as a whole it does not register to any appreciable whole."

Easy Living

RKO, 1949

Cast: Victor Mature (Pete Wilson); Lucille Ball (Anne); Lizabeth Scott (Liza Wilson); Sonny Tufts (Tim "Pappy" McCarr); Lloyd Nolan (Lenahan); Paul Stewart (Dave Argus); Jack Paar (Scoop Spooner); Jeff Donnell (Penny McCarr); Art Baker (Howard Vollmer); Gordon Jones (Bill "Holly" Holloran); Don Beddoe (Jaeger); Richard Erdman (Buddy Morgan); William "Bill" Phillips (Ozzie); Charles Lang (Whitey); Kenny Washington (Benny); Julia Dean (Mrs. Belle Ryan); Everett Glass (Virgil Ryan): Jim Backus (Dr. Franklin); Robert Ellis (Urchin); Michael St. Angel (Gilbert Vollmer); Alex Sharp (Don); Russell Thorson (Hunk Edwards); June Bright (Billy Duane); Edward Kotal (Curly); Audrey Young (Singer); The Los Angeles Rams (Themselves).

Crew: Robert Sparks (Producer); Jacques Tourneur (Director); Irwin Shaw (Story "Education of the Heart"); Charles Schnee (Screenplay); Harry J. Wild (Cinematography); Roy Webb (Music); C. Bakaleinikoff (Musical Director); Albert S. D'Agostino, Alfred Herman (Art Direction); Harley Miller, Darrell Silvera (Set Decorations); Edward Stevenson (Costume Design); Robert Cowan, Lee Greenway, Gordon Bau (Makeup); Russell A. Cully (Special Effects); James Lane, Joel Freeman, Nate D. Slott (Assistant Directors); Clem Portman (Sound); Frederic Knudtson (Editor). Running time: 77 minutes.

Aging pro footballer Pete Wilson (Victor Mature) learns that the coaching job he set his heart on has been offered to his friend Tim McCarr. To make matters worse, he discovers he has a bad heart, but carries on playing, against his doctor's advice, because he fears his social climbing wife Liza will leave him if he is no longer a football hero. The club secretary, Anne, secretly carries a torch for Pete and offers a sympathetic shoulder to help him through his difficulties. Liza strays from the marital home with a rich socialite, but finally returns to Pete when she realizes the error of her selfish ways. Pete accepts her back on his terms and they decide to make a fresh start of it, with Pete taking up another coaching opportunity in a new town.

> "Loving you is like getting kicked in the heart ... only in football I get paid for it."
>
> "Loves not like Football, Baby — One Fumble and You're Through."
>
> "You don't need to be the world's smartest quarterback to know when a woman has been playing offside."

As the song goes, "Love Is a Many Splendored Thing," but not so for Mature in *Easy Living*. With a heart condition in need of tender loving care, he instead has a selfish wife who rips it out, kicks it around the floor and serves it up for breakfast. Lizabeth Scott, what a bad girl you were, but at least she doesn't resort to murder in this film as she did in two of her best film noirs *Dead Reckoning* (1947) and *Too Late for Tears* (1949). Born Emma Matzo, but christened Elizabeth following her appearance in a Broadway show, she dropped the E "just to be different." One of the great femme fatales, she was likened to Lauren Bacall because of a similarity in look and her husky voice. Perhaps the main difference between the two is that you could turn your back on Bacall, but with Scott you'd always be inclined to look over your shoulder to see what she was up to.

Due to familiar Hollywood plot misunderstandings and complications, several of

Aging pro footballer Pete Wilson (Mature) takes time out in the locker room to talk to the press in the Jacques Tourneur sports movie *Easy Living* (RKO, 1949). From left: Mature, Jack Paar (as Scoop Spooner), Sonny Tufts (as Tim "Pappy" McCarr), and Paul Stewart (as Dave Argus).

Mature's on-screen romances, to date, had sometimes bordered on the frosty side, with Louise Platt as feisty as they come in *Captain Caution*, and Betty Grable, Rita Hayworth and Lucille Ball all initially playing hard to get in *Song of the Islands*, *My Gal Sal* and *Seven Days' Leave*, respectively. However, Lizabeth Scott's portrayal of a degenerate social-climbing wife took things to another level in *Easy Living*, with a deliciously icy performance that has poor old hubby Mature making for the bottle to drown his sorrows, while Scott's defiler, a rich silver fox chillingly played by Art Baker, chalks up another penthouse bedroom conquest. Mature's anxiety about the breakdown of his marriage is memorably conveyed in the scene when he says to his wife, "Splitting up with dignity! You give me the book of etiquette for such things, and I'll read it cover to cover."

The film was a great vehicle for Mature, providing another opportunity to stretch himself in an unusual role that required him to express a range of emotions as he sees his ordered life come apart at the seams.

When fellow player Gordon Jones is permanently dropped from the team, facing a bleak future, Mature shows him his sympathetic side when the old trouper exits the stadium, knowing that it could be him next. In contrast, wife Scott casually shrugs him off as a loser while she adjusts her makeup. His compassion and concern for his buddies is clearly observed, but this soon gives way to anxiety, disappointment, despair, inner bitterness and anger as his fears for his health, career and marriage grow by the day. Gone is the cocky, self-assured Mature who nonchantly flips cigarettes into his mouth, exercises his right eyebrow, breathes smoke through his nostrils and tosses coins in the air like a pool-room big shot. Instead, we witness Mature in his most insecure role, portraying a guy on the skids who realizes that attaining an "easy living"' is one thing, sustaining it is quite another.

Complicating his life further, we have Lucille Ball as the club secretary for his team, the New York Chiefs, who holds a torch for him. Will Mature be tempted by the forbidden fruit and succumb himself, or will he rise above it all and give Scott a second chance? On first viewing, I thought that Scott, having been tossed aside like yesterday's newspaper by Baker, would make off with the rest of the New York Chiefs by way of recompense, leaving Mature and Ball to play footsy in the moonlight. But I got it wrong, for in the final scene Mature decides she's worth another try after slapping her silly as a token of his love. After the showdown, he coos, "I never slapped you before, Liza. I probably should have, a long time ago." This has to go down as one of the most shocking "kiss and make up" endings in movie history, and definitely not one for the politically correct brigade.

The movie also finds time for him to strip off in the locker room and show off his manly torso. With his great physique put to good use in *Footlight Serenade*, where he played a boxer, it was only a matter of time before a pro football role came his way. But the last person you would have had down to direct the film was Jacques Tourneur, the master craftsman behind the classic chillers *Cat People* (1942) and *I Walked with a Zombie* (1943). The choice of a football film was even more surprising when you consider that Tourneur knew nothing about the game, once commenting, "I'd never been to a football game. I've never played football: I'm not interested in any sports."[1]

His knowledge of football may have been little, but he certainly knew how to get the best out a cracking supporting cast line-up: Lloyd Nolan, Paul Stewart, Art Baker and Gordon Jones. Most of the football players seen in the film were on loan from L.A. Rams.

To pass the time one day on the RKO set, Mature and some of his co-stars were discussing the difference between Mature's last role as Samson to that of his *Easy Living* character. The discussion contrasted the football player's climactic decision to play it safe and not risk his life on one final game, as opposed to Samson who dared everything for a beautiful face and lost. Mature was very clear which of the two characters he would follow: "I'd string along with the restrained guy who believes in figuring the odds, then in selecting the sensible action in preference to the heroic. In this life a man is constantly confronted with the choice between being a dead hero or merely serving as a pallbearer for a dead hero. Me, I'm the cautious type. I like this world and I don't want to miss a moment of my allotted span."[2]

All the leads were on loan out to RKO for the film, Mature from Fox, Scott from Paramount and Ball from MGM. The film marked a return to RKO for both Mature and Ball, who had last paired up in 1942 for the studio in *Seven Days' Leave* (Ball's last film for RKO before joining MGM). Much had happened in the intervening years, culminating in Howard Hughes purchasing the studio in May 1948. In July of that year, seventy-five percent of the personnel was laid off and production cut to a bare minimum. In mid–July, amidst all this upheaval, *Easy Living*, then titled *Interference*, began filming, completing on August 20. Like RKO, much of the film industry was facing a tough time in 1948 with the sale of television sets gathering pace.

The *New York Times* certainly enjoyed the film, commenting, "The entire cast — particularly Mature, Miss Ball and Lloyd Nolan — give attractive performances and even Lizabeth Scott, as the wife, turns her lip-chewing to advantage." As a whole, *Variety* was disappointed with the film, but did have this to say about the star: "Mature is up to his usual good standard and his personality helps the character he portrays."

Picturegoer: "[C]leverly told and well acted story ... Victor Mature makes a virile and thoroughly credible hero...."

A scene from the film with Mature attired in trenchcoat and fedora appears in *After the Fox* (1966). The tale of an aging pro footballer coming to terms with the end of his career was given an update in 1968 with Charlton Heston's *Number One*.

Samson and Delilah

Paramount, 1949

Cast: Hedy Lamarr (Delilah); Victor Mature (Samson); George Sanders (The Saran of Gaza); Angela Lansbury (Semadar); Henry Wilcoxon (Prince Ahtur); Olive Deering (Miriam); Fay Holden (Hazelelponit); Julia Faye (Haisham); Russ Tamblyn (Saul); William Farnum (Tubal); Lane Chandler (Teresh); Moroni Olsen (Targil); Francis McDonald (Story Teller); William "Wee Willie" Davis (Garmiskar); John Miljan (Lesh Lakish); Arthur Q. Bryan (Fat Philstine Merchant); Kasey Rogers (Spectator); Victor Varconi (Lord of Ashdod); John Parrish (Lord of Garth); Frank Wilcox (Lord of Ekron); Russell Hicks (Lord of Ashkelon); Boyd Davis (First Priest of Dragon); Fritz Leiber (Lord Sharif); Mike Mazurki (Leader of the Philistine Soldiers); Davison Clark (Merchant Prince); George Reeves (Wounded Messenger); Pedro de Cordoba (Bar Simon); Frank Reicher (Village Barber); Colin Tapley (Prince); Charles Evans (Manoah — Samson's Father); Frank Mayo (Master Architect); Charles Meredith (High Priest); Harry Woods (Gammad); Ed Hinton (Makon); Nils Asther, Harry Cording (Princes); Lloyd Whitlock (Chief Scribe); Crauford Kent (Court Astrologer); Stephen Roberts (Bergam).

Crew: Cecil B. DeMille (Producer-Director); Based on the History of Samson and Delilah in the Holy Bible, Judges: 13–16, and the novel *Judge and Fool* by Vladimir Jabotinsky; Jesse Lasky, Jr., Fredric M. Frank (Screenplay); George Barnes (Cinematography); Victor Young (Music); Hans Dreier, Walter H. Tyler (Art Direction); Sam Comer,

Ray Moyer (Set Decorations); Edith Head, Dorothy Jeakins, Gwen Wakeling, Eloise Jensson (Costume Design); Theodore Kosloff (Choreography); Wally Westmore, Harold Lierly, William Woods (Makeup); Gordon Jennings, Paul Lerpae, Devereaux Jennings, Barney Wolff (Special Effects); Edward Salven (Assistant Director); Frank Cordell (Stunt Double for Victor Mature); John Cope, Harry Lindgren (Sound); Anne Bauchens (Editor). Running time: 128 minutes.

For 40 years the Danite people have been under the thumb of the Philistines. Super-strong Danite Samson (Victor Mature) ruffles a few feathers when he falls for Semadar, a Philistine girl, and the couple decide to marry, but she and her father are killed during a brawl between Samson and some of the Philistine guests at the wedding. Semadar's younger sister Delilah harbors a fascination for Samson, now a fugitive, and tries to learn the secret of his great strength which has enabled him to fight and slay a lion barehanded and defeat the Philistine army with nothing more than the jawbone of an ass. She becomes a courtesan of the Philistine ruler, the Saran of Gaza, and sets about to cause the downfall of Samson using her feminine wiles. Eventually she learns that his strength lies in his long hair, which she cuts while he is asleep, before delivering him to his enemies. Set to work as a slave, he is blinded, imprisoned and humiliated by his Philistine captors. But in time he regains his strength when his hair grows back, pushing apart two columns of the Pagan temple he is taken to for further humiliation. This brings the house down, killing Samson and many of the Philistines.

"A story as timeless and tumultuous as the violent age it spreads before you!"
"HISTORY'S MOST BEAUTIFUL AND TREACHEROUS WOMAN!"

The legendary director Cecil B. DeMille once boasted that he could make a great motion picture out of any fifty pages of the Bible, and he was true to his word with his spectacular productions *The Ten Commandments* (1923 and 1956), *King of Kings* (1927), *Sign of the Cross* (1932) and Mature's first foray into the biblical epic *Samson and Delilah* (1949). Demille had planned to make *Samson and Delilah* as early as 1935 with perhaps Henry Wilcoxon as Samsom partnered with Miriam Hopkins, but the project was abandoned.

So much has been written about the film and Mature's contribution that it is difficult to know where to start with this significant chapter in the actor's career, but I guess you can't beat Groucho Marx's comment that he would never go a see a film "where the man's tits are bigger that the woman's." It makes you wonder what he might have come up with if Gary Grant had been chosen to play Samson. Yes, unbelievable as it sounds, Grant was one of DeMille's early considerations for the part, in a list that also included Burt Lancaster (rejected due to a bad back), Douglas Fairbanks, Jr. and Mr. Universe, Steve Reeves.[1] DeMille sponsored talent contests for the role of Samson, but finally settled on Mature after admiring his sincere performance in *Kiss of Death*. Mature wasn't particularly excited when he knew he was in the running for the role, figuring that the director was seeing everyone and now it was his turn. When he was finally summoned to see DeMille, the interview lasted four hours, with the director revealing his extensive knowledge of the actor's career, by which time Mature knew he had nailed the role.[2]

As the story goes, there was only one thing that concerned DeMille about Mature: his weight. Having indulged the life of a star, he was out of shape and overweight by about thirty pounds. But after a few weeks of training sessions, coached by DeMille's longtime associate Henry Wilcoxon, his magnificent torso was back in trim and ready for the camera. Acknowledging that his physique would once again be on show, Mature remarked, "Yes, I, disrobed again, but boy what a part, and what a picture!" To get into shape, Mature also did some mild exercise with horseshoes at Laguna Beach. Within five minutes, he was pale and slightly blue around the mouth and had to call it a day. (Mature was not one for exercise).

During his lengthy conversation with Mature, DeMille mentioned that he was having trouble casting the role of the Saran of Gaza. After the role was described to him, Mature heartily put forward George Sanders, and Sanders it was.[3]

It was during this time that Mature got into the retail television business, selling many discounted sets from his dressing room. When Sanders heard that Mature had recommended him to DeMille, he bought twenty-six television sets from him and sent them out to friends.[4] Mature regarded Sanders as a "truly great actor,"[5] but remembered him as a bit of "a recluse" on set.[6] In the Sanders biography *An Exhausted Life* by Richard Vanderbeets, the author records that Sanders said of the film: "I had a wonderful director in Cecil B. DeMille, and Victor Mature and Hedy Lamarr were easy to work with."[7]

Mature would later acknowledge that *Kiss of Death* and then *Samson and Delilah* were very important to his career, and they helped to secure other good roles in films such as *The Robe* and *Demetrius and the Gladiators*."[8]

The casting of Delilah was also by no means a dead certainty, with the likes of Rita Hayworth, Lana Turner and Ava Gardner down on the director's list as possibilities before, late in the day, it went to Lamarr, who by all accounts impressed the director with her performance in *The Strange Woman* (1946), which co-starred George Sanders.[9] By some accounts, DeMille even considered Betty Hutton for the role.[10] Can you imagine Cary Grant as Samson and Betty Hutton as Delilah?

When she was offered the part, Lamarr asked her agent which star had been selected for Samson, to which he replied, "They're thinking of Victor Mature. But who cares? It's only a body to set off you in the ruins. Muscles and tits sugar-coated with religion. It's for you."[11]

Mature described Lamarr as "gorgeous," adding that "the camera picked up her beauty and mystique." Even though he felt they worked well together, he recalled that she appeared unwell on the set: "Nothing chronic, she was just somehow out of sorts. Let me put it another way: she was not exactly a ball of fire — she just seemed to be loping along."[12] A close friend of Hedy's recalled that the actress did not like Mature. She allegedly complained to DeMille that Mature always worked it that the camera would always be pointing to his face and her back, to which DeMille diplomatically responded, "Do you think there are men in America who would rather look at his face than your ass?"[13]

DeMille selected Angela Lansbury for the role of Semadar, older sister to Delilah, after his original choice Phyllis Calvert became unavailable due to illness.

Casting sewn up, it was time to let cameras roll, with the production getting underway on October 4, scheduled for a ten-week shoot.

In one crucial action scene which allows Samson to show off his strength, he kills a young lion. To make it look as real as possible, DeMille wanted Mature to wrestle the Paramount studio lion, a tame, aging beast called Old Jackie. When DeMille tried to persuade Mature by kidding him that the old lion had no teeth, the star memorably replied, "Well,

I don't want to be gummed to death, either." With the help of a lion skin, and a stunt double, DeMille eventually persuaded Mature to do a few rounds with the beast, and the scene was shot. The scene features one of the great lines in the film when Delilah runs up and hugs Samson after he dispatches the lion, prompting him to yell, "Hey, one cat at a time."

Although looking the part, Mature was always quick to dispel any notions of him being a strong guy in real life, telling one interviewer that a baby could have knocked down the pillars: "I told 'em to make them lightweight. I don't like expending too much physical energy."

Writing for *Life* magazine, John Bainbridge followed cast and crew around during filming, grabbing an interview with Mature in his dressing room where he found the star studying a racing form. When he asked Mature what he thought about his current role, the actor responded. "Jeez, it's great. These whiskers, they're driving me nuts. They put 'em on with glue, spread glue all over my face. It's a great part, really great."[14]

As in *Easy Living* and *Kiss of Death*, Mature convincingly plays a brooding, embittered man with conflicting emotions — indeed, a veritable cauldron of emotions, which gives rise to some great biblically charged dialogue. Betrayed by the women he loves, he says of Delilah, "Your arms were quicksand. Your kiss was death. The name Delilah will be an everlasting curse on the lips of men." And when it's time to destroy the temple in the final scene, he exclaims, "My eyes have seen thy glory, oh God! Now let me die with my enemies."

Adapted from the biblical Book of Judges and made at a reputed cost of $3 million, *Samson and Delilah* was a huge box office hit for Paramount earning $11 million in 1950.[15] It won Academy Awards for Best Art Direction and Best Costume Design. It also received nominations for its cinematography, music score and special effects. The success of the film prompted one critic to suggest that DeMille considered God to be his co-director. In an article for *Picturegoer* magazine, Elliseva Sayers (certainly impressed by the epic) commented, "All the overworked adjectives — spectacular, terrific, awesome, breathtaking — will need to be given a new lease of life to describe the picture. And then they'll miss the mark."

Look: "Victor Mature is probably the only actor in the world who could make Samson's strong-man exploits so believable."

Film Bulletin: "The casting of Hedy Lamarr and Victor Mature in the title roles was inspired. Physically, they are the very prototypes of the Bible characters, and their performances rank with the best they have ever given."

The New York Times: "Victor Mature as Samson is a dashing and dauntless hunk of man whose hair is handsomely tonsured and whose face is as smooth as a baby's cheek."

Samson and Delilah brought new life to the ancient world genre and served as a prototype for the epics that were to follow in the fifties and sixties, with Mature's stoic characterization trailblazing the way for those other epic luminaries Charlton Heston, Stephen Boyd, Yul Brynner and Kirk Douglas.

Wabash Avenue

20th Century–Fox, 1950

Cast: Betty Grable (Ruby Summers); Victor Mature (Andy Clark); Phil Harris (Mike Stanley); Reginald Gardiner (English Eddie); James Barton (Harrigan); Barry Kelley (Bouncer); Margaret Hamilton (Tillie Hutch); Jacqueline Dalya (Cleo); Robin Raymond (Jennie); Hal K. Dawson (Healy); Dorothy Neumann (Reformer); Alexander Pope

(Charlie Saxe); Henry Kulky (Joe Barton); Marie Bryant (Elsa); Collette Lyons (Beulah); Charles Arnt (Horace Carter); Dick Crockett (Bartender); Percy Helton (Ship's Captain); Marion Marshall (Chorus Girl); Walter Long, Billy Daniel (Dancers); John "Skins" Miller (Drunk); George Beranger (Wax Work Attendant); Michael Ross, Red Nichols (Policemen); Douglas Carter (Ferris Wheel Operator).

Crew: William Perlberg (Producer); Henry Koster (Director); Charles Lederer (Story); Charles Lederer, Harry Tugend (Screenplay); Arthur E. Arling (Cinematography); Lionel Newman (Music Director); Mack Gordon, Josef Myrow, Bert Kalmar, and Joe Cooper (Songs); Lyle R. Wheeler, Joseph C. Wright (Art Direction); Paul S. Fox, Thomas Little (Set Decorations); Charles Le Maire (Costume Design); Ben Nye (Makeup); Fred Sersen (Special Effects); Gaston Glass (Assistant Director); Alfred Bruzlin, Roger Heman, Sr. (Sound); Robert L. Simpson (Editor). Running time: 92 minutes.

Singer-dancer Ruby Summers works at the Wabash Avenue casino for owner Mike Stanley, but his plans to keep her there for his own are thwarted when producer Andy Clark (Victor Mature), Mike's former partner, arrives on the scene and takes a fancy to Ruby. The two men maintain a friendly rivalry for Ruby's affections, cheating each other at cards (like the good old days) and during the course of their antics winning and losing their respective business ventures. However, the competition between them really racks up when Andy wants to take Ruby to New York to exploit her full potential in a big Hammerstein show. Mike uses every trick in the book in an effort to keep her, but true love prevails in the end when she does the show and decides that Andy's the one for her.

Mature's last stint in turn-of-the-century America in *My Gal Sal* (1942) saw him emotionally embroiled in on-screen fireworks with love interest Rita Hayworth. For *Wabash Avenue*, he is reunited with Betty Grable and the sparks fly even higher in their love-hate courting ritual, where the trading of insults is taken to an art form. When Grable describes Mature as a big baboon with the smell of a skunk and the heart of a louse, he smugly retorts, "Not bad, I sound like a zoo." And if smart lines weren't enough, we are also treated to some brilliant song and dance routines, Grable's gams, great sets, double dealing par excellence and Mature's lively turn as a hustling promoter who looks like he was born to make with the sassy patter, while decked out in gaudy striped suit and straw hat.

This was Mature at the peak of his game, following on the back of his big office success *Samson and Delilah*. It certainly showed the actor's range, one minute playing a brooding, vulnerable strongman, the next a brash, conceited showman. Grable's best days were perhaps behind her, but the film did give her career a much needed boost after the relative failures of *That Lady in Ermine* (1948) and *The Beautiful Blonde from Bashful Bend* (1949). She was still at the top of the Hollywood salary list.

Originally, *Wabash Avenue* was to be based on the lives of Chicago songwriters Gus and Grace Kahn, but Fox production chief Darryl F. Zanuck decided to keep the title and turn it into a remake of Grable's earlier peak time success *Coney Island* (1943), which co-starred George Montgomery and Cesar Romero as rivals for her affections. The period stayed the same, but the setting was switched from the New York pleasure beach to the Chicago World's Fair. The Khan story would later be made as a vehicle for Doris Day and Danny Thomas under the title *I'll See You in My Dreams* (1951).

Betty had wanted her favorite leading man Dan Dailey to co-star, but he was already working on another film, the musical Western *A Ticket to Tomahawk*. However, she was happy when the studio announced that Mature, her former lover, was down for the role. It was a happy reunion,[1] with both stars showing that they had lost none of the chemistry from their earlier 1942 musical outings in *Song of the Islands* and *Footlight Serenade*. Once again, what Mature lacked in the song and dance department, he more than made up for with his cocky charm and disarming presence. Although it was down to Grable to deliver the show-stopping numbers, Mature did learn to play "Baby, Won't You Say You Love Me" on the piano. Koster had originally planned for Mature to do a dance number with Grable, but Mature soon put an end to that possibility when he showed the director his size 12½ shoes.[2]

Grable may have been thirty-five when she made *Wabash*, but she still looked great as she belted out song after song in some truly memorable dance routines, with much of the choreography partly based on "burlesque moves of the period. Songwriters Mack Gordon and Josef Myrow excelled themselves with a bumper harvest of new songs for the film, which included "Down on Wabash Avenue," "Walking Along with Billy," "Won't You Say You Love Me," "Wilhelmina" (which received an Academy Award nomination for Best Original Song), "May I Tempt You with a Big Red Rosy Apple?" and "Clean Up Chicago." In addition, we also heard "I've Been Floating Down the Old Green River" by Kalmar-Cooper and " I Wish I Could Shimmy Like My Sister Kate" by Armand J. Piron and Peter Bocage. The wonderful choreography came courtesy of Grable's former dance director Billy Daniels, who coached the star in her Paramount films of the 1930s.

Self-assured Andy Clark (Mature, right), accompanied by sidekick English Eddie (Reginald Gardiner), takes in a stage show, while mulling over his next plan to get rich, in the wonderfully nostalgic turn-of-the-century musical *Wabash Avenue* (20th Century–Fox, 1950).

With Grable throwing insults and any available object (including shoes and tomatoes) at Mature, who simply looks on in delighted amusement, the film at times plays like a barrelhouse version of *The Taming of the Shrew*. We even get a hint of a Henry Higgins, Eliza Doolittle relationship as Mature tries to infuse Grable's bad-tempered shimmy dancer with a touch of class, particularly where her wardrobe's concerned. "You know, Miss Summers, you're an awfully nice girl, but there's a couple of things you need to know, including how to dress." After a string of such remarks, Grable simply wants to slap his smug mug in their every encounter, but as is the way with such matters, Mature eventually melts her heart, prompting love rival Phil Harris to deliver the best line in the film when he laments, "I never understand what she sees in a mug like him when she can have a mug like me."

Providing Mature with a great double-dealing partner, the wonderful Harris was certainly at the top of the deck when they were dealing out talent. A successful singer, bandleader, songwriter, jazz musician, actor and comedian, he will be fondly remembered as the voice behind some of the Disney classics, most notably as Baloo in *The Jungle Book* (1967). He was married to Alice Faye, so his inclusion in the cast gave Grable an opportunity to meet up with her old Fox colleague who had retired five years earlier with her family to Palm Springs.

Good value is also provided by James Barton as an Irish drunk who sets the screen alight when he jigs to the lively numbers "Green River" (while swiping unattended drinks) and "Harrrigan." As Mature's sidekick, Reginald Gardiner provides his usual solid, amiable presence in this, his second film with the actor (after *Fury at Furnace Creek*).

A deft hand at light comedy, director Henry Koster really got the best out of all the leads, his brisk direction coaxing a particularly lively performance from Mature. It was a fine performance that owed much to Mature's impeccable comic timing and his natural ability to exude self-assured cockiness.

Born in Berlin, Koster fled the country after hitting a Nazi SA officer who insulted him in a bank. He directed Grable in several films, but his greatest successes were possibly *Harvey* (1950) and Fox's first CinemaScope film *The Robe* (1953), which co-starred Mature.

The film's producer William Perlberg was the man behind many big box office hits including *The Song of Bernadette* (1943), *Miracle on 34th Street* (1947) and *The Country Girl* (1954). Mature received a screen suspension when he refused to take a part in Perlbeg's *Ten Gentlemen from West Point* (1942). Mature said that he'd be happy to play the backwoodsman from Kentucky, (the lead part that went to George Montgomery), but Perlberg had him down for a lesser role. Mature recalled that he was in his dressing room making his first picture for Fox, when he got the telephone call that Perlberg wanted to see him about the part. Still unfamiliar with his new surroundings, Mature inquired as to who Mr. Perlberg was, which sent the actor's agent into a major panic when he heard the news. Anxiously asking Mature what he had said on the phone, Mature casually responded, "All I did to Perlberg was to ask who he is. The only Perlberg I know is a delicatessen in Louisville, Kentucky."[3]

Like *Coney Island*, *Wabash Avenue* was a runaway success, with critics and audiences alike. *Picture Show* raved, "It's vigorous, vulgar, spectacularly staged and beautifully photographed." According to *The New York Times*, "Mr. Mature and Mr. Harris also rate whacks on the back for getting as much tangy humor out of the gentlemen hoodlums as they do. Together with the brilliantined Grable ... they roll up a very considerable wisecrack-decibel score."

Stella

20th Century–Fox, 1950

Cast: Ann Sheridan (Stella Bevans); Victor Mature (Jeff DeMarco); Leif Erickson (Fred Anderson, Jr.); David Wayne (Carl Granger); Randy Stuart (Claire); Marion Marshall (Mary); Frank Fontaine (Don); Evelyn Varden (Flora); Lea Penman (Mrs. Calhoun); Joyce Mackenzie (Peggy Denny); Hobart Cavanaugh (Tim Gross); Charles Halton (Mr. Beeker); Chill Wills (Chief Clark); Mary Bear (Myra); Paul Harvey (Ralph Denny); Larry Keating (Gil Wright); Loreli Vitek (Cigarette Girl); Walter Baldwin (Farmer).

Crew: Sol C. Siegel (Producer); Claude Binyon (Screenwriter-Director); Doris Miles Disney (Novel); Joseph MacDonald (Cinematography); Cyril J. Mockridge (Music); Mark-Lee Kirk, Lyle R. Wheeler (Art Direction); Paul S. Fox, Thomas Little (Set Decorations); Edward Stevenson (Costume Design); Charles Le Maire (Wardrobe); Ben Nye (Makeup); Fred Sersen (Special Effects); Ad Schaumer (Assistant Director); Roger Heman, Sr., E. Clayton Ward (Sound); Harmon Jones (Editor). Running time: 83 minutes.

When a crazy family's uncle, who was always one for the bottle, is accidentally killed during a family picnic, they bury the body in a remote spot, thinking that no one will believe their innocent story concerning his death. When the family's sensible daughter Stella, who was absent from the picnic, finds out what transpired, she is less than impressed with their actions, particularly when she reveals that the insurance company that she works for has a policy with the victim. Armed with this knowledge, family members Carl and Don try to identify every corpse that turns up as their uncle so that they can collect the insurance money. The $20,000 policy brings out snooping insurance investigator Jeff DeMarco (Victor Mature), who falls for Stella during his investigations much to the annoyance of her boss Fred, who wants her for his wife. When it is revealed that the uncle's body was inadvertently buried in an old Indian burial ground, the boys are given steady jobs trying to locate it, amongst the many other bodies, and Stella goes off to make a new life with Jeff.

"Wait'll you see what Ann Sheridan does to Victor Mature in *Stella*!"

Sheridan does what most women do in the first few reels of a Mature movie, stubbornly resists his advances until he finally breaks down her defenses before going in for the clincher. And that's no mean feat where Sheridan was concerned, for if there ever was a sassy gal with enough oomph to match her ready wit, it was this tough, sharp-talking dame.

Stella completed a trio of films with unusual storylines (including *Easy Living* and *Gambling House*) that Mature top-lined in mid-career. All were, to varying degrees, underrated upon their general release, which was unfortunate, because they are all very entertaining in their own way. Each bridged two or three genres, dealing with their themes in an slightly offbeat manner, which perhaps threw audiences of the day, and none more so than the wickedly funny *Stella,* which has been described as screwball, comedy, a black comedy and a straight comedy with shades of noir. But, however you describe it, there is no denying that this is one quirky movie that will hit the funnybone time after time. Director Claude Binyon (a former reporter and screenwriter) had an eye for wit and satire, and *Stella* showcases it to good effect. Binyon will forever be remembered for writing the famous 1929 stock market crash headline for *Variety*, "Wall Street Lays an Egg."

Stella reaffirmed a pattern in Mature's career where he appeared to shift between drama and light comedy with regularity. Such diversity enabled the actor to convey a range of emotions and character traits. In *Stella*, Mature's upbeat insurance investigator, Jeff DeMarco, contrasts sharply with his world-weary, disillusioned characters in both *Easy Living* and *Gambling House*, and, interestingly, it is Sheridan who adopts these characteristics in the film.

Sheridan's perfect comic timing is second to none, and in the selfmocking, laid-back Mature, she found an excellent partner. When Mature quips, "I like women, all women. I never had any trouble with them because I don't take them seriously," she responds, "Has it ever occurred to you, Mr. DeMarco, that to some women you may be actually revolting?" The verbal sparring might be slower than Sheridan's earlier movies such as *Torrid Zone* (1940), which she made with James Cagney, but this is still Sheridan at her best. (Not overly impressed with the movie the *New York Times* did at least acknowledge the exchanges between the two leads, commenting, "Sheridan has a few sharp scenes with Victor Mature.") Sheridan made *Stella* as part of a two-picture deal with *I Was a Male War Bride*.

Sheridan recalled in an interview that although she enjoyed Doris Miles Disney's book *Family Skeleton* from which *Stella* was adapted, she was less impressed with the film itself. Despite a talented cast, she thought the comedy was forced and that there was little screen chemistry between her and Mature.[1] I wonder whether her disappointment was perhaps swayed in any way by the film's poor showing at the box office, because, in my humble opinion, her interaction with Mature and the rest of the cast works a treat—both smooth and relaxed. It is possible that audience dissatisfaction with the end product may be partly attributed to the fact that unconventionally the two leads don't provide the focus in the film, which instead comes from David Wayne in a career best as the wacky brother-in-law who never fails to amuse us with his wild schemes to collect the insurance money.

Wayne was a natural for this type of comedy, but it would be in the world of drama where he would make his most significant impact in films such as *M* (1951) and *Wait Till the Sun Shines, Nellie* (1952). He always sticks in my mind as the Irish cabbie Gus in *Portrait of Jennie* (1948). Former band singer and trombonist Leif Erickson starred in many a similar supporting role before finding fame in the popular television series *The High Chaparral* (1967–71). Two of his three marriages were to actresses (Frances Farmer and Margaret Hayes). At six-foot-four, Erickson continued a trend of supporting actors who were taller than Mature.

In terms of frantic black comedy, *Stella* would certainly make a great box-set with those other two quirky films that wryly deal with corpses, *Arsenic and Old Lace* (1944) and *The Trouble with Harry* (1955). It may not be as polished as these two classics, but it'll definitely bring a smile to your face and linger in your memory for just as long.

Picturegoer magazine (1950): "The film has a neat script and some snappy dialogue, but its cast, good as it is, fails to sweeten its doubtful jokes about death."

Photoplay: "Red-headed Ann and muscle man Vic make a handsome couple."

I'll Get By

20th Century–Fox, 1950

Cast: June Haver (Liza Martin); William Lundigan (William Spencer); Gloria DeHaven (Terry Martin); Dennis Day (Freddy Lee); Harry James (Himself); Thelma Ritter (Miss Murphy); Steve Allen (Peter Pepper); Danny Davenport (Chester Dooley);

Harry Antrim (Mr. Olinville); Tom Hanlon (Announcer); Peggy O'Connor (U.S.O. Girl); Harry Seymour (Stage Manager); Harry Lauter, Don Hicks (Assistant Directors); Charles Tannen (Director); Kathleen Hughes (Secretary); Vincent Renno (Head Waiter); Bob McCord (Commentator); Paul Picerni (Marine Sergeant); Dick Winslow (Cooky Myers); Victor Mature, Jeanne Crain, Dan Dailey, Dick Haymes (Themselves in Cameos).

Crew: William Perlberg (Producer); Richard Sale (Director); Robert Ellis, Pamela Harris, Helen Logan (Screen Story); Mary Loos, Richard Sale (Screenplay); Charles G. Clarke (Cinematography); Lionel Newman (Musical Director), Richard Irvine, Lyle R. Wheeler (Art Direction); Thomas Little, Stuart A. Reiss (Set Decorations); Charles Le Maire, Travilla (Costume Design), Ben Nye, Thomas Tuttle (Makeup); Fred Sersen (Special Effects); Arthur Jacobson (Assistant Director); Harry M. Leonard, George Leverett (Sound); J. Watson Webb, Jr. (Editor). Running time: 83 minutes.

Hard-up song plugger turned music publisher William Spencer teams up with Terry Martin, who has written "Deep in the Heart of Texas," and the two meet and romance a couple of sisters, Liza and Terry Martin. The girls, who sing for the Harry James Band, try to help the boys plug their songs, which eventually proves successful. However, romantic misunderstandings ensue and both couples split up. When war breaks out, the guys join the Marines. They are reunited with the girls who are touring as entertainers in a South Pacific USO show. Along the way the film features guest appearances from the likes of Jeanie Crain, Victor Mature and Dan Dailey.

"Tops in Romance ... Great in its Hilarious Comedy!"
"You've Never Seen Such Song and Sun-Filled
Laugh-Loaded Entertainment!"

Like Mature's previous musical *Wabash Avenue*, *I'll Get By* is a great feel-good musical simply bursting with memorable tunes. Both films were produced by William Perlberg, who certainly knew how to bring new life to previous successes, with *Wabash* essentially a remake of *Coney Island* (1943) and *I'll Get By* providing another take on *Tin Pan Alley* (1940), which starred Alice Faye, Betty Grable, John Payne and Jack Oakie.

Mature shares his cameo appearance with Jeanne Crain, who phones Bill to tell him she would like to sing the George Gershwin number "Yankee Doodle Blues" he has planned for a gala benefit concert. (It's a song Bill has already promised to Liza.) At the end of the call, Mature advises Crain, "Oh, honey, I'm telling you, all you gotta do with this number is dress in red, white and blue and wave." Mature replaced Clifton Webb in this cameo role.

Director Richard Sale started his career writing pulp novels before turning his attentions to screenwriting and directing. He proved himself adept with easygoing Technicolor musicals such as *A Ticket to Tomahawk* (1950), *I'll Get By* (1950) and *The Girl Next Door* (1953)—the latter two showcasing June Haver to best advantage. Haver, a former band singer, was groomed by Fox to be the next Betty Grable, co-starring with Grable in *The Dolly Sisters* (1945). But when her contract ran out in 1953 she left films, entering a convent to become a nun. She was happy for several months before a serious illness forced her to leave that same year. In 1954, she married Fred MacMurray, and later in life found success as an interior decorator.

Mature once said of Haver, "[She] has a quality that's almost unique, it's that young and refreshing. When you get out of the service and come back and see a girl like her walk toward you, you think, 'That's just what I've been waiting to come home to.' She's the epitome of the 'girl next door.' Cute and sweet and wholesome as an apple pie."

William Lundigan studied law and worked as a radio announcer before embarking on a film career which never really progressed beyond "B" status. With his winning smile and handsome features he looked like an amalgam of several actors including John Agar, Steve Forrest and Richard Denning, with perhaps a hint of Gig Young thrown in for good measure. His most notable films include *Pinky* (1949), *I'll Get By* (1950), and the 1951 features *The House on Telegraph Hill*, *I'd Climb the Highest Mountain* and *Love Nest*—the latter with June Haver and Marilyn Monroe.

The daughter of former vaudeville performers, Gloria DeHaven also started out as a band singer before joining MGM, where her vivacious persona was shown to good effect in a number of musicals including *Two Girls and a Sailor* (1944), *Summer Holiday* (1948) and *Two Tickets to Broadway* (1951). She was married to actor John Payne from 1944 to 1950; he was the first of her four husbands. In the Fred Astaire musical *Three Little Words* (1950), she played her own mother Flora Parker DeHaven.

Irish-American singer Dennis Day got his big break working on Jack Benny's radio show in 1939, going on to work with Benny in his television programs, and even got his own radio show in 1946. Like William Lundigan, he first had ideas of taking up a law career before show business beckoned. In addition to singing, he was also an accomplished mimic. He married Peggy Almquist in 1948, and the couple had ten children.

Shot in glorious Technicolor and moving at a lively clip, *I'll Get By* is escapism at its very best, with a clutch of likable, endearing performances and a wealth of great songs including the title song, "Deep in the Heart of Texas," "I Got a Gal from Kalamazoo," "There Will Never Be Another You," "Once in a While," "It's Been a Long, Long Time," "No Love, No Nothing," "Fifth Avenue," "MacNamara's Band," "Yankee Doodle Blues" and "You Make Me Feel So Young"—to list just a few. And added to all this, we have the maestro himself, Harry James, and his magical trumpet. Lionel Newman's musical contribution didn't go unnoticed, his scoring for the film receiving an Oscar nomination (losing out to *Annie Get Your Gun*).

Providing icing to the cake, the supporting cast included the great Thelma Ritter, Steve Allen and Danny Davenport. The unbilled cameos included Jeanne Crain, Victor Mature, Dan Dailey and Reginald Gardiner, who worked with Mature in three other films: *Fury at Furnace Creek*, *Wabash Avenue* and *Androcles and the Lion* (1952).

The New York Times: "*I'll Get By* adds up to a nice, light entertainment, a sort of disk jockey with colored pictures."

Picturegoer: "Musicals dealing with the lives or adventures of music publishers all seem to be much of a muchness so far as the plot is concerned. Here is another conventional example for the collection."

Incidentally, Gloria DeHaven and Dennis Day went on to join Mature in the cameo lineup for *Won Ton Ton, the Dog Who Saved Hollywood* (1976).

Gambling House

RKO, 1950

Cast: Victor Mature (Marc Fury); Terry Moore (Lynn Warren); William Bendix (Joe Farrow); Zachary Charles (Willie); Basil Ruysdael (Judge Ravinek); Donald Randolph (Lloyd Crane); Damian O'Flynn (Ralph Douglas); Cleo Moore (Sally); Ann Doran

(Mrs. Della Lucas); Eleanor Audley (Mrs. Livingston); Gloria Winters (B.J. Warren); Don Haggerty (Sharky); William E. Green (Doctor); Jack Kruschen (Burly Italian Immigrant); Eddie Fields (Fat Man Pickpocket); Victor Paul, Joseph Rogato, Guy Zanette (Italian Immigrants); Kirk Alyn (F.B.I. Man); Sherry Hall (Robbins); Jack Stoney (Detective); Vera Stokes (Station Wagon Driver); Clark Howat (Nick); Leonidas Ossetynski (Mr. Sobieski); Loda Halama (Mrs. Sobieski); Chester Jones (Elevator Attendant); Stanley Price (Gorman).

Crew: Warren Duff (Producer); Ted Tetzlaff (Director); Erwin Gelsey (Story); Marvin Borowsky, Allen Rivkin (Screenplay); Harry J. Wild (Cinematography); Roy Webb (Music); C. Bakaleinikoff (Musical Director); Albert S. D'Agostino, Alfred Herman (Art Direction); Jack Mills, Darrell Silvera (Set Decorations); Michael Woulfe (Costume Design); Mel Berns (Makeup); Phil Brigandi, Clem Portman (Sound); Roland Gross (Editor). Running time: 80 minutes.

Gambler Marc Fury becomes the fall guy for a murder committed by his crime boss Joe Farrow for a $50,000 fee. When self-defense is proven and Marc is cleared, Joe tips off the judge that Marc was born in Italy and his parents were never naturalized. Facing deportation, Marc, with the assistance of pretty social worker Lyn Warrren, begins to realize the value of American citizenship and manages to convince the judge to let him stay in the country. But Joe still wants him out of the picture, sending out the order to have him killed. When Joe and his gang catch up with Marc, the tables are turned on Joe when one of the gang shoots him instead because of his double-crossing ways.

"Here Comes Mature! Shrewd ... charming ... hard ... a gambler."

"The crime-smeared tale of Marc Fury, fall guy, who became a marked man."

"Too Dangerous for a Girl to Fool With! Too Tough for a Mob to Soften!"

When *Gambling House* came to town, Mature's box-office attraction was such that all the publicity guys had to tag on the posters was "Here Comes Mature!" to guarantee an audience. Continuing to star in a steady line of box-office successes, Mature was certainly on a roll, with the social aspects in *Gambling House* giving him another fine opportunity to add to the variety of his characters.

A gem of a sleeper (RKO always seemed to produce them), *Gambling House* is a remake of *Mr. Lucky* (1943), a tale of a cynical gambler who cheats the American War Relief Society before finding redemption; *Mr. Lucky* starred the actor who nearly pipped Mature to the Samson role, Cary Grant. But on this occasion, our hard-boiled gambler is facing deportation after pleading self-defense for a murder committed by his mobster boss.

Opening to a sprawling cityscape of lower Manhattan and Roy Webb's captivating big city score, the film immediately draws you in with its rain-washed sidewalks and a horse-drawn milk wagon making the dawn delivery, while a solitary figure struggles to his apartment, blood dripping from his wounded body. Mature is a tough, unyielding character who doesn't need anything to dull the pain when the doc pulls a slug out of him, while a fellow small-time racketeer illuminates the scene with a hand held-light bulb. Questioning the events that led to him taking a wild slug in a rigged poker game, Mature introduces his character to the audience when he snarls, "Marc Fury, an innocent bystander. You know what I think, Willy? I think I'm a fall guy."

Mature's characters, intrinsically good guys at heart, always lacked the requisite ruthlessness to get to the top in racketeering, making him the perfect patsy in big city thrillers. He played the fall guy in *Kiss of Death*, and could have easily reprised the role of the small-time loser in *Cry of the City* if the honors on that occasion hadn't gone to Richard Conte.

RKO originally had the film scheduled for 1948, but Mature was dissatisfied with the script, and went on to make *Easy Living* instead. In 1950, he still had his concerns about the story, taking a suspension from his Fox contract before RKO agreed to rewrite the script to his satisfaction.[1]

Although the film has noirish undertones, it is essentially a social drama with a romantic sideline, examining immigration laws. Skillfully blending the two genres, director Ted Tetzlaff delivers a tautly paced thriller that makes the most of its black and white staging. An accomplished director of photography before he became a director, Tetzlaff certainly knew how to infuse his films with mood and tension. For his cinematography, he will always be remembered for *I Married a Witch* (1942), *The Enchanted Cottage* (1945) and *Notorious* (1946), with the brilliant thriller *The Window* (1949) his calling card to respectability as a director.

In addition to the obligatory dubious doctor, no film concerning the mob would be complete without a crooked lawyer entering the fold. But high-powered legal types hold no place in Fury's affections as we learn when he contemptuously remarks to one, "I'm not talking to you, you're Farrow's shyster, you'd pick up his spit if he told you to."

In much the same way as Mature's hard character is softened by the love of a good woman in *Kiss of Death*, we witness a similar outcome in *Gambling House,* with his tough exterior gradually melting away in the presence of Terry Moore, who (wise to his smooth-talking ways as a ladies man) informs him that she covered his type in her first psychology semester.

Howard Hughes borrowed Moore, whom he was dating at the time, from Columbia to star alongside Mature. When the filmmakers informed Hughes of their concerns that twenty-year-old Moore was too young to portray a social worker who reforms and wins the heart of Mature's world-weary gangster, he responded, "I don't care. I love the girl."[2]

At five-foot-two, Moore (together with Peggy Cummins in *Moss Rose*) was one of the most petite actresses to star alongside Mature, but what she lacked in height she certainly made up for with her curvaceous figure and perky persona. And in later years, at age 55, she proved that she still had the perfect figure when she posed nude for the August 1984 issue of *Playboy* magazine.

Like Mature, William Bendix started his film career with Hal Roach, and within a year had been nominated for an Academy Award for his part in *Wake Island* (1942). He will also be best remembered for *The Babe Ruth Story* (1948) and the radio and television series *The Life of Riley*—and as the henchman who beats Alan Ladd to a pulp in *The Glass Key* (1942).

With its noir-laden opening, *Gambling House* is superbly bookended with a equally noirish finale, when a cornered Mature talks Bendix's hoods into killing their boss instead of him. Before that fateful moment, Mature stares Bendix straight in the eye and says of the hoods, "Which one of them will get the honor to pull the trigger, because he'll be the one you frame and send to the chair later, while you sit in some nightclub smoking dollar cigars, and hiring some other deadheads to mop up the blood behind you." Endings don't get any better than this one.

Picturegoer (1951): "Story aside, I award a few marks for the acting. Mature looks tough and glares meaningfully in the lead role."

Variety: "Mature gives his role a lot of color."

The *New York Times* thought little of the film: "Put it down as claptrap and the performance of Mr. Mature as another demonstration of an actor doing the best he can with a bad role."

The Las Vegas Story

RKO, 1952

Cast: Jane Russell (Linda Rollins); Victor Mature (Lt. Dave Andrews); Vincent Price (Lloyd Rollins); Hoagy Carmichael (Happy); Brad Dexter (Tom Hubler); Gordon Oliver (Mr. Drucker); Jay C. Flippen (Capt. H.A. Harris); Will Wright (Mike Fogarty); Bill Welsh (Martin); Ray Montgomery (Desk Clerk); Colleen Miller (Mary); Robert J. Wilke (Clayton); Syd Saylor (Matty — Cab Driver); Brooks Benedict (Stickman Dealer); Midge Ware (Chief Money Changer); Paul Frees (District Attorney); Carl Sklover (Dealer); Milton Kibbee (Coroner); Al Murphy (Bartender); Robert Milton (Sheriff); Dorothy Abbott, Jane Easton, Joan Mallory (Waitresses); Mavis Russell (Blonde); Oliver Hartwell (Redcap).

Crew: Robert Sparks (Producer); Robert Stevenson (Director); Jay Dratler (Story); Earl Felton, Harry Essex, Paul Jarrico (Screenplay); Harry J. Wild (Cinematography); Leigh Harline (Music); C. Bakaleinikoff (Musical Director); Hoagy Carmichael, Orrin Tucker (Songs); Albert S. D'Agostino, Feild M. Gray (Art Direction); Darrell Silvera, John Sturtevant (Set Decorations); Howard Greer (Costume Design); Mel Berns (Makeup); Harold E. Wellman (Special Effects); Fred Carson (Stunts); Clem Portman, Earl A. Wolcott (Sound); Frederic Knudtson, George C. Shrader (Editors). Running time: 87 minutes.

Newly married Linda and Lloyd Rollins arrive in Las Vegas, where Linda bumps into an old flame, Police Lieutenant Dave Andrews (Victor Mature), whom she parted with during the war following a misunderstanding. In a hotel casino, Lloyd requests credit, using his wife's expensive diamond necklace as surety. Linda, a former cafe singer in Vegas, visits her old club and meets some old friends, while hubby, who is revealed to be an embezzler, loses a lot of money at the tables. When a casino owner (one that Lloyd was seen arguing with) is found murdered and Linda's necklace is stolen, Lloyd is arrested, but the guilty party turns out to be unscrupulous insurance investigator Thomas Hubler, who has been tailing them and the necklace since they arrived in Vegas. With the game up, Hubler attempts his escape in a car, taking Linda with him, but is eventually cornered and shot by Dave at an abandoned airport. Back in town, Lloyd is extradited on embezzlement charges, leaving Linda to file for divorce and make up for lost time with Dave.

"Las Vegas....

Where everybody plays a game!

And these two play the oldest game on earth ... with a new twist."

This is a cracking 1950s film noir that simply gets better each time you view it. With Jane Russell, Victor Mature, Vincent Price, Hoagy Carmichael, Brad Dexter and Jay C. Flippen in the lineup, embroiled in a lost love thriller set against the backdrop of the gambling mecca of the world, where could you possibly go wrong? Answer: you don't.

Unexpected people "blow in and out" of Lt. Dave Andrews' (Mature) town, including lost love Linda Rollins (Jane Russell), in the Howard Hughes production *The Las Vegas Story* (RKO, 1952).

Having tamed the heart of one no-nonsense dame, Ann Sheridan, in *Stella*, Mature was primed and ready to take on another sensuous wisecracking gal for the Howard Hughes production *The Las Vegas Story*. And this time he was up against the inimitable Jane Russell, perhaps the sexiest woman to have ever graced the silver screen. Wearing a black strapless evening dress adorned with an exquisite diamond necklace (courtesy of Cartier) in an early casino scene, she looks a knockout. Both at the peak of their physiques, Mature and Russell are a well-matched pair as the two former lovers who still hold a torch for each other, simply sizzling together through the Jay Dratler story which was adapted for the screen by Paul Jarrico, Earl Felton and Harry Essex. Jarrico's screen credit was removed by Howard Hughes because the screenwriter had been blacklisted in 1947 after refusing to cooperate with the House Committee on Un-American Activities.[1] The credit was restored, with credits for other films, in 1998 by the Writers Guild of America West.

Dratler's story was originally purchased in 1948 by Warner Brothers, who had Burt Lancaster down for the Mature role. In 1950 RKO acquired the film rights as a vehicle for either Robert Mitchum or Robert Ryan.[2] Any of these three would have been okay in the role of the lovelorn cop, with Lancaster and Ryan, perhaps, up for a more intense performance, which might have appeared slightly out of kilter with the laid-back persona of Russell, Price and Carmichael. The role was actually tailor-made for Mitchum, who enjoyed great chemistry with Russell in their previous outings *His Kind of Woman* (1951) and *Macao*

(1952). Mature shared many similarities with Mitchum, both powerfully built, sleepy-eyed men whose casual style belied hidden depths that only a strong Jane Russell type could tap into. I have to say that although Mature does a fine job in *Vegas*, Mitchum, despite his laconic manner, would have perhaps been a little more believable as a guy yearning for his lost love. Mature had a sentimental side to him, but more often than not he gave the impression of a "love 'em and leave 'em type.

In her autobiography, Jane Russell described Mature as another "Peck's Bad Boy"* who was really a softie inside. She added, "Females were either ladies or tramps to him. And I guess with good reason."[3]

During filming, the cast stayed in Vegas taking in the shows, casinos and generally having a fun time around the pool.[4] One of the film units also took in the sun, filming scenes at the pool of the Flamingo Hotel.[5] The town would always remain one of Mature's favorite places; he told one interviewer, "All the wild stories you've read about Vegas are true, and then some. It's the most fabulous showplace in the world.... But I'll let you into a secret. I don't gamble."[6]

The film may be as lazy as lounging around a hotel pool with a cold beer on a barmy summer's evening but it hits all the right buttons for me. With most noirs set in LA, New York or Frisco, the pacing of the film sits comfortably with its relaxed Vegas setting and laid-back cast. And what other noirs of the '40s and '50s were set in Vegas? Only a handful come to mind, with some more noirish than others: *The Lady Gambles* (1949), *Dark City* (1950) and *Las Vegas Shakedown* (1955). After that, you really start pushing the noir boundaries with entries such as *My Friend Irma Goes West* (1950).

The place may be Vegas, but the script is still hard-boiled noir. When a cabby tells Mature, "Somebody blew into town tonight," Mature responds, "This is a windy town, people blow in, people blow out." And for all his tough guy exterior, he's still a big sap at heart where love is concerned, which we observe in a scene where two lovestruck bobby soxers try to elope. When the father of one of the teenagers asks where he needs to sign to stop the marriage, Mature snarls, "Right under the place where it says I wouldn't give a couple of kids a break."

With its lost love theme, the film has echoes of *Casablanca*, particularly with the lovable Hoagy Carmichael at the piano acting as Russell's confidant. His presence allows us to enjoy three of his wonderful songs, "I Get Along Without You Very Well," "My Resistance Is Low (both sung by Russell) and "The Monkey Song" (inimitably delivered by the great man himself). Mature might not have been in on the singing, but he does get to end the movie in fine style with a spectacular helicopter chase at an abandoned airbase, where we witness a death-defying stunt as the helicopter flies through an open hangar. The shootout at the control tower is also expertly staged, with bad guy Brad Dexter making Mature earn his stripes. Dexter would go on to reprise the role of a self-serving lounge lizard to equal effect in Mature's later feature *Violent Saturday* (1955). This was Mature's second cop role following *Cry of the City*, and he would go on to play law enforcement officers in two other features, *Dangerous Mission* (1954) and *Interpol* (1957).

For all its escapist entertainment, the critics, of the day, were less than impressed:

The *New York Times*: "*The Las Vegas Story* ... is one of those jukebox gambling films that gives the impression of being made up as it goes along."

---

*Peck's Bad Boy was a mischievous fictional lad created by George W. Peck in the late 1880s. Noted for playing tricks on others, including his father, Peck's Bad Boy became a popular term for any incorrigible rule-breaker.

Picturegoer: "One bright spot of the film is an exciting helicopter chase. Another is some singing by Jane Russell."

Maurice Speed Film Review (1952): "Confected, unreal little film about a murder mystery in the gambling town of the title."

Something for the Birds

20th Century–Fox, 1952

Cast: Victor Mature (Steve Bennett); Patricia Neal (Anne Richards); Edmund Gwenn ("Admiral" Johnnie Adams); Larry Keating (Roy Patterson); Gladys Hurlbut (Della Rice); Hugh Sanders (Jim Grady); Christian Rub (Leo Fischer); Wilton Graff (Taylor); Archer MacDonald (T. Courtney Lemmer); Richard Garrick (Chandler); Ian Wolfe (Foster); Russell Gaige (Winthrop); John Brown (Mr. Lund); Camillo Guercio (Duncan); Joan Miller (Mac); Madge Blake (Mrs. Chadwick); Norman Field (Judge); Gordon Nelson (Senator O'Malley); Emmett Vogan (Senator Beecham); John Ayres (Congressman Walker); Charles Watts (Jessup); Rodney Bell (Announcer); Norma Varden (Congresswoman Bates); Leo Curley (Congressman Macy); John Maxwell (Congressman Craig); Elizabeth Flournoy (Receptionist); Herbert Lytton (Captain), Robert Livingston (General); Edmund Cobb (Reporter).

Crew: Samuel G. Engel (Producer); Robert Wise (Director): Alvin M. Josephy, Joseph Petracca, Boris Ingster (Story); Boris Ingster, I.A.L. Diamond (Screenplay); Joseph LaShelle (Cinematography); Sol Kaplan (Music); Lionel Newman (Musical Director); George Patrick, Lyle Wheeler (Art Direction); Thomas Little, Bruce MacDonald (Set Decorations), Eloise Jensson (Costume Design); Charles Le Maire (Costume and Wardrobe); Ben Nye (Makeup); Ray Kellogg (Special Effects); Henry Weinberger (Assistant Director); Harry M. Leonard, Arthur von Kirbach (Sound); Hugh S. Fowler (Editor). Running time: 81 minutes.

Anne Richards comes to Washington to help save the condors of her home state, California. On arrival, she finds a willing ally in kindly old fraud Johnnie Adams, who prints his own invitations to high society parties and is well loved by one and all. She also befriends lobbyist Steve Bennett (Victor Mature), who is working for the oil company that wants to build on the land where the birds live. Difficulties arise when Johnnie is shown to be a charlatan, but eventually Steve comes to the rescue, siding with Ann and Johnnie in their quest to save the birds, by helping to defeat the bill which threatens their existence.

"MR. 880 is BACK — 881 times phonier!"

With Edmund Gwenn, everyone's favorite Santa from the festive 1947 classic *Miracle on 34th Street*, in the cast line-up, all the publicity guys needed to do to reel audiences in to see *Something for the Birds* was plug the star's last film success *Mr. 880* (1950), where he played a lovable old codger who forges dollar bills (the title came from his character's file number with the U.S. Secret Service). Gwenn's whimsical Admiral Johnnie Adams is very much a variation on his Skipper character from *Mr. 880*, which in turn borrowed much from his Kris Kringle in *Miracle on 34th Street*.

As a consequence of Gwenn's quaint, endearing charm, romantic complications between Mature and Patricia Neal take a back seat in this light comedy. However, all the leads acquit themselves very nicely, and there's no loss in face playing second fiddle to a great character actor as Gwenn.

Pleased with the returns from Neal's last film, the classic sci-fi *The Day the Earth Stood Still* (1951), 20th Century–Fox signed her for another two pictures, *Diplomatic Courier* and *Something for the Birds*. Originally titled *Old Sailors Never Die*, *Something for the Birds* was assigned to director Robert Wise. This was his first comedy film and it gave him another opportunity to work with one of his favorite actresses, Neal. At the time she was suffering from the breakdown of her affair with Gary Cooper, losing a lot of weight as a consequence. In the film she appears thin and slightly drawn at times, but this in no way undermines her wonderful performance. According to a 1951 *Hollywood Reporter*, Neal, Mature and Gwenn were not the first stars considered for the parts, with Anne Baxter, Dana Andrews and Victor Moore originally down for the roles.

Combining scenes from Exposition Park and Los Angeles City College with Washington exteriors, the film was shot in four weeks, and by all accounts production was a smooth affair with all the leads going about their business in a professional manner. Stephen Michael Shearer in his wonderful book *Patricia Neal: An Unquiet Life* records that the friendly nature of the cast left Wise and Neal with fond memories of the film. He adds that Wise recalled that it was one Fox film he did not try to get out of.[1] Neal commented that she was delighted

Street-wise lobbyist Steve Bennett (Mature, left) gets a lesson in bird call from T. Courtney Lemmer (Archer MacDonald), while fellow bird enthusiast Anne Richards (Patricia Neal) looks on in awe, in the charming comedy *Something for the Birds* (20th Century–Fox, 1952).

to get the part because it was the first film she featured in where the girl was central in the writing, instead of simply being incidental to the man.[2] She particularly enjoyed working with the gentlemanly Mature.[3]

Mature's wheeler-dealing persona was perhaps a little rich for him to play a straight-hitting, no-frills lawyer, but playing a lobbying attorney who lives by his wits and advances himself through a canny ability to work the system and you have the star in a tailor-made role. The *New York Herald-Tribune* commented: "Both Mr. Mature and Miss Neal turn in neat performances, and it is hard to imagine a likelier sample of the relations grin than Mr. Mature's."

Once again capitalizing on his street-wise savvy (albeit a Washington Street for a change), the film gave Mature another fine opportunity to exercise his natural prowess with a one-liner. When he is accused by a broadcaster of having a pernicious influence, he takes it as a compliment, thinking it good for business, "Makes people think I have more pull than I really do."

According to Mature's view of the world, everyone's a lobbyist in their own sort of way. He lectures Neal, "A lobbyist is someone who disagrees with your views. Anyone who agrees with your views is a patriotic citizen." When Neal counters that she fights for what she believes in and that he only does it for money, Mature responds, "Money happens to be what I believe in."

Questioned about his beliefs, he quips, "I have a few convictions of my own. I'm against slavery, witch burning, cannibalism and head-hunting."

When Neal says that she doesn't understand Washington, Mature responds, "I don't understand the telephone, but it works."

And perhaps the best line arrives when Neal receives a wolf whistle from an onlooker in the Smithsonian, after she reveals a glimpse of leg, prompting Mature to quip, "That's the mating call of the Potomac night owl."

This was Mature's first pairing with an intellectual type, and the second time, since *Stella*, that he has to concede his position to help the flow of true love. And as with most of Mature's female screen encounters, the romantic chemistry works a treat, with both stars conveying their chalk and cheese characters with great sincerity.

The film premiered on October 10, 1952, to mixed reviews:

Variety wrote, "The Samuel G. Engel production uses such familiar names as Victor Mature, Patricia Neal and Edmund Gwenn to top line the cast, and each contributes likeably to answering the demands of Robert Wise's direction and the script."

The New York Times: "It would appear that the director, Robert Wise, whose previous work has been concentrated on the seamier facets of life, was intrigued not with comic comment but with deplorable political expediencies."

The Hollywood Reporter described the film as "a warm, mirthful comedy, rich in satire, that lands several devastating swipes at the Washington scene...."

Picture Show (1952): "Although there is more talk than action in this comedy drama, and it is perhaps a little too American to be thoroughly appreciated, nevertheless many of the witty points made in it will register."

Subject matter—wise, the film is quite a rarity of its time; the only other film that readily comes to mind about the conservation of birdlife is the Christopher Plummer feature *Wind Across the Everglades* (1958).

Million Dollar Mermaid

MGM, 1952

Cast: Esther Williams (Annette Kellerman); Victor Mature (James Sullivan); Walter Pidgeon (Frederick Kellerman); David Brian (Alfred Harper); Donna Corcoran (Annette Kellerman at age 10); Jesse White (Doc Cronnol); Maria Tallchief (Pavlova); Howard Freeman (Aldrich); Charles Watts (Policeman); Wilton Graff (Garvey); Frank Ferguson (Boston Prosecutor); James Bell (Boston Judge); James Flavin (Train Conductor); Willis Bouchey (Movie Director), Adrienne D'Ambricourt (Marie the Housekeeper); Charles Heard (Official); Clive Morgan (Judge); Queenie Leonard (Mrs. Graves); Stuart Torres (Son — John Graves), Leslie Denison (Purser); Wilson Benge (Caretaker); James Aubrey (Pawnbroker); Patrick O'Moore (Master of Ceremonies); Elizabeth Slifer (Soprano); Vernon Downing (Newspaperman); James L. "Tiny" Kelly (Policeman); George Wallace (Bud Willliams); Rod Rogers (Marcellino the Clown); Gordon Richards (Casey).

Crew: Arthur Hornblow, Jr. (Producer); Mervyn LeRoy (Director); Everett Freeman (Screenplay); George J. Folsey (Cinematography); Adolph Deutsch (Music Director); Alexander Courage (Orchestrator); Cedric Gibbons, Jack Martin Smith (Art Direction); Richard Pefferle, Edwin B. Willis (Set Decorations); Walter Plunkett, Helen Rose (Costume Design); William Tuttle (Makeup); A. Arnold Gillespie, Warren Newcombe (Special Effects); Fred Carson (Stunts); Douglas Shearer (Sound); John McSweeney, Jr. (Editor). Running time: 115 minutes.

In 1890s Australia, Annette Kellerman (born with a leg disorder) takes up swimming to build her strength. In adulthood, she has the makings of a champion swimmer, but turns her attention to becoming a ballet dancer. When her father, Frederick, travels to London to take a music teaching job, she accompanies him and along the way meets promoter James Sullivan (Victor Mature), Doc Cronnol and their boxing kangaroo. Tough times fall on Frederick when his job falls through and Annette can't secure work as a dancer. To make her some money, James persuades her to do a publicity stunt: swimming 30 miles down the River Thames. After that they head off to America to make some big money; Annette creates a scandal and a lot of publicity with a one-piece bathing suit. She is then hired by Alfred Harper to be the star of his water ballet revue. After a falling out with James, she becomes romantically attached to Alfred. When she is badly hurt in an accident while making a movie, both James and Alfred visit her in the hospital. When it is clear that she really loves James, Alfred does the gentlemanly thing and steps aside.

To remind us that the top Australian swimmer was once one of the biggest stars in entertainment, the film's introductory comment informs us:

> The great New York Hippodrome is gone, but those who contributed to its fame linger in cherished memory ... Houdini ... Pavlova ... Sousa ... Marceline the clown. And of course the incomparable Annette Kellerman. This is her story.

And who better to bring that story to the silver screen, than that other swimming legend, Esther Williams. There was simply nobody else in Hollywood who could have played it to such perfection, as indeed Mature was the only obvious choice to play the cocky turn-of-the-century promoter, James Sullivan.

Following the success of this movie, musical swimming sensation Wiliiams was coined the "Million Dollar Mermaid" in Hollywood, and aptly used the nickname for the title of her 1999 autobiography. A candid look at her experiences in Hollywood's golden era, the book is a delight for film buffs, focusing on the ups and downs of her career and love life, which included a brief affair with Mature, her *Mermaid* co-star.

Happy-go-lucky promoter James Sullivan (Mature, right) introduces himself to Australian swimmer Annette Kellerman (Esther Williams) and her father Frederick (Walter Pidgeon) during their sea voyage to England in the colorful musical biopic *Million Dollar Mermaid* (MGM, 1952).

Williams described Mature as a big man with a great swagger. She loved his physique, commenting, "I got him and his well-developed pectorals before the peak of his biblical loincloth period." She marveled at how he kept his muscular build considering he would eat anything at any time, fondly recalling how he would knock on her dressing room door at the end of the day and ask if she had any ketchup, which he would put on a piece of cardboard and eat like an hors d'oeuvre.[1]

Williams added that like Bob Mitchum, Mature was one of Howard Hughes' hard-drinking buddies. Mature would often refer to Hughes as the phantom due his habit of appearing briefly on set unannounced, speaking to no one, and slipping away like a skinny ghost.[2]

In addition to being lovers, Williams and Mature became good friends, with the actress crediting Mature, "for making the filmmaking process more exciting than it had ever been." Envious of his sense of freedom, she commented, "Vic was like an overgrown boy, like Peter Pan — or Johnny Weissmuller. He did as he pleased and never felt responsible to anyone."[3]

Williams further records that Annette Kellerman, aged sixty-five at the time, visited the set one day and nodded her approval, commenting that it accurately reflected what backstage at the hippodrome was like. When Williams asked what she thought of her playing her life, Kellerman responded that she had no problem with it, but she would have preferred it if Williiams was Australian, to which Williams replied "I'm the only swimmer in the movies, Miss Kellerman. I'm all you've got."[4]

Another in Mature's long line of hustler types, the part of Kellerman's manager James Sullivan (whom she later married), provided him with a wonderful opportunity to essay a colorful character, brimming with confidence, but prone to moments of self-destructive jealousy. Mature conveys well Sullivan's temperament (according to the Hollywood treatment), particularly when he feels that Kellerman has outgrown him, in one scene reminding her that she is no Joan of Arc but simply a swimmer doing a tank act in his water carnival. Bringing her further down to earth, he disparagingly remarks, "Baby, you're a swimmer. You belong in the water. Wet you're terrific. Dry you're just a nice girl who ought to settle down and get married." When she tells him that if she did get married it wouldn't be to a cheap, stubborn flea circus proprietor, he angrily responds, "This flea circus does all right for the fleas in it, except when they jump out of their cage."

This was the type of role that Mature had off to pat, needing little direction, which is just as well, because according to Williams' recollection, the director Mervyn LeRoy, possibly exhausted from the exertions of his previous movie *Quo Vadis* (1951), just sat back and pretty much let everyone direct themselves.

Busby Berkeley was brought in to direct two of the water extravaganzas, one of which nearly resulted in Williams snapping her spinal cord. In the high dive scene, when she struck the water her head was violently snapped back by the light aluminum crown she was wearing. X-rays later revealed that she had broken three vertebrae in the back of her neck. She was encased in a body cast for six months recuperation, and the filmmakers had to shoot around her. Incidentally, the film that Annette Kellerman is making when she has an accident is titled *Neptune's Daughter*; Williams starred in a film with the same title in 1949.

The film's comic relief is amply provided by Mature's sidekick Jesse White, who helps Mature to hawk around a boxing kangaroo, before moving on to promote Rin Tin Tin as their next animal star attraction. The discovery of the canine sensation by Mature's character was of course a piece of fiction, the real owner and trainer being former airman Lee Duncan. Homage was paid to the dog in Mature's later feature *Won Ton Ton, the Dog That Saved Hollywood* (1976).

Variety thought the film had plenty of high commercial values, among them Williams' nautical prowess and swimsuit-wearing ability. Of her co-stars the review opined: "Victor Mature, Walter Pidgeon and David Brian [all] furnish competent demands of the Everett Freeman script and Mervyn LeRoy's direction."

As Kellerman's father, the Canadian-born Walter Pidgeon is a joy to watch. He is perhaps best remembered for two great films he made in 1941, *Manhunt* and *How Green Was My Valley*, following which he starred opposite Greer Garson in a series of big box office hits including *Blossoms in the Dust* (1941) and *Mrs. Miniver* (1942). As the Hippodrome manager, David Brian is also on fine form. In common with Mature, Brian, a former dancer, served with the Coast Guard during the war. He was usually cast as cold, ruthless types; his most acclaimed role was as a lawyer in *Intruder in the Dust* (1949).

Most of the reviews *for Million Dollar Mermaid* were of the general opinion that a pedestrian script was saved by Williams' swimming and Busby Berkeley's elaborately staged water ballets, which were complimented by George J. Folsey's Oscar-nominated cinematography, and the good musical direction by Adolph Deutsch. Adding to the period atmosphere, the song "Let Me Call You Sweetheart" is used to good effect throughout.

The *New York Times* wrote, "It includes an abundance of Miss Williams and Victor Mature, but it does not include the felicities of a reasonably fascinating script."

Kellerman made several films, in 1916 becoming the first actress to do a nude scene when she appeared in the million dollar production *A Daughter of the Gods* (and I thought Hedy Lamarr got there first in *Ecstasy*). She married her manager James Sullivan in 1912 and they remained married until she died six days after her husband in 1975.

Androcles and the Lion

RKO, 1952

Cast: Jean Simmons (Lavinia); Victor Mature (Captain); Alan Young (Androcles); Robert Newton (Ferrovius); Maurice Evans (Caeser); Elsa Lanchester (Megaera); Reginald Gardiner (Lentulus); Gene Lockhart (Menagerie Keeper); Alan Mowbray (Editor of Gladiators); Noel Willman (Spintho); John Hoyt (Cato); Jim Backus (Centurion); Lowell Gilmore (Metellus); Charles Hall (Town Crier); Larry McGrath (Vendro); Richard Reeves (Secutor); Michael Road (Retiarius); Clint Dorrington (Officer in Forest); Dick Elliott (Ox Cart Driver); Chet Marshall (Call Boy); Woody Strode (The Lion).

Crew: Gabriel Pascal (Producer); Chester Erskine (Director); George Bernard Shaw (Play); Chester Erskine, Ken Englund (Screenplay); Harry Stradling, Sr. (Cinematography); Frederick Hollander (Music); Albert S. D'Agostino, Charles F. Pyke (Art Direction); Al Orenbach, Darrell Silvera (Set Decorations); Emile Santiago (Wardrobe); Mel Berns (Makeup); Linwood G. Dunn (Special Camera Effects); Stubby Kruger, Alex Sharp (Stunts); John L. Cass, Clem Portman (Sound); Roland Gross (Editor). Running time: 98 minutes.

Henpecked animal lover Androcles wins a friend for life when he removes a thorn from a lion's paw. When he and his fellow Christians are rounded up and taken to a Roman arena to be thrown to the lions, he makes a number of other friends including the beautiful Lavinia and strongman Ferrovius. On the journey to the arena, Lavinia falls in love with a handsome Roman captain (Victor Mature) who tries to persuade her to renounce her faith in order to save her life, but she refuses and willingly awaits her fate. In the arena, Ferrovius, against his Christian faith, proves himself a great fighter when pitted against six gladiators, his life and that of the other Christians is spared by Caesar. However, one Christian has to be sent to his death, and Androcles is chosen to face the beast. All ends well when the beast turns out to be the lion he once helped. Having shown great courage in facing the beast, and coming to no harm, Androcles and the lion are also granted their freedom, and wander off into the sunset together.

"Flaming story of history's most fabulous era!"

If you thought Cary Grant as a potential Samson was casting madness, how about Dana Andrews as a Roman Centurion in *Androcles and the Lion*, complete with toga and sandals? That's how it was originally planned when the decision was made to adapt George Bernard Shaw's one-hour play into a film. Howard Hughes apparently gave producer Gabriel Pascal and director Chester Erskine total freedom on the casting front, which would have seen Rex Harrison as Caesar, Dana Andrews as the Roman captain and Harpo Marx as Androcles. However, in the early stages of production, Hughes decided upon a big cast shake-up, replacing Harrison with Maurice Evans, Andrews with Victor Mature and Harpo Marx with Alan Young. At one point, the British actor James Donald was also under consideration for the part of the Roman captain.[1]

The role would have been ideal for Simmons' husband Stewart Granger (had he been in the reckoning), who was no stranger to the work of Shaw and the direction of Pascal, having starred in the U.K. screen adaptation of *Caesar and Cleopatra* in 1945. At the time of production, Granger was making *Scaramouche* at MGM. But that said, Mature's restrained and at times slightly somber acting style lends itself nicely to the troubled and compromised Roman captain who takes no pleasure in escorting the Christians to their fate in the arena. Through Mature's stalwart stance and angst, we see a man torn between duty and the love of a woman. A born pragmatist, with little time for the fervent pursuit of religion, he asks of the Christians, "How is it possible for them to sing when each day brings them closer to death?"

Androcles and the Lion was the first Hollywood filming of a Shaw play, although three of his works had been adapted for the screen in the U.K. including *Pygmalion* (in 1938), *Major Barbara* (in 1941) and *Caesar and Cleopatra* (in 1945)—the latter two directed by the Transylvanian-born Gabriel Pascal. The financial fiasco of *Caesar and Cleopatra* nearly ended Pascal's career, but he was given another opportunity to bring Shaw to the screen when he arrived in Hollywood to produce *Androcles and the Lion*. By this time he was suffering with

Can the handsome Roman captain (Mature) persuade the winsome Christian Lavinia (Jean Simmons) to renounce her faith, and thus be spared a visit to the lions' den in Gabriel Pascal's 1952 RKO version of the George Bernard Shaw fable *Androcles and the Lion*.

cancer and would die two years later in 1954, four years after the death of his friend and mentor Shaw, who died in 1950 at the ripe old age of 94.

Under the yoke of Howard Hughes the film was a long time in the starting blocks, and although it pales in comparison with the previous year's epic, MGM's *Quo Vadis*, which also depicted religious fervor in the early Christian era, there are enough positive aspects to the film to make it well worth a view. In addition to the obvious attractions of Jean Simmons and Mature, the fable exhibits an underlying quirkiness which, carried by a delightful Frederick Hollander music score, is hard to resist.

The secondary storyline with Mature and Simmons as ill-fated lovers works well, dovetailing nicely with the main story which is played mainly for laughs. Mature is suitably stern and compassionate in charge of his Christian prisoners, and sincere and tender in his love scenes with the graceful Simmons. In one enchanting scene his captain elicits a wonderful smile from the winsome Lavinia when he orders the Christians to alter the words of one of their hymns ("Onward Christian Soldiers") during the march to Rome, because the Roman guards are joining in the singing. Looking suitably authoritative and distinguished with a fleck of gray in his hair, he allows the hymn to continue on condition they substitute the words, "Onward Christian Soldiers" with "Throw Us to the Lions."

On his own performance in the film, Mature had this to say: "I often wonder what George Bernard Shaw would have thought of my effort. Personally I did not feel I came off, it really surprised me when fans — and even a few critics — wrote me enthusiastically about my work in the picture."[2]

Demure British beauty Simmons married Stewart Granger in 1950 and accompanied him to Hollywood after a promising start in the British film industry in the well-received films *Great Expectations* (1946) and *Hamlet* (1948). Howard Hughes bought her contract from Rank in 1950 and put her to work in four RKO pictures, two of which co-starred her with Mature: *Androcles and the Lion* (her first Hollywood film) and *Affair with a Stranger* (1953).

When Simmons started work on *Androcles*, Hughes sent the makeup department drawings of how he wanted her lips to look. Simmons was not amused, commenting, "They were very luscious sort of lips, which I kind of resented. You can't draw somebody else's mouth on your mouth."[3]

A court case freed her from the Hughes contract in 1952 and she went on to make some of her most notable films for Fox, including another two features alongside Mature, *The Robe* (1953) and *The Egyptian* (1954). The richly talented actress will always be remembered for her wonderful performances in *Guys and Dolls* (1955), *The Big Country* (1958) and *Spartacus* (1960). In later life, she became depressed with the poor-quality film roles that were being offered to her, and she sought treatment for her alcohol addiction in 1986.

The English-born actor Alan Young makes the role of Androcles his own, injecting it with the requisite amount of wit and whimsy. His dancing with the lion (Woody Strode in a lion suit) in the finale will certainly bring a smile to your face. Starting off in radio, Young is perhaps best remembered for his role as Wilbur Post in the television series *Mister Ed* (1961–1966).

The rest of the cast acquit themselves well, particularly Robert Newton (deliciously over the top as we'd expect), Maurice Evans, Elsa Lanchester, Reginald Gardiner, Gene Lockhart, Alan Mowbray and Mature's close friend Jim Backus.

When the principal photography was over, Hughes decided that the film needed spicing up and introduced a steamy "Vestal Virgin Bathing Sequence," which fell foul of the censors and Pascal, and had to be deleted from the final print. The scene is not entirely lost because it features on the cover of the DVD.

Of Mature's performance, the *Saturday Review* commented, "[H]e plays the handsome Roman captain as if he were captain of a college eleven, and on the losing side at that." *Variety* gave the film a mixed review, but did single out the performances of Simmons and Mature as "worthy of praise." The *New York Times* gave it a rather cool reception overall, noting, "Victor Mature makes a handsome cipher as the Captain of Centurions who loves the girl."

The Glory Brigade

20th Century–Fox, 1953

Cast: Victor Mature (Lt. Sam Pryor); Alexander Scourby (Lt. Niklas); Lee Marvin (Cpl. Bowman); Richard Egan (Sgt. Johnson); Nick Dennis (Cpl. Marakis); Roy Roberts (Sgt. Chuck Anderson); Alvy Moore (Pvt. "Stony" Stone); Russell Evans (Pvt. Taylor); Henry Kulky (Sgt. "Smitty" Smithowsky); Gregg Martell (Pvt. Ryan); Lamont Johnson (Capt. Adams); Carleton Young (Capt. Hal Davis); Frank Gerstle (Maj. Sauer); Stuart Nedd (Lt. Jorgenson); George Michaelides (Pvt. Nemos); John Verros (Capt. Charos); Alberto Morin (Sgt. Lykos); Archer MacDonald (Sgt. Kress); George Saris (Medic); Peter Mamakos (Col. Kallicles); Jonathan Hale (Col. Peterson); Father Nicon D. Patrinakos (Chaplin); Ray Harden (New Zealand Soldier).

Crew: William Bloom (Producer); Robert D. Webb (Director); Franklin Coen (Screenplay); Lucien Ballard (Cinematography); Lionel Newman (Musical Director); Matt Mattox (Choreography); Lewis H. Creber, Lyle R. Wheeler (Art Direction); Fred J. Rode (Set Decorations); Reeder P. Boss, Jesse Munden, Sam Benson (Wardrobe); Ben Nye (Makeup); Ray Kellogg (Special Effects); Eli Dunn (Assistant Director); W.D. Flick, Harry M. Leonard (Sound); Mario Morra (Editor). Running time: 81 minutes.

Lieutenant Sam Pryor (Victor Mature), an American of Greek descent heading a unit of U.S. Combat Engineers, volunteers to lead a regiment of Greeks and American troops into enemy territory on a reconnaissance mission during the Korean War. When the lieutenant loses many of his unit in a skirmish, anti–Greek sentiment sets in, because due to the lack of blood on their bayonets, the lieutenant wrongly assumes that the Greeks are cowards. But when he eventually learns that the Greek soldiers traditionally wipe the blood off their bayonets after battle and that their courage is beyond question, the healthy respect between Americans and Greeks is restored and they pull together, against overwhelming odds, to complete the mission.

> "You'll Never Love So Hard In Your Life ... as these hard-hitting guys hit the dirt ... and come up fighting!"
>
> "You'll Want to Kiss 'em One by One ... Because When It's All Over You'll Have a Heartful of Love for the Handful of Guys Who Became the Glory Brigade"

If you think the taglines are a bit over the top, you should check out the advertising poster for the film — bizarre to say the least. Clearly depicting Greeks and Americans fighting in perfect harmony for the common good, it shows a bunch of combat-ready soldiers doing what can only be described as a kind of military Hokey Cokey as they merrily sing, smile and march along into battle (or possibly the nearest bar).

Looking very much the action-prone, outdoor type, Mature at first glance appears the ideal star for the war film genre, but oddly enough the closest he got to it (prior to *The Glory Brigade*) was as the happy-go-lucky soldier on furlough in the Lucille Ball comedy *Seven Days' Leave* (1942). His lack of participation in the propaganda films that Fox churned out during the war years is perhaps understandable when one considers that the studio had several All-American–looking types who were more representative of the average G.I. Joe — actors like Dana Andrews, George Montgomery and Preston Foster. In contrast, Mature's self-assured characters had a tendency to put themselves first; he was the type of guy you'd happily follow into a burlesque show to catch a glimpse of Grable's pins, but not necessarily someone you'd follow into battle. But by 1953, Mature's rugged looks had hardened and his happy-go-lucky days as a charming ladies man were behind him. His mischievous grin had given way to a more serious, world-weary look that made him the ideal candidate to play a battle-hardened soldier. Added to this, Mature's Mediterranean looks admirably suited him to the part of an U.S. Army lieutenant of Greek parentage in a war film which put its emphasis on how, in times of war, different nationals (in this instance Greeks and Americans) come together, after initial distrust, to fight a common foe.

With an enemy tank fast approaching, left to right, Lt. Sam Pryor (Mature), Cpl. Bowman (Lee Marvin), and Pvt. Stone (Alvy Moore) ponder their next tactical move in *The Glory Brigade* (20th Century–Fox, 1953).

We first learn of Mature's Greek blood when he offers to escort the Greek detachment into enemy territory on a scouting mission, explaining to his commanding officer, "Some of my closest friends are Greeks, including my father." But when, following the massacre of some of his American troops, he suspects the Greeks of cowardice, we witness a more belligerent attitude towards his Greek allies. When addressing Lt. Niklas, he accusingly snarls, "This gun hasn't been fired. What did you fight them with, lieutenant? Slingshots?"

Originally titled *Baptism of Fire*, the film was shot in various locations in Missouri — the Lake of the Ozarks, Fort Leonard Wood near Waynesville (where many soldiers appeared as extras) and Tuscumbia. By all accounts the locals loved Mature, who was very friendly and only too happy to pose for photographs with them. Tragically, while filming at Lake of the Ozarks, special effects crew member Jess Wolf was killed when a demolition charge accidentally exploded beneath his boat. The blast injured two other men.[1]

The film's director, Robert D. Webb, learned his trade as a second-unit director on large-scale productions such as *Captain from Castile* (1947) and *Prince of Foxes* (1949), and was the last person to win in the short-lived Oscar category Best Assistant Director for *In Old Chicago* (1937).

The low budget of the film benefits Mature's characterization, allowing the focus to fall on his sincere, understated performance as opposed to big action scenes. The scene in which he surveys a riverbank strewn with the bodies of many of his platoon members is particularly touching. As we follow his gaze, we observe a facial expression deeply etched with anger, despair and the futility of war. The set pieces of action may be small scale, but they are still effective, allowing Mature to show his courage under fire when he takes out a tank and a machine-gun emplacement with grenades. The emphasis throughout is very much thinking tactically instead of head on confrontations with the greater enemy force. This is borne out in a great little scene where Mature and demolitions expert Lee Marvin set an approaching tank aflame with the use of a drum of "cugas." Mature certainly makes his presence felt in the film, fighting a memorable rearguard action, with the enemy storming towards him in the final scene as the soldiers are rescued by helicopter. And to show that there is no longer any animosity between the two nationalities, Mature lights his cigarette from Alexander Scourby's pipe as the helicopter flies them away to safety, while the enemy forces below are firebombed by American planes.

Fine performances are also given from Scourby, Marvin (wearing glasses), Richard Egan and Nick Dennis. According to studio publicity, Zanuck instructed that all the Greek parts had to be filled with actors of Greek parentage. Being of Greek extraction, Scourby certainly satisfied that condition. Possessing a rich, deep voice, he would go on find his niche as a successful narrator. Marvin was no stranger to combat in real life, receiving the Purple Heart when he was wounded in action during the World War II battle of Saipan. He would of course make his mark in great films such as *The Killers* (1964), *Cat Balou* (1965 — for which he received an Oscar for Best Actor) and *The Dirty Dozen* (1967). Richard Egan served as an Army judo instructor during World War II. Like Mature, he possessed a solid build and rugged look which was put to good use in *Seven Cities of Gold* (1955), *Slaughter on 10th Avenue* (1957) and *The 300 Spartans* (1962). Marvin and Egan would work with Mature again in *Violent Saturday* (1955). Egan also provided support in *Demetrius and the Gladiators*. The real Korean War ended only a month after *The Glory Brigade* was released.

Picturegoer: "You often find incisive characterization in war films of this type. But it isn't so here. For Victor Mature is not a very happy choice as the American officer. His approach to the role seems theatrical."

Variety thought otherwise: "Mature, only familiar marquee name in the cast, excellently sells his rugged character."

The *TV Times Film and Radio Guide* was certainly impressed: "This hard man's Sam Fuller–type war film was in fact directed by Robert D. Webb, who gets strong performances from Victor Mature, Lee Marvin and Alexander Scourby, and keeps his action going at a fast pace..."

Affair with a Stranger

RKO, 1953

Cast: Jean Simmons (Carolyn Parker); Victor Mature (Bill Blakeley); Mary Jo Tarola (Dolly Murray); Monica Lewis (Janet Boothe); Jane Darwell (Ma Stanton); Dabbs Greer (Happy Murray); Wally Vernon (Joe — Taxi Driver); Nicholas Joy (Producer George W. Craig); Olive Carey (Cynthia Craig); Victoria Horne (Mrs. Wallace); Lillian Bronson (Miss Crutcher); George Cleveland (Pop); Billy Chapin (Timmy Wallace, older); Louis Torres (Timmy Wallace, younger); Theodore Von Eltz (Mr. Culpepper); Mary Jane Carey (Edith); Dan Bernaducci (Cab Driver); Frank Wilcox (Dr. Strong); Walter Woolf King (Harry Casino); Jack Lomas (Temple the Policeman); Bob Jellison (Pudgy Man); Chester Jones, James Adamson, Sam McDaniel (Porters); Paul Maxey (Jerry); Fred Graham (Mounted Cop); Alvy Moore (TV Announcer); Eileen Howe (Secretary).

Crew: Robert Sparks (Producer); Roy Rowland (Director); Richard Flournoy (Story and Screenplay); Harry J. Wild (Cinematography); Roy Webb (Music); C. Bakaleinikoff (Musical Director); Albert S. D'Agostino, Feild M. Gray (Art Direction); Darrell Silvera, Clarence Steensen (Set Decorators); Michael Woulfe (Costumes); Mel Berns (Makeup); James W. Lane (Assistant Director); John C. Grubb, Clem Portman (Sound); George Amy (Editor). Running time: 89 minutes.

Conveyed in flashback, the story charts the breakdown of the marriage between playwright Bill Blakeley (Victor Mature) and model Carolyn Parker following a mistaken news item by a gossip columnist that the couple was getting divorced. In the flashbacks recounted by friends of the couple, Bill is struggling to make a living out of writing in New York where he meets and later marries Carolyn, a young model. Living for a while off Carolyn, he eventually gets his big break and becomes a successful playwright, but the idyll of their married life is marred when she loses the baby she is carrying. They adopt a young boy, who Carolyn dotes on, making Bill feel she no longer has any interest in his career. He begins an innocent dalliance with one of the sexy stars from his latest show which leads to a gossip columnist reporting that the marriage is over. When Carolyn hears the news, she takes off to reclaim her man, and all ends well.

"Kiss and run ... that's the game you played ... was it fun?"

What the title and the tagline has to do with this film is anybody's guess. I figure RKO had a ready-made noirish title for all their films whatever the subject matter. It was originally to be released under the equally misleading title *Kiss and Run*, which, to me, gives the impression of a 1960s Tony Curtis battle of the sexes romp. To be fair, the man-eating siren of the piece (Monica Lewis), who tries to steal Mature from his wife, does get to sing "Kiss and Run" to a serious-looking Mature during rehearsals, but that's about as steamy as the affair gets. In the follow-up scene, Mature teaches the show's leading man how to kiss Lewis (like he needed any lessons), with her passionately hanging on to his lips like a limpet mine. But let's not get too bogged down with the weird title, because any film which features Mature alongside the stunning Jean Simmons ticks all the right boxes for me. Mature brings a slightly roguish, tongue-in-cheek charm to his role, which dovetails nicely with Simmons' impish personality.

As if trying to steer the film further into noir territory, RKO shot the film as a series of rain-drenched city flashbacks, which work a treat, but it clearly leaves you wondering where director Roy Rowland was heading with this tale, which was amusingly picked up in recent times by the *Radio Times Guide to Films*, "Watching this is rather like opening a tempting box of chocolates and finding half are missing." The review added that although the film ultimately goes nowhere, having set everything up, it was nonetheless well cast with director Rowland bringing out the best in Mature and Simmons. Fine performances were also delivered by supporting players including Mary Jo Tarola, Monica Lewis, Dabbs Greer, Jane Darwell, Nicholas Joy and Wally Vernon.

Director Roy Rowland had originally planned to become a lawyer before taking a job as a script clerk for MGM. He then went on to become a director, along the way marrying Ruth Cummins, the niece of Louis B. Mayer. He was noted for the series of comedy shorts he made with actor Robert Benchley in the late thirties, as well as full-length features such as *Our Vines Have Tender Grapes* (1945) and *The 5000 Fingers of Dr. T* (1953).

This was second of four screen outings for the team of Mature and Simmons, three set in the ancient world (*Androcles and the Lion, The Robe* and *The Egyptian*). *Affair with a Stranger* gave them a final opportunity to get romantically involved before Simmons turned her attentions to Richard Burton in *The Robe* and Edmund Purdon in *The Egyptian*. Making the most of the opportunity, Mature plants one helluva kiss on an unprepared Simmons in their first encounter on New Year's Eve, prompting her to threaten him with a policeman for his audacity. With a wonderfully mischievous grin, Mature licks his lips after responding, "Say, I think that's a good idea, let's find one." Indeed, Mature eats up all his scenes with his engaging self-assuredness and his impeccable comic timing, which has Simmons aptly summing him up as a handsome, charming tramp.

As savvy as Mature when it comes to romantic sparring, Simmons plays the same sort of trick on him as he played on Grable in *I Wake Up Screaming* (he invited Grable to his room to meet his best gal, suggesting his mother and not his dog) in that she hints that her visiting male friend, Timmy, is a potential suitor, when in fact he is a small boy whom they eventually adopt. Unlike many of his past leading ladies, Simmons doesn't give him the runaround but pretty much falls for him hook, line and sinker after their first encounter.

The role of playwright-producer was a recurring one in Mature's career following in the footsteps of *No, No, Nanette, My Gal Sal,* and *Red, Hot and Blue*. Mature brought a certain vitality to the role of a dreamer who knows one day his luck will change for the better. But to ensure we don't lose sight of the fact that this is, after all, Mature, his character in *Affair with a Stranger* has a weakness for gambling at cards to accompany his talent as a playwright. But nickel-and-dime games don't pay the bills as Mature discovers as he tries to keep body and soul together before his big break. Indeed, the plight of the struggling writer is memorably conveyed in the film, with a hungry Mature cheekily tucking into a roast chicken leg before his host, Simmons, has a chance to invite him to the table.

The desperation of the big lug is further revealed when he visits a restaurant and mixes a soup from hot water and the various condiments on offer — a delightful scene that will, for some reason, forever stay in your mind when the rest of the film has faded. As Mature puts it to Simmons and Mary Jo Tarola, "Y' know, out where I come from, everyone has soup for breakfast, like everyone in New England has pie." Conscious of his lack of income while pounding the typewriter, Mature attempts a spot of housework (complete with apron and brush), while his wife goes out to work, and when things get really tough, he takes a job as a waiter in a restaurant which, with tips, pays more than working as a reporter, as Tarola explains. Another struggling writer, her reporter husband Happy works on a paper during the day and writes his novel in the evening in a cramped apartment.

Despite the film's many attributes, particularly its interesting exposition on the hardships endured in pursuing a dream, its release was met with lukewarm reviews.

Variety: "Miss Simmons is believable in the role of the young wife, but Mature is less than credible as the playwright."

The Robe

20th Century–Fox, 1953

Cast: Richard Burton (Marcellus Gallio); Jean Simmons (Diana); Victor Mature (Demetrius); Michael Rennie (Peter); Jay Robinson (Caligula); Dean Jagger (Justus); Torin Thatcher (Sen. Gallio); Richard Boone (Pontius Pliate); Betta St. John (Miriam); Jeff Morrow (Paulus); Ernest Thesiger (Emperor Tiberius); Dawn Addams (Junia); Leon Askin (Abidor); Frank Pulaski (Quintus); David Leonard (Marcipor); Michael Ansara (Judas); Nicholas Coster (Jonathan); Francis Pierlot (Dodinius); Thomas Browne Henry (Marius); Anthony Eustrel (Sarpedon); Pamela Robinson (Lucia); Helen Beverly (Rebecca); Jay Novello (Tiro); Harry Shearer (David); Emmett Lynn (Nathan); Sally Corner (Cornelia); Rosalind Ivan (Julia); Peter Reynolds (Lucius); George E. Stone (Gracchus); Marc Snow (Auctioneer); George Keymas (Slave); John Doucette (Ship's Mate); Ford Rainey, Sam Gilman (Ship's Captains); Cameron Mitchell (voice of Jesus Christ).

Crew: Frank Ross (Producer); Henry Koster (Director); Lloyd C. Douglas (Novel); Gina Kaus (Adaptation); Philip Dunne (Screenplay); Leon Shamroy (Cinematography); Alfred Newman (Music); George W. Davis, Lyle R. Wheeler (Art Direction); Paul S. Fox, Walter M. Scott (Set Decorations); Emile Santiago (Costumes); Ben Nye (Makeup); Ray Kellogg (Special Effects); Tom Connors, Jr. (Assistant Director); Bernard Freericks, Roger Heman, Sr. (Sound); Barbara McLean (Editor). Running time: 135 minutes.

Under orders from Pontius Pilate, Roman tribune Marcellus Gallio supervises the crucifixion of Jesus Christ. He wins Christ's robe in a dice game, and over time is overwhelmed by its mystical quality, which slowly turns the cynical soldier into a true believer of the Lord. He receives encouragement from his Greek manservant Demetrius (Victor Mature), also a Christian convert following the crucifixion, and the disciple Peter. Back in Rome, he takes up with his childhood sweetheart Diana, informing her of his new faith, which in time provokes the evil emperor Caligula into ordering his execution. Marcellus willingly accepts his date with death and is accompanied by Diana, who prefers to die with her love than live under the tyranny of the emperor.

"The First Picture on the New Miracle Curved Screen!"

"No Special Glasses Needed!"

"The first motion picture in CinemaScope — the modern miracle you see without glasses!"

"The Greatest Story of Love, Faith, and Overwhelming Spectacle!"

The tagline writers certainly went to town in publicizing the first film to be released in the new widescreen process of CinemaScope, and an awe-inspiring spectacle it was. But equally magnificent was Victor Mature's incredible performance as the Greek slave Demetrius, a riveting portrayal that once again reminded us that Mature's strong screen presence was more than matched by his acting prowess when he was handed the right material. Not since *My Darling Clementine* and *Kiss of Death* had we seen the actor deliver a such a powerfully anguished characterization. In common with his tragic Doc Holliday and Nick Bianco, his Demetrius gives the impression of a doomed man, whose well-being or life at some point will be threatened. His Samson, before his tragic end, clearly endured both physical and mental pain in his doomed love life, giving rise to an occasional brooding countenance, but essentially he is a man with a zest for life. By contrast, Demetrius puts himself above indulgent pleasures and simply sees himself as an instrument of God. As Bruce Babington and Peter William Evans put it in their thought-provoking book *Biblical Epics* (which has a whole chapter dedicated to Mature), "*The Robe* exceptionally distances him as far as possible from the sensuality with which he is so often identified...."[1]

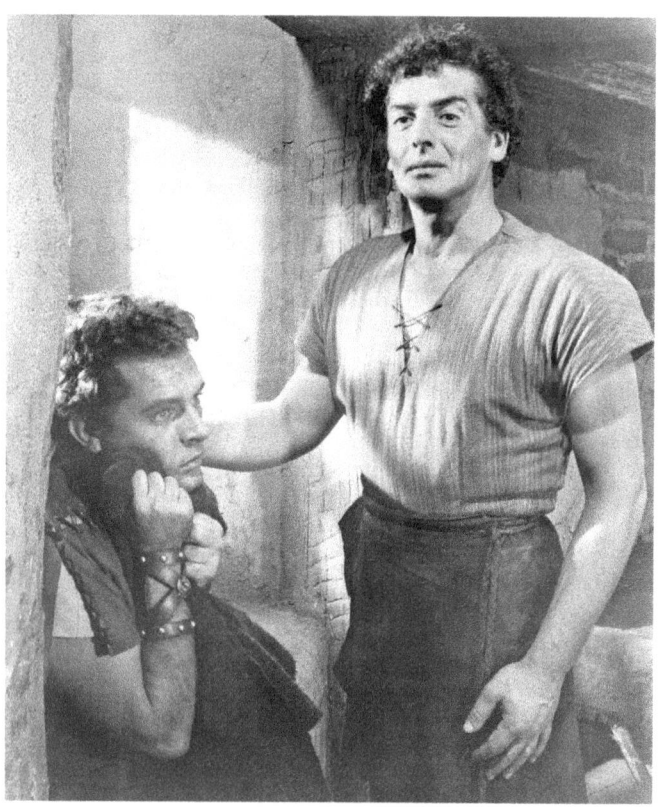

The power of the robe and the strong faith of Greek slave Demetrius (Mature, right) reach out to Roman tribune Marcellus Gallio (Richard Burton) in the first film shot in CinemaScope, *The Robe* (20th Century–Fox, 1953).

Asked by J. Marks in a 1972 interview if he resented never receiving a Oscar, Mature replied that he didn't think he deserved one, and that when he finally gave a performance considered excellent by many (as Demetrius in *The Robe*), Fox production chief Darryl F. Zanuck repeatedly refused to put him up for the nomination as Best Supporting Actor because "he insisted that there were no supporting actors in *The Robe* ... only stars. That was the only thing I ever really liked seeing myself on the screen." One of those impressed was Mike Connolly of *The Hollywood Reporter*, who predicted in January 1954 that both Mature and Jean Simmons would receive Oscar nominations. In fact, Richard Burton was the only star in the film who came away with a nomination (in the Best Actor category).

Zanuck may well have had a point, with all three leads sharing equal prominence in the film, but his refusal to support a Oscar nomination possibly denied Mature his best chance of receiving an award. Many critics viewed this as Mature's finest hour, with some even rating his performance above that of Burton, who played his part in a theatrical manner.

Burton disliked his own performance, describing it as poor. He also hated the way he looked on screen, particularly when attired in historical costumes.[2] One of Burton's few delights in making *The Robe* was working alongside Mature. He would later recall that he marveled at the way Mature was happily aware of his limitations, even rejoicing in them: "He liked to joke that he was no actor and he said he had 60 films to prove it. But against him I looked like an amateur." Burton described a scene when, overcome with religious fervor, he screamed like a girl, whereas Mature just stood there staring heavenward with great conviction. When Burton asked him how he did it and what was he was thinking, Mature replied, "I'm thinking of the money they're paying me." Burton finished his recollection by describing Mature as a wonderful man who taught him how to play craps.[3]

Mature has several such soul-searching scenes in the film, all of which expertly demonstrate his ability to underplay to great effect — and none more so than the scene where he encounters Jesus making his way into Jerusalem. Having caught his gaze as he rides by, Demetrius tells his friend, "I thought he was going to speak, but he didn't. Only his eyes spoke. I think he wants me to follow him." Such awe gives way to despair when at the crucifixion he looks helplessly on. Later, in the pouring rain, he confronts and curses Marcellus for his part in it: "You crucified him. You, my master. Yet you freed me. I'll never serve you again, you Roman pig. Masters of the world, you call yourselves. Thieves! Murderers! Jungle animals! A curse on you! A curse on your empire!" Nobody does a pained, tortured look better than Mature (with the exception of Kirk Douglas, of course) Amusingly, his torture scene in a Roman dungeon established Mature as "the back that launched a thousand whips" in a book dedicated to him, *Lash! The Hundred Great Scenes of Men Being Whipped in the Movies*.

Mature conveys the indignation of his character in an earlier scene when, in answer to another slave's comment that to be a slave in the house of Marcellus is an honor, he sneers that to be a slave anywhere is to be a dog. But Mature doesn't hog all the acting honors, with Michael Rennie in the role of Peter giving another of his wonderfully convincing performances. With his chiseled cheekbones, the former salesman is best remembered for playing the alien Klaatu in the classic sci-fi *The Day the Earth Stood Still* (1951).

Through the expert camerawork of Leon Shamroy and the deft direction of Henry Koster, large set pieces blend well with more intimate scenes, allowing Mature's screen presence to fully register in the new widescreen process. CinemaScope may well have lured many people away from their television sets back to the cinemas, but it was not without its problems as recounted by Jean Simmons, who described the set lights as brutally hot due to the widescreen process' requirement for additional lighting.[4]

The novel *The Robe* was written by ordained Lutheran minister Lloyd C. Douglas, who also wrote the bestselling *Magnificent Obsession* which spawned two Hollywood film adaptations. *The Robe* was originally to have been filmed by RKO in 1948 with Gregory Peck taking the lead role, but Howard Hughes dropped the project when he took over the studio, as he found religious films tedious. Zanuck purchased the film rights as a vehicle for Tyrone Power, but by the time filming commenced Richard Burton had been assigned the role.[5]

Oscar-wise, Burton lost out to William Holden in *Stalag 17* in the Best Actor category.

The film was also nominated for Best Picture, losing out *to From Here to Eternity*, but did pick up awards for art direction-set direction (color) and costume design (color). The film cost $5 million to produce and was the biggest box office earner of 1953, grossing $17.5 million.[6]

Picture Show: This superbly entertaining film marks a stepping stone in film history — it is the first to be shot in CinemaScope, and it scores a great triumph.... The acting is splendid."

Variety: "The performances are consistently good ... Miss Simmons, Burton and Mature are particularly effective..."

The New York Times: "Victor Mature is muscular and moody as the early converted Greek slave."

The Veils of Bagdad

Universal, 1953

Cast: Victor Mature (Antar); Mari Blanchard (Selima); Virginia Field (Rosanna); Guy Rolfe (Kasseim); James Arness (Targut); Gregg Palmer (Osman); Nick Cravat (Ahmed); Ludwig Donath (Kaffar); Jackie Loughery (Handmaiden); Leon Askin (Pasha Hammam); Howard Petrie (Karsh); Charles Arnt (Zapolya); Thomas Browne Henry (Mustapha); Sammy Stein (Abdallah); David Sharpe (Ben Ali); Bobby Blake (Beggar Boy); Glenn Strange (Mik-Kel); Charles Wagenheim (Bedouin Spy); Stuart Whitman (Sergeant); George Lewis (Captain); Dale Van Sickel (Messenger); Ben Welden (Stout Wrestler); Chester Hayes, Thomas A. Renesto, Hans Schnabel, Vic Holbrook (Wrestlers).

Crew: Albert J. Cohen (Producer); George Sherman (Director); William R. Cox (Story and Screenplay); Russell Metty (Cinematography); Joseph Gershenson (Musical Director); Alexander Golitzen, Emrich Nicholson (Art Direction); John P. Austin, Russell A. Gausman (Set Decorations); Rosemary Odell (Costume Design); Bud Westmore (Makeup); Fred Frank (Assistant Director); Leslie I. Carey, Joe Lapis (Sound); Paul Weatherwax (Editor). Running time: 82 minutes.

In 1560, the evil pasha of Bagdad, Hammam, and the equally wicked Vizier Kasseim conspire to use tax money to finance a war against the Ottoman Empire ruled by Suleiman. Enter Suleiman's spy Antar (Victor Mature) and his band of wrestlers and acrobats, who, following a series of action encounters, thwart the pair's plans, killing the vizier and dethroning the pasha. Along the way, Antar romances the vizier's wife Rosanna and the dancing girl Selima, a daughter of a slain hill tribe leader, who is on the hunt for his killer (it turns out to be Hammam). When Antar is named successor to the pasha, he takes Selima as his bride to be, leaving Rosanna to console herself with a handful of gold.

"EXOTIC Adventure ... WHEN PASSIONS RULED
AN EMPIRE THAT ROCKED THE WORLD!"

The Ottoman Empire to be precise, ruled by the great Sultan Suleiman, who would have lost it all were it not for the derring-do of Vic Mature and his merry troupe of wrestlers and acrobats. Oh yes, how we all yearn for those simple, carefree, halcyon days of youth, when the problems of the Orient could be simply resolved in an Arabian Nights costume drama headed by the likes of Mature, Tony Curtis or Rock Hudson, ably assisted, of course, by the odd harem wench, slave girl or belly dancer such as Yvonne De Carlo, Piper Laurie, Rhonda Fleming or in this instance Mari Blanchard.

Having proved his mettle with the Romans in *The Robe*, Mature was more than ready to sort out skullduggery, foul play and intrigue in ancient Bagdad. After the seriousness nature of *The Robe*, a spot of light undemanding entertainment was required, and what better than this tongue in cheek swashbuckler. This time, instead of the drab smock that clothed his frame as the slave Demetrius, Mature had his choice of Universal's extensive wardrobe of colorful Arabian attire to show off his physique. And to ensure we don't forget that muscular torso, Mature strips to the waist for a spot of wrestling with the six-foot-six Arness who, looking completely out of place, continued a long line of supporting males who towered over Mature. For bravery under fire, Arness received the Bronze Star and the Purple Heart after suffering serious injuries to his right leg from German machine-gun fire during the 1944 invasion at Anzio, Italy. He went on to great fame as Marshal Matt Dillon in the television series *Gunsmoke* (1955–1975).

Nineteen fifty-three was a bumper crop for such escapist fare, with *The Veils of Bagdad* tantalizing our taste buds alongside the likes of *The Desert Song, The Golden Blade, Salome, Desert Legion* and *Serpent of the Nile*. Mature's last spot of swashbuckling was at the beginning of his career in Hal Roach's *Captain Caution* (1940), and although the years had rolled by, the star had lost none of his zest for such adventures, even attempting a touch of athleticism when his character swings from chandelier to chandelier during a palace rumble.

As one would expect with such adventures, director George Sherman kept the action going at full gallop, taking a breather now and then to allow Mature to romantically dally with Mari Blanchard and Virginia Field, as his character deliberates whether blondes are more fun than brunettes or vice versa. A former model who suffered from polio as a child, Mari Blanchard found it hard to break away from playing "B" movie exotic types, but in her short career (she died of cancer at age 43) she did give us two memorable performances: as the Venusian queen Allura in *Abbot and Costello Go to Mars* (1953) and as Audie Murphy's love interest in *Destry* (1954). London-born Virginia Field (married three times including to actors Paul Douglas and Willard Parker) is possibly best remembered for her Morgan Le Fay in *A Connecticut Yankee in King Arthur's Court* (1949) and for her supporting performance as Vivien Leigh's fellow ballerina Kitty in *Waterloo Bridge* (1940).

With two such beauties on offer, you'd think Mature would be in seventh heaven, but it takes more than a shapely, scantily clad gal to grab our heroe's attention as we learn when he's introduced to the dancing delights of the mysterious Selima, telling his companion, "I've seen too many dancing girls." When his buddy replies, "But not Selima. You are entranced, my friend," Mature casually responds, "I have often been entranced, but too often disappointed." But with treachery afoot, courtesy of Guy Rolfe, Mature has enough to think about without being distracted by feminine wiles. British character actor Rolfe (once a professional race car driver and boxer) played a variety of roles in his career, but cornered the market in playing sinister villains particularly as Prince John in *Ivanhoe* (1952) and as the *rebel* Karran Khan *in King of the Khyber Rifles* (1953).

Going one better than *Captain Caution*, where fists bettered swords, Mature's merry band in this Arabian adventure awe the sword-wielding villains with their tumbling and acrobatic skills — but with the inimitable Nick Cravat leading the way, what do you expect? Cravat was Burt Lancaster's longtime acrobatic partner and they acted in nine films together, including The *Flame and the Arrow* (1950) and *The Crimson Pirate* (1952). Cravat always played a mute because his thick Brooklyn accent would have been out of place in period costume dramas of this nature.

For those in need of a quick history lesson, Suleiman was not coined the "Magnificent" for nothing, for in addition to his military prowess, he oversaw major developments in law, literature, art and architecture during his 46-year reign. I can just see Mature playing the part of the great leader and, perhaps with the right director and budget, lifting it to the levels of Charlton Heston's El Cid.

Variety: "Neither the players, nor George Sherman's direction are able to make anything of the lines and situations in the trite screen story..."

Leonard Maltin's Movie and Video Guide: "Standard Arabian Nights Costumer, with Mature zestier than most such cardboard heroes."

PS. Watch out for a pre–*Baretta* Robert Blake in a bit role as a beggar boy.

Dangerous Mission

RKO, 1954

Cast: Victor Mature (Matt Hallett); Piper Laurie (Louise Graham); William Bendix (Chief Ranger Joe Parker); Vincent Price (Paul Adams); Betta St. John (Mary Tiller); Harry Cheshire (Mr. Elster); Steve Darrell (Katoonai Tiller); Walter Reed (Ranger Dobson); Marlo Dwyer (Mrs. Elster); Dennis Weaver (Pruitt); George Sherwood (Mr. Jones); Maureen Stephenson (Mrs. Jones); Fritz Apking (Hawthorne); Kem Dibbs (Johnny Yonkers); John Carlyle, Chet Marshall (Bellhops); Frank Griffin (Tedd); Trevor Bardette (Kicking Bear); Virginia Linden (Mrs. Brown); Roy Engel (Hume); Helen Brown (Miss Thorndyke); Frank Wilcox (Jeremiah Kern); Grace Hayle (Mrs. Alvord); Sam Shack, Mike Lally, Ralph Volkie, Craig Moreland (Firefighters).

Crew: Irwin Allen (Producer); Louis King (Director); Horace McCoy, James Edmiston (Story); Horace McCoy, Charles Bennett, W.R. Burnett (Screenplay); William E. Snyder (Cinematography); Roy Webb (Music); C. Bakaleinikoff (Musical Director); Albert S. D'Agostino, Walter E. Keller (Art Direction); Darrell Silvera, John Sturtevant (Set Decorations); Michael Woulfe (Costume Design); Mel Berns (Makeup); Harold E. Wellman (Photographic Effects); James Lane (Assistant Director); Frank McWhorter, Clem Portman (Sound); Frederic Knudtson, Gene Palmer (Editors). Running time: 75 minutes.

After witnessing a gangland killing in a New York nightclub, young Louise Graham flees to Montana's Glacier National Park to escape the mob. Two men, traveling undercover, follow her: federal agent Matt Hallet (Victor Mature), who wants to bring her back to testify in court, and amateur photographer Paul Adams, secretly working for the mob, who wants to silence her through a convenient "accident." As well as vying with Paul for Louise's attention, Matt has to cope with an avalanche and a forest fire. By way of a subplot, park ranger Joe Parker keeps an eye out for an Indian falsely accused of murder. When Paul's murderous intentions are revealed, a climactic chase across a glacier ensues, resulting in Paul's death.

"Avalanche of Action!"

And that's no idle boast, with Mature taking on an avalanche, a forest fire, a square dance (attired in one of the those loud cowboy shirts, as befits the occasion) and a climactic battle on a glacier, all presented in glorious 3-D and lavish Technicolor. And if that wasn't enough, for your entrance fee you also get an unidentified hitman that could be Vincent Price, Vincent Price or perhaps even Vincent Price. Yeah, like you, I made that simple deduction after checking out the publicity poster, which shows Price stomping on Mature's hand as he tries to climb out of a glacier crevasse.

An RKO production, *Dangerous Mission* was never going to pop up at the Academy Awards, unless they dished them out for pure, unadulterated entertainment. For in common with Mature's earlier thriller *The Las Vegas Story*, this film gloriously captures the escapism of mid–1950s Hollywood adventure films, which skillfully combined noirish elements with the great outdoors. Mature would complete a trilogy of such films the following year with the suspense-driven *Violent Saturday*, a classic film which would make a great DVD box companion to the best of the type, *Bad Day at Black Rock* (1955).

With television ruling the roost in the early 1950s, the studios tried to fight back using a number of different film techniques that the little box couldn't offer; enter the 3-D process. Enjoying a "golden era" between 1952 and 1955, the technique was first applied commercially in the Robert Stack African drama *Bwana Devil* (1952). The following year, two films broke new ground with the process, Columbia's *Man in the Dark* and Warner Brothers' *House of Wax*. The latter was the first 3-D feature employing stereophonic sound and also the film which established Vincent Price as a major horror star.

Just as the Dutch scenery stole the show in Mature's wartime thriller *Betrayed* (released later in the year); the same could be said of the breathtaking views of Montana's Glacier National Park in *Dangerous Mission*. Used mainly in back projection, they nonetheless greatly add to the feel of the film, with inviting views of snow-capped peaks, cozy mountain lodges and tranquil lakes, expertly fused with a rousing Roy Webb score, randomly interspersed with snippets from the song "It's Quarter to Three" (which has no relevance to anything in the plot, but it works a treat).

The film reunited Mature with Vincent Price (in their third of four films) and William Bendix (previously seen in *Gambling House*). The film was Piper Laurie's first after leaving her home studio, Universal, presenting her with an early dramatic part after a series of light-weight roles in comedies and costume dramas (usually alongside Tony Curtis). Looking absolutely stunning in Technicolor with her terrific figure, red hair, full lips and hazel eyes, she makes a great love interest for Mature (and initially Price, before he attempts to dump her over a roadside cliff). This was the second time Mature vied with Price for the attention of the leading lady after their love triangle with the equally lovely Jane Russell in *The Las Vegas Story*. Mature may be totally smitten with the cute-nosed beauty, but he's still very much alert to the threat to her life, informing her, "It just occurred to me that I'm in love with a clay pigeon." And reminding us that he is clearly no Astaire on the dance floor, he quips to Laurie, "You know, I have the strangest effect on juke boxes. Every time I start to dance, they stop." (Mature managed to star in five musicals without tapping a toe.) But Mature's smart lines aren't exclusive to Laurie. When Price, equipped with camera, tells him that it's nice to make a hobby pay, Mature responds, "Some people can't even make a living pay." And when park warden Bendix, after discovering Mature's gun, informs him that there is no hunting in the park, he casually remarks, "What sort of hunting could I do with a .38?"

This was the third time Mature played a cop (previously *Cry of the City* and *The Las Vegas Story*) and although the other two included some action sequences, *Dangerous Mission* gave the actor a real opportunity to burst out of his shirt and show off his superhuman

Federal agent Matt Hallett (Mature) keeps a close eye on things, including amateur photographer Paul Adams (Vincent Price), while protecting murder witness Louise Graham (Piper Laurie) from the mob, in the "big outdoors" adventure *Dangerous Mission* (RKO, 1954).

qualities when he manfully grapples with a live wire from a downed power line, escapes a raging forest fire, and hauls Laurie out of a crevasse with just his bare hands and a length of rope.

Producer Irwin Allen went on to become "The Master of Disaster" with a list of such features as long as your arm — most notably *The Poseidon Adventure* (1972) and *The Towering Inferno* (1974). He also created and produced several successful science fiction television shows, including *Voyage to the Bottom of the Sea* (1964–68) and *Lost in Space* (1965–68). Mature and Price worked with the producer again in the colorful drama *The Big Circus* (1959). *Dangerous Mission*'s director, Louis King, a former actor and brother of director Henry King, was a dab hand at adventure films and Westerns, directing several of the Bulldog Drummond films in the 1930s, and proving equally adept at television Westerns in the 1950s.

In an interview with Herb Fagen, Walter Reed (who played Ranger Dobson) recalled how the cast and crew stayed in cabins at the park, with Reed sharing a room with Dennis Weaver. Their room adjoined Mature's, which didn't have a shower or bathtub, so they left the door unlocked to enable Mature to make use of their facilities. On one occasion Reed returned to find the actor not only using the shower but also Reed's razor and other things. Somewhat taken back, he jokingly said, "Victor, when you get to my toothbrush I'm going to close the door and lock it."[1]

Despite a great noir-laden opening scene, exciting action throughout, 3-D, Technicolor, Mature, Price, Laurie and Bendix (and even a small slot for young Dennis Weaver), terrific scenery, and a top-notch finale, the reviews were pretty mixed:

The *New York Times*: "Every so often amid the boredom, an avalanche is let go or a forest fire is set roaring or a fight is fought beside a glacier crevasse."

Variety: "Mature's heroics come over well and Miss Laurie pleases also."

Maurice Speed Film Review: "Routine thriller. "

Picturegoer: "Piper Laurie looks adorable and screams the cutest scream. Victor Mature and Vincent Price make a well matched hero and villain."

Demetrius and the Gladiators

20th Century–Fox, 1954

Cast: Victor Mature (Demetrius); Susan Hayward (Messalina); Michael Rennie (Peter); Debra Paget (Lucia); Anne Bancroft (Paula); Jay Robinson (Caligula); Barry Jones (Claudius); William Marshall (Glycon); Richard Egan (Dardanius); Ernest Borgnine (Strabo); Charles Evans (Cassuis Chaerea); Everett Glass (Kaeso); David Leonard (Marcipor); Karl Davis (Marco); Jeff York (Albus); Carmen de Lavallade (Slave Girl); John Cliff (Varus); Barbara James, Willetta Smith (Specialty Dancers); Selmer Jackson (Senator); Douglas Brooks (Cousin); Fred Graham (Decurion); Dayton Lummis (Magistrate); George Eldredge (Chamberlain); Paul Richards (Prisoner); Ray Spiker, Gilbert Perkins, Mickey Simpson, Paul Stader, Lyle Fox, Dick Sands, Woody Strode (Gladiators); Richard Burton and Jean Simmons (film clip from *The Robe*).

Crew: Frank Ross (Producer); Delmer Daves (Director); Based on characters from the novel *The Robe* by Lloyd C. Douglas; Philip Dunne (Screenplay); Milton R. Krasner (Cinematography); Franz Waxman, Alfred Newman (Music); George W. Davis, Lyle R. Wheeler (Art Direction); Paul S. Fox, Walter M. Scott (Set Decorations); Stephen Papich (Choreography); Charles Le Maire (Costume and Wardrobe); Ben Nye (Makeup); Ray Kellogg (Special Effects); William Eckhardt (Assistant Director); Roger Heman, Sr., Arthur von Kirbach (Sound); Robert Fritch, Dorothy Spencer (Editors). Running time: 101 minutes.

This sequel to *The Robe* continues the story after Marcellas and Diana are executed. Demetrius (Victor Mature) hides the robe from the Romans, but is forced to fight in the arena as a gladiator for the amusement of the emperor Caligula. Due to his faith he defeats his opponents, including the Nubian warrior Glycon, but refuses to kill them, which brings him to the attention of the sensuous Messalina, wife of Claudius. When the innocent Lucia, who is in love with Demetrius, is abused by a group of gladiators at a drunken party and pronounced dead, Demetrius loses his faith and kills each of the gladiators responsible in the arena. In his disillusionment, he becomes an officer of the palace guard and takes Messalina as his lover. In the employ of Caligula, he is instructed to track down the robe so that the emperor can test its magical powers. With the assistance of Peter, he discovers the robe in the hands of Lucia, who is not dead but in a comatose state. Overwhelmed by the discovery that Lucia is still alive, Demetrius regains his faith when she becomes conscious again. Demetrius takes the robe to Caligula to uphold the peace, but Caligula kills a prisoner to see if it will bring him back to life. Incensed, Demetrius tries to attack the emperor and is sent back to the arena to face Caligula's champion, Marco. He once again refuses to fight, but his life is spared when the Praetorian Guard, who regard Demetrius as a hero, kill Marco and the hated Caligula. Claudius is named as the new emperor, and his wayward wife Messlina, who promises to be a faithful wife, takes her place at his side, leaving Demetrius, Peter and Glycon to spread the Christian faith.

> "The Continuation of *The Robe*."
> "It begins where *The Robe* left off!"

With gladiatorial fights galore, a barking mad emperor, and Mature clasping a full-bosomed Susan Hayward to his muscular torso, you'd have thought those publicity guys and gals would have had a field day plugging this movie. But instead, I guess they took the day off, and simply reminded us that it was a continuation of *The Robe*. Which is, of course, very true, and why not cash in on the tremendous box-office success of *The Robe*? But *Demetrius and The Gladiators* charts a rather different course than its predecessor, which was steeped in religiosity. Based on the characters created by Lloyd C. Douglas in *The Robe*, the screenplay for *Demetrius and the Gladiators* opts to dispense with some of the pieties for a more traditional sword-and-sandal approach, emblazoned with all the attendant delights: duels to the death, drunken revelry, heaving bosoms, rippling muscles, Christians

Forever defiant, Greek slave turned champion gladiator Demetrius (Mature) stands up to the mad emperor Caligula in the action-filled spectacle *Demetrius and the Gladiators* (20th Century–Fox, 1954).

being thrown to the lions, dancing girls, and Mature asking Anne Bancroft, "What's a nice girl like you doing at an orgy like this?"

In their book *Biblical Epics*, Bruce Francis Babington and Peter William Evans pretty much summed up Mature's association with the genre: "Victor Mature is the 1950s epic hero, who represents the Titanic clash between the spirit and the flesh, a clash made all the more poignant by signs of flaws and frailties in his massive physique and face, his mannerisms and voice, warning of his propensities to voluptuous enslavement."[1] Of his five forays into the ancient world (the others were *Samson and Delilah*, *Androcles and the Lion*, *The Robe*, and *The Egyptian*), his role in *Demetrius and the Gladiators* possibly best fits this insightful appraisal.

Demetrius, like Samson, commands an inner strength that could prevail against overwhelming odds, whether man or beast, but both men eventually fall prey to treacherous women. However, despite her viperous ways, Samson loves Delilah, whereas Demetrius only succumbs to the inviting flesh of Messalina after his faith is shaken following the assault of Lucia.

Susan Hayward is one class act in the role of the wicked Messalina. She was no stranger to the role of a biblical temptress after her central role in *David and Bathsheba* (1951) opposite Gregory Peck. Hayward and Mature worked equally well, with their torrid love scenes setting the screen alight, but away from the cameras they went their separate ways. By all accounts, Hayward had much on her mind during filming which left her quiet and withdrawn. Her marriage was suffering and she was offended by Darryl F. Zanuck's lack of interest in her performance in the film (apparently all the guys at Fox were focusing their thoughts on the latest sex kitten on the studio block, Marilyn Monroe). As Mature recalled, "After director Delmer Daves yelled 'cut,' she just wandered forlornly back to her dressing room. Susan acted like someone a hundred years old. I didn't know what the trouble was. We were practically on a 'Mr. Mature' and 'Miss Hayward' basis, but it was obvious something was worrying her. We all wished we could help her, but we didn't know how to go about trying."[2]

A Fox press release quoted Mature as saying that Hayward was "Garbo with a difference ... Garbo doesn't talk. Susan talks but reveals very little about herself."[3]

Mature may have spent little time off-camera, with Hayward, but he did take some time out in the company of Ernest Borgnine, who took the part of Strabo, the head of the gladiator school. Still in their full Roman gladiator costumes, the two actors drove to a small sandwich restaurant during a break in filming. When the waitress was somewhat taken back by their entrance, Mature was quick to quip, "What's the matter, don't you serve members of the armed services?"

In his autobiography *I Don't Want to Set the World on Fire, I Just Want to Keep My Nuts Warm*, Borgnine described Hayward as "a doll — beautiful, funny, talented, about as unaffected as a superstar could be." He thought that Mature was pleasant and easy to work with, but he didn't think he took movie acting at all seriously, perhaps preferring the "one take" aspect of stage work from his days at the Pasadena Playhouse.[4]

Sterling support is provided by Michael Rennie (again as Peter), Richard Egan, William Marshall, Barry Jones, Debra Paget, and Jay Robinson, repeating his role as Caligula. After a promising start, Robinson's career went into a tailspin in the late fifties when he got into drugs, but he managed to work his way back into the industry after a stint as a cook and a landlord.

The film grossed $4.25 million in distributors domestic rentals, and was filmed simultaneously with *The Robe* which took $17.5 million in rentals.

The Egyptian

20th Century–Fox, 1954

Cast: Jean Simmons (Merit); Victor Mature (Horemheb); Gene Tierney (Baketamon); Michael Wilding (Akhnaton); Bella Darvi (Nefer); Peter Ustinov (Kaptah); Edmund Purdom (Sinuhe); Judith Evelyn (Taia); Henry Daniell (Mekere); John Carradine (Grave Robber); Carl Benton Reid (Senmut); Tommy Rettig (Thoth); Anitra Stevens (Queen Nefertiti), Peter Reynolds (Sinuhe, aged 10); Donna Martell (Lady-in-waiting); Mimi Gibson (Princess); Carmen De Lavallade (Egyptian Dancer); Harry Thompson (Nubian); George Melford, Lawrence Ryle (Priests); Ian MacDonald (Ship's Captain); Michael Granger (Officer); Don Blackman (Nubian Prince); Mike Mazurki (Death House Foreman); Tyler McDuff (Cadet); Richard Allen (Student in School of Life); Angela Clarke (Kipa); Michael Ansara (Hittite Commander); Edmund Cobb (Patient in Dispensary); Harry Corden (Hittite Officer); Yeghishe Harout (Syrian at Nefer's); Geraldine Bogdonovich (Tavern Waitress).

Crew: Darryl F. Zanuck (Producer); Michael Curtiz (Director); Mika Waltari (Novel); Philip Dunne, Casey Robinson (Screenplay); Leon Shamroy (Cinematography); Bernard Herrmann, Alfred Newman (Music); George W. Davis, Lyle R. Wheeler (Art Direction); Paul S. Fox, Walter M. Scott (Set Decorations); Stephen Papich (Choreography); Charles Le Maire (Costume and Wardrobe); Ben Nye (Makeup); Ray Kellogg (Special Photographic Effects); William Eckhardt (Assistant Director); Alfred Bruzlin, Roger Heman, Sr. (Sound); Barbara McLean (Editor). Running time: 140 minutes.

In pre-Christian times, young Egyptian healer Sinhue and his friend, the low-born Horemheb (Victor Mature), enter into the service of the epileptic Pharaoh Akhnaton. Sinhue, becomes a brilliant physician, drawing the affection of the beautiful barmaid Merit, while Horemheb becomes a powerful soldier. The pharaoh follows the monotheism belief that only one God exists, which angers his priests and puts his life at risk. Sinhue has a brief affair with the Babylonian whore Nefer, but grows weary of her and returns to his true love Merit, who is later killed for being monotheistic. To avert the collapse of the kingdom, Sinhue and Horemheb poison the pharaoh and Horemheb ascends to the throne. Banished by Horemheb and weary of court intrigue, Sinhue disappears into the desert to end his days as a hermit.

"The Most Monumental Achievement in Entertainment History!"

"To Nefer, shameless temptress of Babylon,
he surrendered his parents' hope of immortality."

"I, Sinuhe, The Egyptian, have committed every crime against man,
woman and the Gods!"

"I, Sinuhe, The Egyptian, have forsaken
Eternity for the perfection of love!"

Taken from Finnish author Mika Waltari's 1945 bestselling novel, *The Egyptian* saw Mature back in the ancient world for the fifth and penultimate time (with the exception of his cameo in the 1984 remake of *Samson and Delilah*). In common with his *The Shanghai Gesture*, the film was mauled by many critics, inviting comments that it was more about style than substance. That is perhaps very true, but like *Gesture*, the intoxicating style is such that it simply takes your breath away. With its great cast, lavish sets, stunning costumes, a keen eye for detail, majestic cinematography by Leon Shamroy and awesome music from legendary composers Alfred Newman and Bernard Herrmnan, the film simply oozes period atmosphere, sweeping over you with its unforgettable spectacle.

Stories set in ancient Egypt were few in number by 1954: The silent screen had dabbled with the period, usually under the direction of Cecil B. DeMille (for example, 1923's *The Ten Commandments*), but it took Darryl Zanuck's *The Egyptian* to put some authentic focus on the mysterious land of the pharaohs. But you can bet your bottom dollar that as soon as one studio took a profitable trip down the Nile, others would follow, which certainly gave Fox mogul Zannuck something to think about when he discovered two of his competitors were looking to set their stories against an Egyptian background: MGM's *Valley of the Kings* and Warner Brothers' *Land of the Pharaohs*. In a memo to director Michael Curtis he aired his concerns: "We probably cannot beat *Valley of the Kings*, but I do not care about this so much as it has a modern story, but the Warner picture disturbs me as they have their own color process and can make prints much quicker than we can."[1]

Yes, everyone seemed to be getting in on the act, with Universal offering *Abbott and Costello Meet the Mummy* in 1955 and Cecil B. DeMille remaking *The Ten Commandments* in 1956, using many of the sets, costumes and props from *The Egyptian,* which cost five million dollars to make, much of it going on the 67 sets.

Court intrigue abounds in the sprawling epic ***The Egyptian*** (20th Century–Fox, 1954). From left, Anitra Stevens (as Queen Nefertiti), Michael Wilding (as Akhnaton), Gene Tierney (as Baketamon), and Mature (as Horemheb).

Author Jon Solomon in his book *The Ancient World in the Cinema* wrote favorably of Mature's performance in the film: "Victor Mature plays probably his best and best-suited role of his 'ancient' repertoire.... He is vulgar, brash, demanding, childish, insolent, power-hungry, and unlikable."[2] In the past, many of Mature's roles embraced several of the aforementioned traits, but his characters had always been congenial unlike the ruthless Horemhed, which saw Mature at his most disagreeable. Mature acknowledged this departure from the norm when he jokingly commented that the role of Horemheb was "the greatest switcheroo of my recent career," explaining that in both *The Robe* and *Demetrius and the Gladiators* he was a man who put God above country, while in *The Egyptian* he puts country above God.[3] Horemhed, like Mature's Scarf from *Betrayed*, is a character we initially warm to even though, in the early stages of the film, we are shown little evidence of his true nature. Lowly son of a cheese maker, the ambitious soldier Horemhed is perfectly suited to Mature's brash, swaggering style. He is also one of Mature's few characters with a real chip on his shoulder. Angered by his exclusion from the palace guards because of his poor upbringing, he contemptuously remarks, "Look at the ones they've accepted — mincing, perfumed idiots who carry sunshades and twitter like birds."

Mixing ruthlessness with bravado, Mature's portrayal at times suggests a man slightly deranged by his quest for power. Not quite on the scale as Jay Robinson's Caligula, but certainly pointing in that direction, Mature, by the vigor of his performance, clearly relishes this departure role.

To accompany him in the ancient world, Mature again found himself in the midst of a fine troupe of stars: Edmund Purdom, Jean Simmons, Michael Wilding, Gene Tierney and Peter Ustinov. And let's not forget an impressive cameo by John Carradine as a grave robber who gets the best line in the film with his philosophical thoughts on whether a grave should be marked: "Marked or unmarked, it's all the same. Twenty years to build a pyramid or ten minutes to scrape a hole in the sand. The dead are dead no matter where we put 'em. In the end, the sand conquers all."

Marlon Brando was Zanuck's original choice to play the lead role of the physician Sinuhe, but he turned down the part after reading the script. Farley Granger also rejected the part. Finally it was handed to up-and-coming English actor Edmund Purdom. As Peter Ustinov wryly commented "Brando was no longer part of the cast. He had taken one look at the final script, and become victim of a rare illness, from which he made a miraculous recovery once shooting had begun on his replacement."[4] According to Brando's agent, the star also turned down the part because he hated both the director Michael Curtiz and Zanuck's protégé Bella Darvi, who took the role of the seductress Nefer.

Purdom would go on to star in several other period dramas including *The Prodigal* (1955) and *The King's Thief* (1955). Interestingly, he starred with Jeanne Crain in the Italian spectacle *Nefertiti, Queen of the Nile* (1961), which shared a similar plot and characters to that of *The Egyptian*.

Due to a number of things including the inadequacies of the script and the director's thick Hungarian accent, both Ustinov and Wilding found it difficult to take the film seriously. Ustinov amusingly recalled a scene where Curtiz instructed, "The next shot, Ustinov, you will come running down the hill and visper in the ear of Purdom." Ustinov replied, "What do you want me to whisper?" Enraged, Curtiz snapped back, "Son of a bitch, vot it matters, ven you are vispering in the ear, I'm not hearing anyway."[5]

On the second day of shooting, Wilding described a scene where he and five hundred extras, all dressed in white, were supposed to be staring out over the desert sands. With loudspeaker to hand, Curtiz yelled "Action!" followed by the command "The men in white turn to the left." What he meant was "the *man* in white" (addressing Wilding only), but his accent was so heavy that all five hundred extras turned left and ruined the shot.[6]

For all his shortcomings with the English language, Curtiz was one of the finest directors from Hollywood's golden period, racking up a seemingly endless list of classics including *The Adventures of Robin Hood* (1938), *Angels with Dirty Faces* (1938), *Casablanca* (1942) and *Mildred Pierce* (1945). When he accepted the assignment to direct *The Egyptian*, he was freelancing after having spent twenty-six years at Warner Brothers.

With its long running time, the film would have benefited from more battle scenes, but it did give a good account of ancient Egyptian culture and history. The film has many fascinating elements: the early medical practices of the physician, the introduction of monotheism to Egypt and the first use of iron by the Hittites. (The Hittites were an ancient race who hailed from Anatolia, western Asia, taking in the majority of the republic of Turkey.)

On its release, the film was poorly received by the critics, with the most sustained criticism leveled at Zanuck's then mistress, Polish émigré Bella Darvi (born Bella Weigner). Darvi had known hardship during the war, including time spent in a concentration camp. On her arrival in Hollywood, she went to live with Zanuck and his wife Virginia at their Santa Monica beach house. They renamed her Darvi, which was formed from their first names. She might not have been the greatest actress on the block, but she certainly exuded exotic sensualism. Darvi's lack of professional acting ability clearly annoyed Jean Simmons, who was heard to remark that here was an "actress who Nefer was." After a few films, Darvi, a persistent gambler and drinker, went back to Europe, committing suicide in 1971 at age 43.

Variety wrote favorably of the film, praising many of the performances, describing Mature as a strong asset to the cast and adding, "A hot-tempered man spoiling for a fight and frustrated by the pharaoh's refusal to allow it, Mature shapes Horemheb into a colorful figure."

The *New York Times*: "It glistens with archeological scenery, rumbles deeply with a sense of woe — and moves at the pace of a death march ... Victor Mature bulls and bellows in the small role he has as the hero's soldier pal."

Picturegoer: "Turgid, unconvincing story ... [Mature acts] in let's-tear-the-scenery style..."

In his book *The Ancient World in the Cinema*, Jon Soloman wrote, "By combining authenticity, an intimate, presentation of both the humble, common life and the splendid court life of ancient Egypt, a glimpse into the religious dreams and the military realities of the Eighteenth Dynasty, and an engaging love story, *The Egyptian* succeeds as well as any other nonepic 'ancient' film."

Betrayed

MGM, 1954

Cast: Clark Gable (Col. Pieter Deventer); Lana Turner (Carla Van Oven); Victor Mature (The Scarf); Louis Calhern (Gen. Ten Eyck); O.E. Hasse (Col. Helmuth Dietrich); Wilfred Hyde-White (Gen. Charles Larraby); Ian Carmichael (Capt. Jackie Law-

son); Niall MacGinnis (Blackie); Nora Swinburne (The Scarf's Mother); Roland Culver (Gen. Warsleigh); Leslie Weston (Pop); Christopher Rhodes (Chris); Lily Kann (Jan's Grandmother); Brian Smith (Jan); Anton Diffring (Capt. Von Stanger); Richard Anderson (John); Carl Jaffe (Maj. Plaaten); Wolf Frees (Motorcycle Rider); Peter Swanwick (Fat Major); Nochola Bruce (Dietrich's Lieutenant); Theodore Bikel (German Sergeant); Thomas Heathcote, Glyn Houston, John Glen (Paratrooper Corporals); John Wynn, John Singer, Basil Appleby (Paratroopers); Kenneth Hyde (Instructor); Peter Martin (Freddy Jackson); Mona Washbourne (Waitress), Ferdy Mayne (Luftwaffe Officer).
Crew: Gottfried Reinhardt (Director); Ronald Millar, George Froeschel (Screenplay); Freddie Young (Cinematography); Walter Goehr (Music); Alfred Junge (Art Direction); Pierre Balmain (Costume and Wardrobe); John O'Gorman (Makeup); Tom Howard (Photographic Effects); Peter Price (Assistant Director); A.W. Watkins (Sound); John D. Dunning, Raymond Poulton (Editors). Running time: 108 minutes.

World War II intelligence agent Colonel Pieter Deventer has his suspicions that the beautiful Carla Van Oven is a traitor and is ordered to keep an eye on her. She is sent to Holland to work with the Dutch underground led by The Scarf (Victor Mature), a flamboyant character sporting a bright yellow neck scarf, who previously saved the life of Pieter. Carla poses as a singer to gain the confidence of the Germans, but during the course of her spying activities the underground begins to sustain heavy losses. Thinking that Carla has betrayed them, Pieter is sent in to eliminate her. But he discovers that The Scarf is the real traitor, having changed his allegiance when he found out that his mother had been wrongly accused, and subsequently humiliated by his fellow countrymen, of being a German spy. Tricking The Scarf into a trap, Pieter kills him when he tries to escape, then goes in search of Carla, who is in the straggling ranks of British troops retreating from the disastrous raid on Arnhem.

"Great story of love and war!"
"MGM filmed the mystery of the year in Holland!"
"The Secret Three meet ... one is the betrayer and two the betrayed!"

And what a secret three — Clark Gable, Lana Turner and Victor Mature. Star line-ups don't come any finer, with the big fella (Mature) more than holding his own with two of Hollywood's living legends, who were also one of the silver screen's greatest romantic teams.

Betrayed gave Mature his first opportunity to play in a film set during World War II. The actor had played an ordinary GI getting ready to go overseas in the romantic comedy *Seven Days' Leave*, (1942), and proved his screen battle credentials in *The Glory Brigade* (1953) (set during the Korean War); but films putting him in the thick of World War II action had always eluded him. And, one could argue, *still* eluded him, because instead of playing an American serviceman, Mature added another nationality to his burgeoning repertoire by playing a Dutchman.

Mature and Gable are probably the least likely-looking or indeed likely-sounding Dutchmen ever to step onto a soundstage. In his career, Mature had played Italians, Greeks, Arabs, Indians and even a Viking, and they all lent themselves to his tanned, Mediterranean looks (well, perhaps not the Viking so much). But a Dutchman was a little too ambitious.

Mature wasn't the first star to be considered for the role of the dashing resistance fighter. *The Hollywood Reporter* had Richard Widmark down for the role with Gregory Peck and Ava Gardner originally considered for the Gable and Turner parts. With his light hair and complexion, Widmark would have, perhaps, made a more convincing Dutchman, but just for the record, he made an even more unlikely looking Viking than Mature (remember 1964's *The Long Ships*).

That said, once you've suspended your disbelief with the casting, *Betrayed* is a rattling good spies-and-counterspies whodunit that will hold your attention right to the final reel — is the traitor Mature or Turner? Or, could it possibly be Gable or Louis Calhern, or indeed any one of a wonderful line-up of supporting Brits: Wilfred Hyde-White, Ian Carmichael, Naill MacGinnis and Roland Culver.

Mature might not try hard at being a Dutchman, but he certainly put a lot of spirit into his performance, easily stealing the show from all concerned. For Gable and Turner, this was the last of their four films together, the others being *Honky Tonk* (1941), *Somewhere I'll Find You* (1942), and *Homecoming* (1948). (The last two were also war-based features). German-born director Gottfried Reinhardt had worked as the associate producer on *Homecoming*; *Betrayed,* which had the working title *The True and the Brave*, was his second film as a director. The son of theater director Max Reinhardt, his most notable credits as director include *Invitation* (1952), *Before Sundown* (a 1956 German-made film) and *Town Without Pity* (1961).

Betrayed marked the end of Gable and MGM after his 23-year association with the studio. On his last day, when the film was being re-dubbed, Gable (53 at the time) simply packed his belongings and left the studio with no fanfare. When Gable had reported for work for *Betrayed* in the Netherlands, Lana Turner (who was already there honeymooning with husband number four, actor Lex Barker), had this to say about the actor's imminent departure: "Now his days were numbered at MGM. It was just a matter of time with me, too. The studio could no longer afford us. We were all a little frightened."[1]

Mature would later say many good things about Turner (a girlfriend of his in the '40s), describing her as a sincere, friendly type: "She's really interested in people, concerned about their welfare and happiness. That's her greatest feature."[2]

With the Gina Lollobrigida close-cropped "Italian look" proving all the rage in the mid–1950s, Turner bravely adopted the hair style for her 1954 feature *Flame and the Flesh*, then retained the brunette look for *Betrayed*.[3] But after production wrapped, she dyed it blonde again to keep her fans happy. Mature, also seems to have tried a new look for the film, with his thick black mop of dark hair noticeably more curly than normal. And to make certain that we know that Mature is meant to be Dutch, every time he appears a piece of street organ-grinding music kicks in.

Like his character from *The Veils of Bagdad*, Mature zestfully leaps about the set with amusing abandon, scaling balconies and jumping through windows to rescue Gable and Turner respectively, and in the process spouts some great one-liners courtesy of scriptwriters Ronald Millar and George Froeschel. When Turner tries to focus his thoughts on the war, he gleefully remarks, "War, who cares about the war? Look, Angel, I'm no Boy Scout, I'm in this strictly for the laughs." And when she informs him that London wants to better coordinate his merry band of saboteurs with the Allied war effort, Mature insolently tells her, "You tell London to go coordinate their cockroaches."

During filming in a small Dutch town, the call went out for 300 extras and over 3000 turned up to catch a glimpse of the stars. If for some reason *Betrayed*'s stars don't grab your attention, the wonderful Dutch scenery certainly will, with the impressive location shooting taking in canals, pretty townscapes, windmills and dikes, all captured in glorious Eastman color. And if that's still not enough to whet your appetite, how about Lana Turner singing a sexy rendition of "Johnny Come Home?"

With so much on offer, the critics nevertheless panned it.

Commonweal: "During long parts of it one is never quite sure for whom Clark Gable, Lana Turner and Victor Mature are spying and chasing. But director Gottfried Reinhardt does manage to work up some good suspense at times, and even though your loyalties are splattered all over the place, you get keyed up to quite a pitch."

Newsweek magazine described it as a, "clumsy and over–slow paced piece of melodrama," adding, "Lana Turner and Victor Mature go about their spying and resistance leading with no great conviction, and Clark Gable gives a rather tired, though solid performance as the intelligence officer."

The *TV Times Film & Video Guide*: "Victor Mature ... takes what acting honors are going, as a resistance leader with a mother fixation."

The film was lampooned in the 1984 spy spoof *Top Secret!*, with Christopher Villiers cleverly combining Mature's flamboyant resistance leader with a James Mason voice. Operation Market Garden, and the battle at Arnhem would go on to get the full treatment in Richard Attenborough's epic *A Bridge Too Far* (1977).

Chief Crazy Horse

Universal, 1955

Cast: Victor Mature (Chief Crazy Horse); Suzan Ball (Black Shawl); John Lund (Major Twist); Ray Danton (Little Big Man); Keith Larsen (Flying Hawk); Paul Guilfoyle (Worm); David Janssen (Lt. Colin Cartwright); Robert Warwick (Spotted Tail); James Millican (Gen. George Crook); Morris Ankrum Red Cloud/Conquering Bear); Donald Randolph (Aaron Cartwright); Robert F. Simon (Jeff Mantz); James Westerfield (Caleb Mantz); Stuart Randall (Old Man Afraid); Pat Hogan (Dull Knife); Dennis Weaver (Maj. Carlisle); John Peters (Sgt. Guthrie); Henry Wills (He Dog); Emile Avery (Capt. William Freeman); Willie Hunter, Jr. (Cavalryman); Charles Horvath (Hardy); David Miller (Lieutenant); Robert St. Angelo, Bill Williams (Sergeants); Reg Parton (Doctor).

Crew: William Alland (Producer); Leonard Goldstein (Co-Producer); George Sherman (Director); Gerald Drayson Adams (Story); Gerald Drayson Adams, Franklin Coen (Screenplay); Harold Lipstein (Cinematography); Frank Skinner (Music); Joseph Gershenson (Music Supervisor); Robert F. Boyle, Alexander Golitzen (Art Direction); Russell A. Gausman, Ray Jeffers (Set Decorations); Rosemary Odell (Costume Design); Bud Westmore (Makeup); Marshall Green (Assistant Director); Leslie I. Carey, Corson Jowett (Sound); Al Clark (Editor). Running time: 86 minutes.

On his deathbed, a Lakota Sioux Indian chief predicts that a great warrior will emerge to lead his people to victory against the whites, only to be killed by one of his own. Chief Crazy Horse (Victor Mature) lives out the prophecy, as recalled by his white friend Twist, when Little Big Man, after losing out to Crazy Horse for the hand of Black Shawl, leads villainous traders to gold in the sacred Lakota burial ground in the Black Hills. In the rush for gold, hostilities break out and various treaties are broken. A great military strategist, Crazy Horse wins many battles, including the showdown with General Custer at the Battle of the Little Big Horn. But after the victory, the Indians split up and one by one are defeated and placed into reservations. Given permission to hunt buffalo the traditional way, without guns, by the sympathetic General Cook, Crazy Horse sets out to make preparations, but is fatally stabbed in the back with a bayonet by his soldier guard, Little Big Man, thus fulfilling the prophecy.

> "He Hurled the Lance That Smashed Custer That Historic Day at Little Big Horn!"
>
> "Great Saga of the Fighting Sioux!"

The role of Chief Crazy Horse was Mature's fourth take on a historical character/legendary figure following *My Gal Sal* (Paul Dresser), *My Darling Clementine* (Doc Holliday) and *Samson and Delilah* (Samson). With his craggy, leathery looks, Mature certainly looked the part of the great Sioux leader, and the role provided the actor with another fine opportunity to give an intense, sincere performance as he had done with Doc Holliday, Samson and more recently with Demetrius in *Robe* and *Demetrius and the Gladiator*s. Of all the aforementioned, Demetrius was possibly the closest in terms of characterization, with Mature playing both the Greek slave and Sioux leader as idealistic men, imbued with an inner strength and fierce courage in the face of adversity. They were proud, stalwart men, willing to sacrifice themselves to protect their people and way of life. The disappointment and despair of many broken treaties is indelibly etched into Mature's face as he tries to protect the sacred Black Hills. The actor also convincingly conveys wisdom and leadership in the scenes where Crazy Horse unites the tribes and employs his battle strategies to defeat the cavalry.

Told from the Indians' perspective, *Chief Crazy Horse* is one of the best Indian movies focusing on a great Indian leader, comfortably joining the ranks of *Broken Arrow* (1950), *Geronimo* (1962), etc. All show the Indian in a more sympathetic light, fighting whites who, for the most part, usually want to sell them out to make a quick buck. George Sherman was no stranger to medium-budget Westerns, directing *Battle at Apache Pass* (1952) and a few years later coaxing two sterling performances from Guy Madison in *Reprisal!* (1956) and *The Hard Man* (1957), which incidentally did the rounds as a double bill with Mature's *The Long Haul* (1957).

As John Lund's Major Twist tells us, Crazy Horse was so named because the day he was born, a wild horse rode through the village. In addition to Lund's excellent narration, there are many memorable quotes in the tale, with Mature delivering his lines with deepfelt, visionary conviction: "This is our land ... the sacred land of our fathers. I will fight for it ... and I will die for it!" On the importance of the buffalo hunt, he is equally passionate: "Take this hunt from us and we are no longer Lakotas. We're no longer men. We're nameless and dead."

In the role of Mature's wife Red Shawl, the lovely Susan Ball brings a touch of mellowness to Mature's serious countenance. A second cousin of Lucille Ball, the actress had her leg amputated prior to making *Chief Crazy Horse*, as the consequence of a knee injury sustained in 1953 during a dance number while making *East of Sumatra*. Her leg developed tumors that necessitated the amputation of the limb. In *Chief Crazy Horse*, a double was used for her walking scenes. The film was her last, as she died of cancer (which had spread to her lungs) on August 5, 1955.

Solid support was also provided by John Lund and Ray Danton. The son of a Norwegian glassblower, the handsome, blond, blue-eyed Lund worked in advertising before signing a long-term contract with Paramount. He tended to be cast as stuffed shirts who rarely got the girl, as seen in *High Society* (1956). His most memorable role was perhaps in *A Foreign Affair* (1948). Lund also gave Jeff Chandler's Indian chief, Cochise, a helping hand in *The Battle at Apache Pass*. Ray Danton made his film debut as Little Big Man in

Chief Crazy Horse and would go on to play an Indian in *Yellowstone Kelly* (1959) and *Apache Blood* (1975). Married to Julie Adams, he made his mark with *The Rise and Fall of Legs Diamond* (1960) and *The George Raft Story* (1961). The film additionally enjoyed the presence of a pre–*The Fugitive* David Janssen as a cavalry officer.

Perhaps a little too serious-looking at times and susceptible to heavenly choirs which sway his thinking, Mature's Lakota leader does at least cut a dignified figure, combining strength with vulnerability, and dispensing his lines or downing his foes with ease. Like Samson and Demetrius, Mature's Crazy Horse is a mighty, fearless warrior, taking on three charging Indians on horseback in an early scene and besting Danton in a fight-to-the-death knife duel. But (as with Mature's earlier Western real-life character, Doc Holliday) there's no happy ending, with our hero biting the dust in the final reel, making it Mature's fifth screen death following *The Housekeeper's Daughter*, *My Darling Clementine*, *Samson and Delilah* and *Betrayed*.

In terms of scenic beauty, the film is up there with Mature's *Betrayed* and *Dangerous Mission*, but it would have been a big plus to the film if, against such a majestic backdrop, we'd have seen more of the Battle of the Little Big Horn, instead of just a lot of bugle sounds and gunfire.

Variety was certainly impressed with the film, writing, "With the three topliners doing their characters in good style, the support is also first rate."

Picturegoer: "There is strength in Victor Mature's portrayal of the Indian chief who does not want war so much as freedom for his people."

Herb Fagen's Encyclopedia of Westerns: "Victor Mature plays the famed Lakota Sioux war chief with verve, vigor, and the intuition of a visionary who must lead his people to ultimate triumph against the white man."[1]

Brian Garfield's Western Films: "It's slow until the big climax, but the cast is good (Mature is surprisingly convincing)."

The Epitome of Cool: The Films of Ray Danton by Joseph Fusco: "Mature's tortured expressions convey the challenges faced by the warrior chief, making his death tragic and noble."[2]

The story of the legendary Indian leader was adapted for television in 1996 under the title *Crazy Horse*, with Michael Greyeyes in the title role.

Violent Saturday

20th Century–Fox, 1955

Cast: Victor Mature (Shelley Martin); Richard Egan (Boyd Fairchild); Stephen McNally (Harper); Virginia Leith (Linda Sherman); Tommy Noonan (Harry Reeves); Lee Marvin (Dill); Margaret Hayes (Mrs. Emily Fairchild); J. Carrol Naish (Chapman); Sylvia Sidney (Elsie Braden); Ernest Borgnine (Stadt); Dorothy Patrick (Helen Martin); Billy Chapin (Steve Martin); Brad Dexter (Gill Clayton); Donald Gamble (Bobby); Raymond Greenleaf (Mr. Fairchild); Ricky Murray (Georgie); Robert Adler (Stan); Ann Morrison (Mrs. Stadt); Kevin Corcoran (David Stadt); Donna Corcoran (Anna Stadt); Noreen Corcoran (Mary Stadt); Boyd "Red" Morgan (Slick); Florence Ravenel (Miss Shirley); Harry Seymour (Conductor); Fred Shellac (Signalman); Eilene Bowers (Bank Teller); Dorothy Phillips (Bank Customer); Virginia Carroll (Carol — Martin's Secretary); Joyce Newhard (Dorothy — Librarian); Mack Williams (Drugstore Clerk).

Crew: Buddy Adler (Producer); Richard Fleischer (Director); William L. Heath (Novel); Sydney Boehm (Screenplay); Charles G. Clarke (Cinematography); Hugo Friedhofer (Music); George W. Davis, Lyle R. Wheeler (Art Direction); Chester L. Bayhi (Set Decorations); Kay Nelson (Costume Design); Charles Le Maire (Wardrobe); Ben Nye (Makeup); Ray Kellogg (Special Effects); Joseph E. Rickards (Assistant Director); Harry M. Leonard, E. Clayton Ward (Sound); Louis R. Loeffler (Editor). Running time: 90 minutes.

Three crooks, Harper, Dill and Chapman, arrive in an Arizona mining town planning to rob a bank. As they case the town, several subplots unfold: mine manager Shelley Martin's (Victor Mature) struggle to regain the respect of his son, because (being in a reserved occupation) he didn't fight during the war; playboy Boyd Fairchild's unhappy marriage to Emily; meek bank manager Harry Reeves' secret desire for sexy nurse Linda Sherman; librarian Elsie Braden, who resorts to purse-stealing to pay her debts, and Amish farmer Stadt, who is against violence, but has to resort to it when his family is threatened. When the villains kidnap Shelley (to help with their getaway) after the robbery, he frees himself and bravely thwarts their escape with the help of Stadt, thus winning back his son's respect.

Violent Saturday completed Mature's trilogy of big outdoor crime melodrama's, following *The Las Vegas Story* and *Dangerous Mission,* and what a high note to finish on. In addition to Mature, *The Las Vegas Story* had Jane Russell; *Dangerous Mission,* the delights of 3-D; but *Violent Saturday* trumped them both with three of the best screen villains ever to set foot in small town America, Stephen McNally, Lee Marvin and J. Carrol Naish, who were definitely on par with the dastardly trio of Robert Ryan, Ernest Borgnine and Lee Marvin from the other big crime thriller released the same year, *Bad Day at Black Rock.*

The film (which was produced simultaneously with the publication of the novel) is also injected with a healthy dose of *Peyton Place*-style soap dramatics that will keep you glued to your sets as all the social ills and suppressed desires associated with small town claustrophobia bubble to the surface. Will playboy lush Richard Egan save his wife Margaret Hayes from being a tramp? Will she in turn give country club lothario Brad Dexter another notch on his bedpost? Will purse-stealing librarian Sylvia Sidney take to a life of petty crime? Will Mature's son forgive him for not fighting in the war? Will Amish farmer Ernest Borgnine persist in saying, "I thank thee, neighbor"? Will peeping Tom bank manager Tommy Noonan get to see any more of Virginia Leith undressing? Will she in turn learn to close her curtains while undressing and save Egan from the bottle, who in turn is trying to save his wife from being a tramp? et cetera, et cetera, et cetera—and all this, for the first time, in awesome CinemaScope.

Having played everything from an English gent (*Moss Rose*) to an Indian (*Chief Crazy Horse*), Mature's impressive repertoire had yet to include that of a happily married family man until his role in *Violent Saturday*. Mature had played a family man previously in *Kiss of Death* and *Chief Crazy Horse,* but in both films, tragic circumstances had shattered his family life, with the loss of his wife in the former film, and that of his baby daughter in the latter. *Affair with a Stranger* saw him come close to domestic bliss after he and wife Jean Simmons adopt a child, but when she dotes on the child, to his detriment, the marriage is put under strain. The actor was more associated with roguish man-about-town types and solitary heroes; marriage and Mature were, perhaps, not a natural combination. But by 1955, and at the age of 42, the actor had outgrown his "love 'em and leave 'em" screen persona, and his sincere and credible performance in *Violent Saturday* as a proud, loving father trying to win back the respect of his son was clear evidence that he had turned a corner in his screen career. This becomes clear in the scene where he confides to his boy, "Every dad wants to be a hero to his son, but some of us don't make it."

The role of the doting father also gave Mature the opportunity to showcase a more reflective and vulnerable side to his screen persona, warmly captured in the final scene in the hospital, when he confesses to his son that even heroes experience fear: "Stevie, being scared is only normal and human. No one was ever a 100 percent hero."

Violent Saturday was the first Twentieth Century–Fox film for both producer Buddy Adler and his friend, director Richard Fleischer. In his memoir *Just Tell Me When to Cry*, Fleischer wrote, "Besides being the first CinemaScope picture ever made for under $1 million, it was a damn good movie. Darryl Zanuck, the studio's big boss, was very taken with it, and we—Buddy and I—became sort of heroes."[1]

Fleischer, the son of pioneering American animator Max Fleischer, abandoned medical studies to pursue an interest in drama. He directed RKO shorts before proving himself as a capable director of thrillers and adventure films such as *The Narrow Margin* (1952), *20000 Leagues Under the Sea* (1954), *The Vikings* (1958) and *Compulsion* (1959).

With such a large cast embroiled in several subplots, Fleischer certainly did an expert job in sustaining simmering emotions and tension throughout the film, but it has to said that the one performance that stands out above all others is that of Lee Marvin, an evil killer who treads over a small boy's fingers when he (the boy) accidentally knocks a nasal spray out of Marvin's hand. Such shock value would once again steal the show from Mature, just as Richard Widmark received all the plaudits for pushing a wheelchair-bound old lady down the stairs in *Kiss of Death*. Marvin may well have delivered the stand-out performance, but fellow villain J. Carroll Naish got the best line in the film: He hands a small boy some candy to keep him quiet during the bank raid, telling him, "Stick these in your kisser and go suck on them." Richard Egan came second with his pearl of wisdom, as an explanation for his miserable plight, "Failure breeds success. Success breeds failure."

Several of the cast had worked with Mature before: Marvin (*The Glory Brigade*), Brad Dexter (*The Las Vegas Story*) and Egan and Ernest Borgnine (*Demetrius and the Gladiators*). Borgnine had Mature down as an okay guy, but as he described in his autobiography, he thought the actor had a "me vs. them" attitude toward the studios because of his refusal to dive under a car during an action scene. When the director suggested digging a hole to make it easier, Mature still proved resistant. The actor later told Borgnine that he had refused because he had broken his leg on a motorcycle during a scene in a Columbia movie, and wasn't compensated for it. From then on he adopted a "to hell with them" attitude, and was no longer prepared to do anything remotely dangerous.[2] As it turned out, Mature sustained a back injury while trying to dodge some moving props (an injury that put him out of action for a few days).[3]

The girls were well represented with Virginia Leith, Margaret Hayes and Sylvia Sidney in the cast line-up. Leith's career never really got off the ground, but she secured her screen legacy as the disembodied head in the cult sci-fi film *The Brain That Wouldn't Die* (1962). Hayes' career suffered pretty much the same fate; she is perhaps best remembered for playing a new teacher alongside Glenn Ford in *Blackboard Jungle* (1955). In contrast to her two younger co-stars, veteran sad-eyed actress Sidney enjoyed a long, illustrious career, which included the notable films *City Streets* (1931), *Sabotage* (1936) and *Blood on the Sun* (1945).

Violent Saturday was Mature's last film for Twentieth Century–Fox after a relationship lasting 15 years, and it was definitely a high note to go out on.

Variety: "[It's] a complex but taut melodrama.... [T]he main action of the story stands out as a masterly piece of filmmaking in the meller department. McNally, Marvin and Nash are excellent.... Egan and Mature turn in okay performances."

The New York Times thought the film was a vicious and sadistic account of how a bank robbery is committed. "Victor Mature as the eventual hero is bruising, and Ernest Borgnine as the Amish farmer is a joke. In flat black hat and chin whiskers, he acts as though he's just off the Ark."

Time: "Mature soon becomes marginal when up against Marvin's minimal performance as a loose-lipped killer with a permanent head cold."

Picturegoer: "When the action lets fly, it has the zing of a jet.... Mature is in fine punching form..."

The Last Frontier

Columbia, 1955

Cast: Victor Mature (Jed Cooper); Guy Madison (Capt. Glenn Riordan); Robert Preston (Col. Frank Marston); James Whitmaore (Gus); Anne Bancroft (Corinna Marston); Russell Collins (Capt. Phil Clarke); Peter Whitney (Sgt. Major Decker); Pat Hogan (Mungo); Manuel Donde (Red Cloud); Guy Williams (Lt. Benton); Mickey Kuhn (Luke); William Calles (Spotted Elk); Jack Pennick (Corporal); William Traylor (Soldier); John L. Cason, Robert St. Angelo, Allen Pinson, Reg Parton, Terry Wilson (Sentries).

Crew: William Fadiman (Producer); Anthony Mann (Director); Richard Emery Roberts (novel *The Gilded Rooster*); Philip Yordan, Russell S. Hughes (Screenplay); William C. Mellor (Cinematography); Leigh Harline (Music); Robert Peterson (Art Direction); James Crowe (Set Decorations); Clay Campbell (Makeup); Sam Nelson (Assistant Director); John P. Livadary (Sound); Al Clark (Editor). Running time: 98 minutes.

Relieved of a year's worth of valuable pelts by Indians, trappers Jed Cooper (Victor Mature), Gus and Mungo head to a nearby fort where the uncivilized Jed falls in love with Corinna, the wife of the commanding officer Col. Frank Marston. Due to his reckless leadership, Marston's previous command was wiped out in the Civil War, which still rages. When he plans an ill-conceived attack on a warring tribe, much to the objection of his second in command Captain Riordan, Jed steps in to try and prevent the action which could lead to another slaughter. Marston pursues his offensive against the Indians, and he and Gus are killed in the fighting. The surviving troopers make it back to the fort and the Indians finally retreat. With all-out war with the Indians averted, Jed becomes a sergeant in the troop and, with Marston dead, the road is clear to pursue his romance with Corinna.

"The Men, the Women, the Wilderness of
America's Most Exciting Days!"

"A Rousing Tale of Adventure, Lust and Madness."

The Last Frontier was a major coup for Mature, allowing the actor to come under the direction of one of the best Western directors of the 1950s, Anthony Mann, and also the opportunity to work alongside one of the great actors, Robert Preston — who, like Mature, trained at the Pasadena Community Playhouse.

Just when you thought you had Mature pigeonholed as either the brash, carefree, self-assured man-about-town or dark, brooding type, he again extends his range with another knockout performance. In many ways, Jed is an amalgam of several of his former characters: the wild, naive caveman Tumak (*One Million B.C.*), the excited, childlike boxer Tommy Lundy (*Footlight Serenade*), the lustful Samson (*Samson and Delilah*), the cocky Andy Clark (*Wabash Avenue*), the defiant Demetrius (*The Robe* and *Demetrius and the Gladiators*) and the proud, weather-beaten Crazy Horse (*Chief Crazy Horse*). With such a myriad of personality traits simply bursting to jump out, you simply can't predict how his character will evolve in this riveting tale, which adds greatly to its entertainment value. Mann made the great Westerns *Winchester '73* (1950) and *Man of the West* (1958); and *The Last Frontier* is, in my opinion, certainly up there with the best of them. Mature can't compare with James Stewart or Gary Cooper, but then Stewart and Cooper can't compare with John Wayne or Henry Fonda. They share certain characteristics, but essentially they are all very different. And it has to be said, that there were few other actors at the time who could have done justice to the part of Jed — Burt Lancaster perhaps, or in a pinch Kirk Douglas. But even these two greats would have found it difficult to realistically convey the erratic, childlike nature of the character, which Mature delivered with such natural verve. With his weathered face and wild locks of hair, Mature genuinely looks as if he was brought up in the wilderness, an observation also made by Jeanine Basinger in her thoughtful book on Mann's film career: "Victor Mature is a character worthy of Zola's naturalism. He looks and acts like a huge bear."[1] (I assume this was a compliment.)

Adapted from the Richard Emery Roberts novel *The Gilded Rooster* (also the film's working title), *The Last Frontier* is very much a one-off film. Yes, there are shades of *Fort Apache* (1948) with Henry Fonda's martinet fort commander sharing much with Robert Preston's arrogant Col. Frank Marston, both underestimating the Indian to their peril. And perhaps we can discern traces of Kirk Douglas' contemporary cowboy from *Lonely Are the Brave* (1962) in Mature's mountain man, with both characters free, wild and set in their ways, struggling to come to terms with the spread of so-called civilization. But beyond these two, there is little else to compare, unless we draw even looser linkages with the mountain man-fur trapper genre in general with films such as *The Big Sky* (1952), *The Kentuckian* (1955), *The Trap* (1966), *A Man Called Horse* (1970) and *Jeremiah Johnson* (1972).

Surprisingly, *The Last Frontier*, Mann's only cavalry film, is paid scant regard when it comes to the director's work, perhaps in part because critics find it hard to see beyond Mature's muscular frame and wide grin. Mann wisely tapped into the strengths and nuances of Mature's screen persona, guiding the actor to one of his best performances as possibly the most memorable uncivilized man to hit the screen since the days of Tumak the caveman. The clash of cultures which is prevalent throughout the film is keenly felt due to the excellent support given by Guy Madison, James Whitmore and Anne Bancroft.

Mainly noted for his Westerns, handsome Guy Madison was married to actresses Gail Russell (from 1949 to 1954) and Sheila Connolly (from 1954 to 1964). Like Mature, he served in the Coast Guard during the war. Madison never quite made that major leap into stardom when he took up acting. He gained in popularity via the TV series *Adventures of Wild Bill Hickok* (1951–1958) before heading to Europe in the 1960s to make Spaghetti Westerns and action films.

Although a great actor, major screen success eluded Robert Preston for much of his early career. He once summed it up by saying, "I'd get the best role in every 'B' picture and the second best in the 'A' pictures." But that said, his later films are a great testament to his acting style including *The Dark at the Top of the Stairs* (1960), *The Music Man* (1962), *All the Way Home* (1963) and *Victor Victoria* (1982).

Looking like the long-lost brother of Spencer Tracy, the great supporting actor James Whitmore, who served in the Marines during World War II, chalked up an impressive list of film credits. My favorites have to be his second film *Battleground* (1949), for which he was Oscar-nominated for Best Supporting Actor, and the classic sci-fi *Them!* (1954).

Anne Bancroft needs little by the way of introduction. Her best films include *The Miracle Worker* (1962), for which she received an Oscar for Best Actress, *The Pumpkin Eater* (1964) and *The Graduate* (1967). She had previously worked with Mature in *The Robe,* and although she looks slightly like a fish out of water in *The Last Frontier*, her mere presence is always a welcome addition. (According to *The Hollywood Reporter*, Kathryn Grant was initially down for the role.) Bancroft is notable in Mature's career as the second girl whose face he gets to slap for messing with his head, following in the footsteps of Lizabeth Scott in *Easy Living*.

Mature's mood certainly experiences many changes as he tries to come to grips with his new surroundings and his lust for Bancroft. Through his energetic performance, we really get to relish some of the great dialogue on offer. Swaggering drunk in his first meeting with Bancroft, he says of her husband's photograph, "Say, I guess you have to dress in a fancy uniform like this, to have a woman like you." And in his search for more drink, he presses her, "You must have some whiskey, because the colonel looks like a drinking man."

When accused of not being civilized by Madison, he philosophically responds, "That's what I'm gonna do, I'm gonna find me a woman, make some children, get married and become civilized." And to his bedtime assailant, he snarls, "I smell trouble, and you fill the room with it."

To keep up his quota of overcoming the odds, Mature, in between knocking back his body weight in whiskey, gets to take out three marauding Indians while stranded outside the fort.

Mann was noted for his love of the American landscape and his ability to blend natural vistas with human drama. The *Last Frontier*, with location shooting taking place in Mexico, showcases this talent to full effect, with some amazing panning and tracking shots of the mountain frontier, mostly shot at night, which does much to carry the brooding atmosphere of this underrated film. The views of the fort against this primitive expanse are particularly impressive. Mann left the Western genre in the 1960s and turned his talents to epics such as *El Cid* (1961) and *The Fall of the Roman Empire* (1964) — spectacles that might have featured Mature if made a decade earlier.

Mature certainly looked at home in the great outdoors playing the part of a mountain man, but in real life, apart from the golf course, he was definitely not one for exploring the wilderness, once proclaiming, "I never did see the sense in shuffling round wide open spaces when you've got a nice, comfy apartment with two windows to let in the fresh air."[2]

My thoughts on *The Last Frontier* were summed up aptly by The *Radio Times Guide to Films*: "A majestic and brooding Western..."

Safari

Columbia, 1956

Cast: Victor Mature (Ken Duffield); Janet Leigh (Linda Latham); John Justin (Brian Sinden); Roland Culver (Sir Vincent Brampton); Liam Redmond (Roy Shaw); Orlando Martins (Jerusalem); Earl Cameron (Jeroge); Juma (Odongo); Lionel Ngakane (Kakora); Harry Quashie (O'Keefe); Slim Harris (Renegade); Cy Grant (Masai Chief); John Wynn (Charley); Arthur Lovegrove (Blake); Estelle Brody (Aunty May); Christopher Warbey (Kenny); John Harrison (Wambut); Glyn Lawson (Kikuyu); Frank Singuineau (African); Charles Hayes (Police Inspector); Bartholomew Sketch (Special Mau Mau); John Crook (District Commissioner); Bob Isaacs (Henderson).

Crew: Irving Allen, Albert R. Broccoli (Producers); Adrian D. Worker (Associate Producer); Terence Young (Director); Robert Buckner (Story); Anthony Veiller (Screenplay); John Wilcox (Cinematography); William Alwyn (Music); Muir Mathieson (Music Director); Elliot Scott (Art Direction); Olga Lehmann (Costume Design); Elsa Fennell (Wardrobe) Fred Williamson (Makeup); Frank Holland, Michael Forlong (Assistant Directors): Tony Lower (Sound); Michael Gordon (Editor). Running time: 90 minutes.

Following the death of his son at the hands of the Mau Mau, big game hunter Ken Duffield (Victor Mature) plans to get his revenge on the tribal leader responsible. British millionaire Sir Vincent Brampton, accompanied by his young fiancée Linda, arranges a safari to indulge his passion for lion hunting, but gets more than he bargained for when he is killed as a consequence of his reckless and obsessive manner. Ken finally tracks down and kills the man who murdered his son, and then sets off to start a new life with Linda, the couple having realized that they had strong affections for each other during the trek.

"In Deadly Mau-Mau Land. While Jungle Throbs and Beasts Roar — They Live the Love Adventure That Sets the Dark Continent Aflame!"

"Sensational — Ravaging Mau-Mau, Rampaging Beasts, Raging Jungle Love!"

"All the Splendor and Pageantry of *King Solomon's Mines* — and All Its Mighty Thrills and Love Drama!"

King Solomon's Mines (the 1937 and 1950 versions) is, without doubt, the best jungle adventure ever to grace the silver screen, but that said, *Safari* easily boasts some of the most heightened sexual tension ever put on film, as Janet Leigh and Mature work up a lust-driven sweat, day and night, in the sort of heated courting ritual you'd expect when a former show-girl meets big game hunter in the steamy wilds of Africa.

Set against the background of the Mau Mau uprising, *Safari* is also notable for being shot on location in Kenya when the troubles were far from over. An anti-colonial secret organization, the Mau Mau fought British rule in Kenya between 1952 and 1960, sowing the seeds for Kenyan independence in 1963 (it was one of the last African nations to be granted independence from its European colonizers). *Safari* was one of three films focused on the conflict, along with *Simba* (1955) and *Something of Value* (1957).

Taking the leads, Mature and Leigh satisfied the quota allowance operating at the time, whereupon only two American actors could star in an English-made film. This was Mature's first feature under his six-movie contract with Warwick Films, which capitalized on his big

1956 • The Films   Safari • 129

physical presence in the great outdoors, an imposing presence that was born to be lensed in the widescreen process of CinemaScope.

However, when it came to living in a tent in the big outdoors, Mature was less than happy. When cast and crew set up camp in the bush to begin location filming, Mature opted to stay at his hotel, preferring to take the two-and-a-half-hour drive, each way, to

Mature in a publicity shot from *Safari* (Columbia, 1956).

the set every day. As Leigh recalled in her autobiography *There Really Was a Hollywood*, Mature only gave this up as a bad idea when his hotel was bombed.[1] Leigh further recounted a night when someone was prowling outside the tent she was sharing with her mother, who had accompanied her on location. They were scared that they would be murdered in their beds; Mature eased their concerns when he threw his mattress between their cots and slept there the rest of the night.[2] Mature also revealed his gentlemanly credentials when he accompanied Leigh's mother on the ship taking them back home to the States. As Leigh recalled, "She told me afterward he had been absolutely marvelous to her, treated her like a sister."[3]

Despite his reluctance to rough it in the bush, Mature looks perfect in the role of the big game hunter, sporting large safari hat and khakis. And for the second time (following *Violent Saturday*) we see him in the role of the proud father, a role that also gave him another opportunity to play a tortured, revenge-driven character (as in *Kiss of Death*) after his son is killed by Mau Mau rebels. The total anguish and despair in his eyes when he looks upon his son's dead body grips you like a vise, and is one of the enduring memories of the film; it reprises the futility he conveyed in *The Glory Brigade* when he looked upon his massacred platoon. His world at an end, Mature's sole purpose now is to track down the killers, which leaves him little time for niceties where others are concerned. When Roland Culver tries to contract his services on their first encounter, explaining that he has traveled 4000 miles for this safari, Mature disdainfully replies, "Everyone in Kenya has traveled 4000 miles, it's the only way to get here." And when, en route, Culver shoots a snake of the non-poisonous variety, and accuses Mature of not adequately protecting them, he snarls, "You know as well as I do, you couldn't catch a cold from that snake."

When Leigh pays a social visit to his tent and asks if she can sit down, he replies that there's only the bed, affording her the best line in the film when she angrily pipes back, "Look, junior, I didn't say lie down."

But, as is the way with such things, love eventually blossoms between the two lost souls, after Mature eventually recognizes that perhaps there is more to this gorgeous, hourglass blonde than initially met his eye (although it took Leigh soaping herself in the obligatory great outdoors bathing scene and a bedtime negligee shot to perhaps sway him).

When Leigh later finds herself in great peril, helplessly drifting downstream in dinghy, the great white hunter comes to her rescue. But behind the camera, Mature was wisely having none of it. As Leigh recalled, when director Terence Young instructed Mature to rush into the stream and pick her up, he refused without hesitation, arguing there could be crocodiles in the water. When Young explained that they'd all been scared off by gun-fire before the scene, Mature responded, "What if one of those S.O.B.s is hard of hearing? " which had everyone doubled up with laughter. Mature was finally convinced and the scene was completed.[4] Leigh swallowed some water when the dinghy accidentally overturned, which resulted in her catching a stomach bug that would leave her with a lifelong sensitive abdomen.

Terence Young served as a paratrooper during World War II, and was wounded at the battle of Arnhem. Taken to a Dutch hospital, he was nursed back to health by a 16-year-Dutch girl named Audrey Heenstra, who became better known as Audrey Hepburn. Young went on to direct three of the first four James Bond films, *Dr. No* (1962), *From Russia With Love* (1963) and *Thunderball* (1965), as well as directing Hepburn in *Wait Until Dark* (1967).

The wife of Tony Curtis (from 1951 to 1962) and mother of Jamie Lee Curtis, Janet Leigh secured her place in cinematic history for her Oscar-nominated (supporting) performance in Alfred Hitchcock's *Psycho* (1960). Her dramatic ability was also shown to good effect in *Touch of Evil* (1958) and *The Manchurian Candidate* (1962). Former Royal Air Force pilot Roland Culver's notable credits include *On Approval* (1944) and *Dead of Night* (1945).

Helping to move things along, the excellent William Alwyn score includes trumpet-playing Orlando Martin's catchy tune "We're On Safari" at appropriate intervals.

Picture Show: "It is beautifully photographed, much of it having been taken in Africa, and is well acted..."

The Sharkfighters

United Artists, 1956

Cast: Victor Mature (Lt. Cmdr. Ben Staves); Karen Steele (Martha Staves); James Olson (Ens. Harold Duncan); Philip Coolidge (Lt. Cmdr. Leonard Evans); Claude Akins (Chief "Gordy" Gordon); Rafael Campos (Carlos); George N. Neise (Cmdr. George Zimmer); Nathan Yates (Capt. Ruiz); Jesus Hernandez (Vincente); Master Sgt. Lorin Johns, CPO David Westlein (Themselves), Charles Collingwood (Narrator).

Crew: Samuel Goldwyn, Jr. (Producer); Jerry Hopper (Director); Jo and Art Napoleon (Story); Lawrence Roman, Jonathan Robinson, (Screenplay); Lee Garmes (Cinematography); Jerome Moross (Music); Emil Newman (Musical Director); Russell Shearman (Special Effects); Virgil Hart (Assistant Director); Ralph Hoge (Second Unit Director); Roy Jenson (Stunts); Daniel Mandell (Editor). Running time: 74 minutes.

The movie is set off the coast of Cuba during World War II. Lt. Cmdr Ben Staves (Victor Mature) is assigned to oversee a team of marine biologists, including project leader Leonard Evans and young chemist Harold Duncan, who are trying to create an effective shark repellent for pilots forced to land in the ocean. Having previously lost some of his men to shark attack, Ben wants the project completed as quickly as possible, and is keen to submit a formula before it has been fully tested. When this haste results in the death of an innocent lad, he goes back to the lab to do further research and even uses himself as a guinea pig to prove the effectiveness of the final formula.

"Your Eyes Open Wide with Terror and Excitement!
Man Against Tiger Shark."

"A Peak of Excitement That No Man ... No Camera
has Ever Captured Before!"

"The U.S. Navy's operation 'Shark-Buster' ... Caribbean
adventure that hits like a tidal wave!"

"FIGHTING THE TERROR OF THE SEAS!"

Having tangled with dinosaurs, lions, tigers, Richard Widmark's psycho from *Kiss of Death*, crocodiles and a charging rhino in previous features, Mature now came up against the terror of the seas — the mighty tiger shark. And what an adventure it proved to be, with Mature doing what he does best, defying the odds, and risking all on an experimental shark repellent.

Shot on location in Isla de Pinos and Havana, Cuba, *The Sharkfighters* delivers all the thrills and spills the publicity taglines promised. But, were it not for the efforts of second

132 • *The Sharkfighters*   THE FILMS • 1956

unit director Ralph Hoge, producer Samuel Goldwyn, Jr. would have shelved the project a year before, because he thought it impossible to inject the film with the realism it required. "Even if we can photograph live sharks," he said to Hoge, "how will you manage in the jungles of Isla de Pinos without roads, a deep water port, electricity or housing?" Undeterred, Hoge went ahead to Isla de Pinos and achieved the impossible, bulldozing an airplane runway, hacking a road through the jungle, building sets and accommodations for cast and crew, shipping in batteries and generators, and constructing a steel wire underwater corral which he filled with sharks. In fact, he pretty much did it all apart from act in the film, to which a grateful Goldwyn acknowledged, "He'd have done that, too, if I'd asked him to."[1] Hoge's efforts certainly paid off, enabling Goldwyn to deliver a tension-filled film which explored man's aversion and fear of sharks nearly twenty years before *Jaws* (1975) hit our screens.

Mature's Lt. Cmdr. Ben Staves is the closest the actor got to playing a man of science. But you know intuitively that when he's done with all the painstaking statistics, research and testing, that at some point in the picture he's going to dive into those shark-infested waters with just knife to keep him company. And as the film's pressbook boasted, "There are no rubber sharks, plastic sharks or dead sharks in *The Sharkfighters*— they were all netted live for our entertainment." According to the publicity, Mature, working in a shallow inlet,

With time running out to find a shark repellent, Lt. Cmdr. Ben Staves (Mature) takes to the shark-infested waters as a guinea pig in the Caribbean adventure *The Sharkfighters* (United Artists, 1956).

did all of his own underwater swimming scenes, separated from several live captive sharks by a glass partition.²

Mature was one of those actors who looked a natural in whatever outdoor setting he was in, including the lush Caribbean setting of *The Sharkfighters* (blue waters, golden sands and coconut trees). The idyllic setting was threatened when one Cuban prop man, hearing of the possibility of strong winds, cut all the coconuts down, fearing they could pose a danger to extras working under the trees. Director Jerry Hopper explained he had wanted the coconuts in the film for tropical atmosphere and instructed the man to wire them back to the trees.³

With his hatred of sharks (they killed many of his former crew when his ship was sunk by the Japanese), Mature again assumes the role of someone, slightly unhinged, who is driven purely by revenge, as in his previous film *Safari*. His overzealous quest to rid the waters of sharks is revealed when he uses a rifle to give them a taste of cold lead following one of their experiments. When chief researcher Philip Coolidge asks him what he knows about sharks, Mature snarls, "They got lousy table manners."

Despite his character's aversion to sharks, Mature plays it cool in this tropical outing, in an undemanding role that simply required him to look resolute and determined, while knocking back the occasional cold beer. The rest of the cast including Karen Steele, James Olson and Philip Coolidge, handle their roles with ease, under the deft direction of Hopper. Hopper's film career may have been short-lived before moving into television, but he did manage to coax three fine performances out of that other fine specimen of masculinity, Charlton Heston, in *Pony Express* (1953), *Secret of the Incas* (1954) and *The Private War of Major Benson* (1955).

Former model Karen Steele was born in Hawaii, and earned her first income spearing young sharks lurking in the private cove on the estate of Woolworth heiress Barbara Hutton. Her most critically acclaimed role was as Virginia in *Marty* (1955), but I'll always remember her as Eve McHuron in the *Star Trek* episode "Mudd's Women" (1966).

James Olson made his film debut in *The Sharkfighters*, but had to wait until 1968 to earn the best reviews in his career playing Joanne Woodward's suitor in *Rachel, Rachel*.

Stage and television actor Philip Coolidge was generally underused in films, but did show to good effect in *I Want to Live!* (1958) and *The Tingler* (1959).

The Sharkfighters is the type of adventure yarn that no doubt would have proved equally entertaining with the likes of Richard Egan or Cornel Wilde in the lead, showing off their well-honed torsos, but it did at least give Mature an opportunity to top up his suntan, which would prove beneficial in his next assignment, the role of the Afghan rebel *Zarak*.

Variety felt that Mature carried the film, but due to the limitations of the screenplay, his input was limited to a "walk-through performance."

Picture Show: "Exciting story.... Well photographed and acted."

Zarak

Columbia, 1956

Cast: Victor Mature (Zarak Khan), Michael Wilding (Maj. Michael Ingram); Anita Ekberg (Salma); Bonar Colleano (Biri), Eunice Gayson (Cathy Ingram); Finlay Currie (The Mullah); Peter Illing (Ahmad); Bernard Miles (Hassu); Eddie Byrne (Kasim); Patrick

McGoohan (Moor Larkin); Frederick Valk (Haji Khan); Andre Morell (Maj. Atherton); Harold Goodwin (Sgt. Higgins); Alec Mango (Akbar); Oscar Quitak (Youssuff); George Margo (Chief Jailor); Arnold Marle (Flower Seller); Conrad Phillips (Young Officer).

Crew: Irving Allen, Albert R. Broccoli (Producers); Phil C. Samuel (Associate Producer); Terence Young (Director); A.J. Bevan (Novel *Zarak Khan*); Richard Maibaum (Screenplay); Cyril J. Knowles, Ted Moore, John Wilcox (Cinematography); William Alwyn (Music); Muir Mathieson (Musical Director); John Box, Edward Carrere (Art Direction); Phyllis Dalton (Costume Design); Cliff Richardson (Special Effects); Yakima Canutt, John Gilling (Assistant Directors); Peter Davies (Sound); Alan Osbiston, Bert Rule (Editors). Running time: 94 minutes.

The movie is set in the mountainous North West frontier between British India and Afghanistan in the 1860s. Zarak Khan is nearly flogged to death on his father's instruction as a punishment for his amorous advances towards his father's youngest wife, Salma. Saved by the timely arrival of an elderly Mullah, Zarak leaves the village and becomes the notorious leader of an outlaw gang. A British major, Michael Ingram, is dispatched to capture him, which he succeeds in doing. Zarak makes his escape with the assistance of the sadistic Ahmad, who hates the British. Although adversaries, Ingram and Zarak develop a respect for one another. When Ahmad captures and tortures Ingram, Zarak lays down his life to save him.

"For the Harem Beauty ... Mighty Zarak Fought Half a Continent!"
"Pillage! Plunder! Passion!"

Pillage and plunder, and not a Viking in sight. But who needs bloodthirsty Norsemen chewing up the scenery when you can have marauding brigand cutthroats kicking up a storm on the North West Frontier of British India. Old-fashioned, cliché-riddled, formula-driven, contrived — there can be no doubt, but *Zarak* aspires to little else. There are no moral messages or pretensions, only 94 minutes of good, wholesome action hokum, spiced up by the voluptuous Anita Ekberg, who gyrates and sashays across the desert terrain to great effect. She's definitely worth fighting half a continent for, especially when she does that daring belly dance that will simply make your glasses steam up. The original poster of the film showing a scantily clad Ekberg was banned in the U.K. for "bordering on the obscene."

Having cut a zestful dash as Antar in *The Veils of Bagdad*, Mature again found himself attired in Middle Eastern garb with his Afghan rebel Zarak. But whereas the former was clearly played with tongue in cheek, *Zarak* had a more serious edge to it. Darkly tanned and sporting a goatee, Mature certainly looks the part, and was perhaps, at the time, one of the few actors (in company with Yul Brynner) who could have realistically pulled off the part of an Afghan rebel.

Adapted from A.J. Bevan's novel, *Zarak* was based on a real character, Zarak Khan (the working title of the film), who led a group of rebels operating along the India-Afghanistan frontier opposing the British rule in India. He was granted amnesty by the British when he agreed to spy for them in Burma, which resulted in his capture and execution at the hands of the Japanese. According to a *New York Times* article, Irving Allen altered the historical accuracy of the novel to focus more on character than events, and had initially hoped to secure Errol Flynn's services in the title role.

In his book *Visions of Yesterday*, author Jeffrey Richards wrote, "In the late fifties revival of Imperial cinema there was a group of films centering on the battle of wits between British officers and rebel chieftains and highlighting the mutual respect which develops between them. The prototype of these films is *Zarak*." Richards went on to describe it basically as a "Boys Own Paper" yarn.[1]

In common with Samson and Demetrius, Zarak is lured to his peril by a temptress, in this case the youngest wife of his father. But we are not sure exactly what drives Zarak, other than the possible frustration of losing his love. He seeks not power, friends nor wealth, and like Mature's Dr. Omar from *The Shanghai Gesture* and The Scarf from *Betrayed*, he treats life as if it is a game to be played, not for reward, but to simply partake in the game. This is Mature at his most distant and brooding, languishing in self-pity and enduring inner turmoil

Zarak (Mature) tastes forbidden fruit, in the form of Salma (Anita Ekberg), his father's youngest wife, in the Irving Allen–Albert R. Broccoli production *Zarak* (Columbia, 1956).

for reasons not clearly identified. Constantly immersed in his own thoughts, he has little time or respect for his own compatriots. Not even a writhing, scantily clad Anita Ekberg (singing her nightclub specialty "Climb up the Garden Wall") can tear him away from his deliberations. And when, later, he unknowingly kills the holy man who saved his life, you know, intuitively, that there is to be no happy ending for this lost soul.

Mature is stoicism personified, whether in the thick of battle or under the lash. Steadfast and courageous he boasts, "My father once said I should be flogged to death. He tried, cousin, but he failed." For his open defiance, he is flogged twice in the film, first by his father and then on a second occasion, resulting in his death, to save the life of Wilding (the two rivals having developed a mutual respect for each other).

Lensed in CinemaScope and shot in Morocco under Terence Young's deft direction, the film moves at a brisk pace, with its many action scenes (some borrowed from the 1939 version of *The Four Feathers*) of charging horsemen, rifle-volleying soldiers, and feats of derring-do from both Mature and Wilding as they try to outwit one another. The theme would be picked up again in 1967 with Yul Brynner and Trevor Howard in *The Long Duel*. The realism of the battle scenes was such that the first aid crew were kept busy with both stars and extras suffering injury. Michael Wilding cracked three ribs and Mature suffered a concussion from an ill-timed blow.[2]

Charming leading man Michael Wilding, who was Elizabeth Taylor's second husband (from 1952 to 1957), started out as a commercial artist before the acting bug caught him. He is best remembered for a series of elegant society comedies he made with Anna Neagle, such as *Piccadilly Incident* (1946), *The Courtneys of Curzon Street* (1947), *Spring in Park Lane* (1948) and *Maytime in Mayfair* (1949). He also made two films for Alfred Hitchcock, *Under Capricorn* (1949) and *Stage Fright* (1950).

Zarak may have done little to further Mature's career, or for that matter Michael Wilding's, but it did offer a leg up for Patrick McGoohan, whose glowing mentions in the press for his part of Moor Larkin prompted Rank to star him in *High Tide at Noon* (1957), *Hell Drivers* (1957) and *The Gypsy and the Gentlemen* (1958).[3] He then went on to greater fame in the television series *Danger Man* (1964–1967) and *The Prisoner* (1967–1968).

In the final scene, following the death of Zarak, we are left no wiser as to the reason for his actions. When Larkin comments that even though he was a great fighter, Zarak hated them to the end, Michael responds, "Perhaps so, but if that's true, even greater love hath no man, than that he lay down his life for his enemy."

TV Times Film & Video Guide: "Although never quite credible, this is a colorful adventure yarn…. The film was a hit with the public, although not kindly received by the critics."

The box-office success of the film prompted Warwick to remake it as another Mature feature under the title *The Bandit of Zhobe* (1958).

Interpol

Columbia, 1957

Cast: Victor Mature (Charles Sturgis); Anita Ekberg (Gina Broger); Trevor Howard (Frank McNally); Bonar Colleano (Amalio); Dorothy Alison (Helen); Andre Morell (Commissioner Breckner); Martin Benson (Capt. Varolli); Eric Pohlmann (Etienne Fayala); Peter Illing (Capt. Baris); Sydney Tafler (Curtis); Lionel Murton (Murphy); Sid James (Joe — First Bartender); Danny Green (Second Bartender); Alec Mango (Salko); Marne Maitland (Guido Martinelli); Harold Kasket (Kalish); Van Boolen (Luggage Clerk); Brian Nissen (Alison); Peter Elliot (Badek); Yana (Singer); Charles Lloyd Pack (English Tourist); Al Mulock (Interrogator); Alfred Burke (Vincent Cashling); Maurice Browning (Man with Stick); Cyril Shaps (Warden); Paul Stassino (Customs Inspector); Gaylord Cavallaro (Amalio's Brother); Brian Wilde (The Monk); Russell Waters (Company Man); Richard Molinas (Borgese); Wolfe Morris (Morgue Attendant).

Crew: Irving Allen, Albert R. Broccoli (Producers); Phil C. Samuel (Associate Producer); John Gilling (Director); A.J. Forrest (Story): John Paxton (Screenplay); Ted Moore (Cinematography); Richard Rodney Bennett (Music); Paul Sheriff (Art Direction); Elsa Fennell (Costume Design); Roy Ashton (Makeup); Alec Gibb, Bluey Hill (Assistant Directors); Don Saunders (Sound); Richard Best (Editor). Running time: 92 minutes.

Working alongside Interpol, FBI narcotics agent Charles Sturgis (Victor Mature) is assigned to track down a gang of dope peddlers whose unknown, psychotic leader Frank McNally murdered Sturgis' sister. Smart and ruthless, McNally uses his girlfriend, the beautiful Gina Broger, as a courier. When Gina is finally arrested by Interpol, she helps Sturgis track down his quarry. The pursuit of McNally takes Sturgis to many cities including London, Rome and Athens, before ending up in the docks of New York, where Sturgis finally corners the criminal mastermind, killing him in a shootout as he tries to board a freighter with his $3 million dope consignment.

"This is a picture about DOPE!"
"EXPOSED! The international narcotics kings ... and their women!"
"She looks like an angel ... does the work of the devil!"

Long before Gene Hackman was busting up drug rings in the *French Connection* films (in 1971 and 1975), Mature had his sights on the evil pushers of dope in the brisk little English thriller *Interpol* (1957). Up until this point there had been many fine films addressing the perils of alcohol addiction, but very few associated with drug abuse. Frank Sinatra, James Mason and Cameron Mitchell played characters who had succumbed to drugs in *The Man with the Golden Arm* (1955), *Bigger Than Life* (1956) and *Monkey on My Back* (1957) respectively, and audiences were certainly shocked with the powerful anti-drugs message they conveyed. But aside from these tales of individual addiction, the subject of drug trafficking and the agencies that were set up to fight the illegal trade, was a fertile area yet to be explored by filmmakers. Aspiring English director John Gilling set the ball rolling with this mid-budget crime thriller before going on to make his name in television with several successful series which also enjoyed an international theme such as *The Saint* (1962–1969) and *The Champions* (1968–1969). He will also be remembered for directing several Hammer films including *The Reptile* and *The Plague of the Zombies* (both 1966).

With its headquarters in Lyon, France, Interpol was established in 1927 as an agency to promote the widest possible mutual assistance between all criminal police authorities. One such authority was the U.S. Bureau of Narcotics, here represented by Mature as agent Charles Sturgis, a role that saw the actor on familiar ground as an embittered character seeking revenge on the person who killed his loved one, in this instance his sister, who was strangled by the villain of the piece, played by Trevor Howard.

In his previous Warwick production *Safari*, Mature's personal crusade saw him out to get the Mau Mau killer who murdered his son, a killer who was known to him, but in *Interpol* his adversary is unknown and elusive. Playing against type, Howard snugly fits into the role of the charmingly sinister villain, who delivers his veiled threats and barbed humor brandishing a cigarette holder, clearly paving the way for Charles Grey's Ernst Stavro in *Diamonds Are Forever* (1971). As if, from previous experience, acknowledging that the villains always steal the show (Richard Widmark from *Kiss of Death*, and Richard Conte from *Cry of the City*), Mature offers little acting competition for Howard, going about his part in a surly and straightforward manner. But even a pedestrian Mature grabs your attention, as his world-weary character tries to make sense of it all after the death of his sister. When his boss asks, "Where have you been?" he despondently responds, "Crawling around on my belly in the gutter, looking for dope peddlers, needle pushers — same filthy thing, day in and day out." It's almost as if Mature was weary of playing the good guy, day in and day out, and was desperate to show his darker side, which to certain degrees had found an outlet in *Betrayed*, *The Egyptian* and *Zarak*. Indeed, it would have been a fascinating exercise if the two leads had swapped roles, with Howard, reprising his Major Calloway from *The Third Man*, chasing an evil, grinning, heavy-lidded Mature around the world.

Inactive for much of the previous year (1956), and desperate for a good script, Howard was reluctant to do *Interpol*, commenting about the lead female star, Anita Ekberg, "I

Resourceful FBI agent Charles Sturgis (Mature, right) pumps fellow American Amalio (Bonar Colleano) for information in the scenic crime drama *Interpol* (Columbia, 1957).

thought there was something more worthwhile in life than acting with an ex-beauty queen."¹ The film could have easily been his last. During a chase scene in Rome, the red Mercedes car he was traveling in was spotted by a policeman who, unaware that filming was taking place, fired two shots into it mistaking it, for an identical car that had been involved in a bank robbery the day before. To avoid the press when his car stopped, Howard ran across some electrified railway lines and narrowly escaped being electrocuted.² But the film did have some compensations for the actor: location shooting in Rome and Genoa, and the good company of Mature, with whom Howard had enormous fun both on and off the set. Howard recalled how Mature asked him back to his hotel suite in Rome to discuss a couple of scenes, and on arriving at the room, he found the actor on the bed with three sexy-looking ladies. It was all a set-up, of course, but Mature's Italian girlfriend who turned up unexpectedly shortly thereafter, didn't appreciate the phony orgy joke, throwing all of Mature's clothes out of the window into the crowded piazza below. Looking on with classic British reserve, Howard said to Mature, "You went to all this trouble for me. How very thoughtful."³

Whether playing a hero or villain, Howard was always good value in a film career that gave us the likes of *Brief Encounter* (1945), *The Third Man* (1949), *The Clouded Yellow* (1950) and *Sons and Lovers* (1960), for which he received an Oscar nomination for Best Supporting

Actor, and *Ryan's Daughter* (1970). Miss Sweden of 1951, Anita Ekberg will forever be remembered for cavorting in Rome's Trevi fountain in Fellini's *La dolce vita* (1960).

Preoccupied with chasing the dope king and his associates around the globe, Mature has little time for romantic attachments in the film. And to prove he's not a sap for a pretty face, he tells Howard's moll Ekberg, "The minute I'm tired of chasing you, or anything happens to me, they'll pick you up quicker than a twenty dollar gold piece." When she responds, "I sound fascinating," he snarls, "I stopped being fascinated by dope peddlers a long time ago."

According to an article in the *Daily Sketch* (a U.K. newspaper, later merged into *The Daily Mail*), a hundred guests arrived at the Savoy banquet room to say hello to Mature and Ekberg, but the latter didn't turn up (she'd gone to Elstree Studios for a spot of dubbing). With Scotch in hand, Mature murmured to a reporter, "She should be here. I'm supposed to be at the studios as well. I'm here." Shrugging his shoulders, Mature went on, "But I'm Victor Mature, She's Anita Ekberg. How many films has she made? Two? Or is it three?" Mature had apparently never seen her on screen, which was not unusual as he seldom went to the movies. Mature had good reason to be annoyed; with a 25 percent financial stake in the film, the actor had always courted publicity to help promotion, and Ekberg's absence could have been seen as a rebuff. Later, away from the crowds, Mature talked to the reporter about his two previous wives: "It'll take me ten years to pay off the alimony on mine." That's why, as the article went on, "Mature prefers girlfriends to wives for the time being." Towards the end of the conversation, while eating a steak, Mature was invited on a tour of the Soho clubs by an official and his wife. The actor declined, saying he didn't like clubs, but to appease the official's wife, who was upset by his answer, he cut and offered her a piece of his steak, which prompted her husband to sigh in admiration, "A great guy. A real great guy."[4]

The role of Charles Sturgis was Mature's fourth and last law enforcement officer (after *Cry of the City*, *The Las Vegas Story*, and *Dangerous Mission*). Aimed at an international audience and entitled *Pickup Alley* in America, *Interpol* is, despite its "B" movie credentials, a neat little thriller which grabs your attention like one of those old '50s pulp paperbacks — tawdry and lurid, but great fun.

Variety: "Mature plays it straight as the relentless pursuer, but he doesn't go in for the kid glove treatment."

Picturegoer: "Mature bashes through the business like a sleep-walker who is just marking time until the alarm clock shrills."

TV Times Film and Video Guide: "Victor Mature, frowns and glowers his way through this story."

The Long Haul

Columbia, 1957

Cast: Victor Mature (Harry Miller); Gene Anderson (Connie Miller); Patrick Allen (Joe Easy); Diana Dors (Lynn); Liam Redmond (Casey); Peter Reynolds (Frank); Michael Wade (Butch Miller); Dervis Ward (Mutt); Murray Kash (Jeff); Jameson Clark (MacNaughton); John Harvey (Supt. Macrea); Roland Brand (Army Sergeant); Stanley Rose (Foreman); Barry Raymond (Depot Manager); John Welsh (Doctor); Meire Tzelniker

(Nat Fine); Madge Brindley (Fat Woman); Van Boolen, Harcourt Curacao, Norman Rossington, Martin Shaban, Freddie Watts (Drivers).
Crew: Maxwell Setton (Producer); Tom Morahan (Associate Producer); Ken Hughes (Screenplay and Director); Mervyn Mills (Novel); Basil Emmott (Cinematography); Trevor Duncan (Music); Richard Taylor (Musical Director); John Hoesli (Art Direction); Fred Slark, Ronnie Spencer (Assistant Directors); Tommy Yeardye (Stunt Double); Peter Thornton (Sound); Raymond Poulton (Editor). Running time: 100 minutes.

Ex-serviceman Harry Miller (Victor Mature) wants to return to the States after being demobbed, but is persuaded by his English wife Connie to take a job driving a truck for her uncle's haulage company in Liverpool. As a consequence of interfering with a staged robbery of a fellow driver's cargo, he loses the job. He then gets involved with a smuggling operation run by Joe Easy, and starts an affair with Joe's girlfriend Lynn. Implicated in the death of a friend killed in a fake accident, Harry is hunted by the police, and agrees to transport Joe, Lynn and a truckload of furs to a pre-arranged rendezvous with a freighter off the Scottish coast, which will enable them to flee the country. With the ship in sight, Joe tries to kill Harry, and is himself killed in the fight that ensues. Guilt-ridden, Harry returns home to try and straighten things out with his wife and son. When the police take him into custody, it is with the knowledge that his family will be waiting for him when he is released from prison.

"Mobsters Invade Teamsters!"
"SILK, FLESH AND DYNAMITE!"

Opening credit scenes don't get any better than this one, with a U.S. army truck making its way along the Bavarian highway in the dead of night, wipers working overtime to clear the lashing rain, and all to the pulsating beat of Trevor Duncan's noir-laden music score. So strap yourself in for the rollercoaster ride ahead.

Marking a return to the world of film noir after his last flirtation with the genre *Violent Saturday* (1955), *The Long Haul* saw Mature reprising the role of an essentially good man who, due to human frailties and circumstances beyond his control, falls foul of criminals, much like his characters from *Kiss of Death* and *Gambling House*. Liverpool-born director Ken Hughes skillfully taps into Mature's inherent fallibility and moody countenance, coaxing the actor to one of his best later performances. Hughes was no stranger to the crime genre, directing some great little thrillers including *The House Across the Lake* (1954; U.S. title: *Heatwave*) and *Joe Macbeth* (1955), before going on to make *The Trials of Oscar Wilde* (1960) and *Chitty Chitty Bang Bang* (1968).

A great example of an earthy British noir, *The Long Haul* was filmed in England and Scotland, and gave Mature the opportunity to star alongside the adorable Diana Dors. I can only assume that Warwick Films thought Mature's powerful physique and larger-than-life persona could only be shown to best advantage when opposite top-heavy, curvaceous blondes, having made one film with Janet Leigh, two with Anita Ekberg, and now one with Britain's answer to Marilyn Monroe; Diana Dors. In Dors' latest biography *Hurricane in Mink*, author David Bret records that Robert Mitchum was initially down to play the role of Harry, but his agent persuaded him to drop the project claiming that working with Dors would seriously damage his reputation.[1] It certainly didn't tarnish Mature's reputation from either a personal or professional perspective. The two simply sizzle on screen together, but off-screen they went their separate ways. When Mature was asked if he found his platinum

Trucker Harry Miller (Mature) gets more than he bargained for when he falls for femme fatale Lynn (Diana Dors) in the riveting British film noir *The Long Haul* (Columbia, 1957).

blonde co-star sexy, he replied, "Blonde? I'm color- blind!" Dors in turn thought pretty much the same about Mature, instead preferring his stunt double Tommy Yeardye, with whom she had an affair. In the past, Yeardye has also stunt doubled for Rock Hudson.[2] During filming, Dors found herself the subject of an episode of *This Is Your Life*.

Of the six films Mature made for Warwick Films, this is by far my favorite, with *Safari* in second place. For me the film has many appeals: a great cast (Mature, Dors, Gene Anderson, Patrick Allen and Liam Redmond); great locations, a jazzy score, a topical human dilemma (should he dump his dowdy wife for a blonde bombshell?), wonderfully nostalgic Leyland trucks (the Octopus 8 wheel truck, to be precise) and a thrilling finale where Mature and Allen slug it out. The film is also novel, in that for the first time in his crime film repertoire, Mature is not upstaged by a scene-stealing villain. Patrick Allen makes a great bad guy, but there are no prop accessories like a wheel-chair-bound elderly lady waiting for a fall (*Kiss of Death*), dropped inhaler (*Violent Saturday*) or cigarette holder (*Interpol*) to help the villain grab the limelight. Both Mature and Allen are nicely balanced in a briskly paced tale that holds your attention from beginning to end.

Famous for his distinctive resonant voice, which provided him with a lot of voiceover work, Allen is best remembered for the television series *Crane* (1963–1965) and for one of my favorite British sci-fi films *Night of the Big Heat* (1967; U.S. title: *Island of the Burning*

Damned). He puts his great voice to good use in *The Long Haul*, sounding very much like Richard Basehart, and with his crewcut and cigar jammed in his mouth, he's definitely a dead ringer for that newspaper editor fella whose forever hounding Tobey Maguire in the Spider-Man movies.

As Mature's wife, the wonderful actress Gene Anderson skillfully conveys a downtrodden woman, concealing a deep secret that their son was fathered by Mature's army buddy. Anderson was best known for her television work including several appearances in the *Douglas Fairbanks, Jr. Presents* (1955–1956) productions made at the British National Studios at Borehamwood. She was married to the British actor Edward Judd and they worked together in two films, the crime thriller *The Shakedown* (1960) and the cult science fiction classic *The Day the Earth Caught Fire* (1961). She died in 1965 at age 34. At the time of filming, Anderson told *Picture Show* magazine that she was enjoying her part in *The Long Haul*, commenting, "Romance and human drama play a strong hand in this thriller of lorry life." Mature told the same interviewer, Edith Nepean, that he was no stranger to lorry driving, having driven trucks during his school holidays for his father, a Kentucky businessman.[3]

The film's sleazy, drab, dark surroundings of haulage depots, roadside cafés, soulless highways and guest houses are in complete contrast to Mature's last Warwick production *Interpol*, which took admidst the scenic delights of New York, Lisbon, London, Rome, Naples and Athens. Against the austere surroundings, Mature looms large, his physical presence enhanced by a wardrobe that successively sees him sporting a duffel coat, bomber jacket and a trenchcoat. Like his attire, his moods are constantly changing on a sixpence, but, ever resourceful, he takes all that's thrown at him on the chin. When after leaving the army, his wife persuades him to take a dead end job trucking the highways out of Liverpool, he resignedly tells her, "It looks like I'm gonna quit working for Uncle Sam and start working for Uncle George." And later, up to his neck in haulage skullduggery, transporting a consignment of stolen furs, he snarls at Allen, "Those skins will be so hot, they'll sweat!" On the ten-week filming, which saw him mostly being sloshed with water and beaten up, Mature simply had this to say: "It was no intellectual exercise."

This was Mature's second significant role as father and husband (after *Violent Saturday*), but it was the first time his family man, or indeed any of his characters, would be lured into danger by a femme fatale. With the exception of Hedy Lamarr from *Samson and Delilah* and Lizabeth Scott from *Easy Living*, Mature could usually hold his own where females were concerned, but not so in *The Long Haul*, where his weakness for forbidden fruit is laid bare. Mature's anguished expressions and soul-searching eyes powerfully convey the troubled nature of his character. A tough but vulnerable character, he sometimes gives the impression he might not make it to home base in one piece. But make it home he does, to hand himself into the police, leaving Dors it wrap it all up with a great closing line. When cabbie Sam Kydd asks her, "Back to the docks, miss?" she sums up the grim finality of it all when she dejectedly responds, "Do you know the Congo Club? Just take me there."

It could be argued that the film is simply an updated ... British variation of the Jules Dassin trucker classic *Thieves Highway* (1949) starring Richard Conte (Mature's adversary from *Cry of the City*). Update or not, *The Long Haul* is a wonderfully moody film that deserves greater recognition (few review books refer to it) and, like many of Mature's films, perhaps a reassessment of its cinematic value.

Trucker films are few and far between, so make the most of this one. For me, it sits comfortably alongside the aforementioned *Thieves Highway*. *They Drive by Night* (1940), and the brilliant *Hell Drivers* (1957).

The Long Haul was released on a double-feature with *The Hard Man*, a Western starring Guy Madison, with the tagline, "*The Long Haul* will DELIGHT You — *The Hard Man* Will EXCITE You!" — which led to both films being banned in parts of Europe and America.

Variety: "Mature makes a convincing figure of the straightforward guy who turns cheat on his wife and his work, and Diana Dors gives sufficient reason as the blonde who helps him do it."

Picturegoer: "Dirty work at every crossroads, domestic dissention and Diana Dors, with Victor Mature working that left eyebrow of his overtime…"

The film must have been a brilliant advert for Leyland trucks, as they simply go anywhere, up mountain, down dale and over rocky streams without breaking into a sweat, even with one wheel missing.

No Time to Die (Tank Force)

Columbia, 1958

Cast: Victor Mature (Sgt. David H. Thatcher); Leo Genn (Sgt. Kendall); Bonar Colleano (Polish POW); Anthony Newley (Pvt. "Tiger" Noakes); Alfred Burke (Capt. Ritter); Richard Marner (German Colonel); Martin Boddey (SS Colonel); Percy Herbert (1st English Soldier); Kenneth Cope (2nd English Soldier); Davis Lodge (Maj. Fred Patterson); Sean Kelly (Barlett); Kenneth Fortescue (Cpl. Johnson); Maxwell Shaw (Sheikh); George Coulouris (Italian POW Camp Commandant); Luciana Paluzzi (Carola — Manger of the Lido); Robert Rietty (Alberto); Bob Simmons (Mustapha); Ernest Walder (German Corporal); Peter Elliot (Italian Officer); George Pravda (German Sergeant); Julian Sherrier (2nd Italian Officer); Robert Bruce (Italian Driver); Andreas Malandrinos (Italian Cook); Alan Tilvern (Silverio); Anne Aubrey (Italian Girl).

Crew: Irving Allen, Albert R. Broccoli (Producers); Phil C. Samuel (Associate Producer); Terence Young (Director); Merle Miller (Story); Terence Young, Richard Maibaum (Screenplay); Ted Moore (Cinematography); Kenneth V. Jones (Music); Muir Mathieson (Musical Director); John Box (Art Direction); John McCorry (Costume Design); William Lodge, Tom Smith (Makeup); Cliff Richardson, Roy Whybrow (Special Effects); Bluey Hill (Assistant Director); Alan Pattillo (Sound); Bert Rule (Editor). Running time: 103 minutes.

Sergeant Daniel Thatcher (Victor Mature), an American, is serving with a British tank corps in North Africa during World War II. Following a tank battle, he and most of the unit including Sgt. Kendall and Cpl. Noakes are captured by the Germans and placed in an Italian POW camp. Thatcher, whose wife died in a concentration camp, is wanted by the Nazis following his attempted assassination of Josef Goebbels, Hitler's right-hand man. Thatcher and Kendall escape the camp with several of the men and try to make their way back to Allied lines across the Libyan desert. They are captured by a sheik who supports the Nazis, and Thatcher is tortured before a compassionate German captain helps them to flee the Arab camp. En route, they capture a German tank and head back to their lines pursued by the enemy. Kendal dies of an earlier wound before a massed tank battle in which the British gain a substantial victory. After burying their friend, Thatcher and fellow tanker Noakes hop aboard a British tank to rejoin the fight.

"When Iron Men in Iron Monsters Fought for a Continent!"

"The Titanic Battle of World War II!"
"Hitting the Screen with Irresistible Force!"

Only a handful of actors in the 1950s had the look of an iron man, and Mature was certainly amongst them. His iron man look made him one of the best action stars in the business, whether in Western, costume drama or film noir. However, despite an impressive list of action credits, it wasn't until 1958, when he starred in *No Time to Die*, that he got an opportunity to play an American soldier fighting in World War II. Admittedly, he came close to it in three other wartime features, playing a Dutch resistance fighter in *Betrayed*, a Korean War combatant in The *Glory Brigade*, and a naval officer turned researcher in *The Sharkfighters*. But the role of a fighting soldier in the great conflict had to await Mature's fifth picture under his Warwick Films contract, *No Time to Die*, which was titled *Tank Force* on its American release.

A Yank serving in the British forces was not a new theme for Warwick Films, with Alan Ladd fighting in the British paras in their first feature, *The Red Beret* (1953).* (Tyrone Power kicked it all off in his 1941 wartime flag-waver *A Yank in the RAF*.)

War films involving tanks are always guaranteed to put butts in seats, and even though *No Time to Die* is not in the same class as *Sahara* (1943), *Battle of the Bulge* (1965) or *Kelly's Heroes* (1970), it's still a thoroughly entertaining adventure yarn which, when you throw in a hefty dose of prisoner of war escape antics, makes the perfect film with which to wile away a lazy afternoon. The film has a particularly rousing score by Kenneth V. Jones, who also scored Mature's *The Bandit of Zhobe*.

The film is riddled with familiar situations and clichés, but it excellently showcases Mature's ability to convey steely determination when battling against the odds. Whether under enemy fire or suffering torture, he is a man who will never be broken. A resourceful soldier, he has little time for doing things by the book, or as he dismissively describes it to Leo Genn, "in accordance with King's Regulations." His reckless disregard for danger and his own safety has come about following the death of his wife, a German Jew, in Belsen concentration camp. Her death has left him understandably bitter, angry and humorless. When a fellow soldier enquires as to how he speaks German so well, he snarls, "I used to talk to my wife occasionally. Any objections?"

Like Mature's Zarak, who eventually wins the respect of his British counterpart played by Michael Wilding, his Sgt. Thatcher in *No Time to Die* gains the trust and admiration of the stiff upper lip Sgt. Kendall played by Leo Genn, who initially sees Thatcher as an irresponsible "loose cannon."

The London-born Genn qualified as barrister in 1928 before taking up a theatrical career that led to his film first role in *Immortal Gentleman* (1935). Possessing a memorable velvet voice, he excelled in supporting roles as calm, unflappable types, and was seen at his best in such films as *The Velvet Touch* (1948), *The Wooden Horse* (1950), and his Oscar-nominated role in *Quo Vadis* (1951). Genn also supported Alan Ladd in Warwick's first production *The Red Beret*. After serving in the Royal Artillery during the war, he put his legal experience to good use in the investigation and prosecution of Nazi war crimes perpetrated at the Belsen concentration (coincidently, the same camp where Mature's wife dies in the film).

My father was stationed at the RAF base (RAF Abington Parachute School in Abington, Oxfordshire) when Alan Ladd made The Red Beret. *He not only got his autograph, but he, and some workmates, also played football with the star and crew during break times.*

In addition to Genn, Mature enjoyed the support of Anthony Newley, in a cheeky, chappy role that cemented his position as a screen actor. Many years later when Newley became a big Broadway success with his groundbreaking *Stop the World—I Want to Get Off*, Mature, who had seen the show on several occasions, approached the star in his dressing room and pleaded with him to take out some of the changes that had been introduced, which Mature felt detracted from the show.[1]

The film also featured Alfred Burke as a German captain who hates Nazis. This was his third time in a Mature movie following *The Long Haul* and *Interpol*. He was best known for his role as the down-at-heel private eye Frank Marker in the television series *Public Eye* (1965–1975). And let's not forget Bonar Colleano as a vicious Polish killer, also making his third appearance with Mature following *Zarak* and *Interpol*. Born into a circus family, and typically cast as a wisecracking Yank, always on the make, Colleano is best remembered for films such as *The Way to the Stars* (1945), *Once a Jolly Swagman* (1948) and *Pool of London* (1951). He would go on to make one more film after *Tank Force* before his untimely death in 1958, aged 34, when he crashed his car in Birkenhead, England.

Mature's respect for his fans was clearly highlighted during the making of the film when in Tripoli he was besieged by Italian, French, British and even veiled Arab women asking for his autograph. When he was offered an extra guard at the hotel to keep him from being bothered, he turned it down, explaining, "I figure that I'm the highest paid sergeant in the world. I should make somewhere in the region of $200,000 out of this picture and these people put me in that income bracket. Let 'em all come."

Variety: "Individually the actors turn in competent jobs, but their roles are all overwritten and fall too neatly into slots. Mature is the tough, brash American who really is a hero. Genn is the frightfully decent King's Regulation British sergeant."

Radio Times Guide to Films had pretty much the same to say: "Every racial stereotype in the book stands to attention as Mature lurches from one heroic deed to the next, culminating in a joust with a Panzer tank."

China Doll

United Artists, 1958

Cast: Victor Mature (Capt. Cliff Brandon); Li Hua Li (Shu-Jen); Ward Bond (Father Cairns); Bob Mathias (Capt. Phil Gates); Johnny Desmond (Sgt. Steve Hill); Stuart Whitman (Lt. Dan O'Neill); Elaine Devry (Alice Nichols); Ann McCrea (Mona Perkins); Danny Chang (Ellington); Denver Pyle (Col. Wiley); Don "Red" Barry (Sgt. Hal Foster); Tige Andrews (Cpl. Carlo Menotti); Steve Mitchell (Dave Reisner); Ken Perry (Sgt. Ernie Fleming); Ann Paige (Sally); Gregg Barton (Airman); Bill White, Jr. (Forsyth); Tita Aragon (Shiao-Mee Brandon).

Crew: Frank Borzage (Producer-Director); Robert E. Morrison (Associate Producer); James Benson Nablo, Thomas F. Kelly (Story "Time Is a Memory"); Kitty Buhler (Screenplay); William H. Clothier (Cinematography); Henry Vars (Music); Howard Richmond (Art Direction); Jack Mills (Set Decorations); Angela Alexander, Wesley Jeffries (Costume Design); Layne Britton (Makeup); Lew Borzage (Assistant Director); Fred Carson (Stunts); Earl Crain, Sr. (Sound); Jack Murray (Editor). Running time: 99 minutes.

During World War II in 1943, Air Force captain Cliff Brandon (Victor Mature) is serving in China flying essential supplies to ground troops after the Japanese have cut off all the U.S. supply lines. Weary and disillusioned by the loss of his men after two years of service, he finds his only solace in the contents of a bottle. One drunken evening, he inadvertently purchases the services of a Chinese girl, Shu-Jen, as a housekeeper for three months. Advised by his friend Father Cairns that it would hurt her family's honor if he sent her back, he lets her stay, and in time they fall in love. When he discovers that she is carrying his child, they get married, but tragedy strikes when she arrives at Cliff's new airbase with her baby daughter and is killed in an air attack. When Cliff returns to the base after a mission and learns that Shu-Jen is dead and that the baby is missing, he orders the plane to leave without him. Discovering the baby alive, hidden in a pile of rubble, he places his identification tags in its hands before he is killed manning an anti-aircraft gun during another enemy attack. The child survives the war and spends the next thirteen years in Chinese orphanages before being welcomed to America by the members of her father's old air crew.

"It Splits the China Skies with Its Thunder! The Fighting Tiger ...
Trapped in a Desperate Adventure with the Girl He Bought!"

"China Dynamite. From the Himalayas to the China Sea

... The Battle Adventure

... The Love Adventure

... The Desperate Adventure of the Flying Tiger
and the Girl He Bought!"

The storyline of *China Doll* is probably the most unusual in Mature's film career. The idea of a U.S. flyer unintentionally buying the housekeeping services of a young Chinese girl after a boozy night on the town, then marrying the girl, seems bizarre to say the least. But through sensitive direction and great acting by all concerned, the film actually works, providing Mature with the biggest tearjerker in his film career. That it should expertly tug at your heartstrings should be no great surprise, considering that it was directed by one of the all-time masters of the romantic drama, Frank Borzage. Reaching his career peak in the late silent and early sound era, Borzage pioneered the use of soft focus and gauzed photography, which helped to convey a lush visual romanticism in his films. The idea of love triumphing over adversity was a recurring theme in his work, finding full expression in his *Seventh Heaven* (1927), *Bad Girl* (1931), *A Farewell to Arms* (1932) and *Three Comrades* (1938)—the first two winning him Academy Award for Best Director.

China Doll marked the return of Borzage to film work after a nine-year absence, and once again he found himself pursuing his trademark theme of two lovers trying to sustain their love, this time against a cultural divide and the backdrop of World War II. Borzage and Mature had planned to set up a production company together, but this never came off. Made by John Wayne's Batjac company, *China Doll* (working title: *Time Is a Memory*) was the first of two co-productions between Batjac and Romina Productions. Their second production was *Escort West* (1959), also starring Mature.

With his heroic death at the end of the film, this was probably the first time audiences had to get their handkerchiefs out at a Mature movie. Sure, fans may have come close to tears when Samson toppled the temple or when Chief Crazy Horse went to the happy hunting grounds in the sky, but such larger-than-life historical characters didn't quite get under your skin the way Mature's Capt. Cliff Brandon did. Although embittered and disillusioned, he is essentially just an ordinary guy, looking out for his men as they try to fly the Himalayan Hump—a perilous mission which prompts him to say to his crew, "When your dog tags get back to the States, it's my job to see that you're with them." But it is evident that the strain of command and one too many missions has severely tainted his outlook on life. When his colonel tells him that the world isn't such a bad place to be in, he despondently responds, "Isn't it. colonel? Everyone leaves it, sooner or later."

On his poignant death in the film, Mature had this to say: "It always arouses my fans when I die in a picture. They hate to see a thing like that happen to a wonderful guy like me, and it drives them to write me all sorts of letters of sympathy and commiseration. I like to get mail—especially fan mail."[1]

On the nature of the heroic action roles that took him all around the world, Mature modestly commented, "I am the bravest of the brave." As World War II screen exits go, Mature's forlorn figure, valiantly firing away as Japanese Zeros strafe all around, is up there with the best of them. When I say Zeros, I should say American Corsairs doctored to make them look like Zeros. And while we're on the subject of props, one day during production, riders along U.S. Highway 6, main turnpike to Reno and Las Vegas, found the route peppered with road signs in Chinese calligraphic writing and five hundred Chinese soldiers winding their way to Saugas and Solemint Canyon. This caused a lot of confusion until it

East meets West when tough American flyer Capt. Cliff Brandon (Mature) falls for his housekeeper, the delicate Chinese beauty Shu-Jen (Li Hua Li), in the wartime tearjerker *China Doll* (United Artists, 1958).

was explained they were shooting a scene from the film.[2] It was originally planned that the film would be shot in Formosa, but when Borzage saw the rolling dry-bush terrain of Saugas he thought it favorably matched the photographs he had seen of Kunming in China.

China Doll is more about romance than action, as the two doomed lovers, Mature and Li Hua Li, do their bit for cross-cultural marriages, a theme that was explored in *Love Is a Many-Splendored Thing* (1955) and *Sayonara* (1957). That the story should come over as particularly touching is very much down to the heartfelt performances from both Mature and Li Hua Li, who instill in their characters a great sense of strength, entwined with a fragility that has you rooting for them as we follow their doomed love affair to its tragic conclusion.

After completing several pure action films, Mature clearly relishes the chance to show a more tender side to his character, with his well-meaning but awkward attempts to woo the delicate Li Hua Li coming over as both sincere and touching. In the wrong hands, the love theme could have come over as contrived and clumsy, but under Borzage's deft direction, it works a treat. The director once commented, "Romance is what I want to sell in my pictures, and honest sentiment, too. I want to make women cry. The purpose of good drama is to purge the emotions." I don't know about women, but it certainly had my tear ducts welling up.

Before arriving in America, Li Hua Li was already a big box office star in Southeast Asia, with her own studio and production company. In addition to acting, she wrote, produced and directed her own films. Before turning to acting, co-star Bob Mathias won the Olympic Decathlon in 1948 and 1952. John Wayne, head of Batjac Productions, was grooming him for stardom, but this was not to be and he later went into politics, serving as a Congressman for the state of California. Stuart Whitman was very much cut from the same cloth as Mature, with his thick mop of black hair, beefy build and craggy face. A former boxer and one-time light heavyweight contender, he was nominated for the Academy Award for Best Actor for his role in *The Mark* (1961). His other notable credits include *The Comacheros* (1961) alongside John Wayne, *Those Magnificent Men in Their Flying Machines* (1965) and in the Western television series *Cimarron Strip* (1967–1968). *China Doll* also had a slot for Johnny Desmond, who sprang to stardom as the singer of the Glenn Miller traveling Army Air Forces Orchestra. Ward Bond puts in an excellent performance as a cleric and Mature's confidant.

Variety: "Mature displays his share of love, emotion and humor."

Picturegoer: "For a war film, it is often drearily dull and the script is mostly a pain in the neck. And there seems no good reason why in the end it should be so moving, except for Mature's sincere portrayal of a man who found happiness too late."

In total, Mature would meet his death in nine films, with *China Doll* marking the seventh occasion. But, perhaps more interesting than that, was the fact this was the first time Mature didn't get to kiss the girl. A great believer in Chinese Tradition, Li Hua Li refused to be kissed on screen.[3] Poor old Mature. I guess there are times when one has to suffer for one's art.

Escort West

United Artists, 1959

Cast: Victor Mature (Ben Lassiter); Elaine Stewart (Beth Drury); Faith Domergue (Martha Drury); Reba Waters (Abbey Lassiter); Noah Beery, Jr. (Lt. Jamison); Leo Gordon (Trooper Vogel); Rex Ingram (Nelson Walker); John Hubbard (Lt. Weeks); Harry

Carey, Jr. (Trooper Travis); Slim Pickens (Cpl. Wheeler); Roy Barcroft (Sgt. Doyle); William Ching (Capt. Howard Poole); Ken Curtis (Trooper Burch); Claire Du Brey (Mrs. Kate Fenniman); Syd Saylor (Elwood Fenniman); X Brands (Tago); Chuck Hayward, Charles Soldani (Indians).

Crew: Robert E. Morrison, Nathan H. Edwards (Producers); Francis D. Lyon (Director); Steve Hayes (Story); Leo Gordon, Fred Hartsook (Screenplay); William H. Clothier (Cinematography); Henry Vars (Music); Alfred Ybarra (Art Direction); Mowbray Berkeley (Set Decorations); Elmer Ellsworth, Neva Rames (Costume Design); Layne Britton (Makeup); Dave Koehler (Special Effects); William Beaudine, Jr. (Assistant Director); Fred Carson (Stunts); Earl Crain, Sr. (Sound); Otto Ludwig (Editor). Running time: 75 minutes.

After the American Civil War, former Confederate officer Ben Lassiter (Victor Mature) heads west with his young daughter Abbey to live with his late wife's sister. At a way station they encounter a cavalry patrol that is escorting two sisters, Beth and Mary Drury, to meet an army escort led by Beth's fiancé, Captain Poole. Mary's fiancé was killed by the Confederacy during the war and as a consequence she hates the South. When Ben and Abbey catch up with the patrol at the next way station, they discover that it has been attacked by Modoc Indians; the only survivors are the sisters (hidden in a cellar) and their elderly black servant Nelson, who has been shot in the leg. Two troopers, Vogel and Birch, who were out on patrol at the time, escaped the massacre. Ben makes a litter for Nelson and the party move out, taking the Army payroll which was left behind. During their perilous journey, Ben has to fight off Vogel and Birch (who want the payroll for themselves) as well as warring Modocs, who kill Martha during one encounter. Eventually the group meets up with Captain Poole and his men, who are pinned down by Modoc marksmen, but Ben saves the day when he hunts out and kills the Modoc leader. Having realized that Beth and Ben are in love, Poole steps aside to let the couple begin a new life together.

"Escort West storms through every massacre hell on the map!"

"Rebel on a Rampage!"

Just when you thought Mature had perhaps finally hung up his boots and saddle, after a four-year absence from the Western, he stormed back to delight our oater taste buds with *Escort West*.

Confederate veterans returning home from the American Civil War provided a great backdrop for many a Western tale, and *Escort West* was no exception. Some came back from the conflict vengeful and embittered and, unable to adjust to normal life, went out looking for another reason to vent their anger and frustration like John Wayne in *The Searchers* (1956), Rod Steiger in *Run of the Arrow* (1957) and Clint Eastwood in *The Outlaw Josey Wales*. (1976). Others, like the many Hollywood guises of the James-Younger gang who rode with Quantrill's Raiders during the War, took to a life of crime. In *Horizons West* (1952) with Rock Hudson and Robert Ryan, brothers became pitted against one another on opposing sides of the law.

With his track record of playing characters hellbent on seeking some sort of revenge, for heinous crimes usually committed against his family, Mature might have been expected to play a variation on Wayne's Ethan Edwards' antihero type, bitter and twisted and seeking some form of redemption. But, surprisingly, Mature's ex–Confederate captain, Ben Lassiter, is the complete opposite. He willingly accepts that the South fought and lost, and now it

With the Civil War behind him, former Confederate officer Ben Lassiter finds fresh trouble afoot, while heading west with his daughter Abbey (Reba Waters), in the Western gem *Escort West* (United Artists, 1959).

is time to move on. He has no axe to grind or vengeful quest to pursue, as he simply wants to bring his daughter to Oregon to live with his late wife's sister. And despite all his medals, he is a modest man, telling his daughter who thinks he's a hero, "I'm not a hero, Abbey, I only fought for what I felt to be right."

But we know that it's only a matter of time before this tender, peace-loving man is up to his neck in trouble. And in this Western it comes in all shapes and forms, for as well as rampaging Modocs and renegade soldiers, Mature has to deal with a bitter Faith Domergue, who hates the Confederacy and openly declares it, prompting Mature to tell her, "Look, let's just get one thing straight: We've got a lot of rough country to go over, and I'm not in any mood for a nasty disposition."

Despite being packaged as the next Jane Russell, Faith Domergue's career never quite got off the ground, but she will always be remembered for her on-off relationship with Howard Hughes, and for films such as the Robert Mitchum noir *Where Danger Lives* (1950) and the science fiction films *It Came From Beneath the Sea* and *This Island Earth* (both 1955).

In the early 1950s, MGM signed the shapely Elaine Stewart to a contract with the intention of packaging her as a dark-haired Marilyn Monroe, but like Domergue, her film career remained unfulfilled. She raised many an eyebrow when she posed nude for *Playboy* in September 1959, and rumors abounded in 1958 that she might have been the reason why Mature delayed his marriage to Joy Urwick.

Like Hondo and Shane, Mature's Ben Lassiter is very much the quiet, dignified hero who might not regard himself as a hero, but his courageous deeds, in a series of action scenes, speak for themselves. In face-to-face combat, he first dispenses with one Modoc in a knife duel and, later on, gets the better of another in an exciting duel on horseback, pistols blazing. And if that wasn't enough, he single-handedly carries out an audacious attack on the Modocs in the final reel, throwing a rattlesnake into the face of their leader to gain the ultimate victory.

The film was the second of two co-productions between John Wayne's Batjac and Romina Productions (the first being Mature's *China Doll*). Produced by Wayne's brother Robert E. Morrison and Nate H. Edwards (John Wayne was an uncredited producer), the film was perhaps too small-scale to attract Wayne to the starring role, allowing Mature the opportunity to show a more mellow and dignified side to his screen persona — characteristics that had shown to good effect with his caring family man in *Violent Saturday*. That the film should be tightly edited, to good effect, is no great surprise considering that the director, Francis D. Lyon, was a former editor, winning the Academy Award (with Robert Parrish) for editing one of the greatest boxing films, *Body and Soul* (1947). Moving to directing in the mid-fifties, his films were mainly routine adventures, the best-known being Disney's *The Great Locomotive Chase* (1956). As well as starring in the film, Leo Gordon, everyone's favorite screen heavy, also co-wrote the script. Before making it as a writer and screenwriter, Gordon served time in San Quentin prison for armed robbery. His notable films include *Riot in Cell Block 11* (1954 — filmed in San Quentin) and *Baby Face Nelson* (1957).

Escort West was shot on location at Iverson Ranch in Chatsworth, a desolate corner of the San Fernnado Valley, California. Several weeks of location filming was carried out by a cast and crew of over 200 people. A convoy of forty trucks transported equipment to the site, carefully negotiating a network of barely accessible dirt roads.[1]

The film has much in common with Richard Widmark's excellent Western *The Last Wagon* (1956), with the heroes from both films helping a group of people through the land of hostile Indian, which in *Escort West* came in the form of marauding Modocs — a Native American people who originally lived in the area which is now northeastern California and central Southern Oregon.

In his gray uniform, Mature cuts an impressive figure in the saddle as he attempts to survive clashes with both renegade Yankees and Indians during his perilous journey. But in time-honored fashion, when he meets up with Captain Poole and his men who are pinned down by Modoc marksmen, blue and gray combine forces to fight the common foe, a hard-won unity which provided the basis for such films as *Two Flags West* (1950), *Escape from Fort Bravo* (1953), *Major Dundee* (1965) and *The Undefeated* (1969).

Despite its "B" movie status, this sleeper is a fine, well-crafted Western, in which Mature delivers one of his best understated performances. It definitely deserves wider exposure.

Picturegoer: "Indestructible as ever, Victor Mature oozes blood, guts and the milk of human kindness in a Western as formula as its star's flashing grin in the teeth of adversity."

The Aurum Film Encyclopedia, The Western: "Full of action and well mounted by Lyon with Mature as gruff as can be, the film is a cut above the average Western."

The Bandit of Zhobe

Columbia, 1959

Cast: Victor Mature (Kasim Khan); Anne Aubrey (Zena Crowley); Anthony Newley (Cpl. Stokes); Norman Wooland (Maj. Crowley); Dermot Walsh (Capt. Saunders); Walter Gotell (Azhad); Paul Stassino (Hatti); Larry Taylor (Ahmed); Dennis Shaw (Hussu); Murray Kash (Zecco); Maya Koumani (Tamara); Sean Kelly (Lt. Wylie).

Crew: Irving Allen, Albert R. Broccoli (Producers); Harold Huth (Associate Producer); John Gilling (Director); Richard Maibaum (Story); John Gilling (Screenplay); Ted Moore (Cinematography); Kenneth V. Jones (Music); Muir Mathieson (Musical Director); Duncan Sutherland (Art Direction); Elsa Fennell (Costume Design); Colin Garde (Makeup); Frank Maher (Stunts); Ted Sturgis (Assistant Director); Alan Pattillo (Sound); Bert Rule (Editor). Running time: 80 minutes.

Indian chieftain Kasim Khan (Victor Mature) mistakenly believes that his family was killed by the British, and vows vengeance on the redcoats. However, the real perpetrator is another chieftain, Azhad Khan, whose men were disguised as British troopers when they committed the massacre. Kasim and his men carry out a number of raids on the British and as a result a reward is put on his head. Major Crowley dispatches Lieutenant Wylie to capture Kasim, but during the course of his mission he is murdered at the behest of Azhad, who frames Kasim for the death. Crowley then sets out to bring Kasim to account, and in his endeavors has to cope with his idealistic daughter Zenda, who believes Kasim to be innocent. With Corporal Stokes as an escort, she sets out to locate Kasim but is captured by Azhad en route. Sentenced to burn at the stake, she is rescued by Kasim and taken back to his camp. After much fighting, Kasim and Crowley discover that Azhad is the real villain. Armed with this knowledge, Kasim catches up with Azhad during a battle and strangles him to death, before dying himself from a stab wound.

"Not since *THE SHEIK* ... a lover ... a fighter ...
A MOTION PICTURE ... LIKE THIS!"

"Ruthless! Riotous! Romantic!
She hated his violence ... but she sought him out."

If one chose to be picky, you could argue that we had seen a MOTION PICTURE LIKE THIS only a few years earlier: Mature's first film for Warwick, *Zarak* (1956). The only real difference between the two films is perhaps the leading tagline's suggestion that the romantic aspect of *Zhobe* had more in common with Rudolph Valentino's *The Sheik* (1921) than *Zarak*. In *The Sheik*, the prim and proper English socialite Agnes Ayres falls for the charming sheik played by Valentino, a lustful desire replicated by Anne Aubrey in her quest to tame the mighty warrior Kasim Khan, labeled by his English pursuers "The Bandit of Zhobe."

Aged 46, Mature was certainly no youthful Valentino at this stage in his career, and his character's all-consuming desire to track down those who murdered his wife and son overshadows any romantic possibilities for his noble fighter. Which is a shame, because if ever a feisty Englishwoman looked as if she needed to be whisked away to a Bedouin tent for a thousand and one Arabian nights, it was the beautiful Deborah Kerr look-alike Anne Aubrey. The wonderfully reserved and ladylike Aubrey marked a complete departure from

Mature's previous Warwick leading ladies, who all had a tendency to be blonde and of the sex-kittenish type—Anita Ekberg, Janet Leigh and Diana Dors. Aubrey had featured in Mature's previous Warwick production *No Time to Die* as an Italian girl, but her scenes were cut from the film. With her beauty and talent, it's a shame the actress, who was married to actor Derren Nesbitt, didn't make more of her screen career, which petered out in the early 1960s. But she did at least get an opportunity to work with another Hollywood legend, Robert Taylor, in Warwick's *The Killers of Kilimanjaro*, which also starred Anthony Newley (she appeared with Newley in nine films altogether).

The decision to make *The Bandit of Zhobe* came about because (while making *Zarak*) director Terence Young managed to film half a feature's worth of footage beyond what was needed. Not wanting to waste the footage, producers Broccoli and Allen decided to use it in the guise of another film—enter *The Bandit of Zhobe*.[1] Some of the wardrobe was also reused, with Aubrey wearing the costumes worn by Anita Ekberg in *Zarak*, which prompted the light-hearted comment from the rest of the cast that Aubrey got the role because she was the only girl in England who shared the same vital statistics as Ekberg.[2] (I'm not altogether sure which clothes they shared, because each part was completely different—but it makes for a great little story.) Under the working title *The Bandit*, the film was made at England's Twickenham Studios, with location shooting, according to *The Hollywood Reporter*, taking place in and around Madrid, Spain.

Looking at the material Warwick Productions put Mature's way, it is clear they were not at all interested in playing on the actor's natural ability to convey brash, happy-go-lucky types, the sort of characters he had perfected. Instead, the film company capitalized on his skill in conveying anguish and torment, all with a constant air of melancholy, very much like his character Demetrius. But for all his bitterness and despair, Mature's Kasim is still a noble man at heart, informing Aubrey, "My own father had no respect for bargains or justice, but I do." However, Kasim has little respect for so-called "British justice," as he refers to it, for when Aubrey tells him that justice works slowly, he dismissively asks, "Did it work slowly for me?"

That he should play such tortured souls is not altogether surprising, considering that each of his Warwick characters had good cause to be unhappy, with many simply driven by revenge or the desire for forbidden fruit. In *Zarak*, he is in love with one of his father's wives; in *Safari*, he seeks the Mau Mau killer of his son; in *Interpol*, he hunts the killer of his sister; in *The Long Haul*, his married family man falls for a femme fatale; in *No Time to Die*, he fights the Germans to avenge his wife who died in a concentration camp; and in *The Bandit of Zhobe*, he must take arms against the British whom he, mistakenly, thinks massacred his people including his wife and son. There was precious little opportunity for his characters to show any humor or smug self-assurance in such tragic circumstance. But all is not gloom and doom, for if a sense of levity is required, cue Anthony Newley.

Epitomizing the chirpy Cockney, British actor-singer-composer-director Newley rose to fame on the back of his memorable performance as the Artful Dodger in David Lean's *Oliver Twist* (1948), and after several character roles he went on to greater fame as a pop star and writer of stage musicals. He was married to actresses Ann Lyn and Joan Collins. In the two Mature films in which he appeared, *No Time to Die* and *The Bandit of Zhobe*, he injected some much-needed comic relief into the proceedings, playing a resourceful batman type who's always there to cover your back, come what may. In the best scene in *Zhobe*, during a battle (much of it taken from *Zarak*), he tries to commandeer some dynamite from the ammo store without filling in the necessary paperwork. When he finally convinces the quartermaster to let him have a small box, the latter informs him not to tell anyone else or they'll all be wanting some. Newley also has the best line in the film when, in answer to Major Crowley's query concerning the whereabouts of his daughter, he chirpily responds, "Buying some Persian carpets made in Birmingham."

Zhobe is a better film than its predecessor *Zarak*, chiefly because Mature's hero is better defined, which allows us to gain greater empathy for his plight. Unlike *Zarak*, we know what makes Kasim tick. He is a man driven to avenge the murder of his wife and son. Threatening to divert him from this goal, we also observe a clearly defined heroine, the English Rose, Anne Aubrey.

The clash of cultures between their separate worlds holds our attention, but we intuitively know that they are not destined to ride off into the sunset together. The clashing of cultures was nothing new in Mature's career, with several films touching on the theme, including *One Million B.C.*, *The Shanghai Gesture*, *Moss Rose*, *Androcles and the Lion*, *The Last Frontier*, *The Glory Brigade* and *China Doll*.

In the book *Visions of Yesterday*, the author Jeffrey Richards had this to say about the conflict between cultures in *Zarak* and *The Bandit of Zhobe*: "What is interesting about both these films and fits them into an Imperial scheme is that both assume that the Indians do not have any real grievances against the British and that basically conflict between them was a game which when real danger threatened (Afghan invasion in the case of *Zhobe*) would be abandoned in favor of cooperation against the enemy."

As "boy's own" adventure yarns go, *The Bandit of Zhobe* is an entertaining time-filler which, like a dime novel, shouldn't be taken too seriously. Watch it and be cheerfully reminded of those gallant days on the North West Frontier when "the sun never sets on the British Empire."

Variety: "Indians bite the dust with monotonous regularity in *The Bandit of Zhobe*, a Warwick production with the laments of an old-fashioned American Western.... Victor Mature seems to be getting a little heavy to play the dashing juvenile, and his apparent decision to play his Indian leaders as stoically as possible somewhat cuts down emotional appeal."

Picture Show and *TV Mirror* (1959): "The action of this film moves so fast it's difficult to keep up with."

Radio Times Guide to Films: "Very silly Northwest Frontier romp, with Victor Mature in dark makeup as Kasim Khan…"

TV Times Film and Video Guide: "A fiery 19th century adventure yarn…"

Halliwell's Film Guide: "Tin pot action melodrama in the wake of the rather better *Zarak*."

On a final amusing note, a German publicity poster for the film had Mature sporting a goatee. Sorry, guys, wrong film — the goatee came with *Zarak*. Mature's Kasim was clean-shaven.

The Big Circus

Allied Artists, 1959

Cast: Victor Mature (Henry Jasper "Hank" Whirling); Red Buttons (Randy Sherman); Rhonda Fleming (Helen Harrison); Kathryn Grant (Jeannie Whirling); Vincent Price (Hans Hagenfeld); Gilbert Roland (Zach Colino); Peter Lorre (Skeeter); David Nelson (Tommy Gordon); Adele Mara (Maria "Mama" Colino); Howard McNear (Mr.

Lomax); Charles Watts (Jonathan T. Nelson); Steve Allen (Himself—Cameo Appearance); Nesdon Booth (Jules Borman); Charles Sherlock (Photographer); James Bacon, Geraldine Wall, George Cisar, Kenner G. Kemp (Reporters); James Nolan (Police Lieutenant); John Wald (Commentator at Niagara Falls); Gene Mendez (Wirewalker); Hugo Zacchini (Human Cannonball); The Flying Alexanders (Aerialists); The Ronnie Lewis Trio (High Ladder Equilibrists); Dick Walker (Lion Tamer); The Jungleland Elephants, Tex Carr and his Chimpanzees, and Dick Berg's Movieland Seals.

Crew: Irwin Allen (Producer); Joseph M. Newman (Director); Irwin Allen (Story); Irwin Allen, Charles Bennett, Irving Wallace (Screenplay); Winton C. Hoch (Cinematography); Paul Sawtell, Bert Shefter (Music); Albert S. D'Agostino (Art Direction); Robert Priestley (Set Decorations); Paul Zastupnevich (Costume Design); William Tuttle (Makeup); Robert R. Hoag (Optical Effects); Fred Carson (Stunts); William McGarry (Assistant Director); Conrad Kahn (Sound); Adrienne Fazan (Editor). Running time: 108 minutes.

After parting company with the Borman Brothers with half of their circus, Hank Whirling (Victor Mature) faces many pressures to keep the show from going under. To satisfy the conditions of his bank loan, Randy Sherman is brought in to oversee the circus finances, accompanied by press agent Helen Harrison. Following a series of apparent accidents, including an escaped lion, a train wreck and a circus fire, it becomes clear that there is a saboteur in their midst, hellbent on bringing the circus to a close. Several characters look like possible candidates — Hans Hagenfeld the ringmaster, Skeeter the clown or possibly aerialist Zach Colino, whose wife was killed in the train crash. The circus also has to contend with natural disaster when torrential rains flood several states along their route. To publicize the circus and save it from financial ruin, Zach successfully walks a tightrope above Niagara Falls. The saboteur strikes again when Hank's sister Jeannie secretly makes her debut as an aerialist with the Flying Colinos: Minutes before the act, the saboteur is revealed as fellow aerialist Tommy, who spent some time in an insane asylum and who is now secretly taking orders from the Borman Brothers. Tommy deliberately fails to catch Jeannie, but luckily she is saved. Pursued by Zach, Tommy falls to his death. Disaster averted, Randy takes up with Jeannie and Helen sets her cap at Hank.

"10 Great Stars! 100 Circus Acts! 1001 Spectacular Thrills!"

"YOU are part of THE BIGGEST SHOW IN THE WORLD! The most exciting behind-the-scenes drama of the Big Top ever told!"

Come one, come all and see the ferocious lions, the tinted elephants, the comical clowns, the daring trapeze artist and the larger-than-life Victor Mature in this, his second Irwin Allen production. If there's one type of film that's guaranteed to raise a beaming smile on your face, it's the good old circus (or traveling carnival) film. Wonderfully nostalgic and colorful, they welcome you like a long-lost friend, and akin to candy on a stick, they come in all shapes and sizes. For those looking for big directors, big stars, jumbo-sized budgets and serious storylines, we were presented with extravaganzas such as Cecil B. DeMille's *The Greatest Show on Earth* (1952) with Charlton Heston; Carol Reed's *Trapeze* (1956) with Burt Lancaster and Tony Curtis; and Henry Hathaway's *Circus World* (1964) with John Wayne. For a more low-key affair, we savored the delights of *You Can't Cheat an Honest Man* (1939) and *Carnival Story* (1954); while on a warm-hearted musical note, we enjoyed Disney's *Dumbo* (1941), *Billy Rose's Jumbo* (1962), and *Roustabout* (1964). When more shocks than big-top thrills were called for, we were offered *Circus of Horrors* (1960), *Berserk* (1967), *Vam-*

pire Circus (1971) and *Something Wicked This Way Comes* (1983). And for those looking for something completely off-the-wall, they didn't come any stranger than *Freaks* (1932), *Nightmare Alley* (1947) and *The Woman for Joe* (1955). All great films and highly enjoyable, but my personal favorite has and will always be Irwin Allen's *The Big Circus*. A traveling carnival came to the aid of Mature after a tar-and-feathering incident in *My Gal Sal*, but the actor would have to wait until *The Big Circus* before getting a chance to play the big top. And the role of a circus owner was a part he was born to, perfectly dovetailing with his screen persona as a brash, resilient character with a heart of gold. This was Mature's last big Hollywood film before heading off to Europe for two Italian productions, and then retirement. And what a big, colorful end to a big, colorful Hollywood career. With more than a hint of Romany in his dark, craggy, Mediterranean looks, and sporting a black hat, neckerchief and walking cane, Mature was tailor-made to play a traveling showman with no fixed abode, hardened by the elements and the highs and lows of keeping a big circus on the road. In keeping with many of his action films, Mature again gets to tangle with a mighty beast, on this occasion a lion which has been set loose by the villain of the piece.

What marks this circus film out for me is that, despite its modest budget, it has all the thrills and spills of a big top spectacular, and yet there is a warm, snug comfort about it; it simply refuses to take itself too seriously. All the ingredients of spectacle, drama and humor are there, meticulously measured out and delivered by a superb cast under the skillful direction of Joseph Newman, who gave us the likes of *Red Skies of Montana* (1952), *The Human Jungle* (1954) and the science fiction classic *This Island Earth* (1955).

Underlying the whole show, there is a great whodunit mystery that will keep you hooked and guessing right to the very end. And if that wasn't enough, to ensure we go away with a tune on our lips, the film is buoyed by a memorable Paul Sawtell score, which includes the rousing title tune by Sammy Fain and Paul Francis Webster.

Amongst the fine ensemble, Vincent Price excels as the ringmaster in this, his fourth film with Mature, as does Red Buttons, Rhonda Fleming, Kathyrn Grant (Mrs. Bing Crosby), Gilbert Roland, David Nelson, Adele Maras and Peter Lorre in the role of a clown (a role James Stewart played in the DeMille film). Lorre thoroughly enjoyed playing the clown, coming up with many ideas for his part and the other parts around him, which he would pass on to Mature. (Having put some of his own money into the project, Mature enjoyed script approval and 10 percent of the gross profits.) Mature would in turn forward the suggestions to Irwin Allen, whose usual response was "Fine, tell him to do it."[1] According to some sources, including copyright records, the film is listed as a Saratoga–Vic Mature production, although the actor was not credited on screen as one of the film's producers.[2]

Red Buttons was born Aaron Chwatt, but became known as Red Buttons after his red hair and his loud buttoned uniform as a singing bellhop. His notable films include *Sayonara* (1957), for which he received an Oscar for Best Supporting Actor, *Hatari!* (1961), and *They Shoot Horses, Don't They?* (1969), which earned him an Oscar nomination. (A born comedian, he was quoted as saying, "Elizabeth Taylor has a big heart. She recently built a halfway house for girls who don't want to go all the way.") And what can you say about the stunning Rhonda Fleming, other than "Wow!" She lit up the screen with her appearances in films such as *A Connecticut Yankee in King Arthur's Court* (1949), *Slightly Scarlet* (1956) and *Gunfight at the OK Corral* (1957). With her red hair and green eyes, she looks great alongside the dark-featured Mature, both cutting a statuesque pose and brimming with sensuality.

In many ways, the character of Hank Whirling allows Mature to play himself — a warm, outgoing, gregarious character with a keen eye for publicity and a great affection for children, which we observe when, with a beaming smile, he tells the local kids, much to their delight, that to earn their circus passes they'll first have to water the elephants. And when confronted with obstacles, he is not a man to give up, using his quick thinking to solve their transport crisis following the train crash. With 20 miles of mountainous terrain to cover to reach Niagara the following day, he tells the team, "I got an idea. Two thousand years ago there was a guy named Hannibal who crossed the Alps with the help of 40 elephants. Now when it comes to elephants, we've got Hannibal outnumbered." Ironically, Mature would go on to play the great Carthaginian leader in his next film, *Hannibal* (1960).

Variety: "The role of circus impresario Henry Jasper Whirling is the kind Victor Mature does best."

Picture Show and TV Mirror: "Very colorful and at times a thrilling picture."

Leonard Maltin: "Familiar but well-done circus story with exceptional cast."

The Radio Times Film Guide: "Although clearly hindered by budget limitations, this is a worthy attempt by the studio to break new ground, and rejects the phony romanticism of *The Greatest Show on Earth* to good effect."

Timbuktu

United Artists, 1959

Cast: Victor Mature (Mike Conway); Yvonne De Carlo (Natalie Dufort); George Dolenz (Colonel Charles Dufort); John Dehner (Emir Bhaki); Marcia Henderson (Jeanne Marat); Robert Clarke (Capt. Girard); James Foxx (Lt. Victor Marat); Paul Wexler (Suleyman); Leonard Mudie (Mahomet Adani); Willard Sage (Maj. Leroux); Mark Dana (Capt. Redman); Larry Perron (Dagana); Steve Darrell (Nazir); Larry Chance (Ahmed); Allen Pinson (Sergeant).

Crew: Edward Small (Producer); Jacques Tourneur (Director); Anthony Veiller, Paul Dudley (Screenplay); Maury Gertsman (Cinematography); Gerald Fried (Music); William Glasgow (Art Direction); Darrell Silvera (Set Decorations); Layne Britton (Makeup); Frank Beetson, Jr., Elva Martien (Wardrobe); Alex Weldon, Joe Zomar (Special Effects); Fred Carson (Stunts); Al Westen (Assistant Director); John K. Kean (Sound); Grant Whytock (Editor). Running time: 91 minutes..

The film is set in the French Sudan during the early days of World War II. When France falls into the hands of the Germans, American adventurer Mike Conway (Victor Mature) teams up with Colonel Dufort, of the French Foreign Legion, to put down a Tuareg rebellion, and along the way Conway falls in love with the colonel's wife Natalie. Dealing in the trade of arms, Conway works his way into the confidence of a Tuareg leader in an attempt to rescue a moderate Muslim leader and get him back to Timbuktu to quell an all-out uprising. With the support of Dufort, Conway completes the mission, but Dufort is killed in the process, leaving Natalie free to pursue her love of Conway.

"The Mighty Revolt That Turned the Sahara Red!"
"SEE! The Tarantula Desert Torture!
The Massacre at the Mosque!
The Human Lance-Targets!"

> "It Charges Across the Scalding Sahara! It Storms Through the Temples of Allah! It Sins in the Pagan Palaces!"
>
> "The Hottest Adventure from Here to Timbuktu!"

The last tagline certainly got me tagged, with visions of Mature and De Carlo making out in the desert sands, minus the roar of the pounding surf, of course. For those lacking in imagination, the publicity poster for the film showed our two lovers in a lustful Lancaster–Kerr–like embrace. But that's not to detract from the entertainment value of *Timbuktu*.

Timbuktu was one of the last Hollywood films of director Jacques Tourneur who gave us such classic spinetinglers as *Cat People* (1942), *I Walked with a Zombie* (1943) and *Night of the Demon* (1957). But as we saw with Mature's earlier collaboration with the director, *Easy Living*, a sports movie, there was more to the director that just horror films. With *Timbuktu* he makes a brave attempt to add his two pennies worth to the French Foreign Legion adventure yarn. That genre, to be perfectly frank, was well past its sell by date when this little feature came to town. Ronald Colman kicked off the genre with *Beau Geste* (1926), followed by Gary Cooper in *Morocco* (1930) and *Beau Geste* (1939); Burt Lancaster, Carlos Thompson and Alan Ladd safely tucked it to bed with *Ten Tall Men* (1951), *Fort Algiers* (1953) and *Desert Legion* (1953), respectively. But if you need one last stab at it for old times' sake, who better to play the lead than action star Vic Mature. In the role of a gun-runner, he plays one side off against the other, and spouts such immortal lines as, "I've got the holy man stashed." This is the sort of soldier-of-fortune role that Alan Ladd churned out in stirring action movies such as *China* (1943), *Calcutta* (1947), *Saigon* (1948) and *Thunder in the East* (1953). Like the Ladd characters, Mature's Mike Conway initially comes over as a conscience-free adventurer out to make a quick buck, but as the film unspools we learn that there is more to the man than his big wide hat and his ability to sweep De Carlo off her feet just by raising a lazy eyebrow. Like Mature, De Carlo was probably a bit long in the tooth to be starring in such camp adventure films, but she still looks beautiful and (according to the film's pressbook she did all her own stunt falls from her horse, which is remarkable when you consider that the film amassed the greatest aggregation of Hollywood's best stuntmen in years. Completing 90 stunts in total, they doubled for both the French Colonial troops and the Tuareg Moslem warriors in the exciting desert battle scenes.

De Carlo's real-life husband Bob Morgan, a stuntman, took part in the many stunts. His career was cut short in 1962 when he suffered near-fatal injuries when a train ran over him when filming a stunt in *How the West Was Won*. De Carlo went into substantial debt paying the medical bills when her husband had his left leg amputated as a consequence of the accident. To pay the bills, she took the part of Lily in the successful television show *The Munsters* (1964–1966), which became her most famous role. But let's not forget her enduring performances in *Salome, Where She Danced* (1945), *Criss Cross* (1949), *The Ten Commandments* (1956) and *Band of Angels* (1957).

Mature nearly suffered a serious accident during the filming of *Timbuktu* when his horse reared, and its hindquarters caught the star as it fell.[1] Such mishaps would plague Mature's career, having been injured in *Cry of the City* and *Zarak*, clearly proving that an actor's lot on set was at times a precarious one. Fortunately, Mature emerged unscathed, thus enabling him to fulfill his quota of smart lines, bare torso shots and torture scenes (with a dangling tarantula in this feature). Indeed, the slightly tongue-in-cheek nature of the dialogue keeps the pace moving at a brisk clip, greatly adding to the entertainment on offer. When his shipment is found to contain sewing machines and not rifles, Mature amusingly explains to the colonel, "When times are tough, I whip up a few turbans for the Arabs." And in response to the holy man's "May the blessings of Allah go with you," he says, "I hope they're bulletproof."

Throughout the bullet-strewn proceedings, supporting player George Dolenz, in the role of the colonel, plays it sensitively straight, conveniently biting the dust in the final reel, thus allowing Mature and De Carlo to ride off into the sunset together. Dolenz, who was the father of Mickey Dolenz, tended to play Latin American types in his screen career, and left his mark starring in the television series *The Count of Monte Cristo* (1956).

Chris Fujiwara in his book on Jacques Tourneur *The Cinema of Nightfall*, commented, "*Timbuktu* is an absurd film but one that glows with a special, dismal negative splendor."[2]

Producer Edward Small was less than impressed with the finished product, taking his name of the credits, but not before insisting that Tourneur shoot a series of close-ups of extras with various expressions because the film wasn't long enough. Tourneur recalled his thoughts on these unwelcomed inserts: "[S]uddenly, right in the middle of a battle, you saw more or less bewildered faces for long minutes. People must have said to themselves, 'Tourneur has gone completely gaga.'"[3]

Despite the fun on offer (bewildered faces included), the reviews were pretty poor, with perhaps *Variety* hitting the nail on the head with its comment: "This one is neither better nor worse than a solid program adventure picture such as can be seen on the late show, only Victor Mature's a little older now."

The *New York Times*: "[T]here are no dull moments even if the tension is not exactly unbearable."

Picturegoer: "Victor Mature! Yvonne De Carlo! Gun running in the desert ... need I say more? De Carlo and Mature have been mixed up in these kind of shenanigans so often on the screen that they could probably go through the script in their sleep. And, judging by their performances in this film, maybe they did."

Apparently all points of the compass were considered as titles for the film: *North of Timbuktu*, *East of Timbuktu*, *West of Timbuktu* and *South of Timbuktu*, with *The Road to Timbuktu* even being in contention before they decided to keep it simple with just plain old *Timbuktu*.

Hannibal

Warner Brothers, 1960

Cast: Victor Mature (Hannibal); Gabriele Ferzetti (Fabius Maximus); Rita Gam (Sylvia); Milly Vitale (Danila); Rik Battaglia (Hasdrubal); Franco Silva (Maharbal); Terence Hill (Quintilius); Mirko Ellis (Mago); Andrea Aureli (Gajus Terentius Varro); Andrea Fantasia (Konsul Paulus Emilius); Bud Spencer (Rutario); Franco Dominci (Minitius), Enzo Fiermonte (Announcer in Senate); Andrea Esterhazy (Slave); Piero Tiberi (Hannibal's Son).

Crew: Ottavio Poggi (Producer); Carlo Ludovico Bragaglia, Edgar G. Ulmer (Directors); Ottavio Poggi (Story); Sandro Continenza, Mortimer Braus (Screenplay); Raffaele Masciocchi (Cinematography); Carlo Rustichelli (Music); Ernest Kromberg (Art Direction); Carlo Gentili (Set Decorations); Giancarlo Bartolini Salimbeni (Costume Design);

Mirella Ginnoto (Makeup); Anacleto Giustini (Special Effects); Nino Zanchin (Assistant Director); Raffaele Del Monte, Franco Groppioni (Sound); Renato Cinquini (Editor). Running time: 103 minutes.

In 218 B.C., Carthaginian general Hannibal (Victor Mature) takes his vast army of elephants and troops over the Alps into Italy, hellbent on defeating Rome. He captures Sylvia, the niece of Roman Senator Fabius Maximus, but after discovering that they have feelings for one another, he releases her so she can inform Rome of the might of his army, which crushes the Romans in their first encounter. Hannibal loses the use of one eye, but presses on with his mission to conquer Rome. He remains victorious in battle, but fails to seize the initiative for all-out victory against the Romans. Sylvia meets Hannibal once again but, on return to Rome, she is sentenced to death for high treason, leaving Hannibal to fight on knowing he will never lay claim to Rome.

"Jump On! Hang On! Here Comes the Avenging Hannibal and his Crazed Elephant Army."

"The Mighty Hannibal Hurls His Elephant Army Across Half the World."

"Not in his time! Not in our time! Not in All Time has the world seen such might as the mighty vengeance of HANNIBAL."

As Mature approached the end of his career as a leading man, it was only fitting that he bow out in the genre he was most associated with, "swords and sandals." In the first of two Italian productions (followed by *The Tartars*), he takes the part of the mighty Hannibal. Surprisingly, up until this point, the story of one of history's greatest military leaders was largely overlooked by the film world. Two earlier Italian productions, *Cabiria* (1914) and Mussolini's propaganda film *Scipio Africanus* (1939), were set against the backdrop of the Punic Wars and featured Hannibal, but the emphasis was on other characters, the kidnapped girl Cabira in the former and the Roman Scipio (who was victorious over Hannibal at Rama), in the latter. Next came an MGM musical comedy, *Jupiter's Darling* (1955), which featured Howard Keel as Hannibal and Esther Williams as the love interest. But, for a serious film that sympathetically focused on Hannibal and his battles against the Roman Empire, audiences had to wait until Edgar G. Ulmer's *Hannibal*—film, that despite its low budget, did its bit to put Hannibal back up there with the other great leaders of the ancient world, like Julius Caesar, Alexander the Great and Spartacus.

When an actor is needed to play an epic hero from the ancient world, who better than Victor Mature, proving that at this late stage in his career that he was still a force to be reckoned with. In common with Mature's Samson and Demetrius, Hannibal (bound by the events of history) at times cuts a tragic figure, which perfectly lent itself to Mature's ability to convey shades of despondency in his characters. As Derek Elley noted in his book *The Epic Film*: "Victor Mature's Hannibal is noteworthy: this actor has a sad, stolid quality which accords well with epic characterization, and it is for this reason that Hannibal is best remembered."[1] On the actor's muscular prowess, Bruce Francis Babington and Peter William Evans commented in their book *Biblical Epics* that Mature may well have lacked Burt Lancaster's or Kirk Douglas's fluid athleticism, but "in heroic mood he is more statuesque, his great body a self-contained image of heroism."[2]

Mature certainly does justice to the part, portraying his character with much spirit and conviction, whether discussing battle tactics with his men or in his love scenes with the gorgeous Rita Gam. But that's not to say that *Hannibal* is a great film, far from it. There are times when the screenplay lacks vitality, and the low budget is sometimes revealed in the quality of the sets and the crude battle scenes. But this was very much par for the course with the many historical epics then being produced by Italian studios, which usually starred that other muscular American import, Steve Reeves. But taking into context the period in which they were produced and viewed on their own level, they make for fine entertainment, paving the way for the Spaghetti Westerns which were to follow.

Mature's tired, world-weary look works well here to convey a courageous leader frustrated and constrained by his inability to make good his victories. His pent-up emotions and energy are also put to good use as Hannibal wrestles with the conflict that exists between his professional life as a soldier and that of a lover. This is the sort of epic film where Mature really makes his commanding presence felt, delivering his lines with much pathos and conviction. When one of his men describes the crossing of the Alps in 15 days as a miracle, Mature responds, "[S]eems more like fifteen years. When we started we had 40,000 men, now less than half answer the roll." Mature also does well to express the inner bitterness of his character, informing the mother of his son, who is trying to raise him like him, "I've told you 1000 times, I don't want him to be like me. I never want him to know the meaning of the words hate and revenge."

The film features two major battle scenes with the first showing how the elephants performed in battle, trampling everything in their path. Reflecting the budget, most of this sequence is unfortunately setbound and shot on a small scale, which detracts from the action, but this is more than compensated for in the second battle, which features some wonderful sweeping photography as the armies clash against a broad canvas.

Neatly woven into the major battle and love scenes, Mature, sporting an eye patch, shows his flair for action as his character undergoes a series of challenges and heroic deeds, including lifting a wagon out of a rut using his brute strength, beating off a gang of assassins, fending off a rampaging elephant and fighting a sword duel.

When not wielding his sword, Mature finds time to romance the lovely Rita Gam, before her character faces the death penalty for treason. The American-born Gam had a few notable roles in the U.S.—*The Thief* (1952) and *King of Kings* (1961), before continuing her career in Europe. Mature also received solid support from Gabriele Ferzetti (in the role of Fabius Maximus) who left his mark with films such as *L'Avventura* (1960), *Once Upon a Time in the West* (1968), *The Night Porter* (1974) and *First Action Hero* (1994). Another fine actor to grace the cast was Terence Hill, who would go on to greater fame, with his partner Bud Spencer, in many spaghetti Westerns, most notably *They Call Me Trinity* (1970).

The film employed the services of two directors, Carlo Ludovico Bragaglia and Edgar G. Ulmer. Bragaglia made his mark with Italian adventure films, but is probably best remembered in his native Italy for a series of comedies starring Toto, the Italian stage and screen comedian. The Austrian-born Ulmer secured his legacy with *The Black Cat* (1934), *Detour* (1945) and *The Strange Woman* (1946).

Having lost his love, *Hannibal* ends with narration that tells us that Hannibal went on to fight for endless years in many lands, maybe with a single hope left in him that his son would never know the bitterness of command. It's perhaps a great missed opportunity that the film didn't take the story of Hannibal through to its ultimate conclusion, which would have seen the leader end his own life by taking poison, rather than fall into the hands of his enemies.

After four months filming, Mature summed up the experience in one sentence, claiming, "I got headaches and nausea from riding elephants." (I guess they must have edited that bit, because Mature remains firmly rooted to the ground in my copy of the film).

Variety: "Victor Mature brings physical command to the central role..."

The *TV Times Film and Radio Guide*: "Victor Mature is ideally cast in the title role. No white elephant at the box-office, though: it made a mint."

The Tartars

MGM, 1962

Cast: Victor Mature (Oleg); Orson Welles (Burundai); Liana Orfei (Helga); Arnoldo Foa (Ciu Lang), Luciano Marin (Eric); Bella Cortez (Samia); Furio Meniconi (Sigrun); Folco Lulli (Togrul).

Crew: Riccardo Gualino (Producer); Richard Thorpe (Director); Fernando Baldi (Director of Italian-Dialogue Version); Sabatino Ciuffini, Ambrogio Molteni, Gaio Fratini, Oreste Palella, Domenico Salvati (Screenplay): Amerigo Gengarelli (Cinematography); Renzo Rossellini (Music); Oscar D'Amico, Pasquale Dal Pino (Production Design); Antonio Fratalocchi (Set Decorations); Giovanna Natili (Costume Design); Renato Bomarzi (Makeup); Costel Grozea (Special Effects); Giogio Gentili, Ambrogio Molteni (Assistant Directors); Kurt Doubrowsky (Sound); Maurizio Lucidi (Editor). Running time: 83 minutes.

In medieval times, the Vikings led by Oleg (Victor Mature) expand into the Russian Steppes where they encounter the Tartars, whose chieftain tries to persuade Oleg to join forces with his army to conquer the indigenous Slavic tribes. Oleg refuses and, when the Tartar chieftain is killed, both armies end up taking a female hostage into their camp. Oleg captures the slain chief's daughter Samia, who becomes romantically attached to Oleg's son Eric. The Tartars, now ruled by the chief's brother Burundai, take Oleg's wife Helga, who is brutally treated by her captors. A climactic battle ensues and both Burundai and Oleg are killed. Amidst all this, Eric and Samia head off down the Volga River to start a new life.

"The Tartars vs. the Vikings!"

"Tartars Abduct Viking Beauty!"

"The Proudest ... Most Powerful Warriors That Ever Existed!"

"Orgy Celebrates Conquest!"

"Hide Your Women ... Seize Your Swords ... The Tartars Are Coming!"

To prove he was good for one last historical characterization before hanging up his sword (and sandals), Mature starred in *The Tartars*, a film that put him up against the guy who had stolen his best gal, Rita Hayworth, back in 1943, the one and only Orson Welles. With such bad blood between them, the clashes, bites and scratches would not be confined to those on screen — so let the battle commence!

You have to hand it to those Italian historical spectacles from the 1950s and '60s: Although low-budget and glaringly camp at times, they did boldly go where no filmmaker had gone before. In Mature's previous outing *Hannibal*, we witnessed the rare screen spectacle of Carthaginians fighting Romans, but in the case of *The Tartars*, we are swept away to the Russian Steppes to behold Vikings pitted against Tartars over Slav territory. Of course, such delicious combinations were not entirely unknown, with Richard Widmark's Viking taking on harem girls and Moors in *The Long Ships* (1964), and in later years, Lee Majors' Nordic warrior fighting North American Indians in *The Norseman* (1978). But *The Tartars'* combination enjoyed the added attraction of having two screen legends fighting in opposing camps, Mature and Welles. And if that wasn't enough, the film's director was Richard Thorpe, one of MGM's most revered directors of costume epics, including *Ivanhoe* (1952), *The Prisoner of Zenda* (1952) and *Knights of the Round Table* (1953). Interestingly, Thorpe was the original director of *The Wizard of Oz* (1939), but was taken off the project during production because it was felt that the footage shot lacked the requisite element of fantasy. Thorpe also turned his hand to two Elvis Presley movies *Jailhouse Rock* (1957) and *Fun in Acapulco* (1963).

Both Mature and Welles had their reasons for starring in the film, which essentially boiled down to the paycheck. Mature was building up his nest egg so that he could retire from the screen and play golf all day, while Welles was putting the money away to pay for his next screen project *The Trial* (1962), based on Franz Kafka's novel. Welles took on many such roles, which he felt below him, simply to raise cash to finance his film projects, many of which were never finished or released. Kicking off his film career with the classic *Citizen Kane* (1941), Welles in later years would comment, "I started at the top and worked down."

Historically, the characters played by Mature and Welles existed in different times. Oleg seized Kiev in 882, making it his capital, and then became the undisputed ruler of the Kievan-Novgorodian state when he united the local Slavic and Finnish tribes under his rule. Burundai, a notable Mongol general, participated in the Mongol invasion of Russia and Europe from 1236 to 1242. Still, what's a few hundred years when we're having such fun.

The action is mostly a case of off-screen tit for tat between two screen giants, with equally big egos, trying to get the better of one another. The film's editor, Maurizio Lucidi, who went on to do a lot of work with Welles, recalled how the star stole Mature's scenes by hypnotizing both director and cameraman into focusing on him exclusively, which had the desired effect of winding up Mature.[1] During one incident, according to Barbara Leaming's biography of Welles, an upset Mature raged to the director, "You son of a bitch." When the production assistant, Alessandro Tasca, asked him what was wrong, Mature replied, "You're a son of a bitch, too." Calmly handling the situation, Tasca discovered that Mature was angry because in one scene the director shot two closeups of Welles and only one of him. To satisfy Mature's demand that they should shoot three close ups of him, Tasca shouted to the director to comply, while discreetly whispering to the cameraman only to pretend to shoot the extra shots.[2] In another incident, Welles recalled how Mature had been informed incorrectly by the costume department that he (Welles) would be wearing shoes built up by two inches to make him appear taller. Not to be outdone, Mature got his sandals built up three inches and could hardly walk. Welles further mused that Mature could have saved himself the trouble, if he had only checked the script which had Welles seated on a throne in all their scenes together.[3]

On screen, Mature and Welles certainly hold their own in this tale, and it's hard to say who comes out on top. But if pushed, I'd have to give it to Welles who at least looks the part, as opposed to Mature who, in his black costume, looks more like a Roman than a Viking. Indeed, Mature's dark, powerfully built, Mediterranean look is completely incongruous to the rest of his blonde-haired Viking brethren who, sporting the obligatory cow-horned helmets (which no self-respecting Viking ever wore in battle), look more like a bunch of weedy hippies off to a fancy dress party. Not that this in any way detracts from your enjoyment of the film; if anything, it strangely adds to it in large measures.

A strong, resilient character, Mature's Oleg is not the sort of man to flinch in the face of danger. And he's definitely not the sort you can knock down easily, which we amusingly observe when he puts himself up as a target to help improve the aim of his catapult crew, telling them, "How many times do I have to tell you, you've got to have a target. Now, fire at me." With rocks the size of overripe melons whizzing past his ears, Mature looks defiantly on, and for a moment you think he might try and catch one and toss it back.

Adding to the film's curiosity value, the filmmakers for some obscure reason saw fit to dub Mature's voice in one or two scenes, including the abovementioned catapult sequence when Mature has a go himself at aiming the weapon.

Oleg's wife Helga, played by Liana Orfei, would have been very much at home in Mature's earlier film *The Big Circus*, beginning her career in her father's circus, working as a trapeze artist, acrobat, juggler, and a lion and horse trainer, before making 37 films including Fellini's *I Clowns* (1972).

Filmed in Technicolor on location in Italy and Yugoslavia, *The Tartars'* rousing battle scenes utilized 20,000 men, which included the highly trained Yugoslav cavalry.[4] The battles were filmed in the historic Croatian valley of Grobenicke Polje, and in case of serious injury, of which there were few, ten fully equipped first aid stations were set up along the six and a half mile-long valley, supported by four ambulances. The Viking fortress and Tartar palace were constructed on the outskirts of Zagreb, with other scenes shot on the windswept Dalmatian coast, where a huge tent city was erected.[5] Mature's career may well have been on the wane when making *The Tartars*, but his star presence was still attracting the crowds as witnessed when he was mobbed by frenzied Yugoslav fans when he visited the International Trade fair held in Zagreb. Police were called in to help Mature escape, but despite the mauling, Mature in good humor continued to sign autographs when he managed to make his way out, later commenting, "It's nice to be so popular, even if I did lose every button on my shirt."[6] In another fan-based incident, a young boy watching from the sidelines a sequence in which Mature was grappling with a giant opponent, jumped into the scene and bit his hero's adversary when it looked like Mature was going down to defeat. Mature and director Richard Thorpe saw the amusing aspect of it and decided not to reshoot the scene, leaving the incident in the film as a touch of comedy relief.[7]

To plug the film in America and Britain, the pressbook suggested that local cinema owners find a burly, bearded character and dress him up in the type of costume worn by Orson Welles in the film, and then hire a horse and have him ride around town, suitably bannered. The press kit also included Mature's tips on self-defense, with tip number nine advising that the best defense is to walk away (particularly when confronted by hordes of marauding Tartars, no doubt).

Motion Picture Review: "Orson Welles rolls his eyes and his bulk, Victor Mature leaps about flashing his bare thighs.... [B]oth seem at home in their fancy dress."

Variety: "Watching Mature and Welles one feels the same sense of regret as that inspired by the spectacle of viewing two ex-world heavyweight champions battling it out on the comeback trail for the Eastern Yugoslavian title."

The New York Times: "Big it is — and loud — and gory, and the biggest thing in sight is Mr. Welles as an evil barbarian chief. At this point in his career he looks like a walking house."

After the Fox

United Artists, 1966

Cast: Peter Sellers (Aldo Vanucci); Victor Mature (Tony Powell); Britt Ekland (Gina Romantica); Martin Balsam (Harry); Akim Tamiroff (Okra); Paolo Stoppa (Polio); Tino Buazzelli (Siepi); Mac Ronay (Carlo); Lydia Brazzi (Mamma Vanucci); Lando Buzzanca (Police Chief); Marai Grazia Buccella (Bikini Girl); Maurice Denham (Chief of Interpol); Tiberio Murgia (1st Detective); Francesco De Leone (2nd Detective); Carlo Croccolo (Cafe Owner); Nino Musco (Mayor); Pier Luigi Pizzi (Doctor); Lino Mattera (Singer); Piero Gerlini (1st Jailer); Daniele Vargas (Prosecuting Counsel); Franco Sportelli (Judge); Giustino Durano (Critic); Mimmo Poli (Fat Actor); Enzo Fiermonte (Raymond); Roberto De Simone (Marcel Vignon); Angelo Spaggiari (Felix Kessler).

Crew: John Bryan (Producer); Vittorio De Sica (Director); Neil Simon, Cesare Zavattini (Screenplay); Leonida Barboni (Cinematography); Burt Bacharach (Music Director); Burt Bacharach, Hal David (Song); Mario Garbuglia (Art Director); Piero Tosi (Costume Design); Stuart Freeborn, Amato Garbini (Makeup); Joseph Nathanson (Special Effects); Luisa Alessandri, Franco Cirino (Assistant Directors); Malcolm Cooke, Norman B. Schwartz (Sound); Russell Lloyd (Editor). Running time: 102 minutes.

Italian master thief Aldo Vanucci known as The Fox, who has spent eleven years in and out of prison, makes his escape and hatches a plan to smuggle $3 million of stolen gold from Cairo to Italy. Together with his gang, they unload it from a ship in an Italian coastal village by pretending to film a heist movie. Vanucci plays the part of a flamboyant director, bringing in over-the-hill American matinee actor Tony Powell (Victor Mature) and his agent Harry to add some credibility to the proceedings (Tony and Harry are unaware of Vanucci's real intentions). Vanucci also has to keep an eye on his sister Gina, who he thinks will pick up bad habits due to her movie-struck ways. Following a bout of double-crossing by one of the gang members, the plan to move the gold fails and Vanucci is caught by the police.

"Watch your girl, guard your gold, hold your jewels ... the Fox is loose!"

"You caught the 'Pussycat' ... now chase the Fox!"

For an actor to steal a film from Peter Sellers is quite an achievement, but Mature did precisely that in *After the Fox*, a gloriously funny farce which brought the actor out of early retirement after an absence of four years from the silver screen.

Sending up some of the pretentiousness of the film world, *After the Fox* tapped into Mature's ability to play comedy in any shape or form, here parodying himself as an aging has-been Hollywood star who still thinks he's in his thirties, when in fact he's in his mid-fifties—a look he tries to maintain by boot-polishing his hair black. (Britt Ekland gets it all over her hands and face in one passionate embrace.) Never one to take himself too seriously, Mature gives a performance that is truly memorable, and will have you reeling with laughter every time he appears on screen. Film comebacks don't get any better than this one.

The film was Neil Simon's first screenplay, arriving at a time when the frantic farce was in full bloom with *What's New Pussy Cat* delighting us the previous year and *Casino Royale* the following year, both featuring Peter Sellers, with the latter starring another aging star happy to send himself up, the inimitable David Niven. Sellers' comic genius found an outlet in many films, including *The Ladykillers* (1955), *I'm All Right, Jack* (1959), *Dr. Strangelove* (1963), and, of course, the *Pink Panther* film series (as the bungling Inspector Clouseau).

On paper, *After the Fox* had everything going for it: a Simon script, a $3 million budget, an excellent cast line-up, location shooting on the beautiful isle Ischia in the Bay of Naples, a terrific score by Burt Bacharach and Hal David, and direction by one of the greatest of Italian directors, Vittorio De Sica, who gave us the likes of *Shoe-Shine* (1946), *Bicycle Thieves* (1948) and *Yesterday, Today and Tomorrow* (1963). But for all this, *After the Fox* was poorly received, perhaps reflecting the tension and discord that had surrounded its production. There are several reasons for this disharmony, but it was probably very much a case of too many cooks spoiling the broth, particularly where the screenplay and direction were concerned.

The film was to have been the first from Sellers' new production company, Brookfield, which he set up with John Bryan, a former art director and production designer. But it turned out to be the first and last film the company made when Sellers and Bryan fell out over director De Sica, whom Sellers grew to dislike during the making of the film. (Sellers found De Sica's English too poor to convey his ideas, complaining, "He thinks in Italian, I think in English.") When he tried to get De Sica replaced, Bryan resisted on financial and artistic grounds and, finally fed up with all the infighting, he terminated his business relationship with Sellers.[1] De Sica had little patience for demanding stars and it didn't help matters that he detested Simon's screenplay and Sellers' performance.[2] Simon had originally wanted an Italian actor such as Marcello Mastroianni or Vittorio Gassman to play the Fox, before an agent suggested Sellers. Once signed up, Sellers demanded that Britt Ekland, whom he married in 1964, be cast as Gina, the Fox's sister, even though her accent and looks were wrong for the role. The language problem also proved a headache to Simon, who was saddled with two film editors who spoke no English, which made it difficult for them to understand any of the jokes. To make matters worse, he also had to collaborate with Cesare Zavattini on the screenplay, with both writers having to use interpreters because of the language problem. Simon recalled that he was worried that De Sica's attempts at social comment would not sit comfortably with the broad farce he had originally envisaged.

With so much disharmony in the camp, it appeared that the only person enjoying himself during production was Mature. And in each of his hilarious scenes, it looks like he is well and truly lapping up the self-mockery. The sequence where he gets his manager (Martin Balsam) to punch him in the stomach, to prove he still has what it takes, and then doubles up in pain in the quiet of his room, is well worth the price of admission alone. Another highpoint, superbly capturing his vain posturing, is when the car carrying him and several passengers stalls on a railway track when a train is approaching. Mature's screams give way to smiles when the danger passes, pretending he was never really worried. But the scene that wins hands down for me is when Sellers runs the finished film and gullible Mature takes it all in as if he is truly witnessing an artistic masterpiece.

But surrounded by so much temperament on set, it was only a matter of time before Mature got in on the act. In his 1996 memoir, Simon recalls how Mature got upset when on the first day of shooting on the beach, a driver with a small Fiat was sent to pick him up and deliver him to the set. Mature insisted that his contract clearly stated he was to be driven to all locations in a limousine. When the director heard about this he was furious, but found a white limo just to keep Mature happy. Satisfied that he was getting the star treatment, Mature jumped in and endured a ride that took close to two hours because the car was too big for the narrow, winding road (The Fiat could have made the trip in 35 min-

Master crook Aldo Vannuci (Peter Sellers), in the guise of a flamboyant film director, pulls the wool over the eyes of aging matinee idol Tony Powell (Mature), in the film that proved Mature as a master of self-parody, *After the Fox* (United Artists, 1966).

utes.) When Sellers heard about this, he insisted that he should have a black limo chauffeur him around. De Sica eventually found one on the small isle; it was probably used for funerals, but Sellers was none the wiser.[3]

Mature was quoted as saying, when filming got underway, "[I]f Sellers plays his cards right, I may let him steal the picture." But when he saw the rushes, he told Sheilah Graham, "I suggest you sell your United Artists stock."[4]

Whatever criticisms were directed toward the film, one cannot deny that Mature gave a wonderful performance in a role which memorably played on one of his most engaging qualities, a self-deprecating sense of humor. Nobody laughed at himself more than Mature, and we love him all the more for it.

With his broad grin and deadpan, confused, and at times exasperated look, Mature perfectly enriches Sellers' excellent impression of a vain, posturing Italian director. One scene in particular will have you in stitches, when Sellers' Vanucci tries to buy some time when the gold is delayed. Shooting in a phony neo-realist style, he tells Mature's Tony Powell, "We are ready for the next shot, only in this scene instead of doing nothing, we do something." He then tells Mature and Ekland to run and keep on running, because "No matter how fast you run, you can never run away from yourselves." Completely taken in by all the symbolic nonsense, Tony, who thinks Vanucci is a genius, exclaims, "Ahh! Beautiful!" of the demands made on him.

And lest we forget the Mature of old, the film includes a clip from *Easy Living* in a scene with Lizbeth Scott, showing the actor in familiar 1940s fedora and trenchcoat — trademark garb that Mature's corseted star, Tony Powell dons in the film in an effort to relive the past (wickedly funny). When Mature ditches the garb in one scene, his manager Balsam cries out, "What are you doing, Tony? You can't work without a trenchcoat, that's your trademark," to which Mature replies, "I've got a new trademark, Harry, baby, it's called acting."

Variety: "It is a generous and delightful piece of self-parody and Mature blends well with Sellers and with Martin Balsam..."

The New York Times: "It's pretty much of a mess, this picture. Yes, you'd think it was done by amateurs."

Radio Times Guide to Films: "[T]he best joke of all is Victor Mature as a fading beefcake star, sending up his own image — corsets and all."

TV Times Film & Video Guide: "Victor Mature sends up his own film image nicely as a fading screen idol...."

Time Out: "Marginally enlivened by Mature's witty self-mockery as a beefcake star fretting over his fading charms."

Head

Columbia, 1968

Cast: Peter Tork, Davy Jones, Micky Dolenz, Michael Nesmith (The Monkees); Annette Funicello (Minnie); Timothy Carey (Lord High 'n' Low); Logan Ramsey (Off. Faye Lapid); Abraham Sofaer (The Swami); Vito Scotti (I. Vitteloni); Charles Macaulay (Inspector Shrink); T.C. Jones (Mr. and Mrs. Ace); Charles Irving (Mayor Feedback); William Bagdad (Black Sheik); Percy Helton (Heraldic Messenger); Sonny Liston (Extra); Ray Nitschke (Private One); Carol Doda (Sally Silicone); Frank Zappa (The Critic); June Fairchild (The Jumper); Teri Garr (Testy True); I.J. Jefferson (Lady Pleasure); Victor Mature (The Big Victor); Terry Chambers (Oreh); Mike Burns (Gnihton); Esther Shepard (Rehtom); Kristine Helstoski (Dneirf Lrig); John Hoffman (Dneifxes Eht); Linda Weaver (Yraterces Revol); Jim Hanley (Frodis).

Crew: Bert Schneider (Executive Producer); Jack Nicholson, Bob Rafelson (Producers); Bob Rafelson (Director); Bob Rafelson, Jack Nicholson (Screenplay); Michael Hugo (Cinematography); Ken Thorne (Music Director); Sydney Z. Litwack (Art Direction); Ned Parsons (Set Decorations); Gene Ashman (Costumes and Wardrobe); Toni Basil (Choreographer); Chuck Gaspar (Special Effects); Jon C. Andersen (Assistant Director); Les Fresholtz (Sound); Michael Pozen (Editor). Running time: 86 minutes.

The singing group "The Monkees" travels through a series of pscheldelic adventures (with no plot to speak of) exploring media manipulation. En route they indulge in the satirization of different movie genres and appear as dandruff in the hair of the giant known as the Big Victor (Victor Mature).

"What is HEAD all about? Only John Brockman's shrink knows for sure!"

Like those surreal Beatles films, *A Hard Day's Night* (1964) and *Help!* (1965), *Head* is a wonderful piece of sixties psychedelic slapstick that gets better with every viewing. Watching it for the first time in the mid–1970s, I switched off halfway through, because it bore no resemblance to the television show *The Monkees* that brightened up my early Saturday evenings in the 1960s. But time has been good to it, and I now greatly enjoy its bizarre, dream-like journey that takes in some very funny spoofing on war films, Westerns, desert sagas and musicals. The music (their big hits notably absent) also gets the thumbs-up in my book. And we enjoy cameo appearances from Jack Nicholson (who co-wrote the story with director Bob Rafelson), Teri Garr, Annette Funicello, Frank Zappa, Sonny Liston, Timothy Carey and Ray Nitschke.

The cameo that stands out the most, even though he speaks no dialogue, is that of Victor Mature playing "The Big Victor." In another exercise of self-parody, he gets to show off his glowing sun tan in seven scenes — eight, if you include his magnified eye staring back at Davy Jones through a cabinet mirror in the men's room. We first see him when the guys, playing the part of dandruff, are sucked out of his hair by a giant vacuum cleaner. In his second scene, he appears as a reflection in a mirror, dressed in a safari suit as if he had just stepped off the set of *Safari* or *Timbuktu*. As a grinning giant in a wild west setting, he looms over the Monkees in a third scene, followed by a desert sequence where he sits cross-legged in a director's chair atop a sand dune, presiding over the proceedings, before striking the Monkees with a giant golf club in the fifth scene. Later, we see him watching himself on television as a giant trying to stamp on the Monkees, who are circling around in a Jeep. Finally, with the credits just about to roll, we see him decked out like Sherlock Holmes sitting on the back of a truck transporting the Monkees off the premises in a water-filled tank. Of course, none of this nonsense makes any sense whatsoever, but I still come away laughing each time I watch it.

The same can't be said of audiences in the 1960s, who mostly came away disappointed by the whole affair. (First time round, it mostly went over their heads, I guess — no pun intended.) Many were unhappy with the music, which was far removed from the Monkees' traditional pop sound. Others felt that they had strayed away too far from their familiar, well-groomed public image. The mixed critical reviews all added to a commercial flop, which dealt a severe blow to the Monkees popularity as recording artists. The film was to be the first and last full-length feature for the group.

Bob Rafelson, who created the Monkees along with Bert Schneider, went on to direct Jack Nicholson in several movies including *Five Easy Pieces* (1970), *The Postman Always Rings Twice* (1981) and *Blood and Wine* (1996).

The New York Times was less than impressed, but did concede, "There are some funny moments — an old joke about a regiment of Italian soldiers surrendering to a single man, a policeman posing girlishly before a mirror, a scene in which the boys are cast as dandruff in the hair of a giant Victor Mature...."

Every Little Crook & Nanny

MGM, 1972

Cast: Lynn Redgrave (Nanny); Victor Mature (Carmine Ganucci); Paul Sand (Benny Napkins); Margaret Blye (Stella); Austin Pendleton (Luther); John Astin (Vito Garbugli); Dom DeLuise (Azzecca); Louise Sorel (Marie); Phillip Graves (Lewis); Lou Cutell (Landruncolo); Leopoldo Trieste (Truffatore); Pat Morita (Nonaka); Phil Foster (Lt. Bozzaris);

Pat Harrington, Jr. (Willie Shakespeare); Severn Darden (Dominic); Katherine Victory (Jeanette Kay); Mina Kolb (Ida); Bebe Louie (Sarah); Lee Kafafian (Bobby); Sally Marr (Ida's Mother).

Crew: Leonard J. Ackerman (Producer); Nicky Blair (Associate Producer); Cy Howard (Director); Evan Hunter (Novel); Cy Howard, Jonathan Axelrod, Robert Klane (Screenplay); Phillip Lathrop (Cinematography); Fred Karlin (Music); Philip M. Jefferies (Production Design); James L. Berkey (Set Decorations); Margo Baxley, Buckey Rous (Costume Design); William Turner (Makeup); Ted Schilz (Assistant Director); Bruce Wright, Hal Watkins, Harry W. Tetrick (Sound); Henry Berman (Editor). Running time: 92 minutes.

The studio of British etiquette teacher Miss Poole is taken over by gangster Carmine Ganucci's (Victor Mature) bungling lawyers to use as a bookie joint. She inadvertently becomes a nanny to Ganucci's son Lewis, and hatches a plan to carry out a phony kidnapping of the boy with the intention of using the ransom money to set up a new studio. Assisted by her neurotic pianist Luther, she carries out the plan while Ganucci and his wife Stella are vacationing in Italy. Luther takes the boy to his home where his wife Ida becomes very attached to him. Miss Poole advises one of Ganucci's hoods of the kidnapping and many complications ensue before the boy is safely returned.

"Who would be crazy enough to snatch Carmine Ganucci's kid?"

Having played a variety of small-time crooks in films such as *The Housekeeper's Daughter*, *Kiss of Death* and *Gambling House*, Mature finally got to play Mr. Big in the Cy Howard–Leonard J. Ackerman production *Every Little Crook & Nanny*. With slicked-back hair, and his bronzed middle-aged Italian looks, Mature looked very much the part of underworld czar Carmine Ganucci, a role which brought him out of retirement (for the second time) after a four-year absence from the screen. When asked why he took the role, he answered, "It was too funny a script to turn down."[1] Although excited about the role, Mature told interviewer Aijean Harmetz, "It's just so happened that they caught me when I felt like saying 'Yeah.' If they'd only got me two weeks later, I'd have said 'No.'"[2]

Director Howard was no stranger to fast paced comedies, starting out his career as a comedy writer for radio stars Jack Benny, Danny Thomas and Milton Berle. He co-scripted the popular radio series *My Friend Irma* and wrote the screen version, which saw the debut of Dean Martin and Jerry Lewis. He made his directorial debut with the very funny wedding comedy *Lovers and Other Strangers* (1970), and was once married to Gloria Grahame (from 1954 to 1957).

English actress Lynn Redgrave was equally adept on stage or on screen. Born into an esteemed acting dynasty (she was the daughter of Sir Michael Redgrave and sister to Vanessa Redgrave), she left her mark with her Oscar-nominated performances in *Georgy Girl* (1966 — for Best Actress) *Gods and Monsters* (1998 — for Best Supporting Actress).

As in *After the Fox*, Mature's wonderful flair for self-parody makes each of his scenes count in a crime farce which is amusing but at times, with so many characters and subplots to cover, has a tendency to falter. Helping to move things along, the supporting cast includes Paul Sand, Maggie Blye, Austin Pendleton, John Astin and Dom DeLuise. Most scenes were filmed in Los Angeles and Naples, Italy.

Two running jokes help to liven up the proceedings, with the gangsters repeating the slogan, "There's no such thing as the Mafia," when anyone refers to Ganucci's occupation,

After playing a gangster at the beginning of his career (in *The Housekeeper's Daughter*), Mature reprises the role, this time as an underworld czar, near the end of his screen career in the fast-paced comedy *Every Little Crook & Nanny* (MGM, 1972). From left: Margaret Blye (as Stella), Mature (as Carmine Gannucci), Austin Pendleton (as Luther), and Lynn Redgrave (as Miss Poole).

and Mature saying to his sexpot wife, "Cover up your boobs, Stella, " whenever she appears in public with him. Like Mature's fading star Tony Powell, Ganucci is pretty oblivious to things going on around him, which greatly adds to the film's comedy value. It was this aspect of Ganucci's character which appealed to Mature; he commented in the film's pressbook, "He's a powerful man in his material world, but what makes him funny is his absolute belief in his own absolute power. So many things go on around him in the story, including the kidnapping of his son, without his knowledge — you begin to understand how ignorance breeds arrogance — and it's laughable!"

Having spent several relaxing retirement years at his Rancho Santa Fe home, Mature compared coming back to the regimen of filmmaking to rejoining the military with its confinement and restrictions, and doubted whether if he'd ever make another picture. Laughing, he wrapped up the conversation by saying, "Nobody ever died from loafing."[3] And true to his word, apart from a handful of cameo appearances in the coming years, he didn't play another leading role in a film.

The *New York Times*: "Victor Mature ... seems to be relishing his portrayal of the amiably vulgar, tough underworld big shot..."

Variety: "Mature, in a rare screen appearance, appears to have enjoyed himself enormously, and the feeling is conveyed to an audience."

Radio Times Guide to Films: "A glorious piece of self-guying from Victor Mature illuminates this hit-and-miss comedy, though we don't spend nearly enough time in his company."

Won Ton Ton: The Dog Who Saved Hollywood

Paramount, 1976

Cast: Bruce Dern (Grayson Potchuck); Madeline Kahn (Estie Del Ruth); Art Carney (J.J. Fromberg); Teri Garr (Fluffy Peters); Phil Silvers (Murray Fromberg); Victor Mature (Nick); Dennis Morgan (Tour Guide); Shecky Greene (Tourist); Phil Leeds, Cliff Norton (Dog Catchers); Romo Vincent (Short Order Cook); Sterling Holloway (Old Man on Bus); William "Billy" Benedict (Man on Bus); Dorothy Gulliver (Old Woman on Bus); William Demarest (Studio Gatekeeper); Virginia Mayo (Miss Battley); Henry Youngman (Manny Farber); Rory Calhoun (Philip Hart); Billy Barty (Assistant Director); Henry Wilcoxon (Silent Film Director); Ricardo Montalban (Silent Film Star); Jackie Coogan (Stagehand 1); Aldo Ray (Stubby Stebbins); Ethel Merman (Hedda Parsons); Yvonne De Carlo (Cleaning Woman); Joan Blondell (Landlady); Andy Devine (Priest in Dog Pound); Broderick Crawford (Special Effects Man); Richard Arlen (Silent Film Star 2); Jack La Rue (Silent Film Villain); Dorothy Lamour (Visiting Film Star); Nancy Walker (Mrs. Fromberg); Gloria DeHaven (President's Girl 1); Louis Nye (Radio Interviewer); Johnny Weissmuller (Stagehand 2); Stepin Fetchit (Dancing Butler); Ken Murray (Souvenir Salesman); Rudy Vallee (Autograph Hound); George Jessel (Awards Announcer); Rhonda Fleming (Rhonda Fleming); Ann Miller (President's Girl 2); Dean Stockwell (Paul Lavell); Dick Haymes (James Crawford); Tab Hunter (David Hamilton); Robert Alda (Richard Entwhistle); Eli Mintz (Tailor); Ron Leibman (Rudy Montague); Fritz Feld (Rudy's Butler); Edward Ashley (Second Butler); Kres Mersky (Girl in Arab Film); Jane Connell (Waitress); Janet Blair (President's Girl 3); Dennis Day (Singing Telegraph Man); Mike Mazurki (Studio Guard); The Ritz Brothers (Cleaning Women); Jesse White (Rudy's Agent); Carmel Myers (Woman Journalist); Jack Carter (Male Journalist); Jack Bernardi (Fluffy's Escort); Barbara Nichols (Nick's Girl); Army Archerd (Premiere MC); Fernando Lamas (Premiere Male Star); Zsa Zsa Gabor (Premiere Female Star); Cyd Charisse (President's Girl 4); Huntz Hall (Moving Man); Doodles Weaver (Man in Mexican Film); Pedro Gonzalez Gonzalez (Mexican Projectionist); Edward Le Veque (Prostitute Customer); Edgar Bergen (Professor Quicksand); Ronny Graham (Mark Bennett); Morey Amsterdam, Eddie Foy, Jr. (Custard Pie Stars); Peter Lawford (Slapstick Star); Patricia Morison, Guy Madison (Stars at Screening); Regis Toomey (Burlesque Stagehand); Alice Faye (Secretary at Gate); Ann Rutherford (Grayson's Studio Secretary); Milton Berle (Blind Man); James Brodhead (Priest); John Carradine (Drunk); Keye Luke (Cook in Kitchen); Walter Pidgeon (Grayson's Butler); Augustus von Schumacher (Won Ton Ton).

Crew: David V. Picker, Arnold Schulman, Michael Winner (Producers); Tim Zinnemann (Associate Producer); Michael Winner (Director); Arnold Schulman, Cy Howard (Screenplay); Richard H. Kline (Cinematography); Neal Hefti (Music); Ward Preston (Art Direction); Ned Parsons (Set Decorations); Phil Rhodes (Makeup); Charles Okun (Assistant Director); Terry Rawlings (Sound); Bernard Gribble (Editor). Running time: 92 minutes.

Estie Del Ruth, an aspiring actress, hits the jackpot when the German Shepherd that has been following her becomes a major Hollywood star with the assistance of would-be director Grayson Potchuck and studio boss J.J. Fomberg. But when the public loses interest,

Estie and Grayson are fired and the pooch ends up in a traveling dog show. All ends well when Estie becomes famous in her own right as a comedian and is reunited with the dog.

"Introducing the Dog Who Launched 1000 stars!"

Won Ton Ton: The Dog Who Saved Hollywood was produced at a time in the mid-seventies when films about old Hollywood were in vogue. Some were serious biopics such as *Gable and Lombard* (1976) and *W.C. Fields & Me* (1976), while others like *Won Ton Ton*, *Silent Movie* (1976) and *Nickelodeon* (1976) were comedies which spoofed Hollywood's golden age. The majority, including *Won Ton Ton*, were generally panned on release for a variety of reasons but if ever a film warranted a reappraisal of its fine attributes, it's this very funny satire on the legendary Hollywood pooch Rin Tin Tin. Sure, the movie has its faults, like the fact that the pace can be a little frenetic at times, which makes it difficult for some of the cameos to register, but overall it's a comedic and film buff's delight which deserves a wider audience.

And no film that featured a neverending cavalcade of cameo appearances from former Hollywood stars would have been complete without Victor Mature featuring somewhere in the lineup. He plays a hitman who has been contracted by a temperamental matinee star to take out the dog and its owners, because they prompted the failure of his latest production — a film in which the dog comes to the rescue of Custer at the Little Big Horn. When the star makes a phone call to arrange the hit on the doggie, as he describes it, Mature gets one of the best lines in the film when he responds, " A doggie? I never hit a dog before. I wouldn't know how to charge for a dog. Now what about a horse? I could do you a nice deal on a horse." In his second brief appearance, Mature tries to eliminate Madeline Kahn, but ends up accidentally jumping out of her dressing room window when he bungles his attempt on her life. Cameos don't come any funnier than this one.

Director Michael Winner recalled in his biography, *Winner Takes All*, that working with the old stars, many who had entranced him as a child, was great fun, with each being paid five hundred dollars a day for their services. He added that if each of the stars had signed his script, it would have been one of the greatest pieces of cinema memorabilia ever. He commented that Mature had been one of his screen heroes from the days when he was pushing over temple pillars in *Samson and Delilah*. He added that Mature was the favorite on set because he was the only star who tipped the drivers generously.[1]

Winner was less than enamored with the German Shepherd who took the lead in the film, describing it as an extremely bad-tempered dog who bit practically everybody on the set.[2] The dog also featured in a later Winner film, *Firepower* (1979) playing one of two guard dogs that attack James Coburn and O.J. Simpson. Winner commented that during the making of *Firepower* the dog was now so vicious that it wore a muzzle at all times. The film also featured another cameo by Mature.

Although the dog features in some funny scenes, such when it tries to commit suicide, the real star of the show is undoubtedly the wonderfully animated Madeline Kahn in the role of struggling actress Estie. Her presence and timing is such that she steals most of her scenes. Kahn was nominated for Best Supporting Actress Oscars for her performances in *Paper Moon* (1973) and *Blazing Saddles* (1974). Brooks tapped into her comedic talents in other farces including *Young Frankenstein* (1974) and *High Anxiety* (1977).

Bruce Dern and Art Carney are also in top form, and their running gag with Carney dismissing all of Dern's film ideas, which include the plot scenarios for *Jaws* and *The Exorcist*, is a hoot.

London-born Winner left his mark with films such as *The System* (1964), *The Jokers* (1967) and *Hannibal Brooks* (1969), all starring Oliver Reed. In 1974, he started his successful collaboration with Charles Bronson in the action film *Death Wish*, which spawned four sequels.

The New York Times: "What saves the movie, a jumble of good jokes and bad, chaos and apparently any old thing that came to hand, is Madeline Kahn."

Variety: "[*Won Ton Ton*] leaves no stone unturned in straining for broad, low laughs in the worst possible way; and that's precisely how it succeeds."

Incidentally, Mature promoted Rin Tin Tin in his 1952 musical feature *Million Dollar Mermaid*.

Firepower

ITC/Michael Winner, 1979

Cast: Sophia Loren (Adele Tasca); James Coburn (Jerry Fanon/Eddie); O.J. Simpson (Catlett); Eli Wallach (Sal Hyman); Anthony Franciosa (Dr. Charles Felix); George Grizzard (Leo Gelhorn); Vincent Gardenia (Frank Hull); Fred Stuthman (Halpin); Richard Caldicot (Calman); Frank Singuineau (Manley Reckford); George Touliatos (Stegner); Hank Garrett (Oscar); Conrad Roberts (Lestor); Billy Barty (Dominic Carbone); Jake LaMotta (Nickel Sam); Vincent Beck (Trilling); Dominic Chianese (Orlov); Andrew Duncan (Cooper); Paul D'Amato (Tagua); Paul Garcia (Vito Tasca); Richard Roberts (Dr. Ivo Tasca); Peter Savage (Lawyer); William Trotman (Pathologist); Paula Laurence (Woman Guest); Thom Christopher (Male Guest); Bill Abbott (Reckford's Bodyguard); Sonia Manzano (Air Hostess); Ruth Jaroslow, Elsa Raven (Tourists); Catherine Neilson (Hotel Secretary); Victor Mature (Harold Everett).

Crew: Michael Winner (Producer-Director); Michael Winner, Bill Kelby (Story); Gerald Wilson (Screenplay); Robert Paynter (Cinematography); Gato Barbieri (Music); Robert Gundlach (Art Direction); Simon Wakefield, Robert Coleman (Set Decorations); Joseph G. Aulisi (Costume Design); Richard Mills, Allen Weisinger (Makeup); Al Griswold, Paul Stewart (Special Effects); Joe Marks, Bob Wilkins (Assistant Directors); John Poyner (Sound); "Arnold Crust" [Michael Winner] (Editor). Running time: 104 minutes.

Beautiful Adele Tasca believes her chemist husband was murdered on the orders of wealthy industrialist Stegner, because he was about to expose Stegner's line of bad pharmaceuticals. Adele persuades the Justice Department to pressure mob boss Sal Hyman into enticing her former lover and retired hitman Jerry Fanon back into service to capture Stegner, who hides out in a heavily guarded Caribbean mansion. Fanon, with the assistance of fellow hitman Catlett, carries out the mission and heads back into retirement.

"They'll Blast ... Bulldoze ... or Blow Up anyone who stands in their way!"

And that's no idle boast, with James Coburn and Co. doing exactly that, smoking out the villain of the piece by first setting fire to his luxury Caribbean hideout in Antigua, and when that fails, reducing his second private residence in Curacao to a pile of rubble with a bulldozer. There's definitely nothing subtle about Coburn's calling card in this frenetic tale, which is action all the way with its many explosions and chases, laced with a couple of good twists to hold your attention.

On the subject of explosions, Winner recalled an amusing incident in which they had to blow up a helicopter. A perfect model helicopter, with seven cameras trained on it, was set to fly across the beach by remote control. But the helicopter barely got off the ground before it exploded, having been set off inadvertently by someone on the beach turning on a radio. Unfortunately, none of the cameras caught it, but luckily they had another model helicopter and shot the scene.[1]

If you're not into explosions, which were so much a part of '70s thrillers, then just sit back and soak up the lush Caribbean settings, and of course the attraction of the beautiful Sophia Loren, who in a stunning wardrobe, courtesy of her favorite designer Per Spook, sashays through her scenes in fine style. Some of the outfits were quite revealing, having been designed to make the Caribbean heat more tolerable for Loren. So much so that when she went braless beneath sheer crepes and silks, some of the technical crew retitled the film *Nipplepower*.[2]

With her statuesque body, earthy sex appeal and distinctive Italian looks, it would have been movie heaven to have seen Loren and Mature starring together in one of those epic tales of the ancient world, instead of the brief encounter offered in *Firepower*. Before shooting the scene, Winner met Mature outside the Piere Hotel in New York, informing the actor that his hair had turned green. Mature replied, "I think something went wrong when I dyed it. It's normally white." Winner told him that Loren's face was orange because she insisted upon doing her own makeup, and that the final scene could be described as the orange-faced woman meets the green-haired man.[3]

Loren won a Best Actress Academy Award for her performance in *Two Women* (1961) and (like Mature) was very much at home in epic adventures such as *The Pride and the Passion* (1957), *El Cid* (1961) and *The Fall of the Roman Empire* (1964). Her talent for romantic comedy was showcased to good effect in many features, including *Houseboat* (1958) and *The Millionairess* (1960). After making *Firepower*, Loren returned to Italy, where in 1982 she served seventeen days of a one-month prison sentence for tax evasion.

According to some accounts, Clint Eastwood and Charles Bronson were first considered for the part action hero Jerry Fannon before it went to James Coburn. In Winner's opinion, Bronson turned down the role because he never did a movie with a star leading lady; being insecure, he didn't want the competition.[4]

In common with the likes of Mature and Burt Lancaster, James Coburn had one of the broadest grins in Hollywood, which he used to charming effect as the Bond-like hero in the spy spoofs *Our Man Flint* (1965) and *In Like Flint* (1966). He will also be fondly remembered for *The Magnificent Seven* (1960), *The Great Escape* (1963) and *Cross of Iron* (1977). He won an Academy Award for Best Supporting Actor in *Affliction* (1997), and was the original choice for the role of Hannibal Smith in TV's *The A-Team* before the part went to George Peppard.

Helping to keep the action moving at a lively clip, the fine supporting cast included O.J. Simpson, Eli Wallach, Anthony Franciosa, George Grizzard, Vincent Gardenia and retired boxer Jake La Motta. The film also had a slot for the dog that played the pooch in *Won Ton Ton: The Dog Who Saved Hollywood*, this time playing a vicious guard dog.

The best line in the film: Stegner's head of security tells his business adviser (who wants Loren dead), "I've always noticed it's you rich, soft, pampered people that are most in love with violence. You've never experienced it, you're voyeurs, you just want to see it done."

Having sustained several injuries throughout his film career, Mature was loathe to take any risks on set where his own personal safety was concerned. When he arrived on set to do *Firepower* he told Winner, "I don't do anything active, you know." Musing afterwards, Winner commented, "It was only later I found out that he classified getting out of a car as a major stunt." It was probably for this reason that Mature's cameo appearance is about as brief as they come; it's found at the very end of film, safely distant from any flying bullets or explosions. Playing Harold Everett, the fourth richest man in the world, and dressed in a dinner suit, he is introduced to Loren at a cocktail party, where she informs him that she is attracted to wealthy and powerful men. Clearly taken by her obvious charms, he delivers his only line, "Mrs. Tasker, it's a pleasure," with his customary grin and raising of the left eyebrow. And that said, the credits roll. I thought I was short-changed as far as cameos are concerned, as I was rather hoping that Mature was going to make his brief appearance as one of the villains, perhaps doing a serious take on his Mr. Big from *Every Little Crook and Nanny*. Having reached the end of the film, with no sign of Mature making an entrance, I was just about to rewind to ensure I hadn't accidentally missed him in an earlier scene, when I caught sight of his familiar thick black wavy hair in a party crowd scene before he makes his way towards Loren, in the dying seconds of the film. For this briefest of scenes, Grade paid Mature five thousand dollars.

Winner clearly thought highly of Mature, describing him as a superb person. At the end of the film, Mature asked Winner if he could keep the dinner suit he wore in his scene, prompting Winner to ask him what use could he possibly have for a dinner suit in his home in Ranch Sante Fe. Mature responded that it would come in handy for funerals. When Winner informed him that no one wears a dinner suit at funerals, Mature said, "I do." Mature and Winner corresponded and spoke on the phone for years afterwards, until Mature died in 1999.[5]

Firepower did okay at the box office, but not enough to recover its $8 million cost. Winner enjoyed making it, affectionately describing it as a "pleasant meat-and-potatoes movie."

The *New York Times*: "[T]here's a nice chemistry in the teaming of Miss Loren, Mr. Coburn and Mr. Simpson, each of whom has an unusually physical presence on the screen."

Leonard Maltin: "Another international thriller, with beautiful people in beautiful locations."

Samson and Delilah (TV)

ABC, 1984

Cast: Max von Sydow (Sidka); Belinda Bauer (Delilah); Antony Hamilton (Samson); Stephen Macht (Maluck); Daniel Stern (Micah); Clive Revill (Raul); Jennifer Holmes (Varinia); David Eisner (Arin); David Byrd (Elon); Jose Ferrer (The High Priest); Maria Schell (Deborah); Victor Mature (Manoah); Angelica Aragon (Niji); Rene Ruis (Temple Man); Brandon Scott (Magician); Guy De Saint Cyr (Soldier); Salvador Godinez, Allen Grossman, Tom Lee (Tribe Elders), Philip Guilmant (Governor of Gath); Martin LaSalle (Governor of Ekron); Eduardo Noriega (Governor of Ashdod); Salim Maldonado (Tribe Boy); Ken Smith (High Priest at Wedding).

Crew: Gregory Harrison (Executive Producer); Franklin R. Levy (Producer);

Matthew Rushton (Associate Producer); Lee Philips (Director); Eric Linklatter (Book *Husband of Delilah*); John Gay (Screenplay); Gerry Fisher (Cinematography); Maurice Jarre (Music); Joese Rodriguez Granada (Art Direction); Ed Wittstein (Production Design); Madeline Ann Graneto (Costume Design); Brian McManus (Makeup); George Jay Nicholson, Gabriella Christiani (Editors). Running time: 95 minutes.

A television adaptation of the biblical tale of Samson and his struggles with the Philistines and his passionate affair with the beautiful but treacherous Philistine seductress Delilah, who in this version survives the destruction of the temple to mourn the Hebrew strongman.

Aged 71, Mature decided to return to the biblical epic to round off his screen career. And what could be more appropriate than a remake of the film that really put him at the top, *Samson and Delilah*. Based on the novel *Husband of Delilah* by Eric Linklatter, this television production was shot in Mexico and aired on ABC in the spring of 1984.

At six-foot-two, newcomer Antony Hamilton, who played Samson, was pretty much the same height as Mature, but the similarity between the two actors ended there. Hamilton had a great muscular physique, but his comic-book bodybuilder look was perhaps more suited to Conan the Barbarian than Samson. That aside, Hamilton does play the role with fervor, and his love scenes with Belinda Bauer, in the role of the seductive Delilah, come over well. But the whole affair simply shouts television production, draining the film of any

In his last film, a 1984 telemovie, Mature, right, returned to the biblical tale that made him a huge star, *Samson and Delilah*, but this time playing the strongman's father Manoah to Antony Hamilton's Samson.

real vitality and authenticity. Lending some weight to the proceedings, the film enjoyed solid support from veterans Max von Sydow and Jose Ferrer.

In Mature's previous cameo appearance in *Firepower,* he had little to do except gaze admiring at Sophia Loren. Here, playing Samson's father Manoah, he features in a few more brief scenes, but once again his lines are few, and mostly delivered with a scowl due to his disdain for his son's attraction to Philistine women — Varina and Delilah. Mature's Manoah makes his thoughts crystal clear on the subject of Samson's proposed union with Varina, angrily exclaiming, "This marriage is a plague upon us; all of us will suffer." That he should have married a nice Jewish girl, there can be no dispute, but then we would have missed the spectacles of Samson slaying the Philistine army (all twenty of them in this version) with the jawbone of an ass and the toppling of the Philistine temple.

It is obvious that Mature appreciated the limitations of the production and saw his guest appearance as little more than a paycheck, telling one interviewer, "It was a ridiculous part. I could have phoned it in." John J. O'Connor, who reviewed the film for *TV Weekend,* had similar thoughts when he reported, "Victor Mature has been brought out of retirement to play Samson's father. He manages to look concerned, as well he might."

Director Lee Philips came into the entertainment business as an actor, appearing in *Peyton Place* (1957), *The Hunters* (1958), and *Middle of the Night* (1959) before turning his hand to directing. His impressive list of directorial credits include the television series *The Andy Griffith Show, Peyton Place* and *The Dick Van Dyke Show.*

Antony Hamilton was born in Liverpool but grew up on an Australian sheep farm. Starting out as a ballet dancer, he moved to America to pursue a career as a model, then expanded his career into acting. He starred in the TV series *Cover Up* (1984) and in the 1988 revival of *Mission Impossible.* Openly gay, Hamilton died in 1995, aged 42, from AIDS-related pneumonia.

Australian-born actress Belinda Bauer's career followed a similar path to that of Hamilton, starting out as a ballet dancer and a successful model in New York before turning her talents to acting in film and television. Her film credits include *The American Success Company, Winter Kills* (both made in 1979 and starring Jeff Bridges), *Time Rider: The Adventure of Lyle Swann* (1982) and *Flashdance* (1983). She now works as a psychologist in Los Angeles.

Charlton Heston once said that the epic film is the easiest film to make badly. And perhaps he was right, for what they really need to excel are big budgets, top directors and larger-than-life actors such as Heston, Kirk Douglas and Mature. The golden age of the historical epic, which came to an end with the likes of *Spartacus* (1960), *El Cid* (1961) and *The Fall of the Roman Empire* (1964), had these vital ingredients, and perhaps it was a mite ambitious to try and tell these lofty tales within the confines of television productions. But such thoughts didn't deter another television makeover of the old tale in 1996, this time featuring Eric Thal as Samson and Elizabeth Hurley as Delilah. Once again, this television production has too much of a modern feel to it. In our modern age of computer wizardry, which lends itself to epic sagas, perhaps we will see a new big screen production to rival Mature's 1949 *tour de force.* Following the success of films such as *Gladiator* (2000), *Troy* (2004) and *300* (2006), the big budgets, top directors and audience interest is certainly there, but which modern actor has the screen presence of Victor Mature to make the role of Samson his own? Who has the statuesque physique and noble, weathered look of an ancient warrior, the natural ability to convey strength with vulnerability, sensuality with suppressed emotion, mirthful optimism with heroic melancholia — who else, indeed?

Appendix: Select Radio Appearances

Lux Radio Theater

This hour-long drama show, performed before a live audience, featured many actors in radio adaptations of Broadway plays and Hollywood films (using as many of the original stars from these productions as possible). Aired from 1935 to 1955, the shows were hosted by Cecil B. DeMille and Lionel Barrymore. Lux (soap products) commercials were delivered throughout the show.

Lillian Russell (October 21, 1940). Biographical story of entertainer Lillian Russell, with Mature featuring alongside two of the film's original stars, Alice Faye and Edward Arnold. The 1940 film also starred Don Ameche and Henry Fonda.

Slightly Dangerous (October 25, 1943). Comedy drama about a girl who impersonates a rich man's lost daughter, with Mature, Lana Turner and Gene Lockhart. The 1943 film saw Turner co-starring with Robert Young and Walter Brennan.

Coney Island (September 30, 1946). Mature and Barry Sullivan vie for the affections of singer Betty Grable. Grable reprised her role from the original 1943 film, which also starred George Montgomery and Cesar Romero.

Kiss of Death (January 1, 1948). Mature, Richard Widmark and Coleen Gray teamed again following the success of their 1947 film noir classic about a petty thief (Mature) who turns state's evidence against a psychopathic killer (Widmark) to save his family.

Dressed in his Coast Guard uniform, Mature puts his distinctive, husky voice to good use for the *Lux Radio Theatre* broadcast of *Slightly Dangerous,* which also featured Lana Turner (October 25, 1943).

Wabash Avenue (November 13, 1950). Mature and Betty Grable reprise their roles from the 1950 film, which was essentially a reworking of *Coney Island*.

Samson and Delilah (November 19, 1950). A Biblical tale with strongman Samson falling for the charms of Philistine seductress Delilah, with tragic consequences. Mature and Hedy Lamarr reprised their roles from the 1949 film.

Laura (February 1, 1954). Romantic murder mystery with police detective Mark McPherson (Mature) investigating the supposed murder of Laura Hunt (Gene Tierney). Mature took the role of the lovesick cop played by Dana Andrews in the 1944 film, which also starred Tierney in the title role.

Suspense

A CBS series that aired regularly from 1942 to 1962, focusing on chiller-thriller themes.

Momentum (October 27, 1949). Thriller with Mature as a man who, through a series of accidents, unintentionally kills several people. Written by Cornell Woolrich and E. Jack Neuman.

Black Jack to Kill (December 10, 1951). Thriller with Mature playing a hired killer. Written by David Freidkin and Morton Fine.

The Love and Death of Joaquin Murieta (February 16, 1953). Mature takes the role of the 1850s bandit Joaquin Murieta, who was known as the South-of-the-border Robin Hood. Written by Gil Doud.

The Girl in Car 32 (March 15, 1954). Mature plays a cop who falls in love with the girl he is tailing. Written by E. Jack Neuman and Thomas Walsh.

The Screen Guild Theater

Radio anthology series that ran from 1939 until 1952 with leading actors performing in adaptations of popular films.

Moss Rose (December 8, 1947). Victorian melodrama with Mature and Ethel Barrymore reprising their roles from the 1947 film about a chorus girl who suspects an aristocrat (Mature) of being a murderer.

Kiss of Death (October 28, 1948). Another take on the classic film noir with Mature, Richard Widmark and Coleen Gray, this time supported by Leon Ames. Mature and Widmark performed it again for *Screen Guild Theater* on March 29, 1951.

Fury at Furnace Creek (February 10, 1949). Western with two brothers trying to clear the name of their father, a general accused of causing a massacre. With Mature, Reginald Gardiner and Charles Kemper (reprising their roles from the 1948 film), Barbara Britton and Wendell Corey.

House of Strangers (January 25, 1951). Melodrama about a ruthless banker who uses his sons to promote his schemes. Edward G. Robinson reprised his role from the 1949 film, this time supported by Mature and June Havoc.

Hollywood Star Playhouse

Half-hour dramatic anthology series recreating suspenseful original plays. It ran from 1950 to 1953.

Final Entry (August 21, 1950). Mature plays an ex–Navy officer, accused of cowardice during the Normandy Invasion, who risks his life to save his reputation.

It's Later Than You Think (January 29, 1951). Mature plays a district attorney traveling in a car with a bomb for company.

Skippy Hollywood Theater

A radio show (which promoted Skippy Peanut Butter) that aired from 1941 to 1949.

Angelica (September 24, 1948). Playing an actor, Mature meets and tries to find out more about a mysterious girl.

Hollywood Star Time

Hollywood Star Time, which aired in 1944, initially featured lunch with the stars in RKO's dining room. The 1946–1947 season saw a similar format to the *Lux Radio Theater*, with stars reprising roles from their films.

My Gal Sal (February 20, 1946). Biopic of 1890s songwriter Paul Dresser, with Mature, as in the film, taking the lead role, with June Haver taking the part of his sweetheart played by Rita Hayworth in the film version.

Escape

This anthology series, focusing on adventure drama, was broadcast on CBS between 1947 and 1954.

The Fortune of Vargas (September 21, 1949). Mature finds love and adventure when looking for lost treasure. With William Conrad.

Sealtest Variety Theater

A musical variety and comedy show, hosted by Dorothy Lamour, that aired from 1946 to 1949. Mature guest starred with Eddie Bracken on April 14, 1949, playing men who take their women problems to a psychiatrist. Following advice to change their ways, Bracken becomes a strongman and Mature a timid type when they visit Lamour.

Hedda Hopper's Hollywood

Half-hour radio show hosted by actress–gossip columnist Hedda Hopper, featuring music, talk and star guests performing dramatized excerpts from their films. Mature guest starred with Richard Widmark on December 3, 1950, with both stars discussing why they regarded *Kiss of Death* as their favorite film. The stars also performed a scene from the film.

Notes

Biography

1. Louisville obituary, 1999.
2. Interview with *Courier-Journal* film critic Roger Fristoe, 1984.
3. *Silver Screen*, April 1949.
4. Ibid.
5. *Picture Show*, September 26, 1942.
6. James Robert Parish and Don E. Stanke, *The Swashbucklers* (New York: Arlington House, 1976), 422.
7. *Picture Show*, November 27, 1948.
8. Gladys Hall, "Don't Call Me Glamour Boy" December 1941, source unknown.
9. *Picture Show*, September 1942.
10. *Picture Show* Annual, 1950.
11. *Photoplay*, January 2, 1948.
12. *Picture Show* Annual, 1950.
13. J. Marks, *Interview Magazine*, May 1972.
14. Gladys Hall, "Don't Call Me Glamour Boy," December 1941, source unknown.
15. *Picturegoer*, September 17, 1955.
16. Richard Lewis Ward, *A History of the Hal Roach Studios* (Carbondale: Southern Illinois University Press, 2005), 129.
17. James Robert Parish and Don E. Stanke, *The Swashbucklers* (New York: Arlington House, 1976), 434.
18. Ibid., 441.
19. *Silver Screen*, April 1949.
20. *Photoplay*, January 2, 1948.
21. Ibid.
22. *Picturegoer*, September 17, 1955.
23. Interview with Aljean Harmetz, 1971.
24. Karen Burroughs Hannsberry, *Bad Boys: The Actors of Film Noir* (Jefferson, NC: McFarland, 2003), 442.
25. *The Film Show Annual*, 1954.
26. "I Love My Work," December 1953, source unknown.
27. Interview with Aljean Harmetz, 1971.
28. Esther Williams with Digby Diehl, *Esther Williams—The Million Dollar Mermaid* (New York: Simon & Schuster, 1999), 211–213.
29. *Picture Show*, July 15, 1950.
30. *The Film Show Annual*, 1954.
31. *Picturegoer*, October 9, 1954.
32. *The Film Show Annual*, 1954.
33. Louisville obituary, 1999.
34. U.K. interview with Pip Evans, 1956.

The Housekeeper's Daughter (1939)

1. Brian Kellow, *The Bennetts: An Acting Family* (Lexington: The University Press of Kentucky, 2004), 224–225.
2. J. Marks, *Interview Magazine*, May 1972.
3. Film magazine article, 1942.

One Million B.C. (1940)

1. Eric Gans, *Carole Landis: A Most Beautiful Girl* (Jackson: University Press of Mississippi, 2008), 43.
2. *Silver Screen*, July 1942.
3. Don G. Smith, *Lon Chaney, Jr.: Horror Film Star 1906–1973* (Jefferson, NC: McFarland, 1996), 30.
4. Ibid., 31.

Captain Caution (1940)

1. Turner Classic Movies. News item in *Hollywood Reporter*.

No, No, Nanette (1940)

1. Anna Neagle, *Anna Neagle Says 'There's Always Tomorrow': An Autobiography* (London: W.H. Allen, 1974), 124.
2. James Robert Parish and Don E. Stanke, *The Swashbucklers* (New York: Arlington House, 1976), 428.

The Shanghai Gesture (1941)

1. J. Marks, *Interview Magazine*, May 1972.
2. Michelle Vogel, *Gene Tierney: A Biography* (Jefferson, NC: McFarland, 2005), 55.

I Wake Up Screaming (1941)

1. Tom McGee, *Betty Grable: The Girl with the Million Dollar Legs* (New York: Welcome Rain, 1995), 90.
2. James Robert Parish and Don E. Stanke, *The Swashbucklers* (New York: Arlington House, 1976), 435.
3. Doug Warren, *Betty Grable, The Reluctant Movie Queen* (London: Robson Books, 1982), 68.

Song of the Islands (1942)

1. Tom McGee, *Betty Grable: The Girl with the Million Dollar Legs* (New York: Welcome Rain, 1995), 90.
2. Ibid.
3. Ed Hulse, *The Films of Betty Grable* (Burbank: Riverwood Press, 1996), 119.
4. Rudy Behlmer, *Memo from Darryl Zanuck: The Golden Years at Twentieth Century–Fox* (New York: Grove Press, 1993), 49.

My Gal Sal (1942)

1. Gene Ringgold, *The Films of Rita Hayworth* (New York: Citadel Press, 1974),134–135.
2. *Hollywood Reporter*, December 1941.
3. Ibid.
4. Barbara Leaming, *If This Was Happiness: A Biography of Rita Hayworth* (London: Weidenfeld and Nicholson, 1989), 53.
5. Ibid.
6. Phil Silvers with Robert Saffron, *The Man Who Was Bilko: The Autobiography of Phil Silvers* (London & New York: W.H. Allen, 1974), 118–119.

Footlight Serenade (1942)

1. Tom McGee, *Betty Grable: The Girl with the Million Dollar Legs* (New York: Welcome Rain, 1995), 99.
2. Phil Silvers with Robert Saffron, *The Man Who Was Bilko: The Autobiography of Phil Silvers* (London & New York: W.H. Allen, 1974), 120.
3. Ed Hulse, *The Films of Betty Grable* (Burbank: Riverwood Press, 1996), 122.
4. Ibid.
5. Phil Silvers with Robert Saffron, *The Man Who Was Bilko: The Autobiography of Phil Silvers* (London & New York: W.H. Allen, 1974), 119.

Seven Days' Leave (1942)

1. Cindy De La Hoz, *Lucy at the Movies* (Philadelphia: Running Press, 2007), 230.
2. Stefan Kanfer, *Ball of Fire: The Tumultuous Life and Comic Art of Lucille Ball* (London: Faber and Faber, 2003), 85.
3. Ibid., 83.
4. Ibid.
5. Kathleen Brady, *Lucille: The Life of Lucille Ball* (New York: Billboard Books, 2001), 129.

My Darling Clementine (1946)

1. Joseph McBride, *Searching for John Ford: A Life* (New York: St. Martin's Press, 2001), 111–112.
2. Rudy Behlmer, *Memo from Darryl Zanuck: The Golden Years at Twentieth Century–Fox* (New York: Grove Press, 1993), 101.
3. Scott Eyman, *Print the Legend: The Life and Times of John Ford* (Baltimore: The John Hopkins University Press, 1999), 311.
4. Ibid.
5. Rudy Behlmer, *Memo from Darryl Zanuck: The Golden Years at Twentieth Century–Fox* (New York: Grove Press, 1993), 102.
6. Joseph McBride, *Searching for John Ford: A Life* (New York: St. Martin's Press, 2001), 433.
7. Scott Eyman, *Print the Legend: The Life and Times of John Ford* (Baltimore: The John Hopkins University Press, 1999), 313–314.

Moss Rose (1947)

1. Lucy Chase Williams, *The Complete Films of Vincent Price* (New York: Citadel Press, 1998), 104.
2. Ibid.
3. *Mose Rose* pressbook.

Kiss of Death (1947)

1. Rudy Behlmer, *Memo from Darryl Zanuck: The Golden Years at Twentieth Century–Fox* (New York: Grove Press, 1993), 114.
2. Doug McClelland, *Forties Film Talk* (Jefferson, NC: McFarland,1992).
3. Ibid.
4. Karen Burroughs Hannsberry, *Bad Boys: The Actors of Film Noir* (Jefferson, NC: McFarland, 2003), 441.
5. Kingsley Canham, "Hathaway's Films," *Focus on Film*, No. 7, 1971.
6. *Photoplay*, January 2, 1948.

Fury at Furnace Creek (1948)

1. Studio publicity release, Academy of Motion Picture Arts and Sciences.

Cry of the City (1948)

1. J. Greco, *The File on Robert Siodmak in Hollywood: 1941-1951* Dissertation.com, 1999, 108.
2. James Robert Parish and Don E. Stanke, *The Swashbucklers* (New York, Arlington House, 1976), 447
3. *Cry of the City* pressbook.

4. Ibid.

Red, Hot and Blue (1949)

1. Betty Hutton with Carl Bruno and Michael Mayer, *Backstage You Can Have My Own Story* (Palm Springs: The Betty Hutton Estate, 2009), 221.

Easy Living (1949)

1. Chris Fujiwara, *Jacques Tourneur: The Cinema of Nightfall* (Baltimore: John Hopkins University Press, 2000), 158.
2. *Silver Screen*, April 1949.

Samson and Delilah (1949)

1. Stephen Michael Shearer, *Beautiful: The Life of Hedy Lamarr* (New York: Thomas Dunne Books, St. Martin's Press), 229.
2. Doug McClelland, *Forties Film Talk* (Jefferson, NC: McFarland,1992).
3. Ibid.
4. Richard Vanderbeets, *George Sanders: An Exhausted Life* (London, Robson Books, 1991),134.
5. Ibid., 81.
6. Ibid.,122.
7. Ibid., 149.
8. Doug McClelland, *Forties Film Talk* (Jefferson, NC: McFarland,1992).
9. Ruth Barton, *Hedy Lamarr: The Most Beautiful Woman in Film* (Lexington: The University Press of Kentucky, 2010), 169.
10. Stephen Michael Shearer, *Beautiful: The Life of Hedy Lamarr* (New York: Thomas Dunne Books, St. Martin's Press), 229.
11. Hedy Lamarr, *Ecstasy and Me. My Life as a Woman* (London: W.H. Allen, 1967), 133.
12. Ruth Barton, *Hedy Lamarr: The Most Beautiful Woman in Film* (Lexington: The University Press of Kentucky, 2010), 172.
13. Stephen Michael Shearer, *Beautiful: The Life of Hedy Lamarr* (New York, Thomas Dunne Books, St. Martin's Press), 239.
14. Ibid., 389.
15. Ruth Barton, *Hedy Lamarr: The Most Beautiful Woman in Film* (Lexington: The University Press of Kentucky, 2010), 174.

Wabash Avenue (1950)

1. Tom McGee, *Betty Grable: The Girl with the Million Dollar Legs* (New York: Welcome Rain, 1995), 168.
2. Ibid., 163.
3. Interview with Aljean Harmetz, 1971.

Stella (1950)

1. Margie Schultz, *Ann Sheridan: A Bio-Bibliography* (Westport, CT: Greenwood Press, 1997), 210.

Gambling House (1950)

1. James Robert Parish and Don E. Stanke, *The Swashbucklers* (New York: Arlington House, 1976), 454–455.
2. Peter Harry Brown and Pat H. Broeske, *Howard Hughes: The Untold Story* (London: Little, Brown, 1996), 240–241.

The Las Vegas Story (1952)

1. Peter Harry Brown and Pat H. Broeske, *Howard Hughes: The Untold Story* (London: Little, Brown, 1996), 281
2. Studio press release, 1950.
3. Jane Russell, *Jane Russell: An Autobiography* (London: Sidgwick & Jackson, 1986), 122.
4. Victoria Price, *Vincent Price: A Daughter's Biography* (London: Sidwick & Jackson, 1999), 210.
5. *Picturegoer*, May 10, 1952.
6. *Picturegoer*, September 24, 1955.

Something for the Birds (1952)

1. Stephen Michael Shearer, *Patricia Neal: An Unquiet Life* (Lexington: The University Press of Kentucky, 2006),135.
2. Ibid., 136.
3. Ibid., 135.

Million Dollar Mermaid (1952)

1. Esther Williams with Digby Diehl, *Esther Williams—The Million Dollar Mermaid* (New York: Simon & Schuster, 1999), 211.
2. Ibid., 211–213.
3. Ibid., 212.
4. Ibid., 214.

Androcles and the Lion (1952)

1. James Robert Parish and Don E. Stanke, *The Swashbucklers* (New York: Arlington House, 1976), 456.
2. *Picture Show Annual*, circa 1952.
3. Peter Harry Brown and Pat H. Broeske, *Howard Hughes: The Untold Story* (London: Little, Brown, 1996), 241.

The Glory Brigade (1953)

1. Robert J. Lentz, *Korean War Filmography* (Jefferson, NC: McFarland, 2003), 137.

The Robe (1953)

1. Bruce Francis Babington and Peter William Evans, *Biblical Epics: Sacred Narrative in the Hollywood Cinema* (Manchester: Manchester University Press, 1993), 236.
2. Michael Munn, *Richard Burton, Prince of Players* (London, JR Books, 2008), 78.
3 Ibid., 79–80.
4. Eric Niderost, "Victor Mature. The "Beefcake King" and Underrated Actor" *Classic Images*, No. 237, March 1995, 20.
5. Ibid.
6. Neil Doyle, "Victor Mature: Beautiful Hunk of Man," *Classic Images*, September 2001, 9.

Dangerous Mission (1954)

1. Turner Classic Movies website.

Demetrius and the Gladiators (1954)

1. Bruce Francis Babington and Peter William Evans, *Biblical Epics: Sacred Narrative in the Hollywood Cinema* (Manchester: Manchester University Press, 1993), 229.
2. Beverly Linet, *Susan Hayward: Portrait of a Survivor* (New York: Atheneum, 1980), 144.
3. Kim R. Holston, *Susan Hayward* (Jefferson, NC: McFarland, 2009), 100–101.
4. Ernest Borgnine, *I Don't Want to Set the World on Fire, I Just Want to Keep My Nuts Warm. An Autobiography* (London: JR Books, 2009), 86.

The Egyptian (1954)

1. Rudy Behlmer, *Memo from Darryl Zanuck: The Golden Years at Twentieth Century–Fox* (New York: Grove Press, 1993), 242.
2. Jon Solomon, *The Ancient World in the Cinema* (New Haven: Yale University Press, 2001), 247.
3. James Robert Parish and Don E. Stanke, *The Swashbucklers* (New York: Arlington House, 1976), 464.
4. Peter Ustinov, *Peter Ustinov: Dear Me* (London: Book Club Associates, 1977), 193.
5. John Miller, *Peter Ustinov: The Gift of Laughter* (London: Weidenfeld & Nicolson, 2002), 83.
6. Michael Wilding with Pamela Wilcox, *Michael Wilding: Apple Sauce* (London: George Allen & Unwin, 1982), 107.

Betrayed (1954)

1. Jane Ellen Wayne, *Clark Gable: Portrait of a Misfit* (London: Robson Books, 1993), 264.
2. Victor Mature, "What I like About Women" source unknown.
3. Cheryl Crane with Cindy De La Hoz, *Lana: The Memories, the Myths, the Movies* (Philadelphia: Running Press, 2008), 316.

Chief Crazy Horse (1955)

1. Herb Fagen, *The Encylopedia of Westerns* (New York: Fact on File, 2003), 86.
2. Joseph Fusco, *The Epitome of Cool: The Films of Ray Danton* (Albany, GA: BearManor Media, 2010), 25.

Violent Saturday (1955)

1. Richard Fleischer, *Just Tell Me When To Cry: A Memoir* (New York: Carroll & Graf,1993),15.
2. Ernest Borgnine, *I Don't Want to Set the World on Fire, I Just Want to Keep My Nuts Warm: An Autobiography* (London: JR Books, 2009), 86.
3. James Robert Parish and Don E. Stanke, *The Swashbucklers* (New York: Arlington House, 1976), 466.

The Last Frontier (1955)

1. Jeanine Basinger, *Anthony Mann* (Middleton, CT: Wesleyan University Press, 2007), 109.
2. U.K. interview with Pip Evans, 1954.

Safari (1956)

1. Janet Leigh, *There Always Was a Hollywood: An Autobiography* (New York: Doubleday, 1984), 191.
2. Ibid., 195.
3. Ibid., 198.
4. Ibid., 194.

The Sharkfighters (1956)

1. *The Sharkfighters* pressbook.
2. Ibid.
3. Ibid.

Zarak (1956)

1. Jeffrey Richards, *Visions of Yesterday* (London: Routledge & Kegan Paul, 1973), 206.
2. *The TV Times Film & Video Guide* (London: Mandarin, 1995), 809.
3. Roger Langley, *Patrick McGoohan: Danger Man or Prisoner?* (Sheffield, England: Tomahawk Press, 2007), 54.

Interpol (1957)

1. Michael Munn, *Trevor Howard: The Man and His Films* (London: Robson Books, 1989), 61.

2. Vivienne Knight, *Trevor Howard: A Gentleman and a Player* (London: Muller, Blond & White, 1986), 122–123.
3. Terence Pettigrew, *Trevor Howard: A Personal Biography* (London: Peter Owen, 2001),176.
4. Matt White, *Dailey Sketch*, August 20, 1956.

The Long Haul (1957)

1. David Bret, *Diana Dors: Hurricane in Mink* (London: JR Roberts, 2010), 114.
2. Damon Wise, *Come By Sunday: The Fabulous Ruined Life of Diana Dors* (London: Sidgwick & Jackson, 1998), 157.
3. *Picture Show*, June 22, 1957.

No Time to Die (1958)

1. Garth Bardsley, *The Biography of Anthony Newley: Stop the World* (London: Oberon Books, 2003), 101.

China Doll (1958)

1. *China Doll* pressbook.
2. Ibid.
3. Ibid.

Escort West (1959)

1. *Escort West* pressbook.

The Bandit of Zhobe (1959)

1. Garth Bardsley, *The Biography of Anthony Newley: Stop the World* (London: Oberon Books, 2003), 62.
2. Ibid., 63.

The Big Circus (1959)

1. Stephen D. Youngkin, *The Lost One: A Life of Peter Lorre* (Lexington: The University Press of Kentucky, 2005), 398.
2. Turner Classic Movies website.

Timbuktu (1959)

1. *Timbuktu* pressbook.
2. Chris Fujiwara, *Jacques Tourneur: The Cinema of Nightfall* (Baltimore: John Hopkins University Press, 2000), 262
3. Ibid., 263.

Hannibal (1960)

1. Derek Elley, *The Epic Film, Myth and History* (London: Routledge & Kegan Paul, 1984), 85.
2. Bruce Francis Babington and Peter William Evans, *Biblical Epics: Sacred Narrative in the Hollywood Cinema* (Manchester: Manchester University Press, 1993), 229.

The Tartars (1962)

1. Charles Higham, *Orson Welles: The Rise and Fall of an American Genius* (London: New English Library, 1986), 305.
2. Barbara Leaming, *Orson Welles: A Biography* (London: Weidenfeld and Nicholson, 1989).
3. Orson Welles and Peter Bogdanovich, *This Is Orson Welles* (London: Harper Collins, 1993), 266–267.
4. *The Tartars* pressbook.
5. Ibid.
6. Ibid.
7. Ibid.

After the Fox (1966)

1. Ed Sikov, *Mr. Strangelove: A Biography of Peter Sellers* (London: Sidgwick & Jackson, 2002), 238–240.
2. Ibid., 238.
3. Neil Simon, *Neil Simon Rewrites: A Memoir* (New York: Simon & Schuster, 1996), 211–212.
4. Ed Sikov, *Mr. Strangelove: A Biography of Peter Sellers* (London: Sidgwick & Jackson, 2002), 240.

Every Little Crook & Nanny (1972)

1. *Every Little Crook & Nanny* pressbook.
2. J. Marks, *Interview Magazine*, May 1972.
3. *Every Little Crook & Nanny* pressbook.

Won Ton Ton: The Dog Who Saved Hollywood (1976)

1. Michael Winner, *Winner Takes All: A Life of Sorts* (London: Robson Books, 2004), 231–232.
2. Ibid., 205.

Firepower (1979)

1. Michael Winner, *Winner Takes All: A Life of Sorts* (London: Robson Books, 2004), 231
2. Warren G. Harris, *Sophia Loren: A Biography* (New York: Simon & Schuster, 1998), 317.
3. Michael Winner, *Winner Takes All: A Life of Sorts* (London: Robson Books, 2004), 232.
4. Ibid., 224.
5. Ibid., 232.

Bibliography

Anderson, Christopher P. *A Star Is a Star Is a Star! The Lives and Loves of Susan Hayward*. London: Robson Books, 1982.

Andrews, Bart, and Thomas J. Watson. *Loving Lucy: An Illustrated Tribute To Lucille Ball*. New York: St. Martin's Griffin, 1980.

Aylesworth, Thomas G. *Broadway to Hollywood*. Twickenham, Middlesex: Hamlyn, 1985.

Babington, Bruce Francis, and Peter William Evans. *Biblical Epics: Sacred Narrative in the Hollywood Cinema*. Manchester: Manchester University Press,1993.

Bardsley, Garth. *The Biography of Anthony Newley: Stop the World*. London: Oberon Books, 2003.

Barson, Michael. *The Illustrated Who's Who of Hollywood Directors. Volume 1: The Sound Era*. New York: Noonday Press,1995.

Barton, Ruth. *Hedy Lamarr: The Most Beautiful Woman in Film*. Lexington: The University Press of Kentucky, 2010.

Basinger, Jeanine. *Anthony Mann*. Middleton, CT: Wesleyan University Press, 2007.

Baxter, Peter. *Sternberg*. London: BFI, 1980.

Behlmer, Rudy. *Memo from Darryl Zanuck: The Golden Years at Twentieth Century–Fox*. New York: Grove Press, 1993.

Behlmer, Rudy, ed. and annotator, Polly Platt, interviewer *Henry Hathaway: A Director's Guild of America Oral History*. Lanham, MD: Scarecrow Press, 2001

Bergan, Ronald. *Sports in the Movies*. London and New York: Proteus Books, 1982.

_____. *The United Artists Story*. New York: Crown, 1986.

Billman, Larry. *Betty Grable: A Bio-Bibliography*. Westport, CT: Greenwood Press, 1993.

Bondanella, Peter. *Hollywood Italians: Dagos, Pallokas, Romeos, Wise Guys, and Sopranos*. New York: Continuum, 2006.

Borgnine, Ernest. *I Don't Want to Set the World on Fire, I Just Want to Keep My Nuts Warm: An Autobiography*. London: JR Books, 2009.

Brady, Kathleen. *Lucille: The Life of Lucille Ball*. New York: Billboard Books, 2001.

Bret, David. *Diana Dors: Hurricane in Mink*. London: JR Roberts, 2010.

Brode, Douglas. *The Films of the Fifties*. New York: Citadel Press, 1976.

Buhle, Paul, and *Dave Wagner. Blacklisted. The Film Lover's Guide to the Hollywood Blacklist*. New York: Palgrave Macmillan, 2003.

Cameron, Ian. *Adventure in the Movies*. New York: Crescent Books, 1973, 1974.

Carnes, Mark C., ed. *Past Imperfect: History According to the Movies*. New York: Owl Books, 1996.

Chibnall, Steve, and Brian McFarlane. *The British "B" Film*. London: BFI, 2009.

Crane, Cheryl, with Cindy De La Hoz. *Lana: The Memories, the Myths, the Movies*. Philadelphia: Running Press, 2008.

Crowther, Bruce. *Film Noir: Reflections in a Dark Mirror*. London: Virgin, 1988,1990.

Custen, George F. *Twentieth Century's Fox: Darryl F. Zanuck and the Culture of Hollywood*. New York: Basic Books, 1997.

Darby, William. *Anthony Mann: The Film Career*. Jefferson, NC: McFarland, 2009.

De Carlo, Yvonne. *Yvonne: An Autobiography*. New York: St. Martin's Press, 1987.

De La Hoz, Cindy. *Lucy at the Movies*. Philadelphia: Running Press, 2007.

Eames, John Douglas. *The MGM Story*. London: Octopus Books, 1975.

_____. *The Paramount Story*. London: Octopus Books, 1985.

The editors of *Consumer Guide* and Jay A. Brown. *Rating the Movies*. Skokie, Illinois, 1982, 1983, 1984, 1985, 1986, 1987.

Eldridge, David. *Hollywood's History Films*. London. New York: I.B. Tauris, 2006.

Everson, William K. *The Films of Hal Roach*. New York: The Museum of Modern Art, 1971. Distributed by New York Graphic Society, Ltd.

Eyman, Scott. *Print the Legend: The Life and Times*

of John Ford. Baltimore: The John Hopkins University Press, 1999.

Fagen, Herb. *The Encylopedia of Westerns*. New York: Fact on File, 2003.

Feret, Bill. *Lure of the Tropix: A Pictorial History of The Tropic Temptress in Films, Serials and Comics*. London and New York: Proteus Books, 1984.

Fleischer, Richard. *Just Tell Me When to Cry: A Memoir*. New York: Carroll & Graf, 1993.

Frank, Alan. *Frank's 500: The Thriller Film Guide*. London: B.T. Batsford, 1997.

Fraser, George MacDonald. *The Hollywood History of the World*. London: Michael Joseph, 1988, 1989.

Fujiwara, Chris. *Jacques Tourneur: The Cinema of Nightfall*. Baltimore: The John Hopkins University Press, 2000.

Fusco, Joseph. *The Epitome of Cool: The Films of Ray Danton*. Albany, GA: BearManor Media, 2010.

Gans, Eric. *Carole Landis: A Most Beautiful Girl*. Jackson: University Press of Mississippi, 2008.

Garfield, Brian. *Western Films: A Complete Guide*. London: Da Capo Press, 1982.

Gottfried, Martin. *Balancing Act: The Authorized Biography of Angela Lansbury*. Boston: Little, Brown, 1999.

The Great Movie Stars: The International Years. New York: Hill and Wang, 1980.

The *Great Movie Stars: The International Years*, 2. London: Warner Books, 1989.

Greco, J. *The File on Robert Siodmak in Hollywood: 1941–1951*. Dissertation.com, 1999.

Hagen, Ray, and Laura Wagner. *Killer Tomatoes: Fifteen Tough Film Dames*. Jefferson, NC: McFarland, 2004.

Halliwell, Leslie. *Halliwell's Film Guide*, 10th ed. London: Harper Collins, 1994.

Hannsberry, Karen Burroughs. *Bad Boys: The Actors of Film Noir*. Jefferson, NC: McFarland, 2003.

Hardy, Phil. *The Aurum Film Encyclopedia. The Western*. London: Aurum Press, 1983, 1991, 1995.

_____. *The Aurum Film Encyclopedia. Gangsters*. London: Aurum Press, 1998.

_____, ed. *The BFI Companion to Crime*. London: Cassel, 1997.

Harper, Sue, and Vincent Porter. *British Cinema of the 1950s: The Decline of Deference*. Oxford: Oxford University Press, 2003.

Harris, Warren G. *Sophia Loren: A Biography*. New York: Simon & Schuster, 1998.

Higham, Charles. *Cecil B. DeMile*. New York: Dell, 1973.

_____. *Orson Welles: The Rise and Fall of an American Genius*. London: New English Library, 1986.

Hirschhorn, Clive. *The Columbia Story*. London: Octopus Books, 1989.

_____. *The Hollywood Musical*. Octopus Books, 1981.

_____. *The Universal Story*. London: Octopus Books, 1983.

_____. *The Warner Bros. Story*. London: Octopus Books, 1979.

Holston, Kim. *Richard Widmark: A Bio-Bibliography*. Westport, CT: Greenwood Press.

_____. *Susan Hayward*. Jefferson, NC: McFarland, 2009.

Howard, James. *The Complete Films of Orson Welles*. New York: Citadel Press, 1991.

Hulse, Ed. *The Films of Betty Grable*. Burbank: Riverwood Press, 1996.

Hutton, Betty, with Carl Bruno and Michael Mayer. *Backstage You Can Have: My Own Story*. Palm Springs: The Betty Hutton Estate, 2009.

Jewell, Richard B., with Vernon Harbin. *The RKO Story*. London: Octopus Books, 1982.

Kael, Pauline. *5001 Nights at the Movies*. New York: Owl Books, 1982, 1984, 1991.

Kanfer, Stefan. *Ball of Fire: The Tumultuous Life and Comic Art of Lucille Ball*. London: Faber and Faber, 2003.

Katz, Ephraim. *The Macmillan International Film Guide Encyclopedia*. New York: Macmillan, 1998.

Kellow, Brian. *The Bennetts: An Acting Family*. Lexington: The University Press of Kentucky, 2004.

Kinnard, Roy, and Tim Davis. *Divine Images: A History of Jesus on the Screen*. New York: Citadel Press, 1992.

Knight, Vivienne. *Trevor Howard: A Gentleman and a Player*. London: Muller, Blond & White, 1986.

Kobal, John. *A History of Movie Musicals: Gotta Sing Gotta Dance*. Spring Books, 1988.

_____. *Rita Hayworth: The Time, the Place and the Woman*. London: W.H. Allen, 1977.

Laguardia, Robert, and Gene Archi. Red: *The Tempestuous Life of Susan Hayward*. London: Robson Books, 1985.

Lamarr, Hedy. *Ecstasy and Me: My Life as a Woman*. London: W.H. Allen, 1967.

Langley, Roger. *Patrick McGoohan: Danger Man or Prisoner?* Sheffield, England: Tomahawk Press, 2007.

Leaming, Barbara. *If This Was Happiness: A Biography of Rita Hayworth*. London, Weidenfeld and Nicholson, 1989.

Leigh, Janet. *There Always Was a Hollywood: An Autobiography*. New York: Doubleday, 1984.

Lentz, Robert J. *Korean War Filmography*. Jefferson, NC: McFarland, 2003.

_____. *Lee Marvin: His Films and Career*. Jefferson, NC: McFarland, 2000, 2005.

Linet, Beverly. *Susan Hayward: Portrait of a Survivor*. New York: Atheneum, 1980.

Maltin, Leonard. *Leonard Maltin's Movie and Video Guide*. New York: Signet, 1996

McBride, Joseph. *Searching for John Ford: A Life*. New York: St. Martin's Press, 2001.

McGee, Tom. *Betty Grable: The Girl with the Million Dollar Legs.* New York: Welcome Rain, 1995.
Miller, John. *Peter Ustinov: The Gift of Laughter.* London: Weidenfeld & Nicolson, 2002.
Milne, Tom, ed. *The Time Out Film Guide,* 3d ed. New York: Penguin, 1989, 1991, 1993.
Morella, Joe, and Edward Z. Epstein. *Lana: The Public and Private Lives of Miss Turner.* London: W.H. Allen, 1983.
Morella, Joe, and Edward Z. Epstein. *Jane Wyman: A Biography.* London: Robert Hale, 1986.
Moreno, Eduardo. *The Films of Susan Hayward.* New York: Citadel Press, 1979.
Muller, Eddie. *Dames: The Wicked Women of Film Noir.* New York: Regan Books, 2001.
Munn, Michael. *Richard Burton: Prince of Players.* London: JR Books, 2008.
_____. *Trevor Howard: The Man and His Films.* London: Robson Books, 1989.
Neagle, Anna. *Anna Neagle Says 'There's Always Tomorrow' : An Autobiography.* London: W.H. Allen, 1974.
Newman, Kim. *Wild West Movies or How The West Was Found, Won, Lost, Lied About, Filmed and Forgotten.* London: Bloomsbury, 1990.
Ottoson, Robert. *A Reference Guide to the American Film Noir: 1940–1958.* Metuchen, NJ: Scarecrow Press, 1981.
Parish, James Robert, and Don E. Stanke. *The Swashbucklers.* New Rochelle, NY: Arlington House, 1976.
Parish, James Robert, and Michael R. Pitts. *The Great Western Pictures.* Metuchen, NJ: Scarecrow Press, Inc., 1976.
Pastos, Spero. *Pin-Up: The Tragedy of Betty Grable.* New York: Berkley Books, 1987.
Peary, Danny. *Cult Movie Stars.* London: Simon & Schuster, 1991.
Pettigrew, Terence. *Trevor Howard: A Personal Biography.* London: Peter Owen, 2001.
Place, J.A. *The Western Films of John Ford.* New York: Citadel Press, 1974.
Price, Victoria. *Vincent Price: A Daughter's Biography.* London: Sidwick & Jackson, 1999.
Quinlan, David. *Illustrated Directory of Film Star.* London: B.T. Batsford, 1981.
_____. *Quinlan's Illustrated Directory of Film Character Actors.* London: B.T. Batsford, 1985, 1997.
_____. *Quinlan's Film Directors.* London: B.T. Batsford, 1999.
Radio Times Guide to Films. London: BBC Worldwide, 2000.
Richards, Jeffrey. *Visions of Yesterday.* London: Routledge & Kegan Paul, 1973.
Ringgold, Gene. *The Films of Rita Hayworth.* New York: Citadel Press, 1974.
Ringgold, Gene, and Dewitt Bodeen. *The Complete Films of Cecil B. DeMille.* New York: Citadel Press, 1969.
Russell, Jane. *Jane Russell: An Autobiography.* London: Sidgwick & Jackson, 1986.
Schultz, Margie. *Ann Sheridan: A Bio-Bibliography.* Westport, Connecticut, Greenwood Press, 1997.
Selby, Spencer. *Dark City: The Film Noir.* Jefferson, NC: McFarland, 1984.
Shearer, Stephen Michael. *Beautiful: The Life of Hedy Lamarr.* New York: Thomas Dunne Books, St. Martin's Press, 2010.
_____. *Patricia Neal: An Unquiet Life.* Lexington: The University Press of Kentucky, 2006.
Shipman, David. *The Great Movie Stars: The International Years.* New York: St. Martin's Press, 1972.
Sikov, Ed. *Mr. Strangelove: A Biography of Peter Sellers.* London: Sidgwick & Jackson, 2002.
Silver, Alain, and Elizabeth Ward, eds. *Film Noir: An Encyclopedic Reference to the American Style.* 3d ed. Woodstock, NY: Overlook Press, 1979, 1992.
Silvers, Phil, with Robert Saffron. *The Man Who Was Bilko: The Autobiography of Phil Silvers.* London & New York: W.H. Allen, 1974.
Simon, Neil. *Neil Simon Rewrites: A Memoir.* New York: Simon & Schuster, 1996.
Sinclair, Andrew. *John Ford.* London: George Allen & Unwin, 1979.
Smith, Don G., *Lon Chaney, Jr.: Horror Film Star, 1906–1973.* Jefferson, NC: McFarland, 1996.
Solomon, Jon. *The Ancient World in the Cinema.* New Haven: Yale University Press, 2001.
Spicer, Andrew. *Film Noir.* Harlow, Essex: Longman, 2002.
Tanitch, Robert. *Blockbusters! 70 years of Best-Selling Movies.* London: BT Batsford, 2000.
Thomas, Tony. *The Complete Films of Henry Fonda.* New York: Citadel Press, 1983.
Thomas, Tony. *Howard Hughes in Hollywood.* New York: Citadel Press, 1985.
Thomas, Tony, and Aubrey Solomon. *The Films of 20th Century–Fox: A Pictorial History.* New York: Citadel Press, 1979.
Thomson, David. *The New Biographical Dictionary of Film.* New York: Alfred A. Knopf, 2002.
TV Times Film & Video Guide. Selected by David Quinlan. London: Madarin, 1995.
Ustinov, Peter. *Peter Ustinov: Dear Me.* London: Book Club Associates, 1977.
Valentino, Lou. *The Films of Lana Turner.* New York: Citadel Press, 1976.
Vanderbeets, Richard. *George Sanders: An Exhausted Life.* London: Robson Books, 1991.
Vinson, James. *The International Dictionary of Films and Filmmakers — Actors and Actresses.* London, Papermac, 1986.
Vogel, Michelle. *Gene Tierney: A Biography.* Jefferson, NC: McFarland, 2005.

Ward, Richard Lewis. *A History of the Hal Roach Studios*. Carbondale: Southern Illinois University Press, 2005.
Warren, Doug. *Betty Grable: The Reluctant Movie Queen*. London: Robson Books, 1982.
Wayne, Jane Ellen. *Clark Gable: Portrait of a Misfit*. London: Robson Books, 1993.
_____. *Lana: The Life and Loves of Lana Turner*. New York. St. Martin's Press, 1995.
Welles, Orson and Peter Bogdanovich. *This is Orson Welles*. London: Harper Collins, 1993.
Wilding, Michael, with Pamela Wilcox. *Michael Wilding: Apple Sauce*. London: George Allen & Unwin, 1982.
Williams, Esther, with Digby Diehl. *Esther Williams—The Million Dollar Mermaid*. New York: Simon & Schuster, 1999.
Williams, Lucy Chase. *The Complete Films of Vincent Price*. New York: Citadel Press, 1998.
Winner, Michael. *Winner Takes All: A Life of Sorts*. London: Robson Books, 2004.
Winters, Shelley. *Shelley*. St. Albans, Herts: Granada, 1980.
Wise, Damon. *Come By Sunday: The Fabulous Ruined Life of Diana Dors*. London: Sidgwick & Jackson, 1998.
Young, Christopher. *The Films of Hedy Lamarr*. New York: Citadel Press, 1978.
Youngkin, Stephen D. *The Lost One: A Life of Peter Lorre*. Lexington: The University Press of Kentucky, 2005.
Youngin, Stephen D, James Bigwood, and Raymond Cabana, Jr. *The Films of Peter Lorre*. New York: Citadel Press, 1982.

Miscellaneous

China Doll.
Cry of the City.
Doyle, Neil. "Victor Mature: Beautiful Hunk of Man." *Classic Images*, September 2001.
Escort West.
Every Little Crook and Nanny.
F. Maurice Speed Film Review.
Film Show Annual.
Focus on Film.
The Glory Brigade.
Internet databases—eg., IMDb and Wikipedia.
Moss Rose.
Niderost, Eric. "Victor Mature. The 'Beefcake King' and Underatted Actor." *Classic Images*, No 237, March 1995.
Photoplay.
Picture Show Magazine and Annual.
Picturegoer Magazine and Annual.
Pressbooks.
Samson and Delilah.
The Sharkfighters.
Silver Screen.
The Tartars.
Timbuktu.
Turner Classic Movies website.
Victor Mature Fan Club website (Shannon).

Index

Abbot, Bill 174
Abbot, Dorothy 68, 86
Abbot, John 35
Abbot and Costello Meet the Mummy 115
ABC 176
Academy Award 13, 17, 29, 38, 43, 46, 49, 55, 60, 76, 83, 85, 94, 100, 104, 105, 109, 127, 130, 138, 144, 145, 148, 151, 156, 173, 175
Ackerman, Leonard J. 170
Adams, Dawn 103
Adams, Gerald Drayson 120
Adamson, James 101
Adler, Buddy 123, 124
Adler, Robert 59, 62, 122
Affair with a Stranger 16, 97, 101–103, 123
After the Fox 3, 20, 49, 73, 165–168
Aguglia, Mimi 64
Ahern, Lloyd 65
Akins, Claude 131
Alberni, Luis 23
Alda, Robert 172
Alessandri, Luisa 165
Alexander, Angela 145
Algiers 36
Alison, Dorothy 136
Alland, William 120
Allen, Irving 128, 134, 135, 136, 143, 152, 153, 155
Allen, Irwin 108, 110, 155, 156
Allen, Patrick 139, 141
Allen, Ricca 26
Allen, Richard 114
Allen, Steve 83, 155
Allied Artists 20, 154
Almquist, Peggy 83
Alwyn, William 128, 131, 134
Alyn, Kirk 84
Amateau, Rod 59
Ameche, Don 34, 43, 44, 179
Ames, Leon 180
Amsterdam, Morey 172

Amy, George 101
Anderson, Gene 139, 141, 142
Anderson, Jon C. 168
Anderson, Richard 118
Andre, Charles 50
Andrews, Dana 7, 51, 90, 96, 99, 180
Andrews, Stanley 44
Andrews, Tige 145
Androcles and the Lion 16, 83, 95–98, 113, 154
Angelica 181
Angels with Dirty Faces 66
Ankrum, Morris 39, 120
Ansara, Michael 103, 114
Antrim, Harry 82
Apking, Fritz 108
Appleby, Basil 118
Aragon, Angelica 176
Aragon, Tita 145
Arden, Eve 32, 35
"Are You Kidding" 49
Arlen, Richard 172
Arling, Arthur E. 77
Arnaz, Desi 50
Arness, James 106, 107
Arnold, Edward 178
Arnt, Charles 44, 77, 106
Arsenic and Old Lace 81
Arthur, George M. 50
Arthur, Jean 24
Ashley, Edward 172
Ashman, Gene 168
Ashton, Roy 136
Askin, Leon 103, 106
Asther, Nils 40, 73
Astin, John 169, 170
Ates, Roscoe 29
Attenborough, Richard 120
Aubrey, Anne 143, 152
Aubrey, James 92
Audley, Eleanor 84
Aulisi, Joseph G. 174
Aureli, Andres 159
Austin, John P. 106
Avery, Emile 120

Axelrod, Jonathan 170
Ayres, John 89

Babington, Bruce Francis 104, 113, 160
"Baby, Won't You Say You Love Me" 78
Bacall, Lauren 70
Bacharach, Burt 165, 166
Bachelin, Franz 68
Back to Methuselah 9
Backus, Jim 13, 21, 70, 95, 97
Bacon, Irving 47
Bacon, James 155
Bad Day at Black Rock 123
Baer, Max 48
Bagdad, William 168
Bainbridge, John 76
Bakaleinkoff, C. 50, 70, 84, 86, 101, 108
Baker, Art 70, 72
Baker, George 26
Baldi, Fernando 162
Baldwin, Walter 64, 80
Ball, Lucille 12, 39, 50, 70, 72, 73, 99, 121
Ball, Susan 120, 121
Ballard, Lucien 98
Balmain, Pierre 118
Balsam, Martin 165, 166, 168
Bancroft, Anne 111, 112, 125, 126, 127
The Bandit of Zhobe 20, 136, 144, 152–154
Bands, X 149
Barbier, George 41
Barbieri, Gato 174
Barboni, Leonida 165
Barcroft, Roy 149
Bardette, Trevor 108
Barnes, George 73
Barnett, Griff 62
Barrat, Robert 29
Barris, Harry 47
Barry, Don "Red" 145
Barrymore, Ethel 56, 58, 180

191

Barton, Gregg 145
Barton, James 76, 79
Barty, Billy 172, 174
Baseheart, Richard 142
Basevi, James 52
Basil, Toni 168
Basinger, Jeanine 125
Basserman, Albert 35
Bassler, Robert 44
Batjac Film Company 145, 148, 151
Battaglia, Rik 159
Battle at Apache Pass 121
Battle of the Bulge 39, 144
Bau, Gordon 70
Bauchens, Anne 73
Bauer, Belinda 176, 177, 178
Baxley, Margo 170
Baxter, Anne 53, 89
Baxter, John 29
Baxter, Lex 119
Bayhi, Chester L. 123
Bear, Mary 80
Beatty, May 39
Beaudine, William, Jr. 149
Beck, Vincent 174
Beddoe, Don 70
Beery, Wallace 34
Beetson, Frank, Jr. 157
Bell, James 92
Bell, Rodney 89
Benchley, Robert 102
Bendix, William 16, 83, 85, 108, 109
Benedict, Brooks 86
Benedict, William "Billy" 172
Benge, Wilson 92
Bennett, Charles 108, 155
Bennett, Joan 8, 23, 24, 26
Bennett, Richard Rodney 136
Benson, Martin 136
Benson, Sam 98
Beranger, George 77
Bergen, Edgar 172
Bergman, Ingrid 48
Berkeley, Busby 94
Berkeley, Mowbray 149
Berkey, James L. 170
Berle, Milton 172
Berman, Henry 170
Bernaducci, Dan 101
Bernardi, Jack 172
Berns, Mel 84, 86, 95, 101, 108
Berry, Dorothy Stanbridge (third wife) 14, 19
Berry, Noah, Jr. 148
Best, Richard 136
Betrayed 18, 109, 116, 117–120, 122, 135, 144
Bevan, A.J. 134
Bevan, Billy 56
Beverly, Helen 103

The Big Circus 110, 154–157
Bikel, Theodore 118
Binyon, Claude 80
Birkenhead, England 145
Black, Harry 23, 26
Black Jack to Kill 180
Blackman, Don 114
Blair, Janet 172
Blair, Nicky 170
Blake, Bobby 106
Blake, Madge 89
Blake, Oliver 64
Blake, Robert 108
Blanchard, Mari 106, 107
Blondell, Joan 172
Blood and Sand 44
Bloom, William 98
Blore, Eric 35
"Blue and Gray" 46
"Blue Shadows" 44
Blye, Margaret 169, 170, 171
Blystone, Jasper 65
Bocage, Peter 78
Boddey, Martin 143
Boehm, Sydney 123
Boerner, Charles 68
Bogdonovich, Geraldine 114
Bois, Curt 44
Bomarzi, Renato 162
Bond, James 19, 49, 130
Bond, Lilian 23
Bond, Ward 52, 55, 145, 148
Boolen, Van 136, 140
Boone, Richard 41, 103
Booth, Charles G. 62
Booth, Nesdon 155
Borgnine, Ernest 111, 122, 123, 124
Borowsky, Marvin 84
Borzage, Frank 19, 145, 146, 148
Borzage, Lew 145
Boss, Reeder P. 98
Bouchey, Willis 92
Bowers, Eilene 122
Bowers, William 50
Box, John 134, 143
Boyd, Stephen 76
Boyer, Charles 36
Boyle, Robert F. 120
Bracken, Eddie 68, 181
Braddock, Well "The Cinderella Man" 48
Bragaglia, Carlo Ludovico 161
Brand, Roland 139
Brando, Marlon 116
Braus, Mortimer 159
Brazzi, Lydia 165
Brendel, El 29
Brennan, Walter 52, 55
Bret, David 140
Brian, David 92, 94
Bridge, Al 62
A Bridge Too Far 120

Brigandi, Phil 84
Briggs, Howard 62
Bright, June 70
Brindley, Madge 140
Britannia Mews 57
Britton, Barbara 180
Britton, Layne 145, 149, 157
Broadbent, Aida 33
Broadhead, James 172
Broadway 9, 10, 34, 36, 38, 39, 69
Broccoli, Albert "Chubby" 19, 128, 134, 135, 136, 143, 152
Broderick, Helen 32, 35
Brodine, Norbert 23, 26, 29, 59, 60
Brody, Estelle 128
Broken Arrow 121
Bronson, Charles 172, 175
Bronson, Lillian 101
The Brooklyn Daily Eagle 52
Brooks, Douglas 111
Brooks, Phyllis 35, 38
Brown, Gilmor 7
Brown, Helen 108
Brown, John 89
Brown, Les 50, 51
Browning, Maurice 136
Bruce, Nichola 118
Bruce, Robert 143
Bruzlin, Alfred 44, 77, 114
Bryan, Arthur Q. 73
Bryan, John 165, 166
Bryant, Marie 77
Bryd, David 176
Bryne, Eddie 133
Brynner, Yul 43, 134, 135, 176
Buazzelli, Tino 165
Buccella, Marai Grazia 165
Buckner, Robert 128
Budd, Norman 26
Buhler, Kitty 145
Burke, Alfred 136, 143, 145
Burnett, W.R. 108
Burns, Mike 168
Burroughs, Edgar Rice 26
Burton, Richard 17, 102, 103, 104, 105, 111
Busch, Niven 56
Buttolph, David 56, 57, 59
Buttons, Red 154, 156
Buzzanca, Lando 165
Bwana Devil 108

Cabiria 160
Cabot, Bruce 29, 30, 32
Caesar and Cleopatra 96
Cagney, James 66, 81
Caldicot, Richard 174
Calhern, Louis 117, 119
Calhoun, Rory 172
Call Northside 67

Callender, Romaine 29
Calles, William 125
Calvert, Phyllis 75
Cameron, Earl 128
Campbell, Clay 125
Campbell, Johnny 20
Campos, Rafael 131
Canutt, Yakina 134
Captain Caution 9, 17, 29–32, 72, 107
Care, Leslie I. 106
Carey, Harry, Jr. 149
Carey, Leslie I. 120
Carey, Mary Jane 101
Carey, Olive 101
Carey, Timothy 168, 169
Carlson, Richard 9, 32, 33, 34, 35, 49
Carlyle, John 108
Carmichael, Ian 117, 119
Carmichael, Hoagy 16, 86, 88
Carney, Art 172, 173
Carr, Bernard 23, 26
Carradine, John 114, 116, 172
Carrere, Edward 134
Carrillo, Leo 29, 30, 32
Carroll, Virginia 122
Carson, Fred 86, 92, 145, 149, 155, 157
Carson, John L. 125
Carter, Douglas 77
Carter, Harry 59, 62
Carter, Jack 172
Caruso, David 62
Casablanca 36, 88
Casino Royale 165
Cass, John L. 95
Cassini, Oleg 35, 38
Castle, Dolores 64
Catlett, Walter 44
Cavallaro, Gaylord 136
Cavanaugh, Hobart 80
CBS 180
Cesar, Irving 33
The Chair for Martin Rome 65
Chambers, Terry 168
Chance, Larry 157
Chandler, Chick 39
Chandler, Jeff 121
Chandler, Lane 73
Chaney, Lon, Jr. 26, 27, 28
Chang, Danny 145
Chaplin, Billy 101, 122
Chaplin, Charlie 26, 43
Charisse, Cyd 172
Charles, Zachery 83
Chase, Charlie 25
Chesebro, George 62
Cheshire, Harry 108
Chianese, Dominic 174
Chief Crazy Horse 18, 120–122, 123, 126

China Doll 2, 19, 51, 145–148, 151, 154
Ching, William 149
Christey, Ken 64
Christiani, Gabriella 177
Christopher, Thom 174
Cinemascope 104, 123, 129, 135
Cinquini, Renato 160
Cirano, Franco 165
Circus World 155
Cisar, George 155
Ciuffini, Sabatino 162
Clare, Bernice 34
Clark, Al 120, 125
Clark, Buddy 50
Clark, Carroll 50
Clark, Davidson 64, 73
Clark, Fred 62, 63, 64, 67
Clark, Mamo 26
Clarke, Angela 114
Clarke, Charles G. 82, 122
Clarke, Donald Henderson 23
Clarke, James B. 56
Clarke, Jameson 139
Clarke, Robert 157
"Clean Up Chicago" 78
Cleveland, George 62, 101
Cliff, John 111
Clifford, Ruth 64
"Climb Up the Garden Wall" 135
Clothier, William H. 145, 149
Cobb, Edmund 62, 89, 114
Coburn, James 20, 172, 174, 175, 176
"Cockeyed Mayor of Kaunakakai" 44
Coen, Albert J. 106
Coen, Franklin 98, 120
Coghlan, Frank 47
Cohn, Harry 50
Coleman, Robert 174
Coleman, William H. 68
Colleano, Bonar 133, 136, 137, 143, 145
Collingham, Charles 131
Collins, Anthony 33
Collins, Joan 153
Collins, Russell 125
Colman, Ronald 158
Colton, John 35, 38
Columbia Pictures 19, 44, 45, 50, 85, 109, 125, 128, 129, 136, 137, 139, 141, 143, 152, 168
"Come Tell Me What's Your Answer (Yes or No)" 46
Comer, Sam 68, 73
Commonweal 120
Conan Doyle, Sir Arthur 26
Coney Island 77, 82
"Coney Island" (radio) 179, 180
Conlan, Frank 52
Connell, Jane 172

Connolly, Mike 103
Connolly, Sheila 126
Connors, Tom 103
Conrad, William 181
Conte, Richard 40, 64, 65, 66, 142
Conti, Albert 44
Continenza, Sandro 159
"The Convict and the Bird" 46
Coogan, Jackie 172
Cook, Elisha, Jr. 25, 39, 41
Cook, Tommy 64
Cooke, Malcolm 165
Coolee, Ann 29
Coolidge, Philip 131, 133
Cooper, Gary 90, 158
Cooper, Joe 77
Cooper, Kalmar 78
Cope, John 73
Cope, Kenneth 143
Corcoran, Donna 92
Corcoran, Noreen 122
Cordell, Frank 73
Corden, Harry 114
Cording, Harry 73
Cordone, Amy 41
Corey, Wendell 180
Corner, Sally 103
Corrigan, Lloyd 29
Cortes, Mapy 50, 51
Cortez, Bella 162
Coster, Nicholas 103
Cotten, Joseph 58, 60
Coulouris, George 143
Courage, Alexander 92
Cover Girl 45
Cowan, Robert 70
Cox, William R. 106
Coxen, Edward 26
Crain, Earl, Sr. 145, 149
Crain, Jeanne 41, 53, 82, 83, 116
Cravat, Nick 106, 107
Craven, James 47
Crawford, Broderick 172
Creber, Lewis H. 98
Cregar, Laird 11, 39, 40
The Crime of Laura Saurelle 56, 57
Crisler, B.R. 29
Croccolo, Carlo 165
Crockett, Dick 77
Cronjager, Edward 39
Crook, John 128
Crowe, James 125
Crowther, Bosley 35
"Crust," Arnold (Michael Winner) 174
Cry of the City 13, 40, 64–68, 85, 88, 109, 139, 142, 158
Cuba 19
Cully, Russell A. 70
Culver, Roland 128, 130, 131

194 • Index

Cummings, Irving 44, 45
Cummins, Peggy 13, 56, 57, 58, 85
Cummins, Robert 43
Cummins, Ruth 102
Curacao, Harcourt 140
Curley, Leo 89
Currie, Finlay 133
Curson, Frank 13
Curtis, Ken 149
Curtis, Tony 106, 109, 130, 155
Curtiz, Michael 114, 115, 116, 117
Cutell, Lou 169

D'Agostino, Albert S. 50, 70, 84, 86, 95, 101, 108, 155
Dailey, Dan 77, 82, 83
Daily Film Renter 58
The Daily Mail 139
The Daily Sketch 139
Dalio, Marcel 35
Dalmatoff, Michael 35
Dal Pino, Pasquale 162
Dalton, Phyllis 134
Dalya, Jacqueline 26, 76
D'Amato, Paul 174
D'Ambricourt, Adrienne 92
D'Amico, Oscar 162
Dangerous Mission 17, 82, 108–111, 122, 123, 139
Daniel, Billy 77
Daniell, Henry 114
Daniels, Billy 78
Danton, Ray 120, 121
Darden, Severn 170
Darrell, Steve 108, 157
Darvi, Bella 17, 114, 116, 117
Darwell, Jane 52, 55, 101, 102
Dassin, Jules 142
Daugherty, Herschel 68
A Daughter of the Gods 95
Davenport, Danny 81, 83
Daves, Delmer 17, 111
David, Hal 165, 166
David and Bathsheba 113
Davidson, William B. 52
Davies, Peter 134
Davis, Boyd 73
Davis, George W. 103, 111, 114, 123
Davis, Joan 43
Davis, Karl 111
Davis, William "Wee Willie" 73
Dawson, Hal K. 41, 76
Day, Dennis 81, 83, 172
Day, Doris 34, 77
Day, Richard 39, 41, 44, 47, 56
Dean, Julia 70
De Brulier, Nigel 26
De Carlo, Yvonne 20, 107, 157, 158, 159, 172
de Cordoba, Pedro 73
"Deep in the Heart of Texas" 83

Deering, Olive 73
De Filippi, Amedeo 23
De Grasse, Robert 50
Dehaven, Gloria 81, 172
Dehner, John 157
Dekker, Albert 62, 63
De Lavallade, Carmen 111, 114
De Leone, Francesco 165
Del Mar Hotel, Hollywood 17
Del Monte, Raffaele 160
DeLuise, Dom 169, 170
Demarest, William 68, 69, 70, 172
Demetrius and the Gladiators 17, 75, 111–113, 116, 121, 124, 126
DeMille, Cecil B. 14, 69, 73, 74, 75, 76, 115, 155
Denham, Morris 165
Denison, Leslie 92
Dennis, Nick 98, 100
Dern, Bruce 172, 173
De Saint Cyr, Guy 176
The Desert Legion 107
The Desert Song 107
De Sica, Vittorio 165, 166
De Simone, Roberto 165
Desmond, Johnny 145, 148
Dettaven, Gloria 83
Deutsch, Adolph 92, 94
Devine, Andy 172
Devry, Elaine 145
Dexter, Brad 86, 88, 122, 123, 124
Diamond, I.A.L. 89
Dibbs, Kem 108
Dick Berg's Movieland Seals 155
Dietrich, Marlene 36, 37
Diffring, Anton 118
Dilson, John 47
Disney, Doris Miles 80, 81
Dobbs, George 47
Doda, Carol 168
Dolenz, George 157, 159
Dolenz, Micky 168
Domergue, Faith 19, 148, 150
Dominci, Franco 159
Donah, Ludwig 106
Donald, James 95
Donde, Manuel 125
Donlevy, Brian 59, 60
Donnell, Jeff 70
Doran, Ann 83
Dorr, Lester 68
Dorrington, Clint 95
Dors, Diana 19, 139, 140, 142, 143, 153
Doubrowsky, Kurt 162
Doucette, John 103
Doud, Gil 180
Douglas, Gordon 23
Douglas, Kirk 76, 105, 125, 160, 178

Douglas, Lloyd C. 103, 105, 111, 112
Dowd, Ross 68
"Down on Ami Oni Oni Isle" 44
"Down on Wabash Avenue" 78
Downing, Vernon 92
Downs, Cathy 52, 63, 64
Dragonwyck 57
Dratler, Jay 86, 87
Dreir, Hans 68, 73
Dreiser, Theodore 44
Dresser, Paul 44, 45, 46, 47, 121, 181
Du Brey, Claire 149
Dudley, Paul 157
Duff, Warren 84
Dugan, Tom 23
Duncan, Andrew 174
Duncan, Lee 94
Duncan, Trevor 140
Dunn, Eli 98
Dunn, Linwood G. 95
Dunne, Irene 44
Dunne, Philip 103, 111, 114
Dunning, John D. 118
Dunnock, Mildred 59
Durano, Giustino 165
Durante, Jimmy 69
Dwyer, Marlo 108
Dyne, Michael 56

Earl, Kenneth 47, 50
Earp, Wyatt 13, 52, 53
East of Sumatra 121
Easton, Jane 86
Eastwood, Clint 149, 175
Easy Living 14, 48, 51, 70–73, 76, 80, 81, 85, 158, 168
Eckardt, William 52, 111, 114
Ecstasy 95
Edmiston, James 108
Education of the Heart 70
Edwards, Edgar 26
Edwards, Nate H. 149, 157
Edwards, Ralph 50, 51
Egan, Richard 13, 98, 100, 113, 122, 123, 124
The Egyptian 17, 97, 102, 113, 114–117
Eisner, David 176
Ekberg, Anita 133, 134, 135, 136, 137, 139, 140, 153
Ekland, Britt 165, 166
El Cid 108, 178
Eldredge, George 111
Elley, Derek 160
Elliot, Dick 95
Elliot, Peter 136, 143
Ellis, Mirko 159
Ellis, Robert 41, 47, 70, 82
Ellsworth, Elmer 149
Elstree Studios (UK) 34

Emerson, Hope 64, 67
Emmott, Basil 140
Engel, Roy 108
Engel, Samuel G. 52, 89, 91
England, Ken 33, 95
England, Paul 56
Erdman, Richard 70
Erikson, Leif 80, 81
Erskine, Chester 95
Escape 181
Escort West 2, 19, 146, 148–151
Essex, Harry 86, 87
Esterhazy, Andrea 159
Eustrel, Anthony 103
Evans, Bud 13
Evans, Charles 73, 111
Evans, Ella 13
Evans, Frances (first wife) 8
Evans, Maurice 95, 96, 97
Evans, Peter William 104, 113, 160
Evans, Russell 98
Evelyn, Judith 114
Every Little Crook and Nanny 20, 169–172, 176
Eyman, Scott 55

Fadiman, William 125
Fagen, Herb 110, 122
Fain, Sammy 156
Fairbanks, Douglas, Jr. 30, 54, 74
Fairchild, June 168
The Fall of the Roman Empire 178
Fanny by Gaslight 57
Fantasia, Andrea 159
Fapp, Daniel L. 68
Farnum, William 73
Farrow, John 68, 69
Farrow, Mia 69
Faye, Alice 9, 40, 43, 44, 79, 82, 172, 179
Faye, Julia 68, 73
Fazan, Adrienne 155
Feld, Fritz 172
Fellow, Robert 68
Felton, Earl 86, 87
Fennell, Elsa 128, 136, 152
Ferguson, Frank 92
Ferrer, Jose 176, 178
Ferzetti, Gabriele 159, 162
Fetchit, Stepin 172
Field, Norman 89
Field, Virginia 196, 107
Fields, Eddie 83
The Fiend Who Walked the West 62
Fiermonte, Enzo 159, 165
"Fifth Avenue" 83
Filauri, Antonio 64
Fillmore, Clyde 35
Film Bulletin 76
Final Entry 181
Fine, Morton 180

Firepower 20, 173, 174–176, 178
Fisher, Gerry 177
Fisher, Mary Gale 26
Fisher, Steve 39
The Flamingo Hotel, Las Vegas 88
Flavin, James 11, 92
Fleischer, Richard 123, 124
Fleming, Rhonda 107, 154, 156, 172
Flick, W.D. 59, 98
Flippen, Jay C. 86
Flournoy, Elizabeth 89
Flournoy, Richard 101
Flying Elephants 26
Flynn, Errol 9, 30, 34, 134
Foa, Arnoldo 162
Folsey, George J. 92, 94
Fonda, Henry 13, 50, 52, 53, 55, 126, 179
Fontaine, Frank 80
Footlight Serenade 12, 34, 40, 46, 47–49, 69, 72, 77, 126
Ford, Francis 52
Ford, Glenn 124
Ford, John 13, 52, 53, 54, 64, 65
Ford, Wallace 50
Forlong, Michael 128
Forrest, A.J. 136
Fort Apache 126
Fort Leonard Wood, Missouri 100
Fortescue, Kenneth 143
The Fortunes of Vargas 181
Foster, Harve 29
Foster, Phil 169
Foster, Preston 51, 99
The Four Feathers 135
Four Men and a Prayer 64
Fowler, Hugh S. 89
Fox, Earle 52
Fox, Lyle 111
Fox, Paul S. 56, 77, 80, 103 111, 114
Foy, Eddie, Jr. 172
Fracone, Tiny 64
Franciosa, Anthony 174, 175
Frank, Fred 106
Frank, Fredric M. 73
Fratalocchi, Antonio 162
Fratini, Gaio 162
Freeborn, Stuart 165
Freeman, Everett 92, 94
Freeman, Joel 70
Freeman, Howard 64, 92
Freericks, Bernard 39, 47
Frees, Paul 86
Freidkin, David 180
The French Connection 137
Fresholtz, Les 168
Frickert, Joseph 26
Fried, Gerald 157
Friedhofer, Hugo 123

Fritch, Robert 111
Froeschal, George 118, 119
Frontier Marshal 53, 55
Fujiwara, Chris 159
Fuller, Leyland 59
Funicello, Annette 168, 169
Furthman, Jules 35, 56
Fury at Furnace Creek 14, 62–64, 79
"Fury at Furnace Creek" (radio) 180
Fusco, Joseph 122

Gable, Clark 18, 40, 117, 119, 120
Gabor, Zsa Zsa 172
Gage, Ben 46
Gaige, Russell 89
Galli, Rosina 23
Gam, Rita 159, 161, 162
Gamble, Donald 122
Gambling House 80, 81, 83–86, 109, 140, 170
Garbini, Amato 165
Garbuglia, Mario 165
Garcia, Paul 174
Garde, Betty 64
Garde, Colin 152
Gardenia, Vincent 174, 175
Gardiner, Reginald 62, 64, 76, 78, 79, 83, 95, 97, 180
Gardner, Ava 75, 118
Garfield, Brian 122
Gargan, William 23, 25, 39
Garmes, Lee 47, 131
Garner, Dan 52
Garr, Teri 168, 169, 172
Garrett, Hank 174
Garrick, Richard 89
Garth, David 62, 64
Garvin, Gene 68
Gaslight 57
Gasper, Chuck 168
Gassman, Vittorio 166
Gausman, Russell A. 106, 120
Gay, John 176
Gaye, Gregory 39, 44
Gayson, Eunice 133
Gelsey, Erwin 84
Gengarelli, Amerigo 162
Genn, Leo 143, 144
Gentili, Carlo 159
Gentili, Giogio 162
George H. Tingley Public School 5
Gerlini, Piero 165
Geronimo 120
Gershenson, Joseph 106, 120
Gerstle, Frank 98
Gertsman, Maury 157
Gibb, Alec 136, 137
Gibbons, Cedric 92
Gibson, Mimi 114

Gilbert, Billy 32, 41
Gilda 45
The Gilded Rooster 125, 126
Gillespie, A. Arnold 92
Gilling, John 134, 136, 152
Gilman, Sam 103
Gilmour, Lowell 95
Ginnoto, Mirella 160
The Girl in Car 32 180
Giustini, Anacleto 160
Gladiator 178
Glasgow, William 157
Glass, Everett 70, 111
Glass, Gaston 77
Gleason, Adda 26
Gleason, James 44, 46, 47, 49
Glen, John 118
Glenwood Springs, Colorado 53
The Glory Brigade 17, 51, 98–101, 118, 124, 130, 144, 154
Gluskin, Lud 23
Goddard, Paulette 24
Goer, Walter 118
The Golden Blade 107
Goldinez, Salvador 176
Goldstein, Leonard 120
Goldwyn, Samuel, Jr. 131, 132
Golitzen, Alexander 106, 120
Gone with the Wind 24, 38
Gonzalez, Pedro Gonzalez 172
Goodwin, Harold 134
Gordon, Leo 148, 149, 151
Gordon, Mack 41, 77, 78
Gordon, Mary 32
Gordon, Michael 128
Gotell, Walter 152
Grade, Sir Lew 176
Graff, Wilton 89, 92
Graham, Fred 101, 111
Graham, Ronny 172
Graham, Sheila 167
Granada, Joese Rodriguez 177
Graneto, Madeline Anu 177
Granger, Farley 116
Granger, Michael 114
Granger, Stewart 96, 97
Grant, Cary 74, 84, 95
Grant, Cy 128
Grant, Elspeth 11
Grant, Kathryn 127, 154, 156
Grassini, Marilee 59
Grauman's Chinese Theatre 21
Graves, Phillip 169
Gray, Coleen 59, 60, 61, 62, 63, 64, 179, 180
Gray, Feild M. 86, 101
The Great Dictator 43
Greco, J. 65
Green, Danny 136
Green, Marshall 120
Green, Shecky 172
Green, William E. 84

"Green River" 79
Greene, Richard 58, 64
Greenleaf, Raymond 122
Greenway, Lee 70
Greer, Dabbs 101, 102
Greer, Howard 86
Grenzbach, Hugo 68
Grey, Charles 137
Greyeyes, Michael 122
Gribble, Bernard 172
Griffin, Frank 108
Griffiths, D.W. 26, 27, 28, 29
Griswold, Al 174
Grizzard, George 174, 175
Grobenicke Polje, Croatia 164
Groppioni, Franco 160
Gross, Roland 84, 95
Grossman, Allen 176
Grossman, Eugene 52, 62, 65
Grozea, Costel 162
Grubb, John C. 101
Gualino, Riccardo 162
Guercio, Camillo 89
Guilfoyle, Paul 120
Guilmant, Philip 176
Gulliver, Dorothy 172
Gundlach, Robert 174
Guttman, Henry 68

Hackman, Gene 137
Hageman, Richard 35, 38
Haggerty, Don 83
Hal Roach Film Studio 8
Halama, Loda 84
Hale, Creighton 26
Hale, Jonathan 98
Hall, Ben 26, 52
Hall, Charles D. 23, 26, 29, 95
Hall, Gladys 40
Hall, Huntz 172
Hall, Jon 28
Hall, Sherry 84
Halliwell, Leslie 26, 154
Halton, Charles 80
Hamilton, Antony 20, 176, 177, 178
Hamilton, Margaret 76b
Hamlet 69
Hampton, Grayce 35
Hanley, Jim 168
Hanlon, Tom 82
Hannibal 20, 157, 159–162
Hanson, Aleth "Speed" 52
Harbach, Otto A. 33
A Hard Day's Night 168
The Hard Man 143
Harden, Ray 98
Harline, Leigh 86, 125
Harmetz, Ajean 21, 170
Harout, Yeghishe 114
"Harrigan" 78
Harrington, Pat, Jr. 170

Harris, Pamela 82
Harris, Phil 76, 79
Harris, Slim 128
Harrison, Gregory 176
Harrison, John 128
Harrison, Rex 28, 95
Hart, Virgil 131
Hartsook, Fred 149
Hartwell, Oliver 86
Harvey, John 139
Harvey, Paul 80
Hasse, O.E. 117
Hathway, Henry 13, 59, 60, 61, 155
Hattie, Hilo 41, 43
Havana, Cuba 131
Haver, June 81, 82, 83, 181
Havoc, June 68, 69, 180
"Hawaiian War Chant" 44
Hayes, Charles 128
Hayes, Chester 106
Hayes, Margaret 122, 123, 124
Hayes, Peter Lind 50, 51
Hayes, Steve 149
Hayle, Grace 108
Haymes, Dick 45, 82, 172
Hays Office 38
Hayward, Susan 11, 17, 112, 113
Haywood, Chuck 149
Hayworth, Rita 2, 12, 20, 39, 44, 45, 46, 50, 51, 52, 72, 75, 77, 162, 181
Head 20, 168–169
Head, Edith 68, 74
Heard, Charles 92
Heath, William L. 122
Heathcote, Thomas 118
Hecht, Ben 59, 60, 67
Hedda Hopper's Hollywood 181
Hefti, Neal 172
Heinemann, Eda 59
Hell Drivers 142
Hellman, Sam 52
Help! 168
Helseth, Henry Edward 65, 66
Helstoski, Kristine 168
Helton, Percy 68, 69, 77, 168
Heman, Roger, Sr. 39, 41, 44, 47, 52, 56, 59, 65, 77, 80, 103, 111, 114
Henderson, Charles 47
Henry, Thomas Browne 103, 106
Hepburn, Audrey 128
Herbert, Lew 59
Herbert, Percy 143
Herczeg, Geza 35
"Here You Are" 46
Herman, Alfred 70, 84
Hermann, Bernard 114
Hernandez, Jesus 131
Heston, Charlton 73, 76, 108, 133, 155, 178

Heymann, Werner R. 26, 29
Hicks, Don 82
Hicks, Russell 32, 73
Hide-White, Wilfred 117
Hill, Al 62
Hill, Bluey 136, 143
Hill, Terence 159, 161
Hinton, Ed 73
His Prehistoric Past 26
Hitchcock, Alfred 65
Hoag, Robert R. 155
Hoch, Winton C. 155
Hoesli, John 140
Hoffman, John 168
Hogan, Pat 120, 125
Hoge, Ralph 131, 132
Hogsett, Albert 47, 62, 65
Holbrook, Vic 106
Holcombe, Herbert 59
Holden, Fay 73
Holden, William 105
Holland, Arthur 59
Holland, Frank 128
Hollander, Frederick 95, 97
Holliday, Doc 2, 13, 52, 53, 54, 60, 62, 104, 121
Holloway, Sterling 170
Hollywood 1, 5, 6, 7, 9, 10, 12, 13, 16, 24, 25, 27, 33, 34, 36, 39, 40, 46, 48, 64, 65, 66, 69, 92, 96, 97, 118, 149, 158, 173, 175
The Hollywood Reporter 64, 90, 91, 104, 118, 127, 153
Hollywood Star Playhouse 180
Hollywood Star Time 181
Hollywood Star Turn 16
Holman, Harry 50
Holmes, Jennifer 176
Holmes, Kenneth 33
Holmes, Taylor 59
Holt, Tim 52, 55
"Home on the Range" 44
Hope, Bob 69
Hopkins, Miriam 74
Hopper, Hedda 181
Hopper, Jerry 131, 133
Hornblow, Arthur, Jr. 92
Horne, Victoria 101
Horvath, Charles 120
Hot Spot 39; see also *I Wake Up Screaming*
House Committee on Un-American Activities 87
House of Strangers 180
The Housekeeper's Daughter 8, 23–26
Houston, Glyn 118
Houston, John 38
Howard, Cy 170, 172
Howard, Harold 26
Howard, Tom 118

Howard, Trevor 19, 135, 136, 137, 138
Howat, Clark 84
Howe, Eileen 101
Hoyt, John 95
Hubbard, John 23, 26, 28, 148
Hubert, Rene 52, 56, 62
Hudson, Rock 106, 141, 149
Hughes, Howard 70, 85, 87, 93, 95, 97, 105, 150
Hughes, Kathleen 82
Hughes, Ken 140
Hughes, Leigh 125
Hugo, Mauritz 62
Hugo, Michael 168
Humberstone, H. Bruce 39, 40, 62
Hunter, Evan 170
Hunter, Tab 172
Hunter, Willie, Jr. 120
Hurlbut, Gladys 89
Hurley, Elizabeth 178
Huston, Walter 35, 38
Huth, Harold 152
Hutton, Betty 3, 14, 68, 69, 70, 75
Hyams, John 23
Hyde, Kenneth 118

"I Get Along Without You Very Well" 16, 88
"I Got a Gal from Kalamazoo" 83
"I Heard the Birdies Sing" 49
"I Wake Up" 69
I Wake Up Screaming 11, 28, 39–41, 43, 45, 62, 65, 67, 102
"I Want to Be Happy" 34
I Was a Male War Bride 81
"I Wish I Could Shimmy Like My Sister Kate" 78
"If You Wants Me" 46
"I'll Be Marching to a Love Song" 49
I'll Get By 16, 81–83
I'll See You in My Dreams 77
Illing, Peter 13, 136
"I'm Still Crazy for You" 49
The Incorrigible One 6
Ingersoll, Thomas 64
Ingram, Rex 148
Ingster, Boris 89
Interpol 19, 88, 136–139, 141, 142, 145, 153
Ireland, John 52, 55
Irene 34
Irvine, Richard 82
Irving, Charles 168
Isaacs, Bob 128
Ischia, Bay of Naples 166
"I'se Your Honey" 46
Isla de Pinos 131
I.T.C. 174

"It's a Quarter to Three" 109
"It's Been a Long, Long Time" 83
It's Later Than You Think 181
Ivan, Rosalind 103
Ivano, Paul 35
"I've Been Floating Down the Old Green River" 78
Iverson Ranch, California 151

Jabotinsky, Vladimir 73
Jackson, Henry 62
Jackson, Selmer 111
Jacobson, Arthur 82
Jaffe, Carl 118
Jagger, Dean 103
James, Barbara 111
James, Harry 81, 83
James, Rian 23
James, Sid 136
Jamison, Bud 29
Janssen, David 120
Jaroslow, Ruth 174
Jarre, Maurice 177
Jarrico, Paul 86, 87
Jassy 57
Jaws 132
Jeakins, Dorothy 74
Jefferies, Philip M. 170
Jefferson, I.J. 168
Jeffries, Wesley 145
Jellison, Bob 101
Jenks, Si 62
Jennings, Devereaux 74
Jennings, Gordon 74
Jenson, Roy 131
Jensson, Eloise 74, 89
Jessel, George 172
"Johnny Come Home" 119
Johns, Master Sgt. Lorin 131
Johnson, Lamont 98
Jones, Barry 111, 113
Jones, Chester 84, 101
Jones, Davy 168, 169
Jones, Gordon 70, 72
Jones, Grover 29
Jones, Harmon 65, 80
Jones, Kenneth V. 143, 144
Jones, T.C. 168
Josephy, Alvin M. 89
Joslyn, Allyn 89
Jowett, Corson 120
Joy, Nicholas 101, 102
Judd, Edward 142
Juma 128
Junge, Alfred 118
The Jungleland Elephants 155
Jupiter's Darling 160
Juran, Nathan 39
Justin, John 128

Kadison, Harry 59
Kafafian, Lee 170

Kahn, Conrad 155
Kahn, Grace 77
Kahn, Gus 77
Kahn, Madeline 172, 173
Kalmar, Bert 77
Kann, Lily 118
Kaplan, Sol 89
Karlin, Fred 170
Karnes, Robert 59, 64
Kash, Murray 152, 157
Kasket, Harold 136
Kaus, Gina 103
Kean, John K. 157
Keating, Larry 80, 89
Keaton, Buster 26
Keel, Howard 160
Kelby, Bill 174
Keller, Walter E. 108
Kellerman, Annette 92, 93
Kellog, Ray 89, 98, 103, 111, 114, 123
Kelly, Barry 68, 76
Kelly, Gene 45, 49
Kelly, James L. "Tiny" 92
Kelly, John 44
Kelly, Sean 143, 152
Kelly, Thomas F. 145
Kelly's Heroes 144
Kemp, Hal 10
Kemp, Helen 10
Kemp, Kenner G. 155
Kemp, Martha Stephenson (second wife) 9, 12
Kemper, Charles 62, 63, 64, 180
Kenab, Utah 64
Kenab Movie Fort 64
Kennedy, King 50
Kent, Crauford 73
Kent, Dorothea 32
Kenya, Africa 19, 128
Kenyon, Curtis 50
Kerr, Charles 35
Keymas, George 103
Kibbee, Milton 86
Kinematograph Weekly 58
King, Henry 110
King, Louis 108, 110
King, Walter Woofe 101
The King and I 43
King Kong 29, 30
King's Rhapsody 34
Kirk, 1Mark-1Lee 56, 80
Kiss of Death 2, 3, 16, 40, 59–62, 63, 64, 65, 67, 74, 75, 76, 85, 104, 123, 124, 131, 140, 141, 170, 179, 180, 181
Klane, Robert 170
Kline, Richard H. 172
Knowles, Cyril J. 134
Knudtson, Frederic 70, 86, 108
Koehler, Dave 149
Kohler, Fred 59, 62

Kolb, Mina 170
Kosloff, Theodore 74
Koster, Henry 77, 78, 79, 103, 105
Kotal, Edward 70
Koumani, Maya 152
Kramer, Arthur 59
Krasner, Milton R. 111
Kroeger, Berry 64, 67
Kromberg, Ernest 159
Kruger, Stubby 95
Kruschen, Jack 68, 83
Kuhn, Mickey 125
Kulky, Henry 77, 98

LaBarba, Fidel 47
Ladd, Alan 29, 32, 158
Lady in the Dark 9, 10, 35
Lake, Stuart N. 52
Lake of the Ozarks, Missouri 100
Lally, Mike 108
Lamarr, Hedy 14, 25, 73, 95, 142, 180
Lamas, Fernando 172
LaMotta, Jake 174, 175
Lamour, Dorothy 42, 172, 181
Lancaster, Burt 73, 87, 107, 126, 155, 158, 160, 175
Lancaster, Elsa 95, 97
Land of the Pharaohs 115
"Land on Your Feet" 49
The Land That Time Forgot 26
Landis, Carole, 8, 9, 11, 26, 27, 38, 40, 41, 44, 46
Lane, Charles 39, 70
Lane, James 70, 101
Lane, Jane 108
Lang, Fritz 25, 45
Lang, June 47
Lang, Walter 41, 43, 44
Langan, Barbara 17
Langlan, Glenn 62, 63
Lansbury, Angela 73, 75
Lansing, Ernest 65
Lapis, Joe 106
Larsen, Keith 120
La Rue, Jack 172
The Las Vegas Story 16, 86–89, 109, 123, 124
LaSalle, Martin 176
LaShelle, Joseph 89
Lasky, Jessie, Jr. 73
The Last Frontier 19, 125–127, 154
Lathrop, Phillip 170
"Laura" (radio) 180
Laurel and Hardy 25, 26
Laurence, Paula 174
Laurie, Piper 17, 106, 108, 109, 110
Lauter, Harry 82
The Law and Martin Rome 65

Lawford, Peter 172
Lawrence, Gertrude 9, 10
Lawrence, Marc 23, 25
Lawson, Glyn 128
Leaming, Barbara 163
LeBaron, Willam 41, 47
Lebedeff, Ivan 35
Lederer, Charles 59, 68, 77
Lee, Tom 176
Leeds, Phil 172
Lehmann, Olga 128
Leiber, Fritz 73
Leibman, Ron 172
Leigh, Janet 19, 128, 130, 140, 153
Leigh, Vivien 24
Leith, Virginia 122, 124
Le Maire, Charles 56, 59, 62, 77, 80, 82, 89, 111, 114, 123
Leonard, David 103, 111
Leonard, Harry M. 62, 82, 89, 98, 123
Leonard, Queenie 92
Leonard Maltin's Movie and Video Guide 108, 157, 176
LeRoy, Mervyn 92, 94
Lerpae, Paul 73
Leven, Boris 35, 38
Le Veque, Edward 172
Leverett, George 82
Levy, Franklin R. 176
Lewis, George 106
Lewis, Monica 101, 102
Leyland Trucks 141, 143
Li, Li Hua 145, 147, 148
Libby, Fred 52
Lierly, Harold 73
Life (magazine) 6, 76
Lilacs in the Spring 34
Lilley, Joseph J. 68
Lillian, Russell 179
Linden, Virginia 108
Lindgren, Harry 73
Linklatter, Eric 177
Lipsky, Eleazar 59
Lipsrein, Harold 120
Lishman, Harold 41
Liston, Sonny 168, 169
Little, Thomas 39, 41, 44, 47, 52, 56, 59, 62, 77, 80, 82, 89
Litwack, Sydney Z. 168
Livadary, John P. 125
"Living High" 49
Livingstone, Robert 89
"Liza Jane" 46
Lloyd, Harold 25
Lloyd, Russell 165
Lloyds of London (insurance) 48
Lockhart, Gene 95, 97, 179
Lodge, Davis 143
Lodge, William 143
The Lodger 40, 57
Loeffler, Louis R. 123

Loesser, Frank 50, 68, 69, 70
Logan, Helen 41, 47, 82
Lollobrigida, Gina 119
Lomas, Jack 101
London, England 19
Lonely Are the Brave 126
Long, Walter 77
The Long Duel 135
The Long Haul 19, 121, 139–143, 145, 153
The Long Ships 119, 163
Look (magazine) 76
Loos, Mary 82
Loren, Sophia 20, 172, 175, 176
Lorre, Peter 25, 154, 156
Los Angeles 12, 16, 67, 88, 170
The Los Angeles Examiner 67
The Los Angeles Rams 70, 72
The Lost World 26, 29
Lougherty, Jackie 106
Louie, Bebe 170
Louisville, Kentucky 5, 6, 7, 8, 61, 79
The Love and Death of Joaquin Murieta 180
Lovegrove, Arthur 128
Lower, Tony 128
Lucidi, Maurizio 162, 163
Luick, Earl 47
Luke, Keye 172
Lulli, Folco 162
Lummins, Dayton 111
Lund, John 120, 121
Lundigan, William 81, 83
Lux Radio Theater 179, 181
Lyn, Ann 153
Lynn, Emmett 103
Lyon, Francis D. 149, 151
Lyons, Collette 77
Lytton, Herbert 89

Macaulay, Charles 168
MacDonald, Archer 89, 90, 98
MacDonald, Bruce 89
MacDonald, Ian 114
MacDonald, J. Farrell 52, 62
MacDonald, Joseph 52, 56
MacGinnis, Niall 118, 119
Macht, Stephen 176
Mack, Wilbur 47
MacKenzie, Joyce 80
MacMurray, Fred 82
"MacNamara's Band" 83
Madel, Frank 33
Madeleine 57
Madison, Guy 120, 125, 126, 143, 172
Madrid, Spain 153
Maguire, Tobey 142
Maher, Frank 152
Maibaum, Richard 134, 152
Maitland, Marne 136

Majors, Lee 163
Maladrinos, Andreas 143
Malden, Karl 59
Maldonado, Salim 176
Mallory, Joan 86
"Maluna Malolo Mawaena" 44
Mamakos, Peter 98
The Man in the Iron Mask 24
Mandell, Daniel 131
Mander, Miles 29, 32
Mango, Alex 134, 136
Mann, Anthony 125
Mann, Iris 59
Mann, Stanley 56
Manners, Audrey 26
Man's Genesis 26
Manzano, Sonia 174
Mapes, Ted 62
Mara, Adele 154
Marchak, John 68
Margo, George 134
Marin, Luciano 162
Maris, Mona 44
Markey, Gene 56
Marks, J. 104
Marks, Joe 174
Marle, Arnold 134
Marley, John 59
Marner, Richard 143
Marr, Sally 170
Marshall, Chet 95
Marshall, Marion 77, 80
Marshall, Trudy 47
Marshall, William 111, 113
Martell, Cregg 59, 98
Martell, Donna 114
Martien, Elva 157
Martin, Freddy 50, 51
Martin, Orlando 131
Martin, Peter 118
Marvin, Lee 40, 98, 99, 100, 101, 122, 123, 125
Marx, Groucho 74
Marx, Harpo 95, 96
Masciocchi, Raffaele 159
Mason, James 120, 137
Mastroianni, Marcello 166
Mathias, Bob 145, 148
Mathieson, Muir 128, 134, 143
Mattera, Lino 165
Mattox, Matt 98
Mature, Clara (mother) 2, 5, 12
Mature, Marcellus George (father) 5, 6, 11
Mature, Victor: birth of daughter 21; contract with Hal Roach 8; death of father 11; death of mother 20; fifth marriage 21; first marriage 8; fourth marriage 20; move to Hollywood 6; passion for golf 18; retail television business 14;

retirement 20; second marriage 9; third marriage 14; United States Coast Guard 12
Mature, Victoria (daughter) 21
Mau, Mau 128, 130, 137, 153
Maurice Speed Film Review 64, 68, 89
Maxey, Paul 101
Maxwell, John 89
"May I Tempt You with a Big Red Rosy Apple" 78
Mayer, Louis B. 102
Maynard, Kermit 62
Mayne, Ferdy 118
Mayo, Frank 73
Mayo, Virginia 172
Mazurki, Mike 35, 73, 114, 172
McCord, Bob 82
McCorry, John 143
McCoy, Horace 108
McCrea, Ann 145
McDaniel, Sam 101
McDonald, Francis 73
McDuff, Tyler 114
McGarry, William 155
McGoohan, Patrick 134, 136
McGrath, Larry 95
McGuire, Macy 50, 51
McHugh, Jimmy 50
McIntyre, Leila 23
McKay, Norman 59
McLean, Barbara 114
McManus, Brian 177
McNally, Stephen 122, 123
McNear, Howard 154
McSweeney, John, Jr. 92
McWhorter, Frank 108
"Me and My Fella" 46
Medina, Patricia 56, 58
Meek, Donald 23, 25
Melford, George 114
Mellor, William C. 125
Mendez, Gene 155
Meniconi, Furio 162
Menjou, Adolphe 23, 25
Mercer, Jim 47
Mercier, Louis 52
Meredith, Charles 73
Merman, Ethel 69, 172
Mersky, Kres 172
Metty, Russell 33, 106
Mexico 127, 177
MGM 1 (Metro-1Goldwyn-1Mayer) 18, 30, 45, 51, 73, 83, 92, 93, 96, 97, 102, 115, 118, 119, 150, 160, 162, 163, 169, 170
Miami, Florida 12
Michaelides, George 98
"Midnight at the Masquerade" 46
Miles, Bernard 133
Milestone, Lewis 30

Miley, Jerry 62
Miljan, John 73
Milland, Ray 69
Millar, Ronald 118, 119
Miller, Ann 172
Miller, Colleen 86
Miller, David 120
Miller, Harley 70
Miller, Joan 64, 89
Miller, John "Skins" 77
Miller, Merle 143
Miller, Seton 44
Miller, Winston 52, 62
Millican, James 120
Million Dollar Mermaid 13, 16, 34, 92–95, 174
Mills, Jack 84, 145
Mills, Mervyn 140
Mills, Richard 174
Milton, Robert 86
Mintz, Eli 172
Miracle on the 34th Street 48, 89
Mr. Lucky 84
"Mr. Volunteer" 46
Mitchell, Cameron 103, 137
Mitchell, Millard 59
Mitchell, Steve 145
Mitchell, Thomas 41, 42
Mitchum, Robert 2, 87, 88, 93, 140, 150
Mockridge, Cyril J. 39, 52, 80
Moffatt, Margaret 44
Molinas, Richard 136
Molteni, Ambogio 162
Momentum 180
"The Monkees" 20, 168, 169
"The Monkey Song" 16, 88
Monroe, Marilyn 140, 150
Montalban, Ricardo 172
Montana Glacier National Park 17, 109
Montgomery, George 44, 51, 64, 77, 79, 99, 179
Montgomery, Jack 52
Montgomery, Ray 86
Moore, Alvy 98, 99, 101
Moore, Cleo 83
Moore, Ted 134
Moore, Terry 16, 83, 85, 136, 152
Moore, Victor 90
Morahan, Tom 140
Moreland, Craig 108
Moreland, Mantan 47
Morell, Andre 134, 136
Morgan, Bob 158
Morgan, Boyd "Red" 122
Morgan, Dennis 172
Morgan, Gene 23
Morin, Alberto 98
Morison, Patricia 60, 172
Morita, Pat 169
Morocco 135

Moross, Jerome 131
Morra, Mario 98
Morris, Wolfe 136
Morrison, Ann 122
Morrison, Robert E. 145, 149, 151
Morrow, Jeff 103
Moss Rose 13, 56–58, 123, 154
"Moss Ross" (radio) 180
Motion Picture Review 164
Mowbray, Alan 39, 52, 95, 97
Moyer, Ray 73
Mudie, Leonard 157
Mulock, Al 136
Munden, Jesse 98
Munson, Ona 35, 36, 38
Murgia, Tiberio 165
Murphy, Al 86
Murphy, Richard 65
Murray, Jack 145
Murray, Ken 172
Murray, Ricky 122
Murton, Lionel 136
Musco, Nino 165
My Brother Paul 44
My Darling Clementine 2, 52–56, 59, 63, 104, 121, 122
My Gal Sal 2, 12, 16, 28, 34, 44–47, 72, 102, 121, 156, 181
"My Gal Sal" 46
"My Resistance Is Low" 16, 88
Myers, Carmel 172
Myrow, Josef 77, 78

Nablo, James Benson 145
Nagel, Conrad 26
Naish, J. Carrol 122, 123, 124
The Naked City 67
Napoleon, Art 131
Napoleon, Jo 131
Nathanson, Joseph 165
Natili, Giovanna 162
Neagle, Anna 9, 32, 33, 34, 49, 68
Neal, Patricia 16, 89, 90, 91
Nedd, Stuart 98
Nefertiti, Queen of the Nile 116
Negley, Howard 62
Neilson, Catherine 174
Neise, George N. 131
Nelson, David 154, 156
Nelson, Gordon 89
Nelson, Kay 123
Nelson, Sam 125
Nepean, Edith 142
Neptune's Daughter 94
Nesmith, Michael 168
Neuman, Jack E. 180
Neumann, Dorothy 76
New York (city) 9, 13, 61, 65, 67, 88
The New York Herald Tribune 13, 61, 91

The New York Post 9, 29, 30
The New York Sun 13, 55
The New York Times 8, 29, 32, 43, 46, 52, 57, 64, 67, 68, 70, 73, 76, 79, 83, 86, 88, 91, 95, 98, 105, 111, 117, 125, 134, 159, 164, 168, 171, 173, 176
The New York World-Telegram 9, 30
Newcom, James E. 29
Newcombe, Warren 92
Newhard, Joyce 122
Newley, Anthony 143, 145, 152, 153
Newman, Alfred 41, 46, 52, 56, 62, 65, 67, 103, 111, 114
Newman, Emil 131
Newman, Joseph M. 155, 156
Newman, Lionel 77, 82, 83, 89, 98
Newsweek 49
Newton, Robert 95, 97
Next Time I Marry 50
Ngakane, Lionel 128
Nichols, Barbara 172
Nichols, Red 77
Nicholson, Emrich 106
Nicholson, George Jay 177
Nicholson, Jack 168, 169
Nigh, Jane 64, 68
Night of the Big Heat 141
A Night to Remember 30
Nissen, Brian 136
Nitschke, Ray 168, 169
Niven, David 64, 165
"No Love, No Nothing" 83
No, No Nanette 9, 32–35, 43, 68, 69, 102
"No, No Nanette" 34
No Time to Die 51, 143–145, 153
Nolan, James 155
Nolan, Lloyd 70, 72, 73
Noonan, Tommy 122, 123
Noriega, Eduardo 176
The Norsemen 163
Northpole, John 26
Northwest Passage 30
Norton, Cliff 172
Novack, Mickell 26
Novello, Jay 103
"Now That I Need You" 69
Noyes, Jack 35
Number One 73
Nye, Ben 52, 56, 62, 65, 77, 80, 82,
Nye, Louis 172
Nyitray, Emil 33

Oakie, Jack 41, 42, 43, 82
O'Brien, George 53
O'Brien, Pat 66

"O'Brien Has Gone Hawaiian" 44
O'Connor, John 178
O'Connor, Peggy 82
Odell, Rosemary 106, 120
Of Men and Mice 28, 30
O'Flynn, Damian 83
O'Gorman, John 118
"Oh, the Pity of it All" 46
O'Hara, Maureen 30
O'Hara, Scarlett 24, 44
Ohman, Phil 29
Ohrenbach, Michael 50
Okun, Charles 172
Old Jackie 75
Oliver, Gordon 86
Olsen, Moroni 73
Olson, James 131, 133
O'Malley, J. Pat 29
O'Moore, Patrick 56, 92
"On the Banks of the Wabash" 46
"On the Great White Way" 46
"Once in a While" 83
One Million B.C. 8, 26–29, 30
One Million Years B.C. (1966) 28
Orenbach, Al 95
Orfei, Liana 162, 163
Orth, Frank 39, 44, 47, 62
Osbiston, Alan 134
Osbourne, Ted 29
Osbourne, Vivienne 29
O'Shea, Oscar 62
Ossentynski, Leonidas 84
O'Sullivan, Maureen 28, 69
Our Gang 25
Ouspenskaya, Maria 35
"Over the Rainbow" 41

Paar, Jack 70
Pack, Charles Lloyd 136
Paget, Debra 64, 67, 111, 113
Paige, Ann 145
Palance, Jack 41
Palange, Ince 26
Palella, Oreste 162
Palmer, Ernest 41, 44
Palmer, Gene 108
Palmer, Gregg 106
Paluzzi, Luciana 143
Pan, Hermes 44, 46, 47, 48
Papich, Stephen 111, 114
Paramount Pictures 14, 15, 42, 68, 70, 73, 75, 76, 78, 121, 172
Parish, John 151
Parks, Eddie 64
Parrish, John 73
Parsons, Louella 12
Parsons, Ned 168, 172
Parton, Reg 120, 125
Pascal, Gabriel 95, 96, 98
Pasedena Play House 7, 8, 25, 113, 126
Paths of Glory 7
Patrick, Dorothy 122
Patrick, George 89
Patrinakos, Father Nicon D. 98
Pattillo, Alan 143, 152
Paul, Victor 83
Paxton, John 136
Payne, John 34, 43, 47, 48, 49, 82, 83
Paynter, Robert 174
Pearce, Guy 39, 41, 44, 47
Peary, Harold 50, 51
Peck, Gregory 113, 118
Pefferle, Richard 92
Pendleton, Austin 169, 170, 171
Penman, Lea 80
Pennrick, Jack 125
Peppard, George 175
Per Spook 175
Perkins, Gil 52, 111
Perlberg, William 77, 79, 82
Perron, Larry 157
Perry, Ken 145
Peters, Jean 41
Peters, John 120
Peterson, Robert 125
Petracca, Joseph 89
Petrie, Howard 106
The Philadelphia Story 35, 43
Philips, Lee 177, 178
Phillips, Conrad 134
Phillips, Dorothy 122
Phillips, Wendell 59
Phillips, William "Bill" 70
Photoplay (magazine) 81
Picerni, Paul 82
Pickens, Slim 149
Picker, David V. 172
Pickup Alley see *Interpol*
Picture Show (magazine) 79, 91, 105, 131, 133, 142
Picture Show and TV Mirror (magazine) 154
Picturegoer (magazine) 10, 11, 47, 70, 73, 76, 81, 83, 85, 89, 100, 117, 122, 125, 139, 143, 148
Pidgeon, Walter 92, 93, 94, 172
Pierlot, Francis 103
Pinson, Allen 125, 157
Piron, Armand, Jr. 78
Pirosh, Robert 41
Pitts, ZaSu 32, 34, 35
Pizzi, Pier Luigi 165
Platt, Louise 29, 30, 32, 72
Playboy (magazine) 85, 150
Plummer, Christopher 91
Plunkett, Walter 29, 92
Poggi, Ottavio 159
Pohlmann, Eric 136
Polard, Alex 41
Poli, Mimmo 165
Pope, Alexander 76
Pope, Patricia 26
Porter, Lillian 41
Portman, Clem 70, 84, 86, 95, 101, 108
Poulton, Raymond 118, 140
Power, Tyrone 16, 30, 54, 63, 105, 144
Poyner, John 174
Pozen, Michael 168
Pravda, George 143
Pressburger, Arnold 35
Pressburger, Fred 35
Preston, Robert 7, 125
Preston, Ward 172
Price, Peter 118
Price, Stanley 84
Price, Vincent 13, 54, 56, 64, 86, 108, 109, 110, 154, 156
Priestly, Robert 155
Pulaski, Frank 103
Purdom, Edmund 17, 102, 114, 116
Pyke, Charles F. 95
Pyle, Denver 145

Quashie, Harry 128
Queen Elizabeth II 18
Quitak, Harry 128
Quo Vadis 94, 97

The Radio Times Guide to Films 41, 49, 50, 68, 102, 145, 154, 157, 168, 172
Rafelson, Bob 168, 169
Raft, George 40
Rainey, Ford 103
Rainger, Ralph 46, 47, 49
Raksin, David 62
Rameau, Emil 64
Rames, Neva 149
Ramsey, Lord 168
Ramsey, Walt 8
Rancho Santa Fe 18, 21, 171, 176
Randall, Stuart 120
Randall, William 23, 26
Randall, William M., Jr. 29
Randolph, Donald 83, 120
Rank Films 136
Rasumny, Mikhail 35
Ratoff, Gregory 47, 48, 56, 57
Raven, Elsa 174
Ravenel, Florence 122
Rawlings, Terry 172
Ray, Aldo 172
Raymond, Barry 139
Raymond, Robin 76
Reagan, Ronald 49
The Red Beret 144
Red, Hot and Blue 3, 14, 68–70, 102
Redgrave, Lynn 20, 169, 171

Redmond, Harry, Jr. 35
Redmond, Liam 128, 139, 141
Reed, Carol 155
Reed, Donna 53
Reed, Oliver 174
Reed, Tom 56
Reed, Walter 50, 108, 110
Reeves, George 73
Reeves, Richard 95
Reeves, Steve 19, 74, 161
Reicher, Frank 73
Reid, Carl Benton 114
Reid, Elliot 41
Reinhardt, Gottfried 118, 119, 120
Reiss, Stuart A. 82
Remisoff, Nicolai 29
Renesto, Thomas A. 106
Renie 50
Rennie, Michael 103, 105, 111, 113
Renno, Vincent 82
Rettig, Tommy 114
Revill, Clive 176
Reynolds, Peter 103, 114, 139
Rhodes, Christopher 118
Rhodes, Phil 172
Rich, Dick 11
Richards, Addison 50
Richards, Gordon 92
Richards, Jeffrey 134, 154
Richards, Lloyd 33
Richards, Paul 111
Richardson, Cliff 134, 143
Richardson, John 28
Richmond, Howard 145
Rickard, Joseph E. 122
Rietty, Robert 143
Rin Tin Tin 94, 173, 174
Ring, Cyril 39
Ritter, Thelma 81, 83
The Ritz Brothers 172
Rivero, Lorraine 26
Rivkin, Allen 83
RKO 9, 12, 14, 16, 32, 33, 34, 50, 52, 70, 71, 72, 73, 83, 85, 86, 95, 96, 101, 102, 105, 108, 109, 110, 124
Roach, Hal 8, 9, 11, 23, 24, 25, 26, 28, 29, 30, 32, 34, 38, 40, 85, 87
Roach, Hal, Jr. 26, 27
Road, Michael 95
The Robe 2, 17, 75, 79, 97, 102, 103–106, 107, 112, 113, 116, 121, 126, 127
Roberts, Conrad 174
Roberts, Kenneth 29, 30
Roberts, Richard 174
Roberts, Richard Emery 125
Roberts, Roy 52, 62, 63, 98
Roberts, Stephen 73
Robertson, Chuck 62
Robertson, Stuart 32

Robertson, Willard 62
Robin, Leo 46, 47, 49
Robinson, Casey 114
Robinson, Edward G. 25, 60, 180
Robinson, Jay 103, 111, 113, 116
Robinson, Jonathan 131
Robinson, Pamela 103
Robles, Rudy 41
Rock, Felippa 56
Rode, Fred J. 98
Roesch, Douglas J. 16
Rogato, Joseph 83
Rogers, Ginger 35
Rogers, Hazel 35
Rogers, Kasey 73
Rogers, Rod 92
Roland, Gilbert 154, 156
Rolfe, Guy 106, 107
Roman, Lawrence 131
Romanoff's Resturant 54
Romero, Cesar 40, 60, 77, 179
Romina Productions 145, 151
Ronay, Mac 165
Roper, Jack 48
Rose, Helen 92
Rose, Stanley 139
Ross, Anthony 59
Ross, Claudette 64
Ross, Frank 8, 103, 111
Ross, Michael 77
Rossellini, Renzo 162
Rossington, Norman 140
Rous, Buckey 170
Rowland, Roy 101, 102
Royce, Lynn & Vanya 50
Royer 35
Rub, Christian 89
Ruis, Rene 176
Rule, Bert 134, 143, 152
Ruman, Sam 50
Rushton, Matthew 177
Russell, Gail 126
Russell, Jane 16, 86, 87, 88, 89, 109, 123, 150
Russell, Mavis 86
Rustichelli, Carlo 159
Rutherford, Ann 172
Rutherford, Jack 59
Ruysdael, Basil 83
Ryan, Robert 87, 123, 149
Ryan, Tim 11
Ryle, Lawrence 114

Safari 19, 128–131, 133, 137, 141, 153, 169
Sage, Willard 157
Sahara 144
St. Angel, Michael 70
St. Angelo, Robert 120
St. John, Betta 103
St. John, Mary 108
St. Joseph's Academy, Bardstown 5

St. Paul's Parochial School 5
St. Xavier Parochial School 5
Sale, Richard 82
Salimbeni, Bartolini 159
Salome 107
Salven, Edward 73
Salvi, Emimmo 162
Samson and Delilah 2, 14, 15, 16, 17, 69, 72, 73–76, 77, 113, 121, 126, 142, 173
"Samson and Delilah" (radio) 180
Samson and Delilah (TV) 20, 176–178
Samuel, Phil C. 134, 136, 143
Sand, Paul 169, 170
Sanders, George 73, 75
Sanders, Hugh 89
Sands, Dick 111
Sanford, Lee 59
San Francisco 67, 88
San Quentin 151
Santiago, Emile 95, 103
Saris, George 98
The Saturday Review 98
Saunders, Don 136
Savage, Carol 56
Savage, Peter 174
Savonarola, Elena 64
The Savoy, London 139
Sawtell, Paul 155, 156
Sayers, Elliseva 76
Saylor, Syd 86, 149
Sayonara 145
Scarlet Street 25
Schaumer, Ad 56, 80
Schell, Maria 176
Schilz, Ted 170
Schnabel, Hans 106
Schnee, Charles 70
Schneider, Bert 168, 169
Schrank, Joseph 41
Schroeder, Jules 8
Schulman, Arnold 172
Schwartz, Norman B. 165
Scipio Africanus 160
Scott, Brandon 176
Scott, Elliot 128
Scott, Gordon 20
Scott, Lizabeth 14, 70, 71, 72, 73, 127, 142, 168
Scott, Randoph 53
Scott, Walter M. 111, 114
Scotti, Vitto 64, 168
Scourby, Alexander 98, 100, 101
The Screen Guild Theatre 62, 64, 180
Sealtest Variety Theatre 181
Seawright, Roy 23, 26, 29
Sebena, Loretta G. (fifth wife) 21
Self Portrait: Gene Tierney 38
Sell, Bernard C. 59

Sellers, Peter 3, 20, 165, 166, 167, 168
Seltzer, Jules 8
Sennett, Max 30
Sgt. Bilko 46, 51
Serpent of the Nile 107
Sersen, Fred 52, 56, 59, 62, 65, 77, 80, 82
Setton, Maxwell 140
Seven, Clifford 29
Seven Days Leave 12, 34, 50–52, 72, 73, 99, 118
The Seventh Veil 57
Seymour, Harry 82, 122
Shaban, Martin 140
Shack, Sam 108
Shamroy, Leon 103, 105, 114
Shane 41
Shanghai 36
The Shanghai Gesture 110, 11, 35–39, 43, 55, 57, 65, 114, 135, 154
The Sharkfighters 19, 131–133, 144
Sharp, Alex 70, 95
Sharpe, David 106
Shaps, Cyril 136
Shaw, Dennis 152
Shaw, George Bernard 9, 16, 95, 96, 97
Shaw, Irwin 70
Shaw, Maxwell 143
Shayne, Konstantin 64
Shearer, Douglas 92
Shearer, Harry 103
Shearer, Stephen Michael 90
Shearing, Joseph 56
Shearman, Russell 131
Sheerwood, George 108
Shefter, Bert 155
The Sheik 152
Shellac, Fred 122
Shelton, Don 68
Shepard, Esther 168
Sheridan, Ann 16, 80, 81, 87
Sheridan, Michael 64
Sheriff, Paul 136
Sherlock, Charles 155
Sherman, George 106, 107, 120, 121
Sherrier, Julian 143
Shirley, Anne 49
Shrader, George C. 86
Sidney, Sylvia 122, 123, 124
Siegel, Sol C. 65, 80
Silva, Franco 159
Silver and Ward 41, 61
Silvera, Darrell 33, 50, 70, 84, 86, 95, 101, 108, 157
Silverheels, Jay 62
Silvers, Phil 44, 46, 47, 48, 49, 172
Simba 128

Simmons, Bob 143
Simmons, Jean 16, 17, 95, 96, 97, 101, 102, 103, 104, 105, 111, 114, 116, 117, 123
Simms, Ginny 50
Simon, F. Robert 120
Simon, Neil 20, 165, 166
Simpson, Mickey 52, 111
Simpson, O.J. 173, 174, 175, 176
Simpson, Robert L. 39, 41, 44, 47, 62, 77
Simpson, Russell 52
Sinatra, Frank 137
"Sing Me a Song of the Islands" 42, 44
Sing, Sing (penitentiary) 13, 61
Singer, John 118
Singuineau, Frank 128, 174
Siodmak, Robert 65, 67
Sketch, Bartholomew 128
Skinner, Frank 120
Skippy Hollywood Theater 181
Skylover, Carl 86
Slark, Fred 140
Slifer, Elizabeth 92
Slightly Dangerous 179
Slott, Nate D. 70
Small, Edward 157, 159
Smart, J. Scott 59
Smith, Art 68
Smith, Brian 118
Smith, Howard 59
Smith, Jack Martin 92
Smith, Ken 176
Smith, Tom 143
Smith, Willetta 111
Snow, Mark 103
Snyder, Ray 26
Snyder, William E. 108
Sofaer, Abraham 168
Soldani, Charles 149
Soloman, Jon 116, 117
Something for the Birds 3, 12, 16, 40, 89–92
Something of Value 128
Song of the Islands 2, 41–44, 72, 77
Sorel, Louise 169
Spaggiari, Angelo 165
Sparks, Robert 70, 86, 101
Spartacus 178
Spence, Ralph 50, 51
Spencer, Bud 47, 159, 161
Spencer, Dorothy 52, 111
Spencer, Ronnie 140
Sperling, Milton 39, 42
Spiker, Ray 111
Sportelli, Franco 165
Stack, Robert 108
Stader, Paul 111
Stagecoach 32
Stallone, Sylvester 20

Stang, Arnold 50
Stark, Michael 64
Starling, Lynn 47
Stassino, Paul 136, 152
Steele, Karen 131, 133
Steensen, Clarence 101
Steiger, Rod 149
Stein, Sammy 106
Steinbeck, John 28
Stella 3, 16, 80–81, 87, 91
Stephenson, Maureen 108
Stern, Daniel 176
Sternberg, Abe 59
Sterns, John 59
Stevens, Anitra 114, 115
Stevens, Charles 52, 62, 63
Stevens, Onslow 68
Stevenson, Edward 33, 70, 80
Stevenson, Robert 86
Stewart, Elaine 19, 148, 150
Stewart, James 54, 126
Stewart, Paul 70, 71, 72
Stockwell, Dean 172
Stokes, Vera 84
Stone, Bobby 41
Stone, George E. 23, 25, 103
Stoney, Jack 84
Stoppa, Paolo 165
Storey, June 64
Stradling, Harry, Sr. 95
Strange, Glenn 106
The Strange Woman 75
The Strawberry Blonde 45
Street Scene (film score) 41, 67
Strode, Woody 95, 97, 111
Stuart, Randy 80
Stubbs, Chuck 26
Sturgis, Ted 152
Sturtevant, John 86, 108
Stuthman, Fred 174
Suleiman, Sultan 106, 108
Sullivan, Barry 179
Sullivan, James 92, 94, 95
Suspense 16, 180
Sutherland, Duncan 152
Sutton, John 44, 46
"Swanee River" 44
Swanwick, Peter 118
Swinburne, Nora 117

Tafler, Sydney 136
"Take a Little One-Step" 34
Tallchief, Maria 92
Talman, William 13, 68, 69
Tamara 32
Tamblyn, Russ 73
Tamiroff, Akim 165
Tank Force see *No Time to Die*
Tannen, Charles 47, 64, 82
Tarola, Mary Jo 101, 102
The Tartars 20, 160, 160–165
Tarzan and His Mate 28

Tasca, Alessandro 163
Taylor, Dwight 39
Taylor, Elizabeth 136
Taylor, Larry 152
Taylor, Libby 44
Taylor, Robert 40, 153
"Tea for Two" 34
Teal, Ray 62
Temple, Shirley 30
The Ten Commandments 115
Ten Gentlemen from West Point 79
Tetzlaff, Ted 84, 85
Texas, Temple 59
Thal, Eric 178
Thatcher, Torin 103
"That's Loyalty" 69
Thelby, Rosemary 26
"There Will Never Be Another You" 83
There's Always Tomorrow (Anna Neagle's autobiography) 34
Thesiger, Ernest 103
Thieves Highway 142
The Third Man 59
Thomas, Danny 77
Thompson, Harry 114
Thorley, Victor 59
Thorne, Ken 168
Thornton, Peter 140
Thorpe, Richard 162, 163, 164
Thorson, Russsell 70
Three Ages 26
Tiberi, Piero 159
Tiernan, Lawrence 59
Tierney, Gene 35, 37, 38, 39, 114, 116, 180
Tilvern, Alan 143
Timbuktu 20, 64, 157–159, 169
Time (magazine) 61, 125
Time Is a Memory 145
Time Out Film Guide 67, 168
Tin Pan Alley 82
To Quito and Back 8
Tombes, Andrew 29, 44
The Tombs (New York City) 61
Toomey, Reg 172
Top Secret 120
Topper (series) 25, 35
Tork, Peter 168
Torres, Louis 101
Torres, Stuart 92
Tosi, Piero 165
Touch of Evil 40
Touliatos, George 174
Tourneur, Jacques 14, 70, 71, 72, 157, 159
Tracy, Spencer 30
Travilla 82
Traylor, William 125
The Treasure of the Sierra Madre 38
Trieste, Leopoldo 169

Tripoli 145
Trotman, William 174
The Trouble with Harry 81
Tucker, Orrin 86
Tuffs, Sonny 70, 71
Tugend, Harry 77
Tunberg, Karl 44
Tuscumbia, Missouri 100
Tuttle, Thomas 82
Tuttle, William 92
The TV Times Film and Video Guide 41, 101, 120, 136, 139, 154, 162, 168
20th Century–Fox 11, 12, 13, 14, 16, 18, 21, 28, 39, 41, 43, 44, 45, 46, 50, 51, 53, 57, 59, 62, 63, 64, 67, 73, 76, 77, 78, 79, 81, 82, 85, 89, 90, 97, 98, 99, 103, 104, 111, 112
Twickenham Studios (UK) 153
Tyler, Walter H. 73

Ulmer, Edgar G. 159, 160, 161
United Artists 19, 20, 23, 24, 26, 27, 29, 30, 35, 37, 38, 131, 132, 145, 147, 150, 157
United States Coast Guard 12, 13
Universal Pictures 65, 106, 107, 109, 115, 120
Urecal, Minerva 62
Urwick, Adrienne Joy (fourth wife) 20, 150
Ustinov, Peter 114, 116

Valee, Rudy 172
Valk, Frederick 134
Valley of the Kings 115
Van, Frankie 47
Vanderbeets, Richard 73
Van Sickel, Dale 106
Vanya *see* Royce, Lynn
Van Zandt, Philip 68
Varconi, Victor 73
Varden, Evelyn 80
Varden, Norma 89
Vargas, Daniele 165
Variety 13, 26, 32, 35, 41, 44, 49, 55, 58, 61, 70, 73, 80, 86, 91, 94, 98, 101, 105, 108, 111, 117, 121, 124, 133, 139, 143, 145, 148, 154, 157, 159, 162, 164, 168, 172, 173
Vars, Henry 145, 149
Vatentino, Rudolph 152
Veiller, Anthony 128, 157
The Veils of Bagdad 17, 106–108, 119, 134
Verebes, Erno 68
Vernon, Wally 101, 102
Verros, John 98
Vicki 41

Victor, Charles 50, 51
Victory, Katherine 170
Villiers, Christopher 120
Vincent, Romo 172
Violent Saturday 18, 40, 88, 100, 109
Vitale, Joseph 68
Vitale, Milly 159
Vitek, Loreli 80
Vogan, Emmett 89
Volkie, Ralph 108
Vollmoller, Karl 35
Von Eltz, Theodore 101
von Kirbach, Arthur 111
Von Schumacher, Augustus 172
von Sydow, Max 176, 178
Vuolo, Tito 59, 64

Wabash Avenue 2, 16, 34, 40, 76–80, 82, 83,
"Wabash Avenue" (radio) 180
Wade, Michael 139
Wagenheim, Charles 106
Wakefield, Simon 174
Wakeling, Gwen 39, 41, 44, 74
Walburn, Raymond 68, 69
Wald, John 155
Walder, Ernest 143
Walker, Dick 155
Walker, Nancy 172
Walker, Vernon L. 33, 50
"Walking Along with Billy" 78
Wall, Geraldine 155
Wallace, George 92
Wallace, Irving 155
Wallace, Richard 29, 30
Wallach, Eli 174, 175
Walsh, Arthur 52
Walsh, Dermot 152
Walsh, Thomas 180
Waltari, Mika 114
Walters, Charles 50
Wanger, Walter 25
Warbey, Christopher 128
Ward, Clayton 41, 80, 123
Ward, Dervis 139
Ware, Darrell 44
Ware, Midge 86
Warner Brothers 34, 87, 115, 117, 159
Warren, Eda 68
Warren, Harry 41
Warwick, Robert 62, 120
Warwick Film Productions 19, 128, 137, 140, 142, 144, 152, 153, 154
Washbourne, Mona 118
Washington 90, 91
Washington, Kenny 70
Waters, Reba 148, 150
Waters, Russell 136
Watkin, Pierre 29

Watkins, Al 170
Watkins, A.W. 118
Watts, Charles 89, 92, 155
Watts, Freddie 140
Waxman, Franz 111
Wayne, David 3, 80, 81
Wayne, John 30, 69, 146, 148, 149, 151, 155
Weatherwax, Paul 106
Weaver, Dennis 108, 110, 120
Weaver, Doodles 172
Weaver, Linda 168
Webb, Clifton 82
Webb, J. Watson, Jr. 59, 82
Webb, Robert D. 98, 100
Webb, Roy 70, 84, 101, 108, 109
Webster, Paul Francis 156
Weinberger, Henry 89
Weisenger, Allen 174
Weissmuller, Johnny 28, 93, 172
Welch, Raquel 28
Welden, Ben 106
Weldon, Alex 157
Welles, Orson 12, 20, 40, 45, 46, 162, 163
Wellman, Harold E. 86, 108
Welsh, Bill 86
Welsh, John 139
"We're on Safari" 131
West, Mae 44
Westen, Al 157
Westerfield, James 120
Westlein, CPO David 131
Westmore, Bud 106, 120
Westmore, Wally 68, 73
Weston, Leslie 117
Wexler, Paul 157
What's New Pussy Cat 165
Wheeler, Lyle, R. 52, 59, 62, 65, 77, 80, 82, 89, 98, 103, 111, 114, 123
Whelan, Tim 50
"Where Has My Hubby Gone?" 34
White, Bill, Jr. 145
White, Jesse 59, 92, 94, 172
White Collar Girl 47
Whitlock, Lloyd 73
Whitman, Stuart 106, 145, 148
Whitmore, James 125, 126, 127
Whitney, Peter 125
Whybrow, Roy 143
Whylock, Grant 157
Widmark, Richard 13, 40, 59, 60, 61, 62, 118, 131, 163, 179, 180, 181
Wilcox, Frank 73, 101, 108

Wilcox, Herbert 33, 34, 35
Wilcox, John 128, 134
Wilcoxon, Henry 73, 75, 172
Wild, Harry J. 70, 84, 86, 101
Wilde, Brian 136
Wilde, Hagar 68,
Wilding, Michael 114, 115, 116, 117, 133, 135, 144
"Wilhelmina" 78
Wilke, Robert J. 86
Wilkerson, Guy 62, 125
Wilkins, Bob 174
Williams, Bill 120
Williams, Elmo 33
Williams, Esther 16, 46, 92, 93, 94, 144, 152, 153, 154, 160
Williams, Lawrence P. 33
Williams, Mack 122
Williams, Rhys 56
Williamson, Fred 128
Willis, Edwin B 92
Willman, Noel 95
Wills, Chill 80
Wills, Henry 120
Wilson, Gerald 174
Wilson, Gilbert 56
Wilson, Harry 26
Wilson, Terry 125
Winchel, Walter 69
Wind Across the Everglades 91
Winner, Michael 20, 172, 173, 174, 176
Winslow, Dick 82
Winsten, Archer 9
Winston, Sam 35
Winters, Gloria 84
Winters, Roland 64
Winters, Shelley 64, 67
Wise, Robert 50, 89, 90, 91, 100
Withers, Grant 52
Wittstein, Ed 177
Wolcott, Earl A. 86
Wolf, Jeff 100
Wolfe, Ian 89
Wolff, Barney 73
The Woman in the Window 25
Won Ton Ton, the Dog Who Saved Hollywood 20, 83, 94, 172–174, 175
Wong, Bruce 41
"Won't You Say You Love Me" 78
Wood, Allen 47
Wood, Bill
Wood, Peggy 23, 25
Woode, Margo 56
Woods, Harry 52, 73
Woods, William 73

Woodward, Joanne 133
Wooland, Norman 152
Woolrich, Cornell 180
Worker, Adrian D. 128
Woulfe, Michael 84, 101, 108
Wright, Bruce 170
Wright, Cobina 47
Wright, Joseph C. 41, 44, 77
Wright, Will 86
Wyman, Jane 47, 49
Wynn, John 118, 128
Wynn, Nan 46

Yana 136
A *Yank in the RAF* 144
"Yankee Doodle Blues" 83
Yankee Doodle Dandy 46
Yates, Nathan 131
Ybarra, Alfred 149
Yeardye, Tommy 140, 141
Yordan, Philip 125
York, Jeff 111
"You Make Me Feel So Young" 83
Youmans, Vincent 33
Young, Alan 95, 96, 97
Young, Audrey 70
Young, Carleton 98
Young, Freddie 118
Young, Loretta 64
Young, Robert 179
Young, Roland 32, 35
Young, Terence 128, 130, 134, 135, 143, 153
Young, Victor 73
Youngman, Henry 172
Yugoslavia 20, 164
Yuma, USA 8

Zacchini, Hugo 155
Zagreb, Croatai 184
Zanchin, Nino 160
Zanette, Guy 84
Zanuck, Darryl 16, 39, 40, 42, 43, 47, 48, 53, 54, 59, 60, 67, 77, 100, 104, 105, 113, 114, 115, 116, 117, 124, 133
Zappa, Frank 168, 169
Zarak 19, 133–136, 144, 145, 153, 154, 158
Zarak Khan (novel) 134, 152, 153
Zastupnevich, Paul 155
Zavattini, Cesare 165, 166
Ziegler, William 23
Zinnerman, Tim 172
Zomar, Joe 157
Zucco, George 56

www.ingramcontent.com/pod-product-compliance
Ingram Content Group UK Ltd.
Pitfield, Milton Keynes, MK11 3LW, UK
UKHW050527150426
5217IPUK00026B/1827